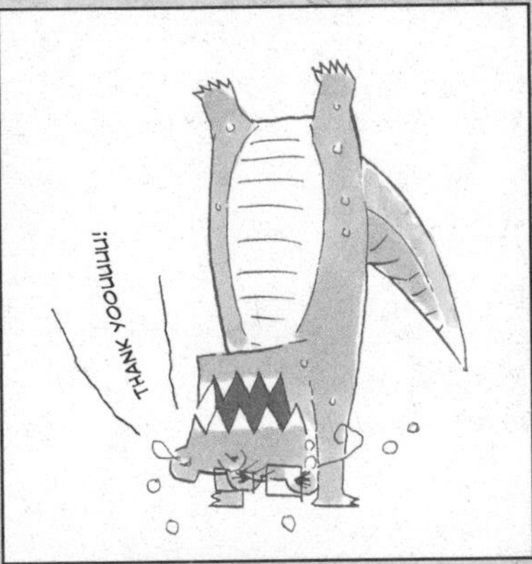
THANK YOOUUUUU!

KOYOHARU GOTOUGE

I did it! I'm Gotouge. I got comments from Togashi Sensei on the *obi*!* It's like a dream! My stomach hurts! Thank you very much to Togashi Sensei, everyone rooting for me, and everyone who helps out. I'll work as hard as I can!

*The *obi* is a paper band found on Japanese books.

DEMON SLAYER:
KIMETSU NO YAIBA
VOLUME 4
Shonen Jump Edition

Story and Art by
KOYOHARU GOTOUGE

KIMETSU NO YAIBA
© 2016 by Koyoharu Gotouge
All rights reserved. First published in Japan
in 2016 by SHUEISHA Inc., Tokyo. English
translation rights arranged by SHUEISHA Inc.

TRANSLATION John Werry

ENGLISH ADAPTATION Stan!

TOUCH-UP ART & LETTERING John Hunt

DESIGN Adam Grano

EDITOR Mike Montesa

Printed in the U.S.A.

Published by VIZ Media, LLC
P.O. Box 77010
San Francisco, CA 94107

11
First printing, January 2019
Eleventh printing, July 2021

DEMON SLAYER

KIMETSU NO YAIBA

4

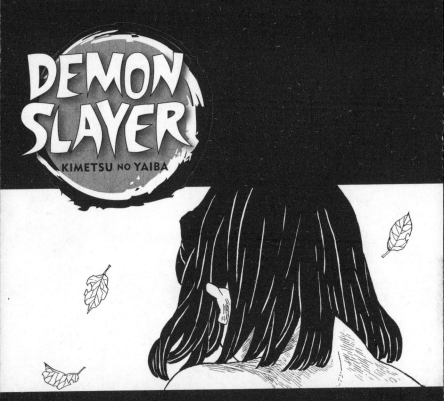

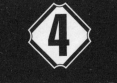

ROBUST BLADE

KOYOHARU
GOTOUGE

CHARACTERS

TANJIRO KAMADO

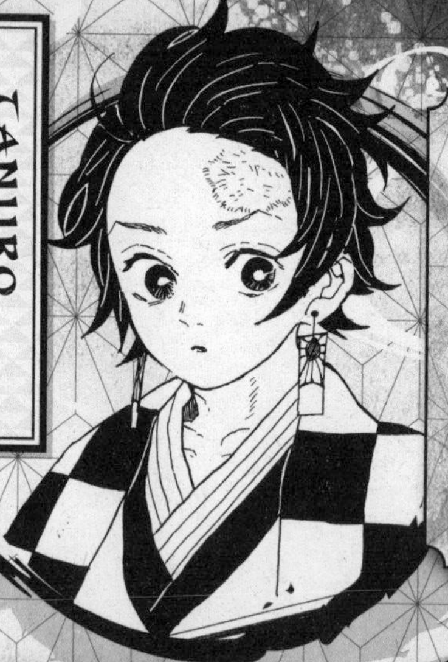

A kind boy who saved his sister when the rest of his family was killed. Now he seeks revenge. He can smell the scent of demons and his opponents' weaknesses.

NEZUKO KAMADO

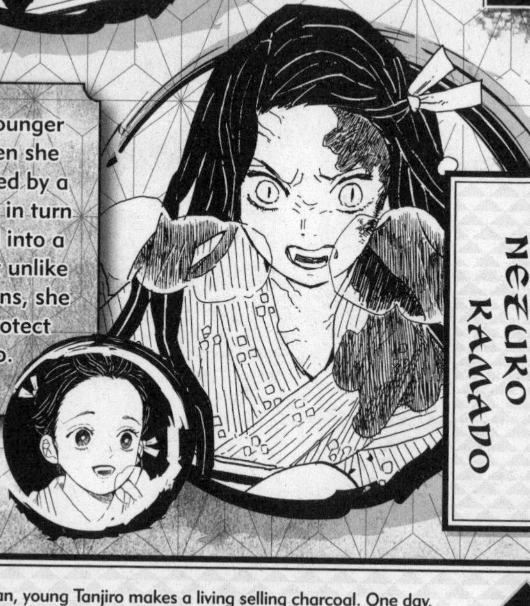

Tanjiro's younger sister. When she was attacked by a demon, she in turn was turned into a demon, but unlike other demons, she tries to protect Tanjiro.

STORY

In Taisho-era Japan, young Tanjiro makes a living selling charcoal. One day, demons kill his family and turn his younger sister Nezuko into a demon. Tanjiro and Nezuko set out to find a way to return Nezuko to human form and defeat Kibutsuji, the demon who killed their family! Having finished training with Urokodaki and completing Final Selection for the Demon Slayer Corps, Tanjiro accepts a mission and brings Nezuko with him. During the mission, Tanjiro encounters his most hated enemy, Kibutsuji, but the demon escapes. Then Tanjiro meets Tamayo and Yushiro, who are demons but also want to kill Kibutsuji. They provide Tanjiro with a clue as to how Nezuko may return to being human. Later, he bumps into Zenitsu Agatsuma, whom he first met during the Final Selection, then heads out on his next mission. Tanjiro defeats a demon who wields a tsuzumi drum, and then finds Zenitsu under attack by a boy wearing a wild boar's hide!

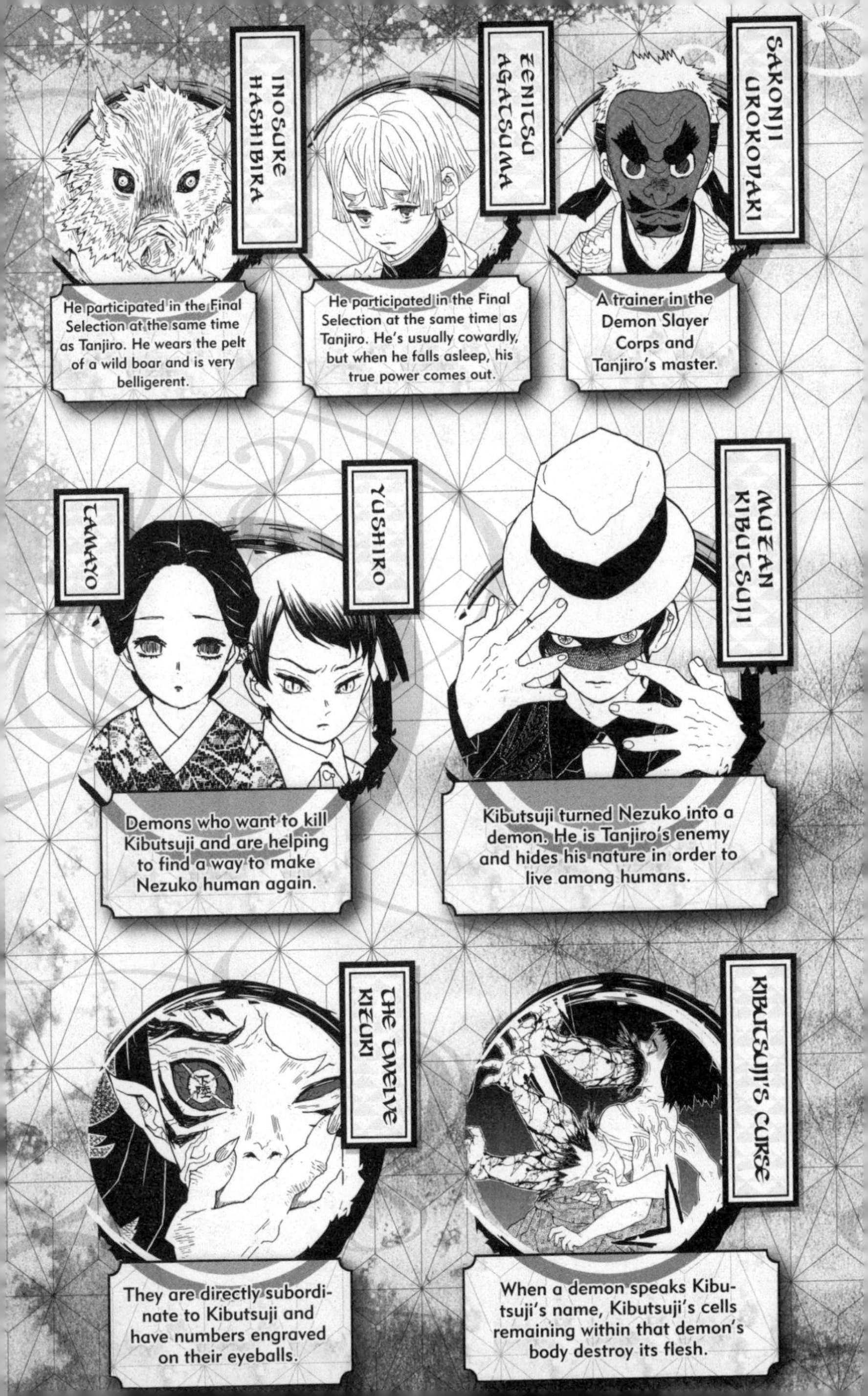
SAKONJI UROKODAKI
A trainer in the Demon Slayer Corps and Tanjiro's master.
ZENITSU AGATSUMA
He participated in the Final Selection at the same time as Tanjiro. He's usually cowardly, but when he falls asleep, his true power comes out.
INOSUKE HASHIBIRA
He participated in the Final Selection at the same time as Tanjiro. He wears the pelt of a wild boar and is very belligerent.
MUZAN KIBUTSUJI
Kibutsuji turned Nezuko into a demon. He is Tanjiro's enemy and hides his nature in order to live among humans.
YUSHIRO
TAMAYO
Demons who want to kill Kibutsuji and are helping to find a way to make Nezuko human again.
KIBUTSUJI'S CURSE
When a demon speaks Kibutsuji's name, Kibutsuji's cells remaining within that demon's body destroy its flesh.
THE TWELVE KIZUKI
They are directly subordinate to Kibutsuji and have numbers engraved on their eyeballs.

CONTENTS

DEMON SLAYER!
KIMETSU NO YAIBA

4

ROBUST BLADE

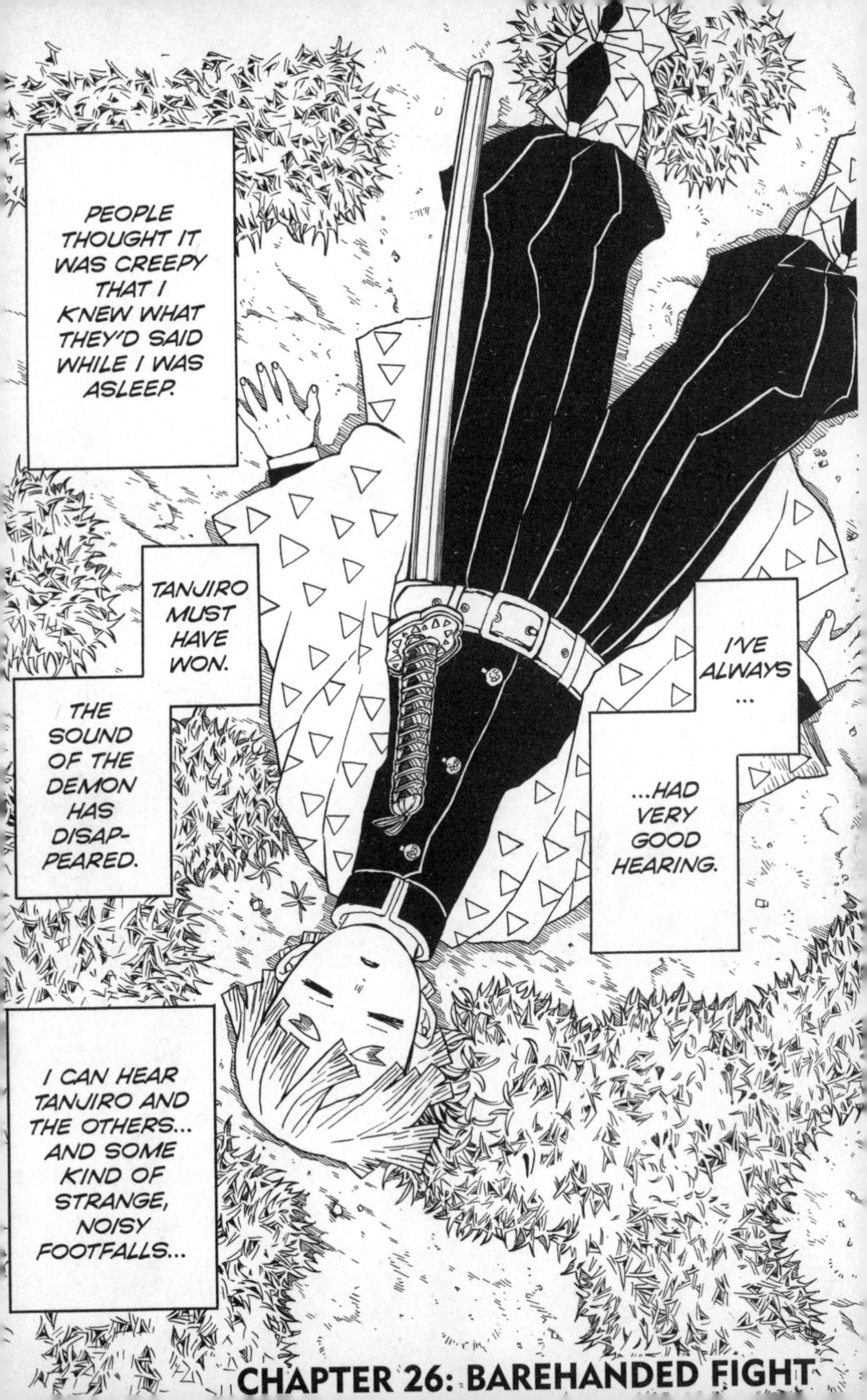
I'VE ALWAYS...
...HAD VERY GOOD HEARING.
PEOPLE THOUGHT IT WAS CREEPY THAT I KNEW WHAT THEY'D SAID WHILE I WAS ASLEEP.
TANJIRO MUST HAVE WON.
THE SOUND OF THE DEMON HAS DISAPPEARED.
I CAN HEAR TANJIRO AND THE OTHERS... AND SOME KIND OF STRANGE, NOISY FOOTFALLS...

CHAPTER 26: BAREHANDED FIGHT

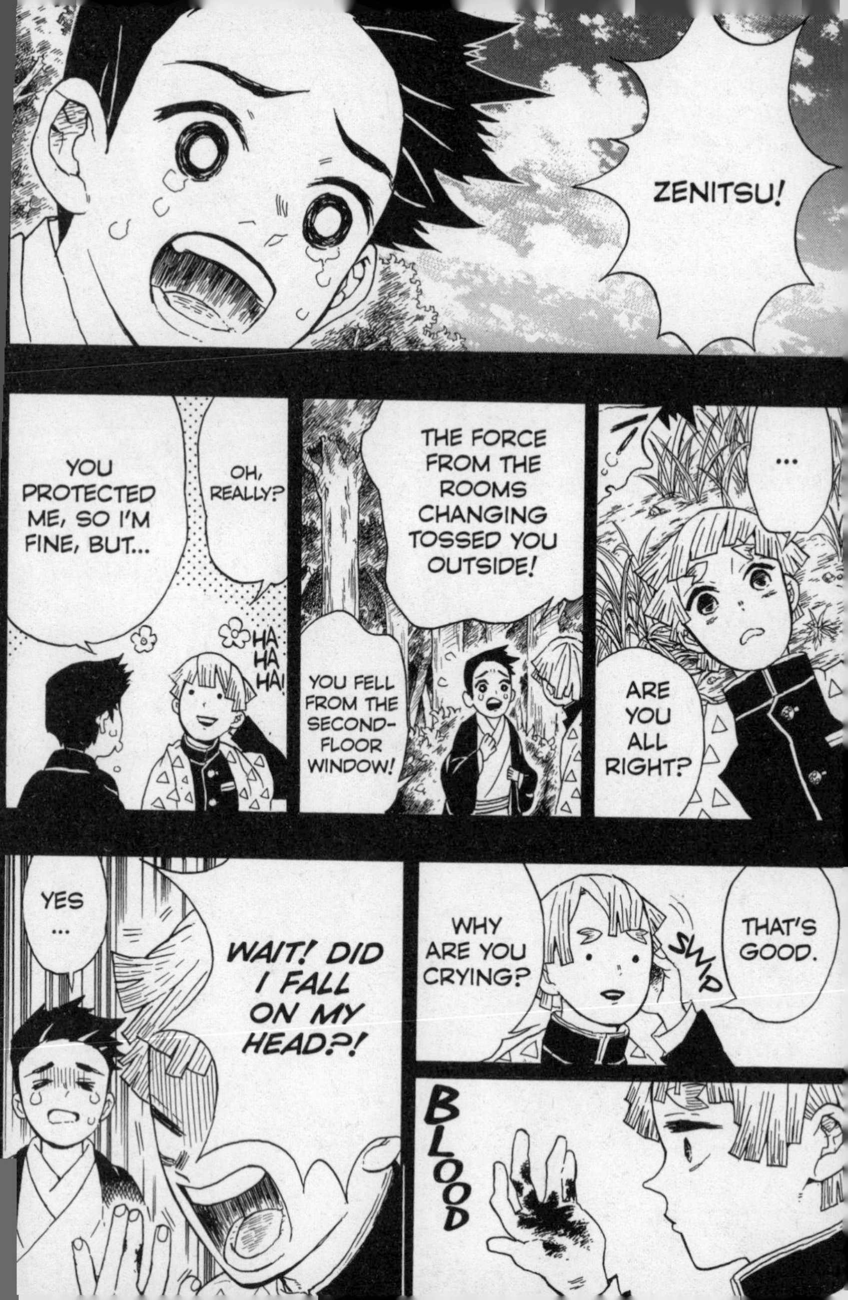
ZENITSU!
...
ARE YOU ALL RIGHT?
THE FORCE FROM THE ROOMS CHANGING TOSSED YOU OUTSIDE!
YOU FELL FROM THE SECOND-FLOOR WINDOW!
OH, REALLY?
YOU PROTECTED ME, SO I'M FINE, BUT...
HA HA HA!
THAT'S GOOD.
SWIP
WHY ARE YOU CRYING?
BLOOD
WAIT! DID I FALL ON MY HEAD?!
YES ...

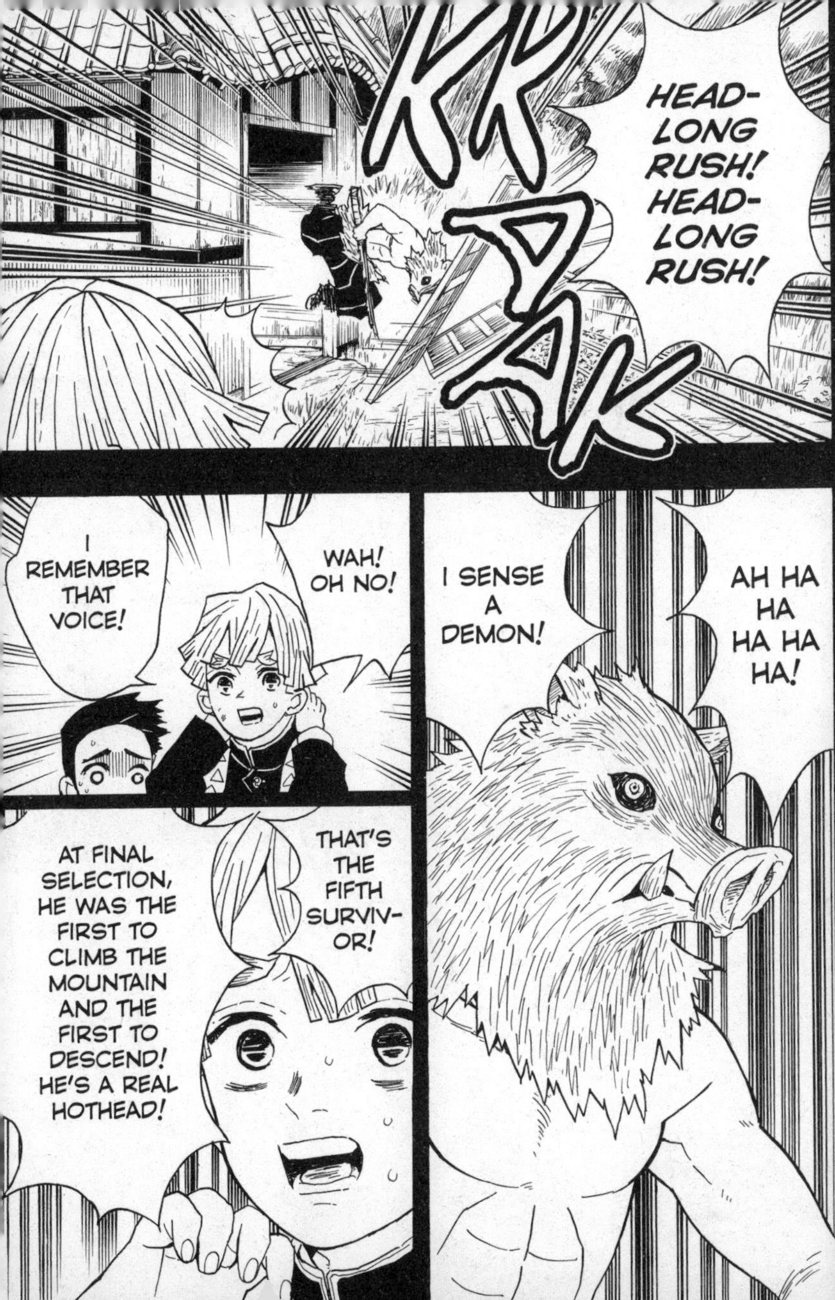
HEAD-LONG RUSH! HEAD-LONG RUSH!
KRAAK
AH HA HA HA HA HA!
I SENSE A DEMON!
WAH! OH NO!
I REMEMBER THAT VOICE!
THAT'S THE FIFTH SURVIVOR!
AT FINAL SELECTION, HE WAS THE FIRST TO CLIMB THE MOUNTAIN AND THE FIRST TO DESCEND! HE'S A REAL HOTHEAD!

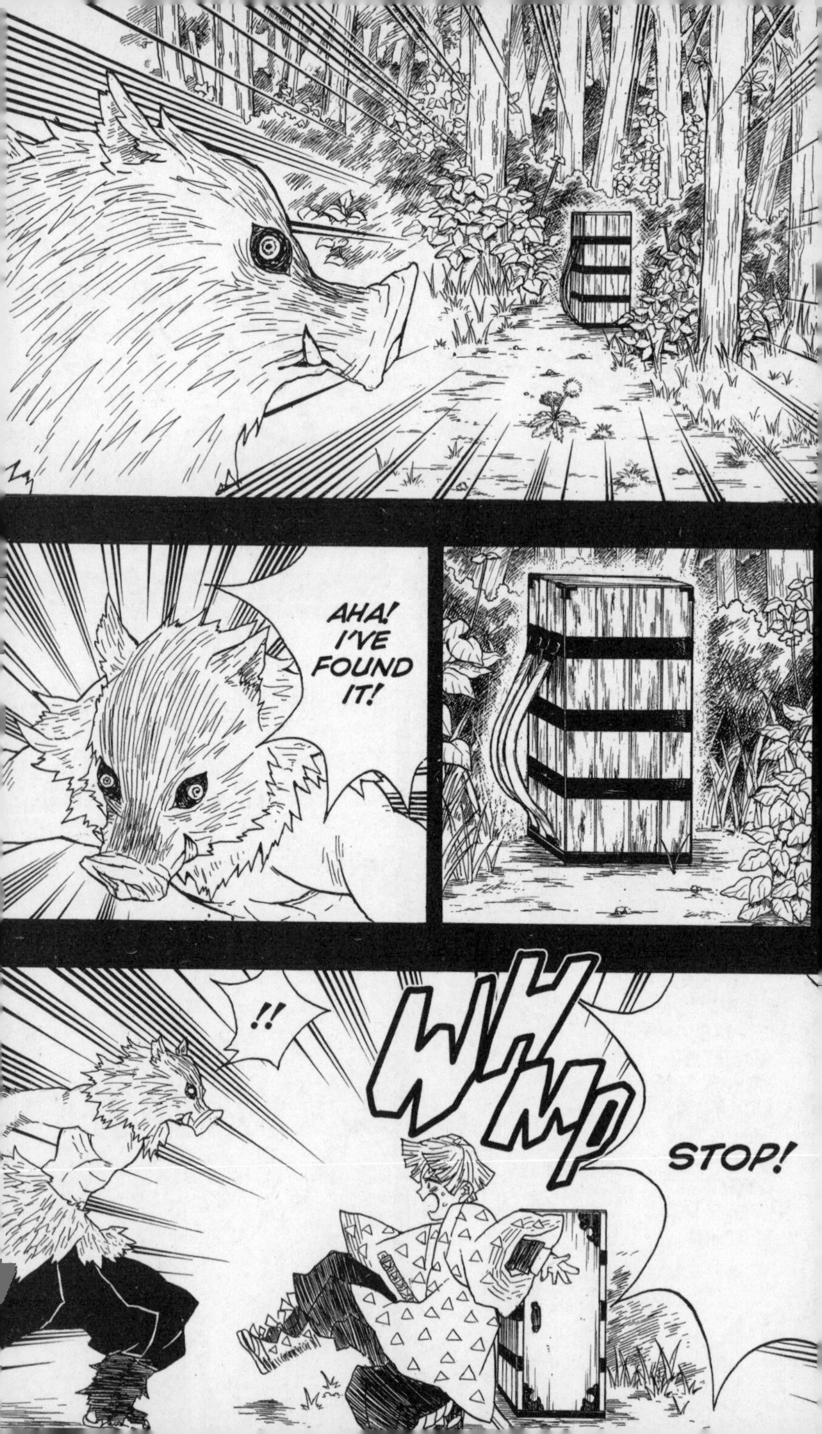
AHA! I'VE FOUND IT!
!!
WHMP
STOP!

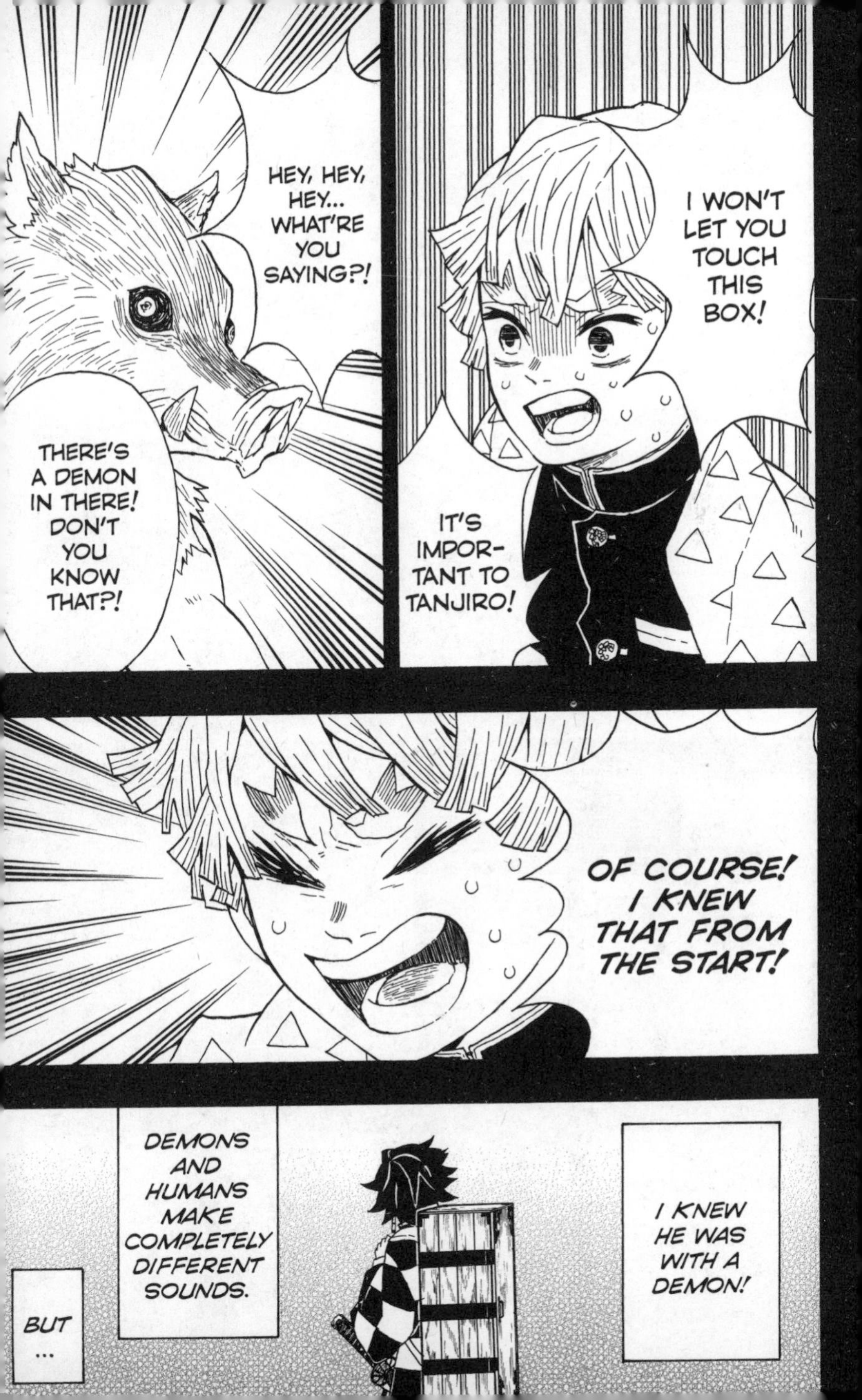
I WON'T LET YOU TOUCH THIS BOX!
IT'S IMPOR-TANT TO TANJIRO!
HEY, HEY, HEY... WHAT'RE YOU SAYING?!
THERE'S A DEMON IN THERE! DON'T YOU KNOW THAT?!
OF COURSE! I KNEW THAT FROM THE START!
I KNEW HE WAS WITH A DEMON!
DEMONS AND HUMANS MAKE COMPLETELY DIFFERENT SOUNDS.
BUT ...

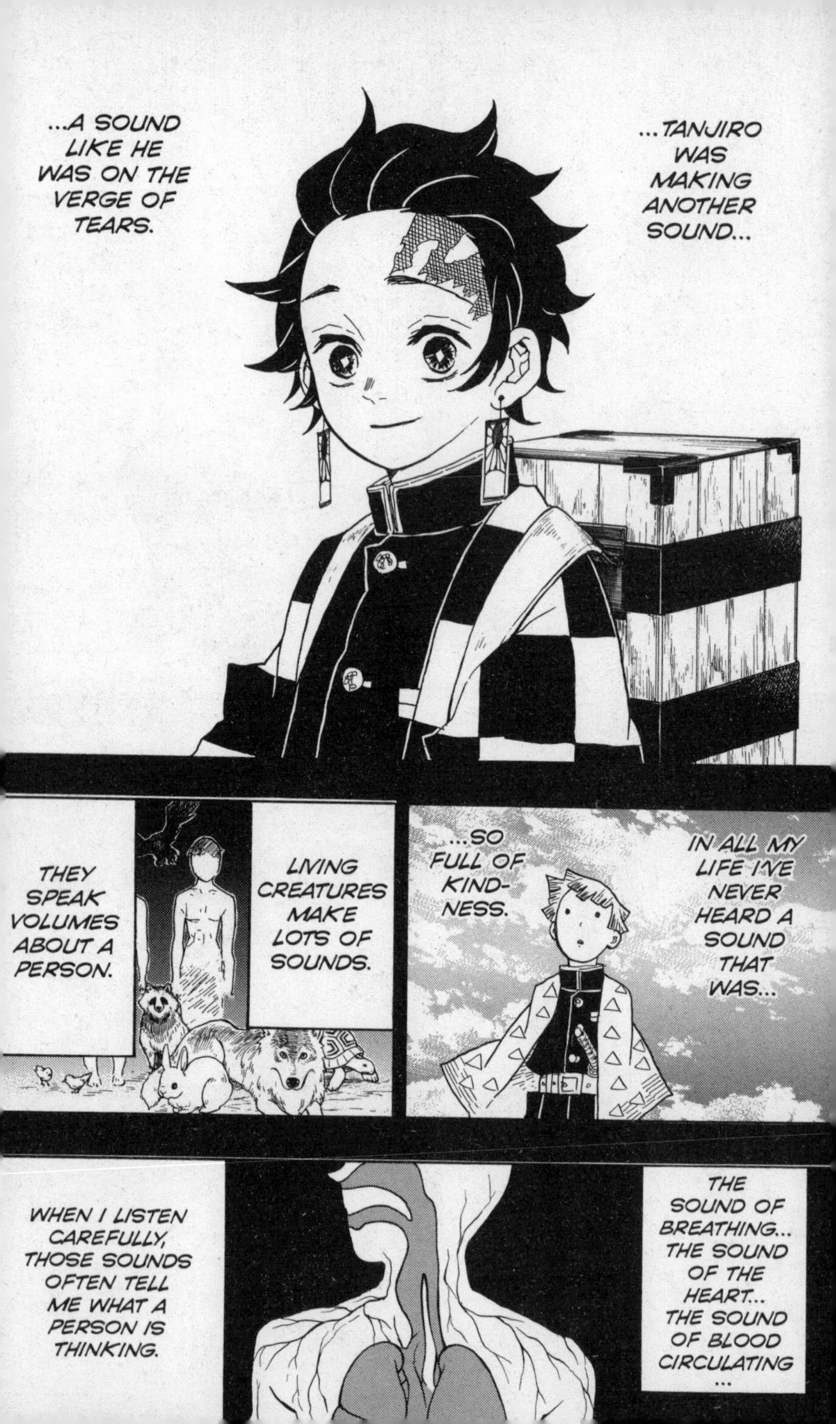

...TANJIRO WAS MAKING ANOTHER SOUND...
...A SOUND LIKE HE WAS ON THE VERGE OF TEARS.
IN ALL MY LIFE I'VE NEVER HEARD A SOUND THAT WAS...
...SO FULL OF KINDNESS.
LIVING CREATURES MAKE LOTS OF SOUNDS.
THEY SPEAK VOLUMES ABOUT A PERSON.
THE SOUND OF BREATHING... THE SOUND OF THE HEART... THE SOUND OF BLOOD CIRCULATING...
WHEN I LISTEN CAREFULLY, THOSE SOUNDS OFTEN TELL ME WHAT A PERSON IS THINKING.

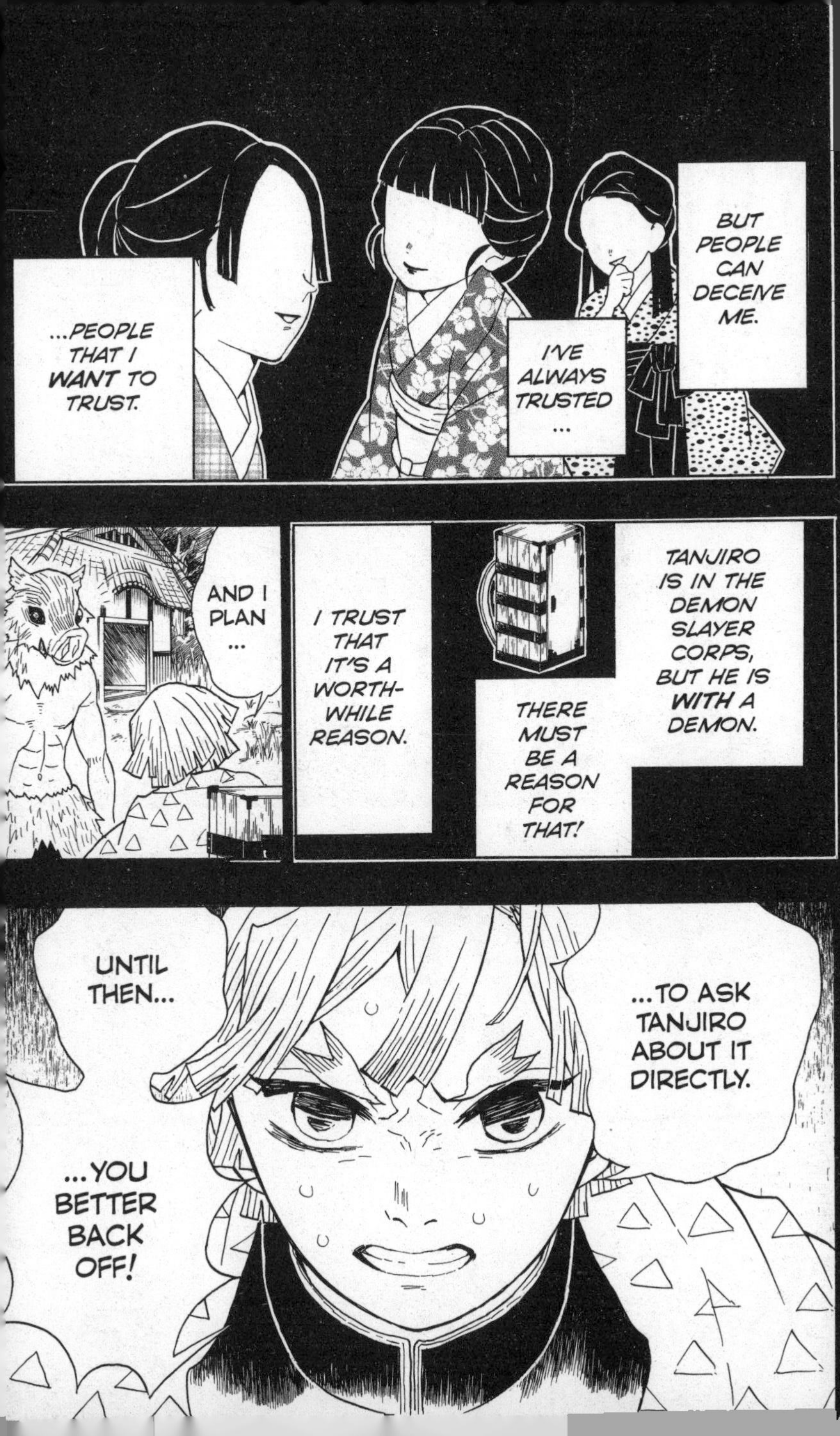
BUT PEOPLE CAN DECEIVE ME.
I'VE ALWAYS TRUSTED ...
...PEOPLE THAT I *WANT* TO TRUST.
TANJIRO IS IN THE DEMON SLAYER CORPS, BUT HE IS *WITH A* DEMON.
THERE MUST BE A REASON FOR THAT!
I TRUST THAT IT'S A WORTH-WHILE REASON.
AND I PLAN ...
...TO ASK TANJIRO ABOUT IT DIRECTLY.
UNTIL THEN...
...YOU BETTER BACK OFF!

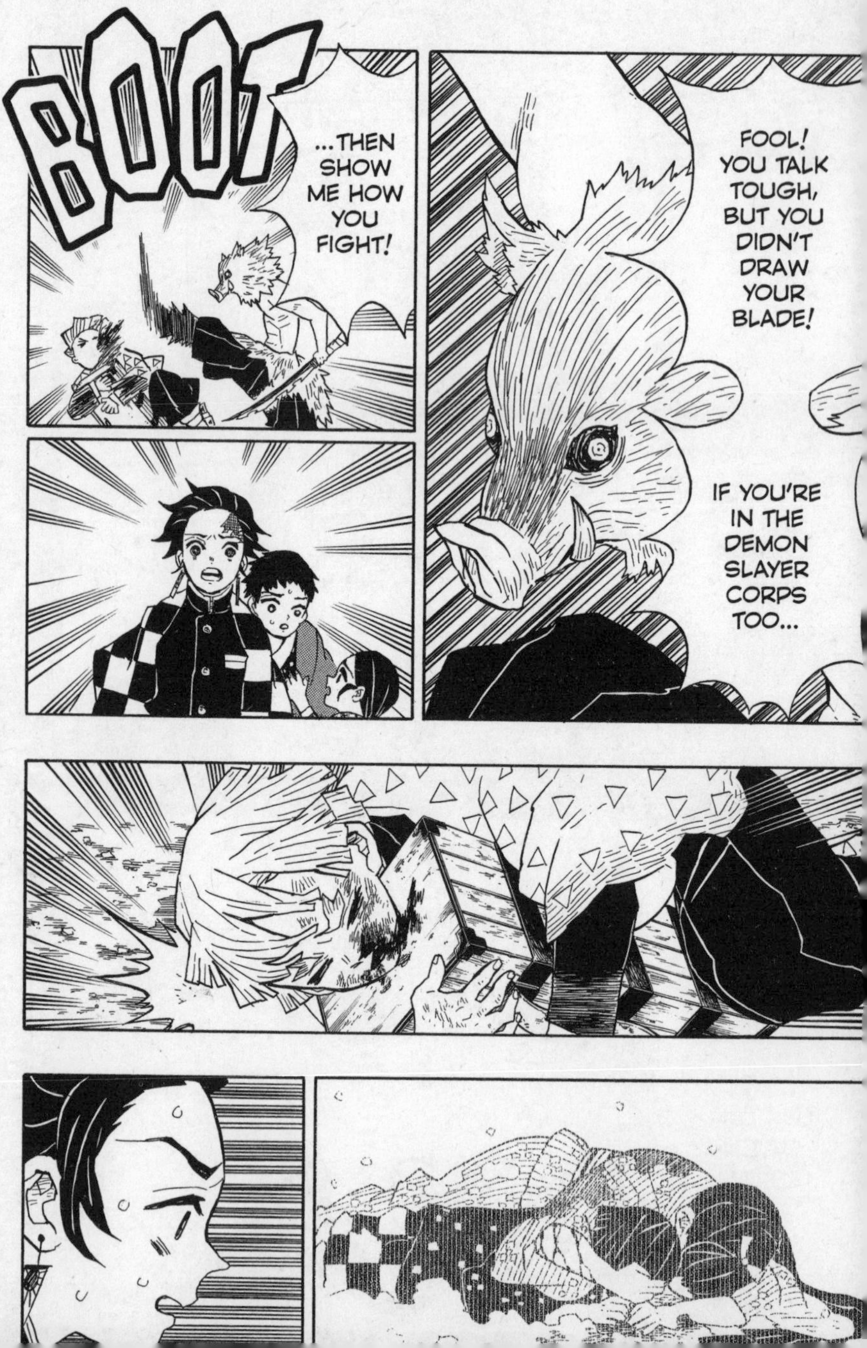
FOOL! YOU TALK TOUGH, BUT YOU DIDN'T DRAW YOUR BLADE!
IF YOU'RE IN THE DEMON SLAYER CORPS TOO...
...THEN SHOW ME HOW YOU FIGHT!
BOOT

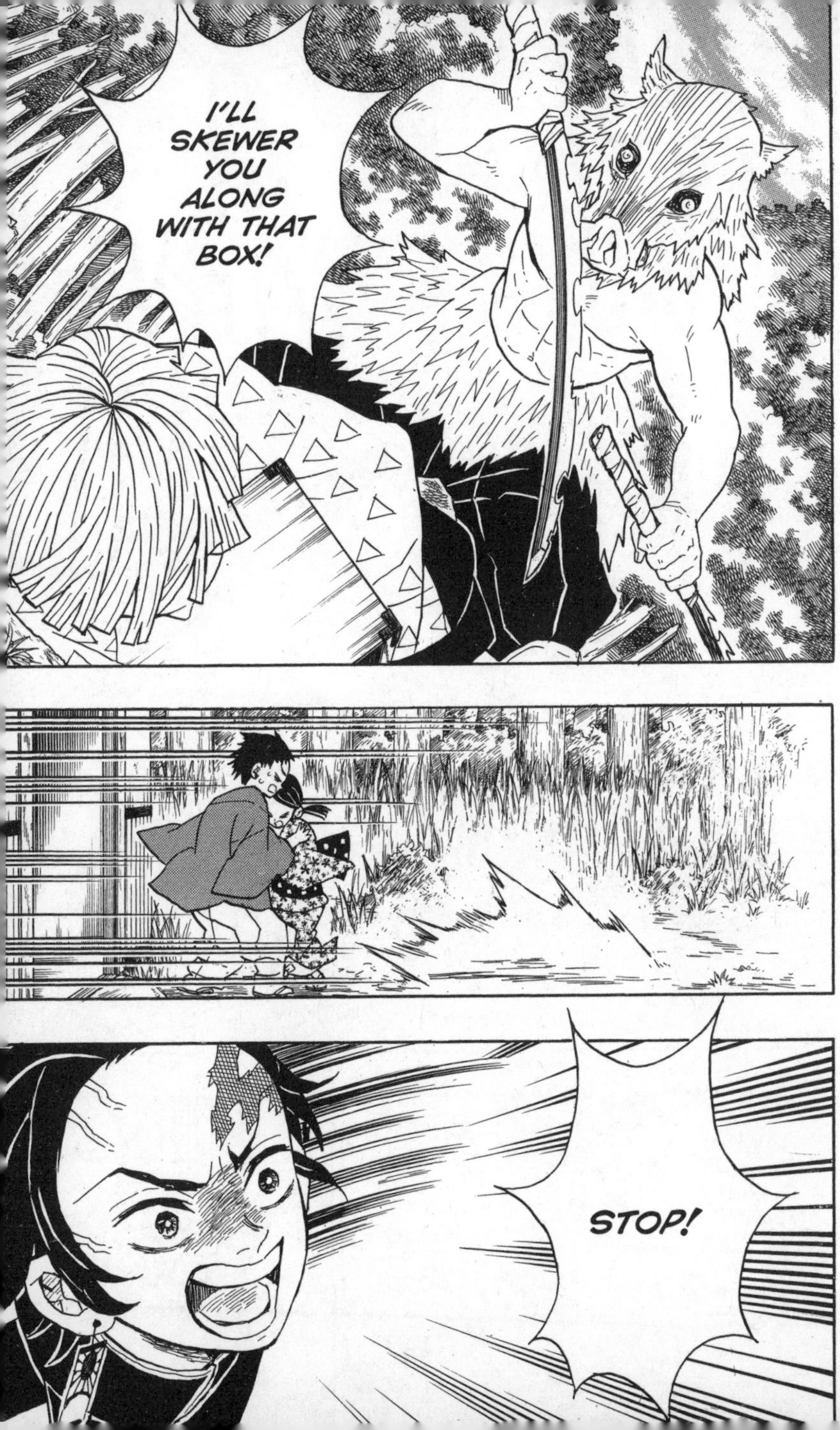
I'LL SKEWER YOU ALONG WITH THAT BOX!
STOP!

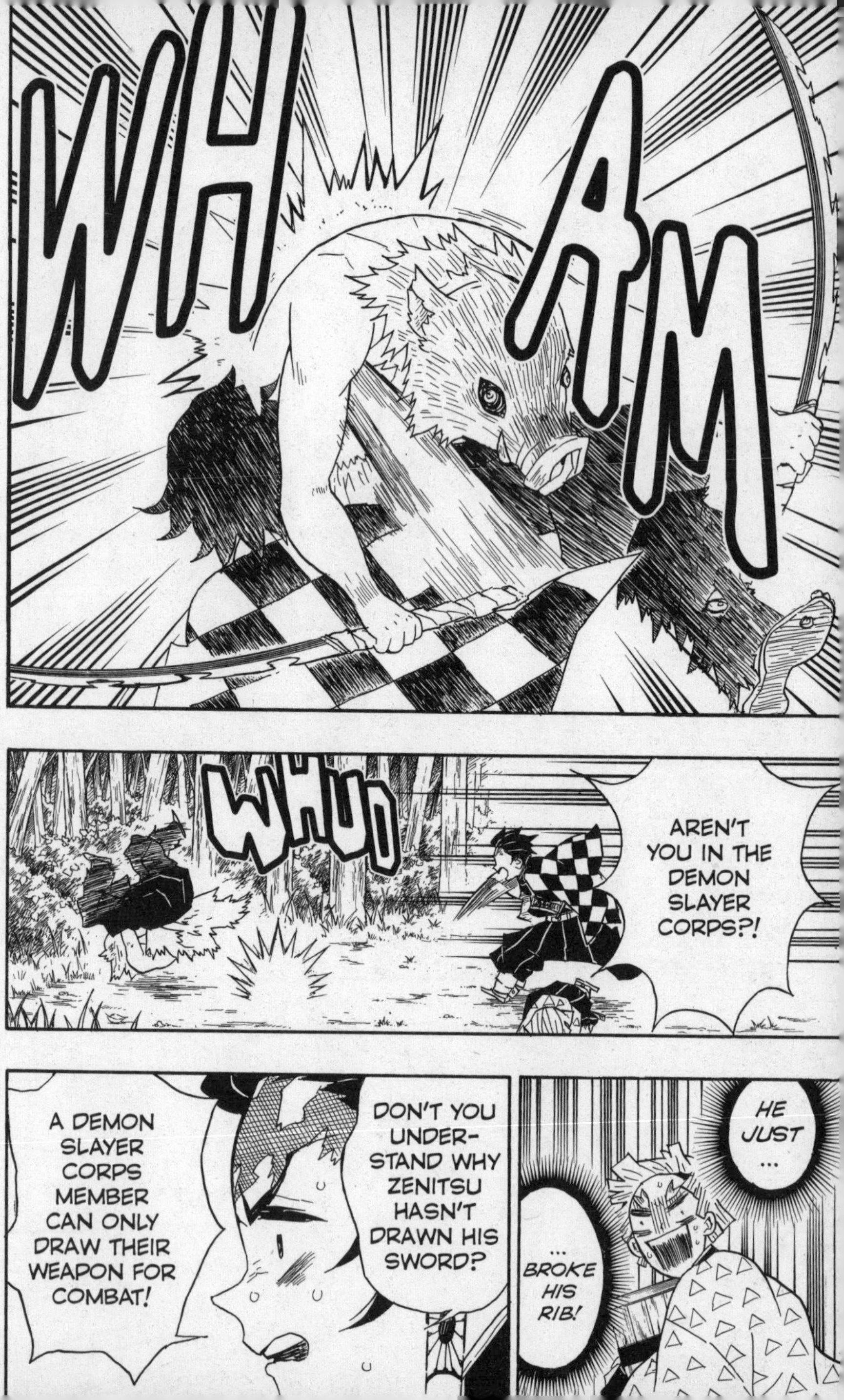
WHAM
ARE'NT YOU IN THE DEMON SLAYER CORPS?!
WHUD
HE JUST ...
... BROKE HIS RIB!
DON'T YOU UNDER-STAND WHY ZENITSU HASN'T DRAWN HIS SWORD?
A DEMON SLAYER CORPS MEMBER CAN ONLY DRAW THEIR WEAPON FOR COMBAT!

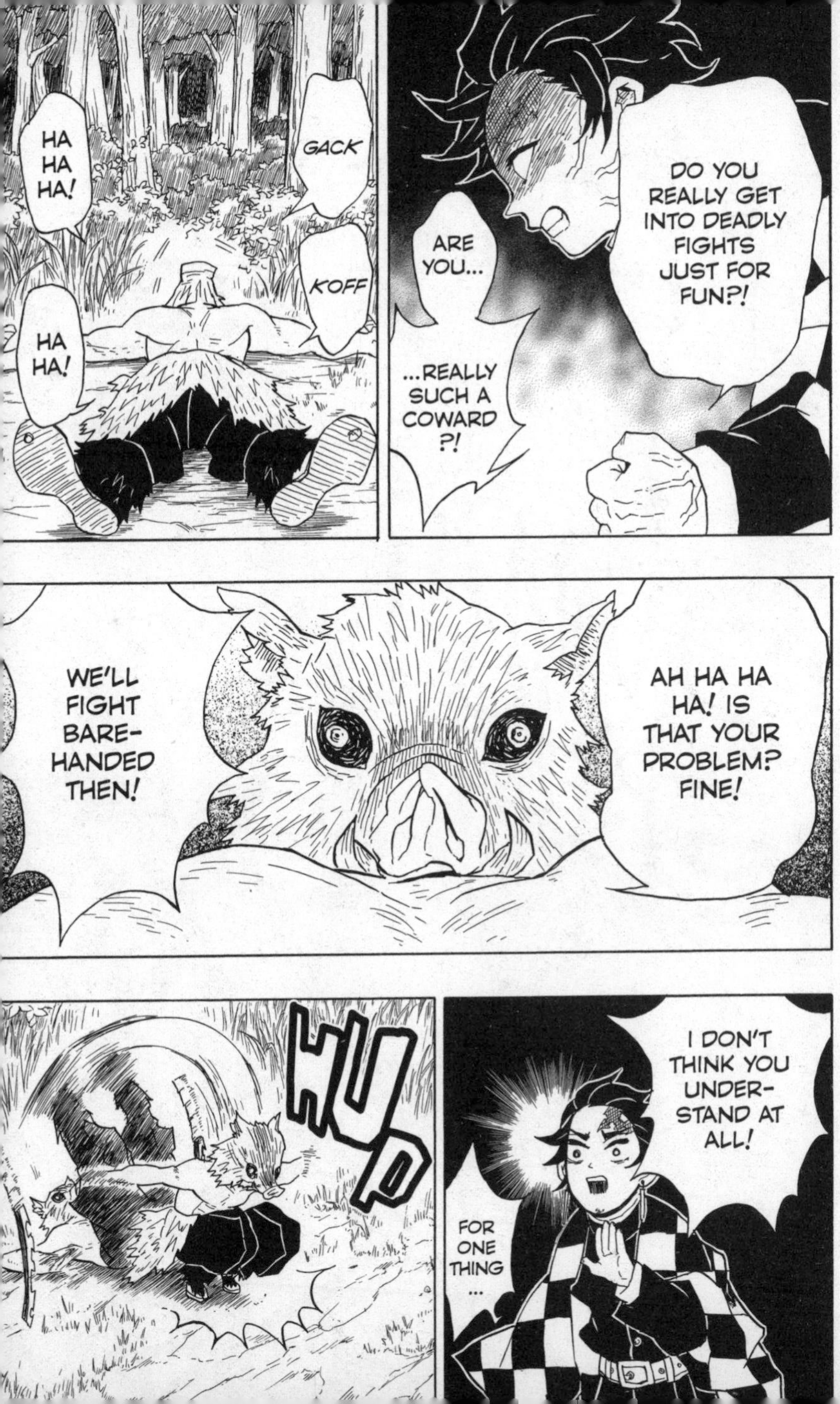
DO YOU REALLY GET INTO DEADLY FIGHTS JUST FOR FUN?!
ARE YOU...
...REALLY SUCH A COWARD ?!
GACK
KOFF
HA HA HA!
HA HA!
AH HA HA HA! IS THAT YOUR PROBLEM? FINE!
WE'LL FIGHT BARE-HANDED THEN!
I DON'T THINK YOU UNDER-STAND AT ALL!
FOR ONE THING ...
HUP

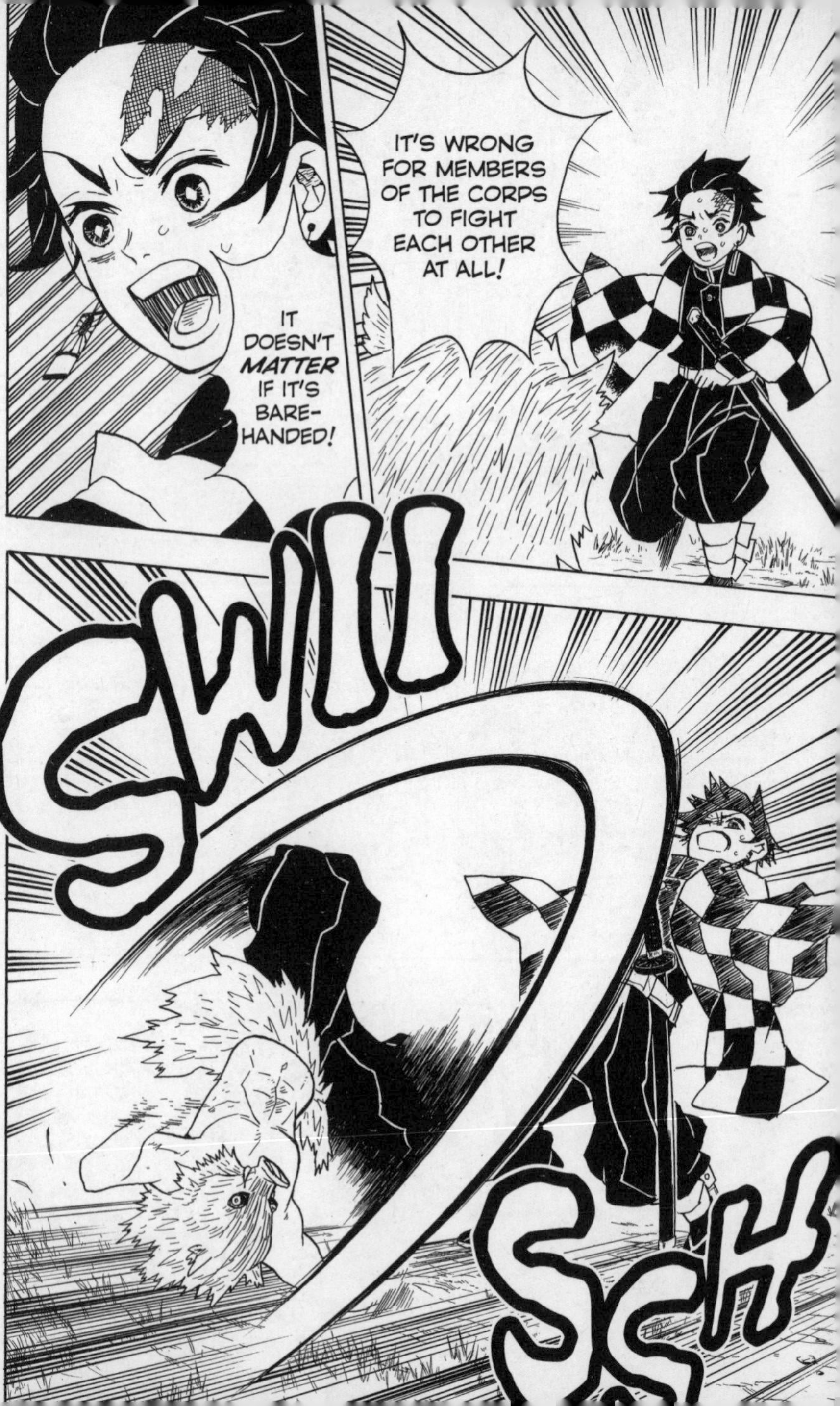
IT'S WRONG FOR MEMBERS OF THE CORPS TO FIGHT EACH OTHER AT ALL!
IT DOESN'T *MATTER* IF IT'S BARE-HANDED!
SWIII
SCH

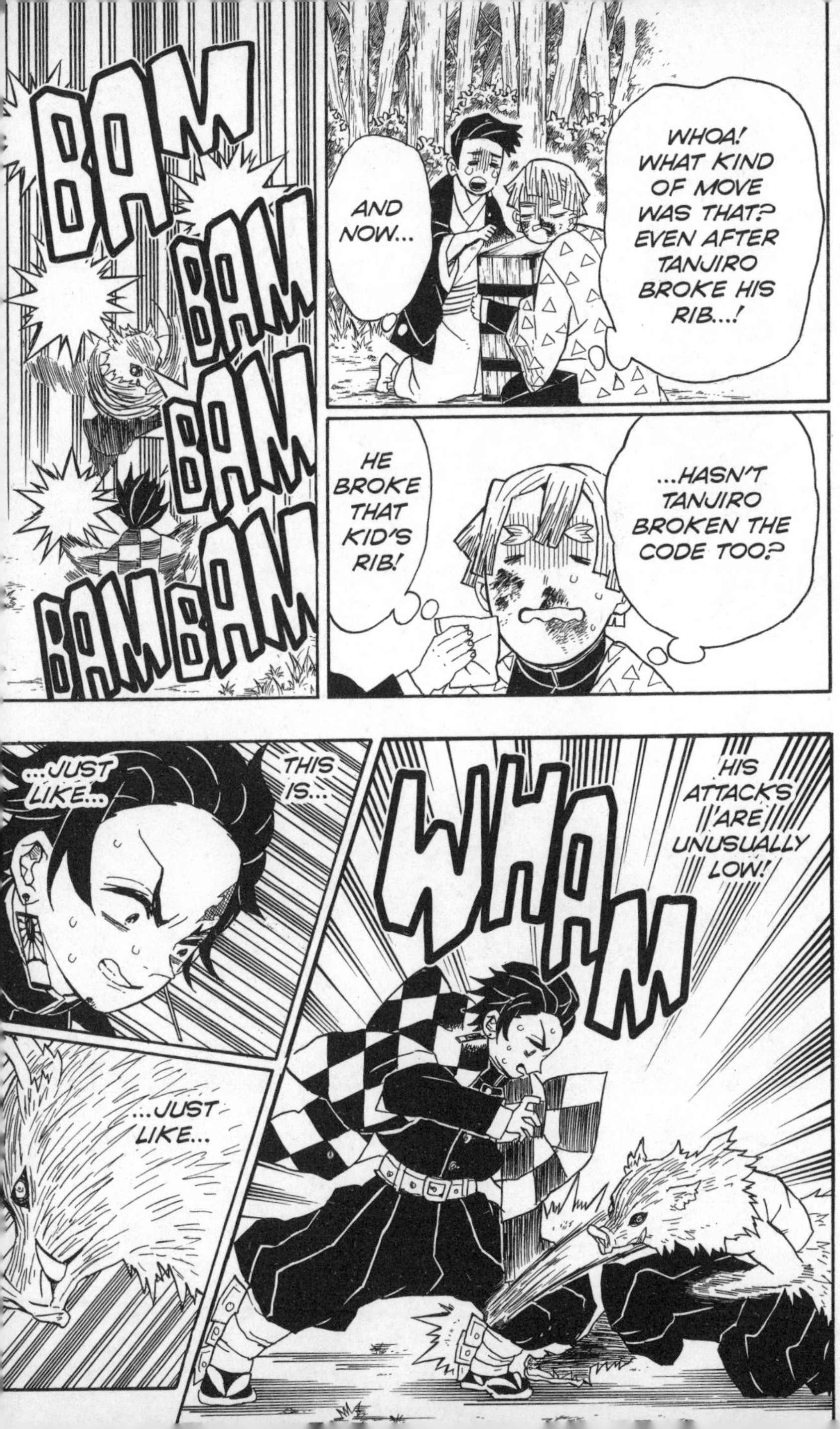
WHOA! WHAT KIND OF MOVE WAS THAT? EVEN AFTER TANJIRO BROKE HIS RIB...!
AND NOW...
...HASN'T TANJIRO BROKEN THE CODE TOO?
HE BROKE THAT KID'S RIB!
BAM
BAM
BAM
BAM BAM
HIS ATTACKS ARE UNUSUALLY LOW!
WHAM
THIS IS...
...JUST LIKE...
...JUST LIKE...

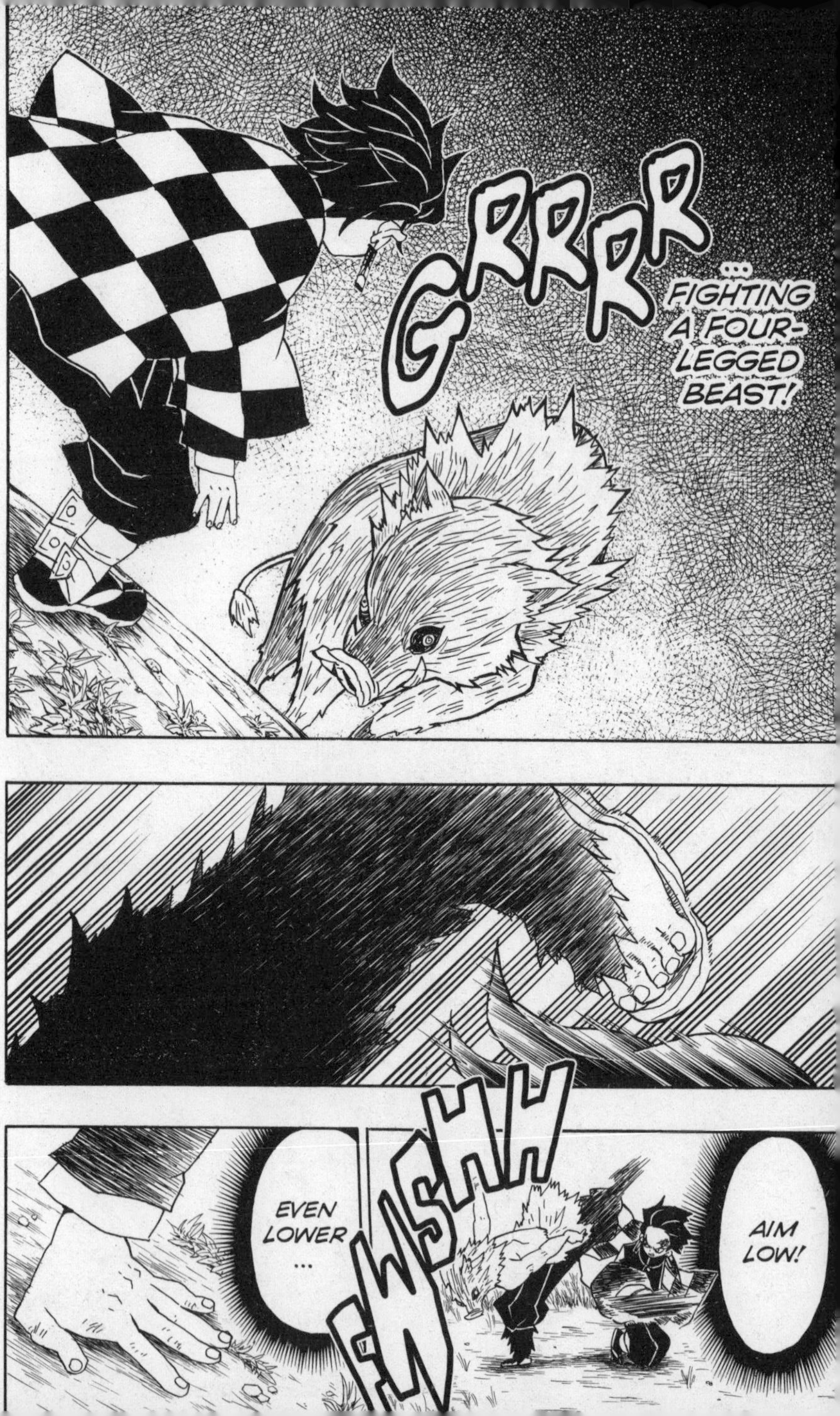
GRRRR
...FIGHTING A FOUR-LEGGED BEAST!
AIM LOW!
FWSHH
EVEN LOWER ...

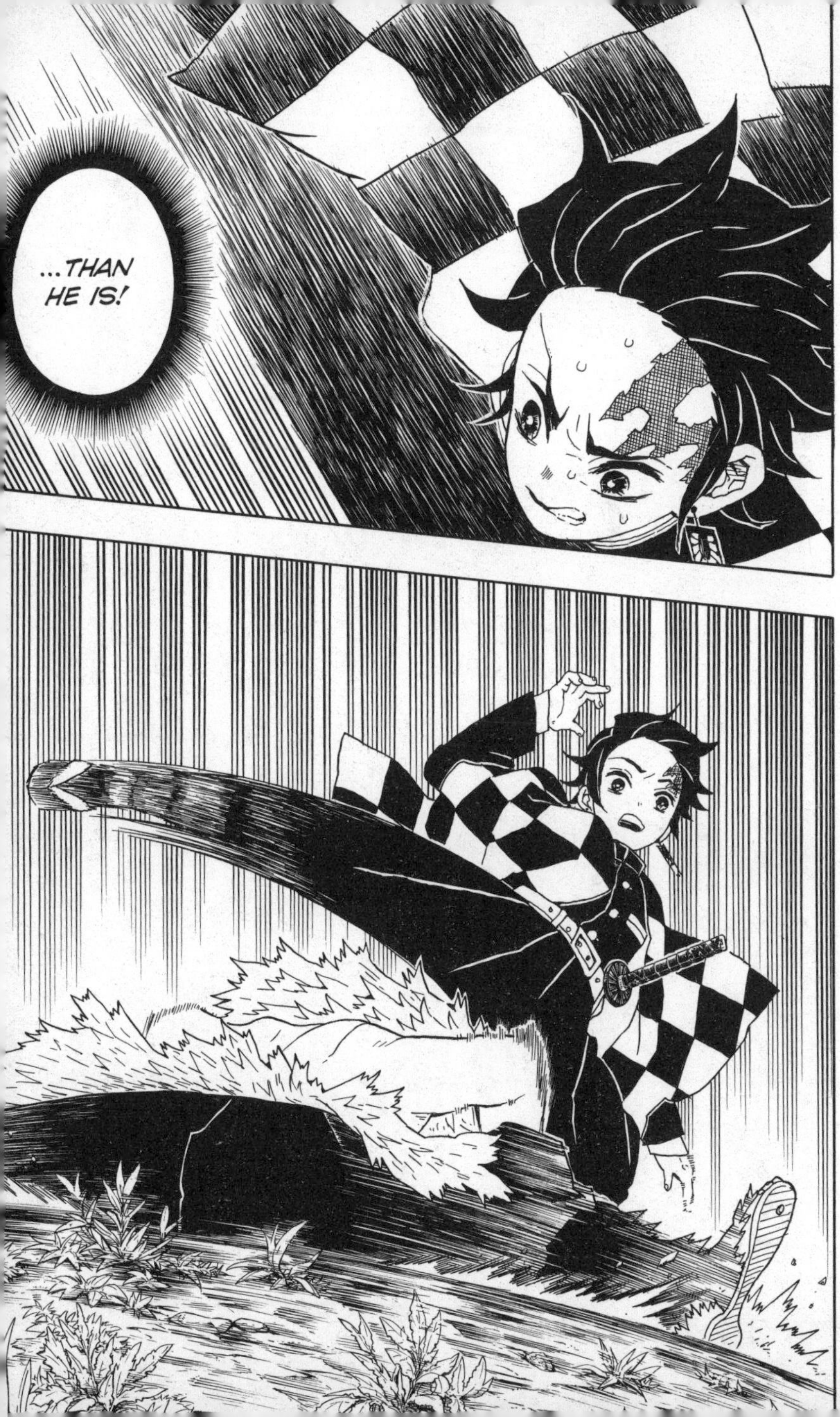
...THAN HE IS!

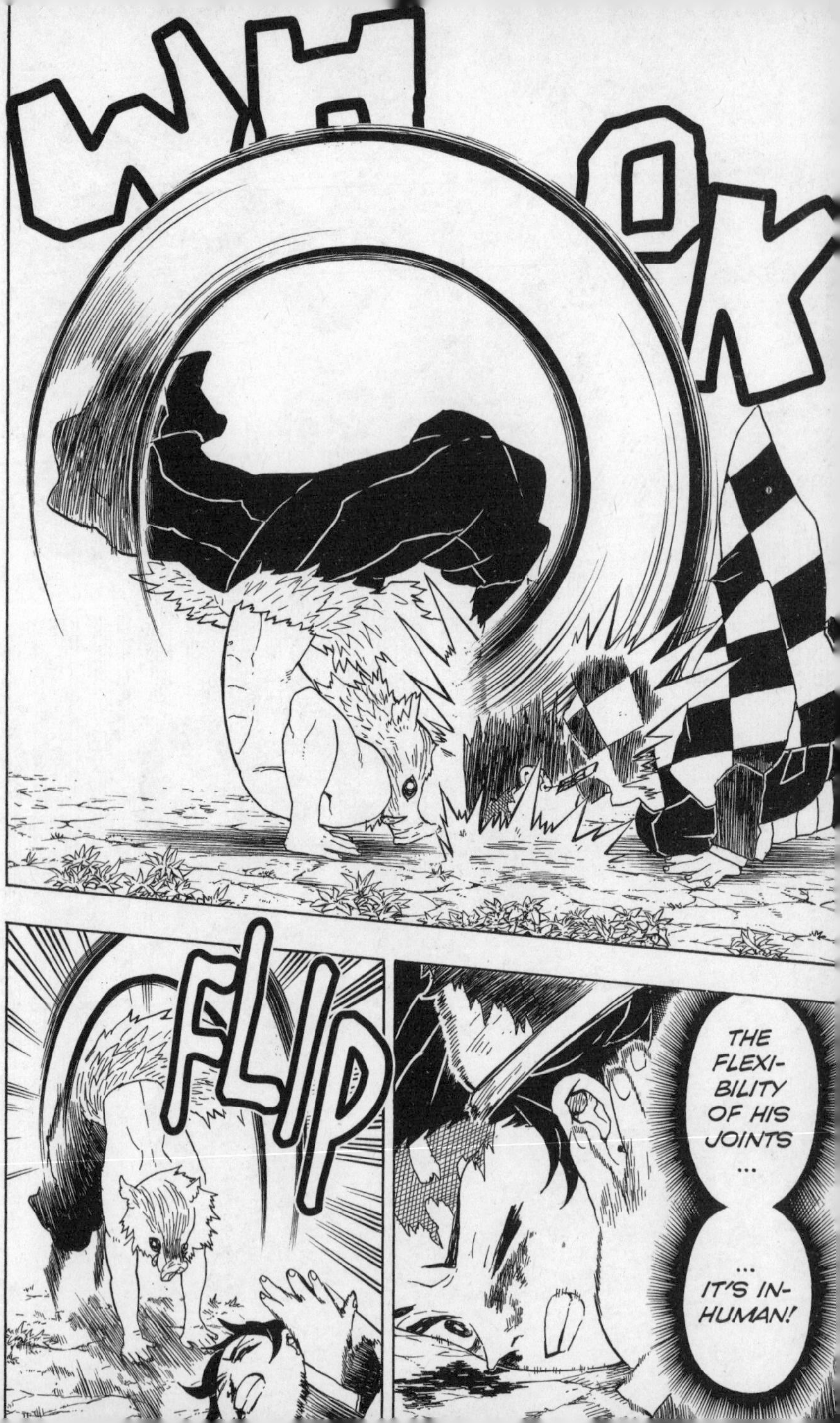
WH OK
THE FLEXI-BILITY OF HIS JOINTS ...
... IT'S IN-HUMAN!
FLIP

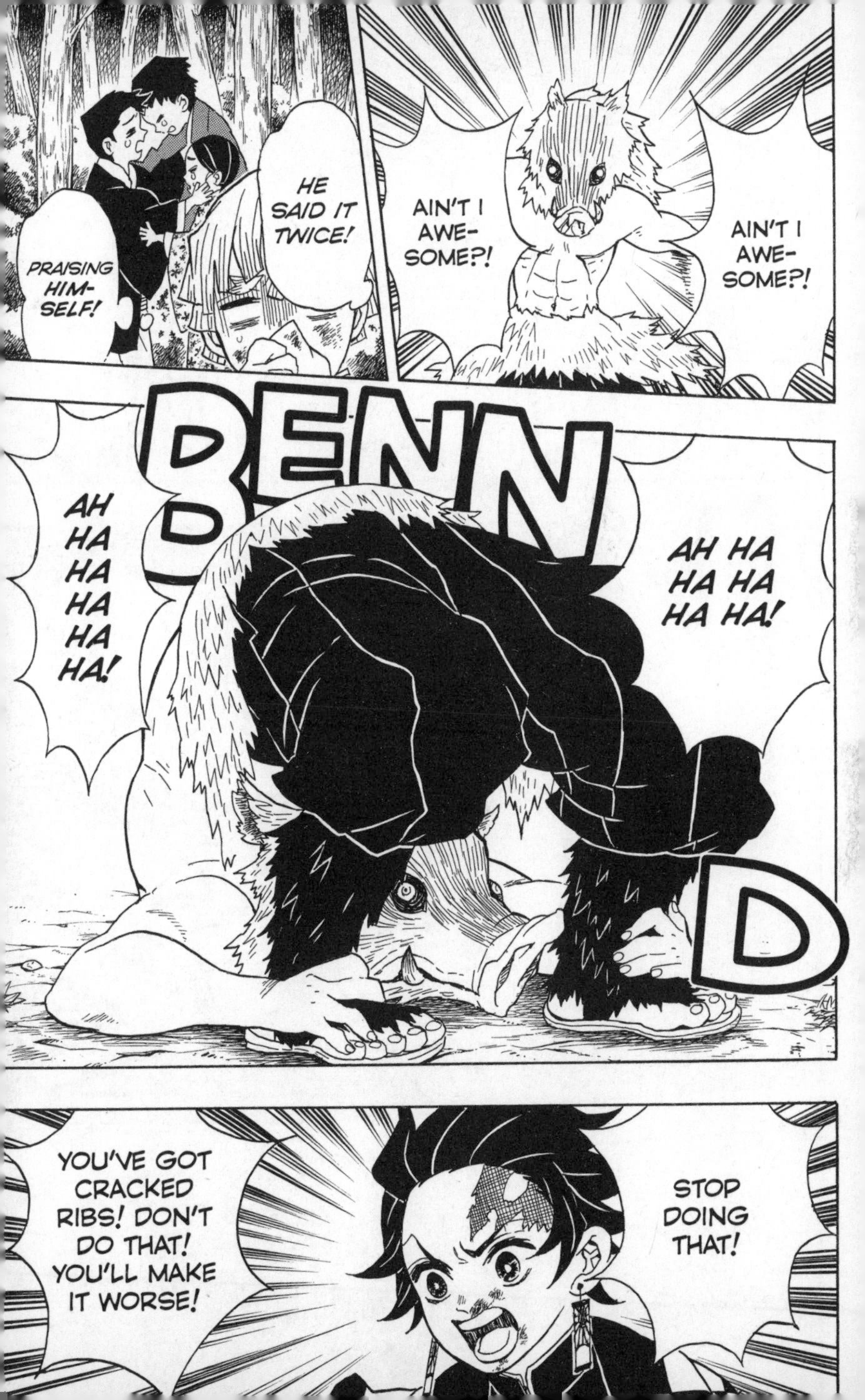
AIN'T I AWE-SOME?!
AIN'T I AWE-SOME?!
HE SAID IT TWICE!
PRAISING HIM-SELF!
BENN D
AH HA HA HA HA HA!
AH HA HA HA HA HA HA HA HA!
STOP DOING THAT!
YOU'VE GOT CRACKED RIBS! DON'T DO THAT! YOU'LL MAKE IT WORSE!

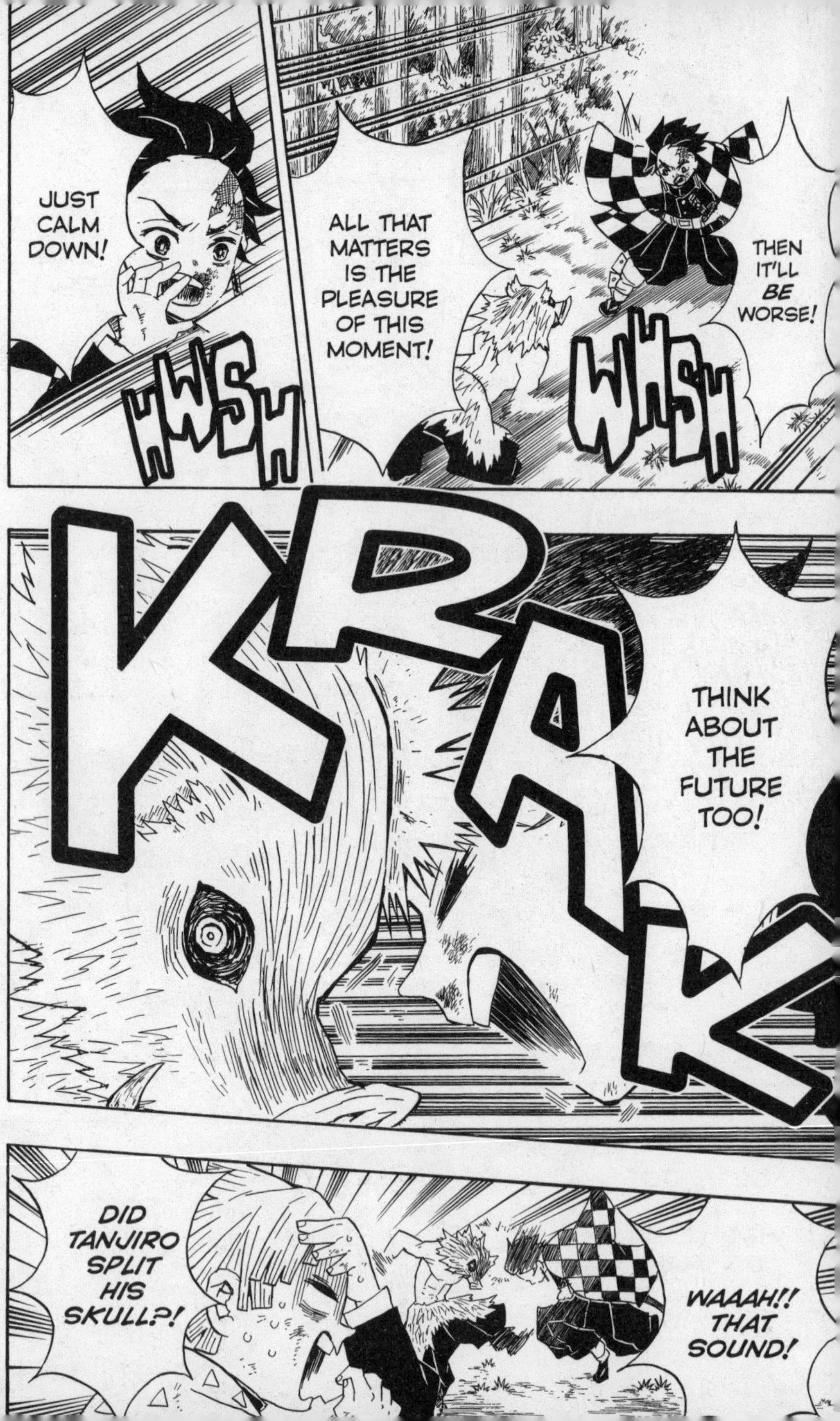
THEN IT'LL *BE* WORSE!
WHSH
ALL THAT MATTERS IS THE PLEASURE OF THIS MOMENT!
JUST CALM DOWN!
WHSH
THINK ABOUT THE FUTURE TOO!
KRAK
WAAAH!! THAT SOUND!
DID TANJIRO SPLIT HIS SKULL?!

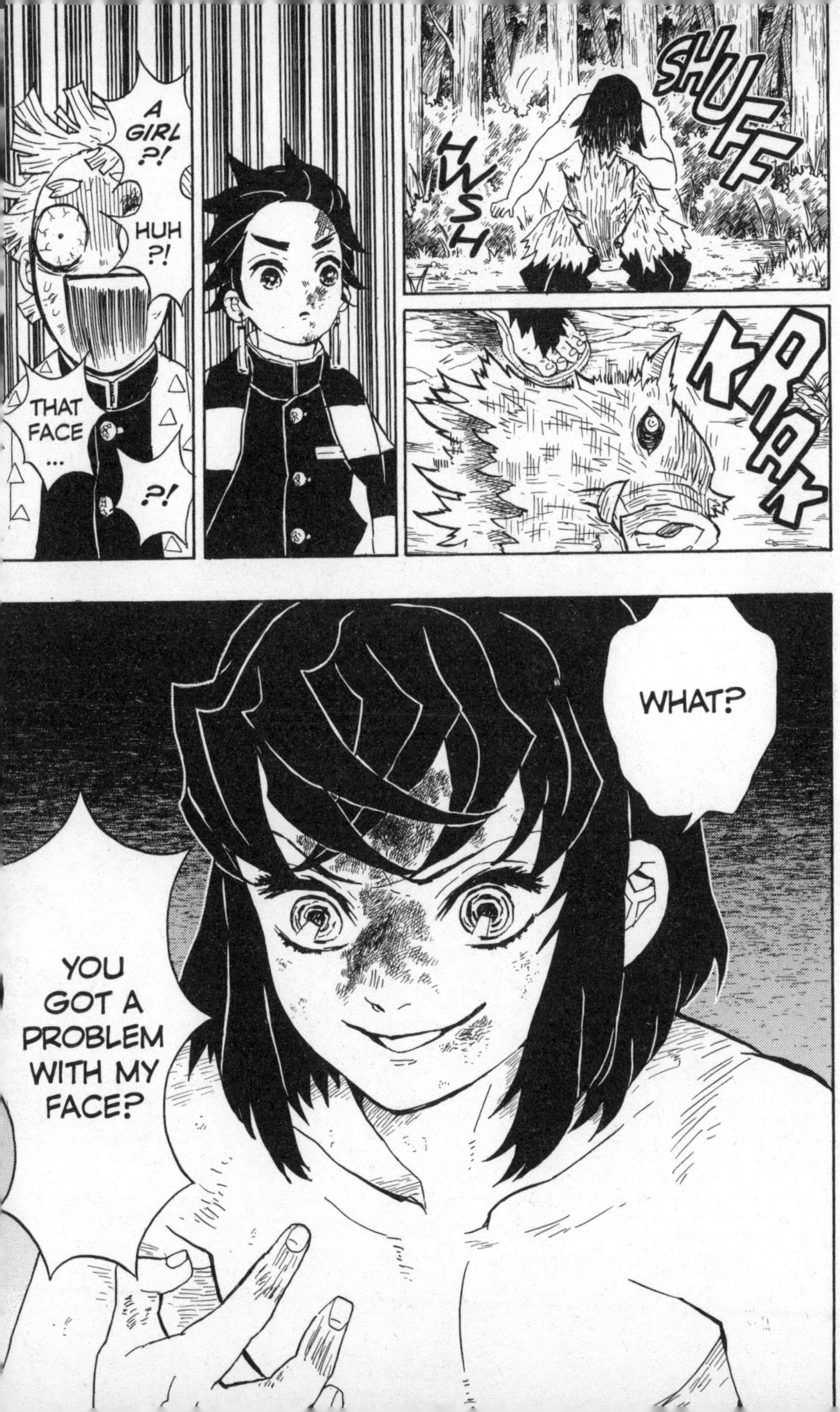
SHUFF
HWSH
KRAK
A GIRL ?!
HUH ?!
THAT FACE ...
?!
WHAT?
YOU GOT A PROBLEM WITH MY FACE?

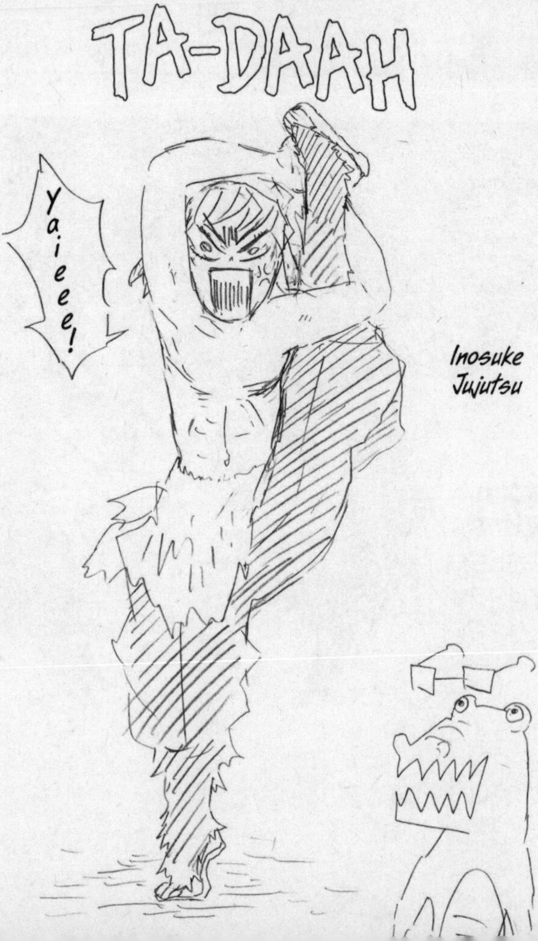
TA-DAAH
Inosuke Jujutsu
Yaieee!

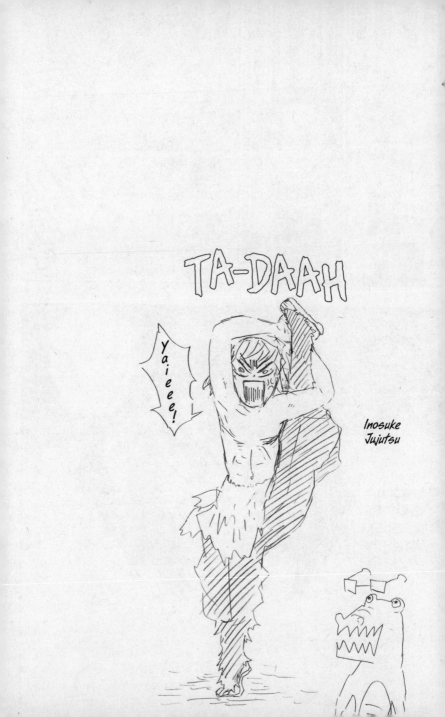

CHAPTER 27: INOSUKE HASHIBIRA

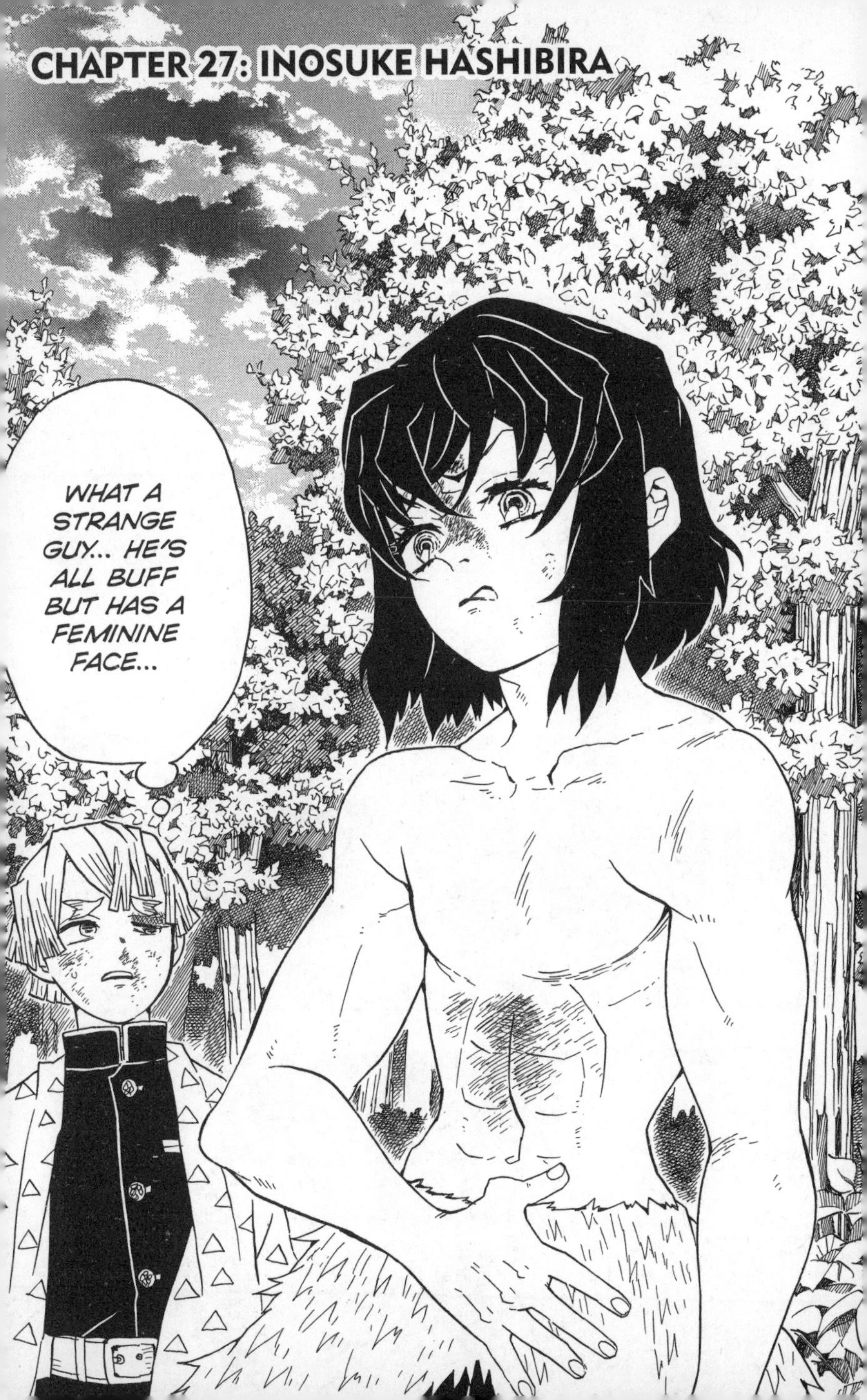
WHAT A STRANGE GUY... HE'S ALL BUFF BUT HAS A FEMININE FACE...

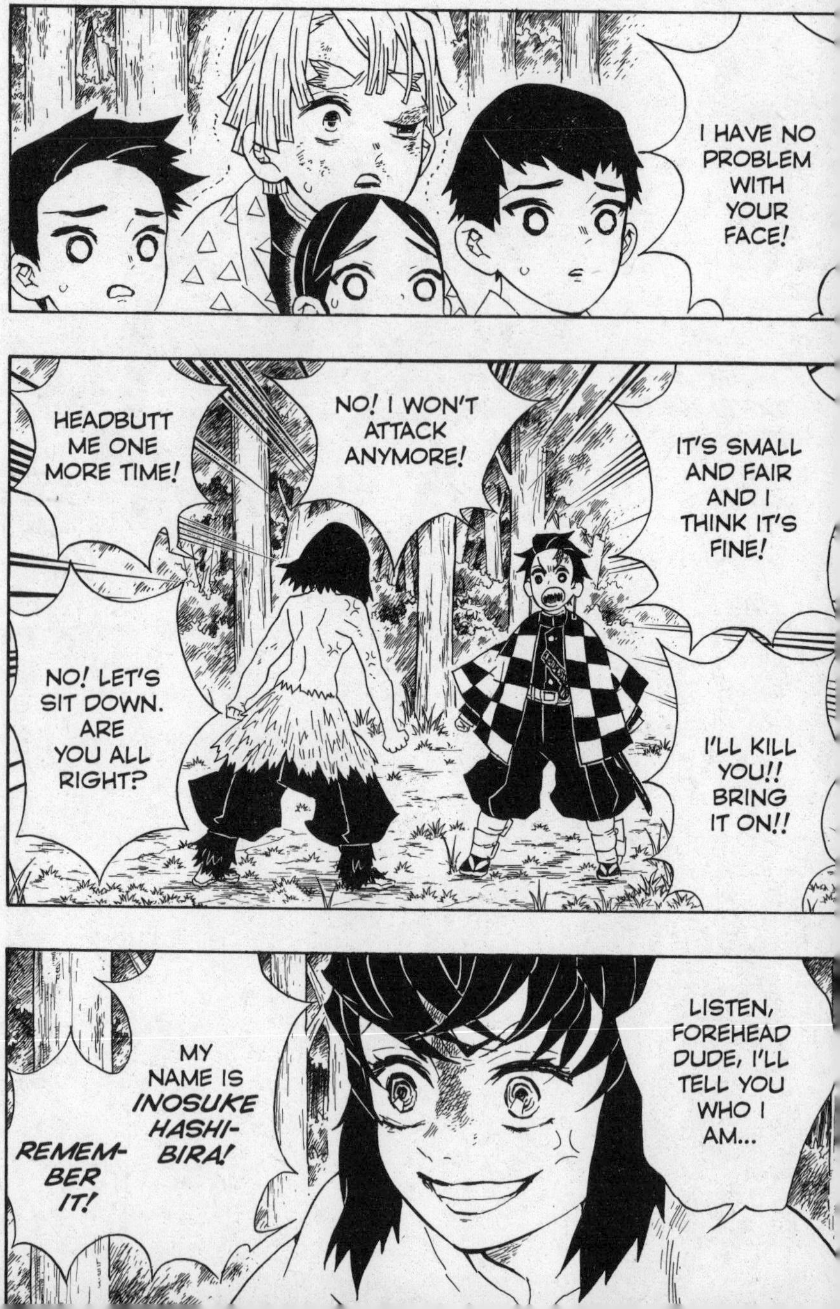
I HAVE NO PROBLEM WITH YOUR FACE!
IT'S SMALL AND FAIR AND I THINK IT'S FINE!
NO! I WON'T ATTACK ANYMORE!
HEADBUTT ME ONE MORE TIME!
I'LL KILL YOU!! BRING IT ON!!
NO! LET'S SIT DOWN. ARE YOU ALL RIGHT?
LISTEN, FOREHEAD DUDE, I'LL TELL YOU WHO I AM...
MY NAME IS *INOSUKE HASHI-BIRA!*
REMEM-BER IT!

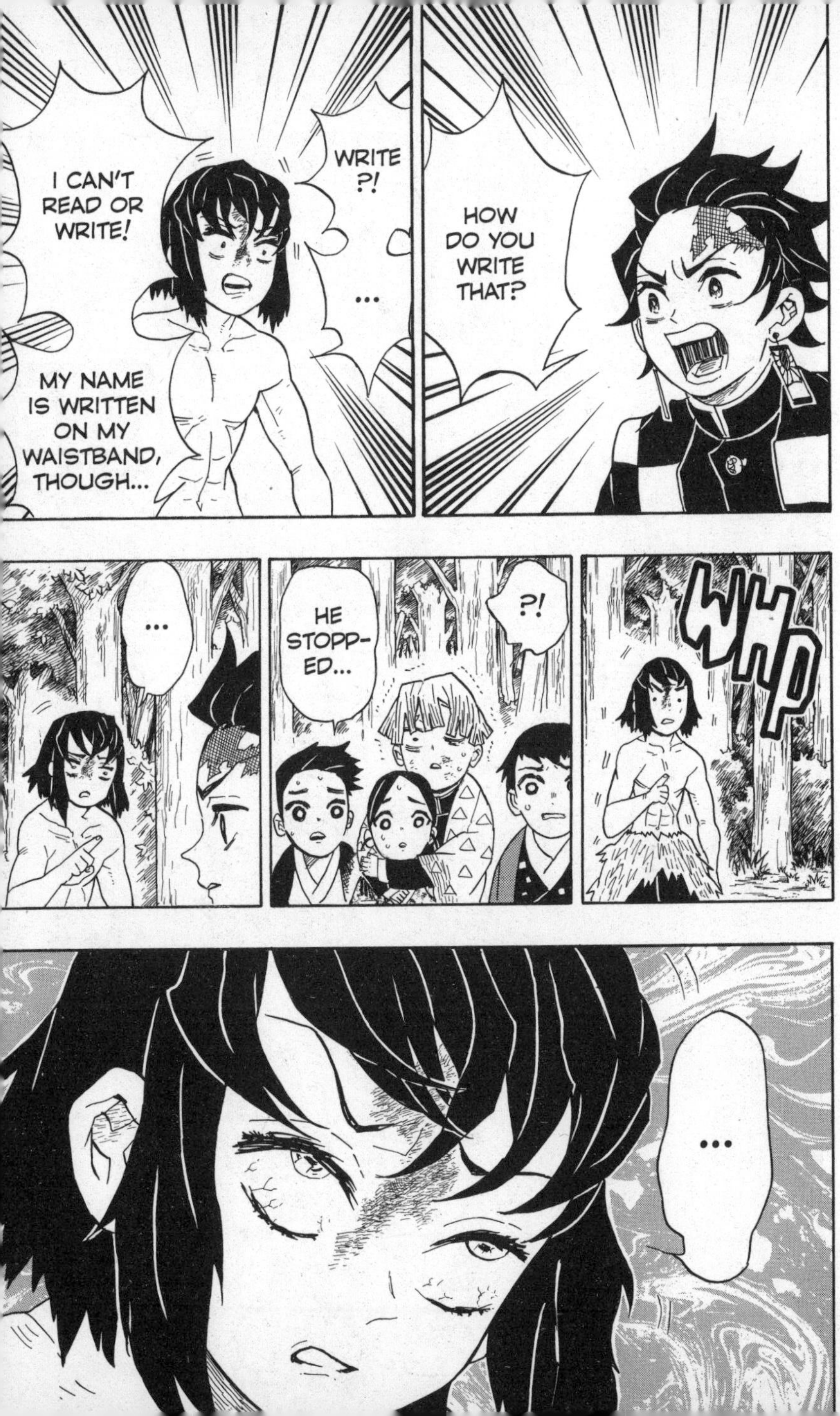
HOW DO YOU WRITE THAT?
WRITE ?!
I CAN'T READ OR WRITE!
...
MY NAME IS WRITTEN ON MY WAISTBAND, THOUGH...
WHP
?!
HE STOPP-ED...
...
...

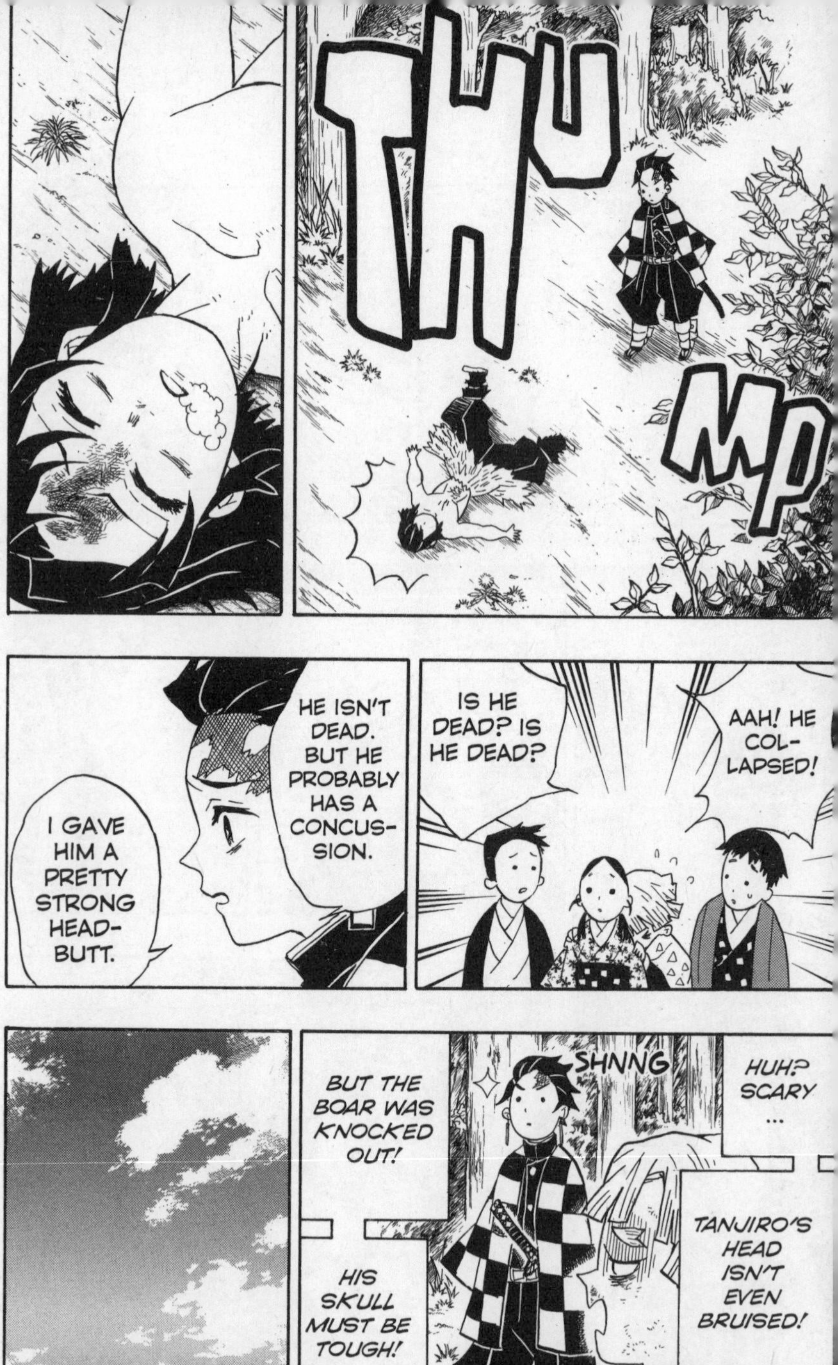
THUMP
AAH! HE COL-LAPSED!
IS HE DEAD? IS HE DEAD?
HE ISN'T DEAD. BUT HE PROBABLY HAS A CONCUSSION.
I GAVE HIM A PRETTY STRONG HEAD-BUTT.
HUH? SCARY ...
SHNNG
BUT THE BOAR WAS KNOCKED OUT!
TANJIRO'S HEAD ISN'T EVEN BRUISED!
HIS SKULL MUST BE TOUGH!

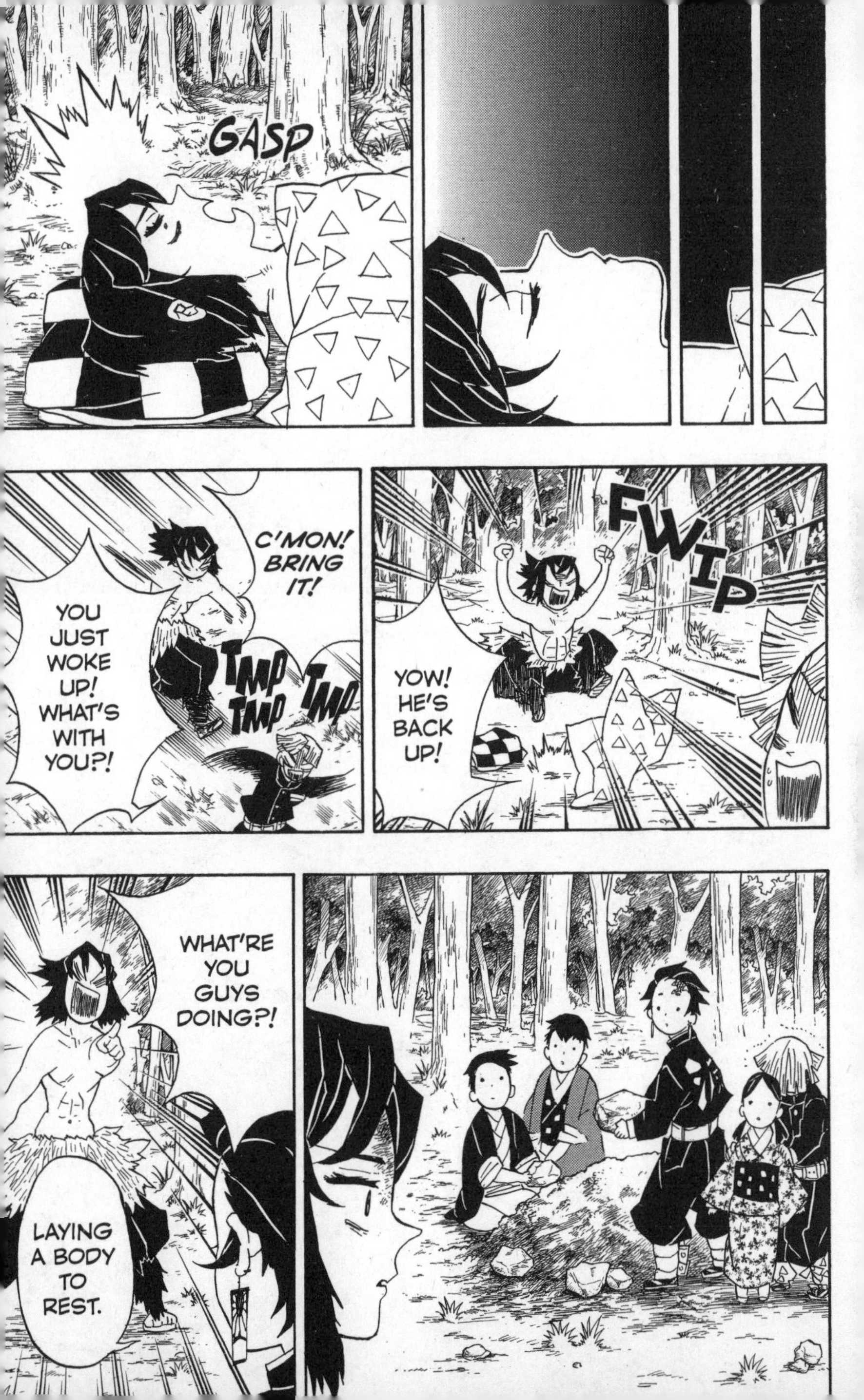
GASP
FWIP
YOW! HE'S BACK UP!
C'MON! BRING IT!
YOU JUST WOKE UP! WHAT'S WITH YOU?!
TMP TMP TMP
WHAT'RE YOU GUYS DOING?!
LAYING A BODY TO REST.

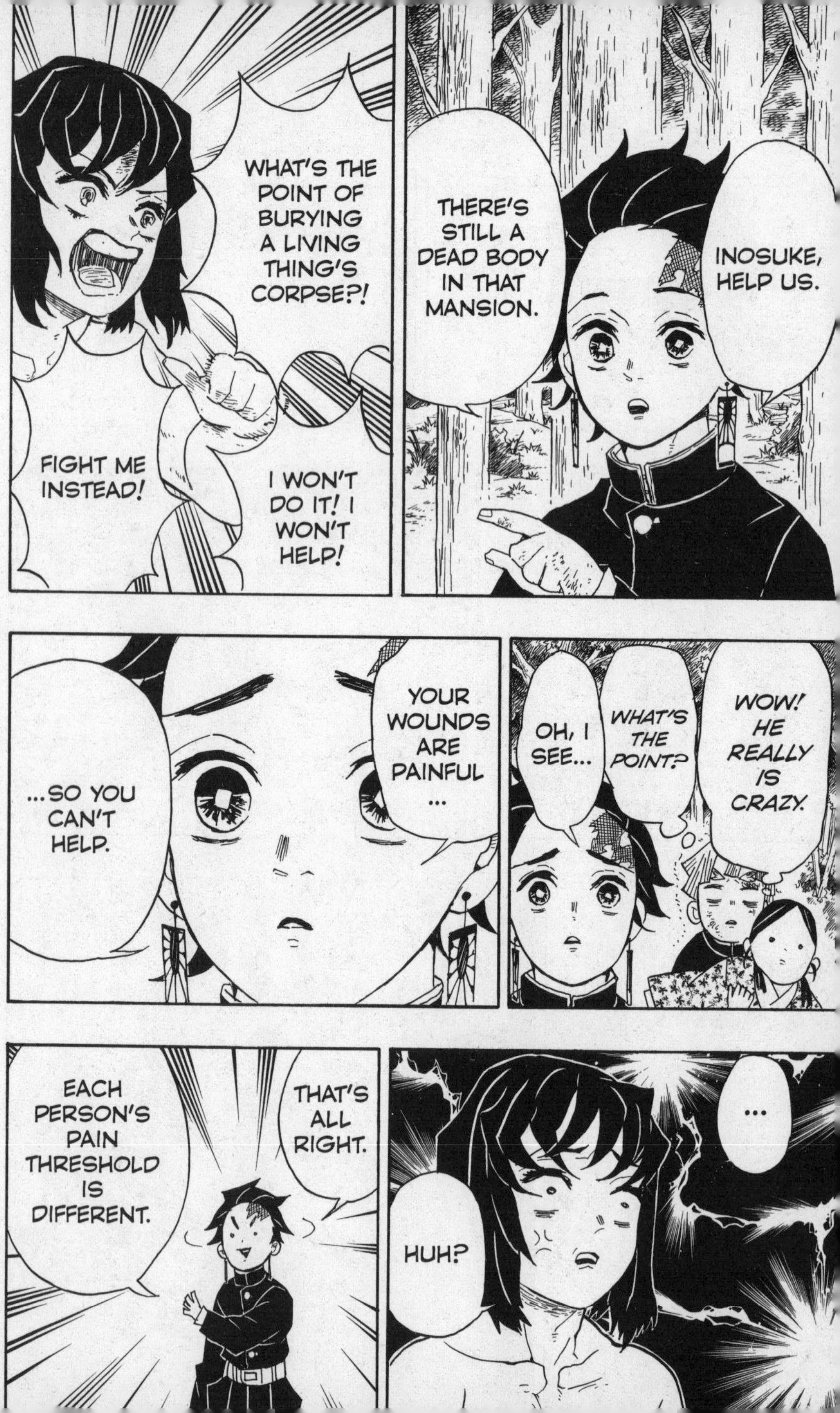
INOSUKE, HELP US.
THERE'S STILL A DEAD BODY IN THAT MANSION.
WHAT'S THE POINT OF BURYING A LIVING THING'S CORPSE?!
I WON'T DO IT! I WON'T HELP!
FIGHT ME INSTEAD!
WOW! HE REALLY IS CRAZY.
WHAT'S THE POINT?
OH, I SEE...
YOUR WOUNDS ARE PAINFUL ...
...SO YOU CAN'T HELP.
...
HUH?
THAT'S ALL RIGHT.
EACH PERSON'S PAIN THRESHOLD IS DIFFERENT.

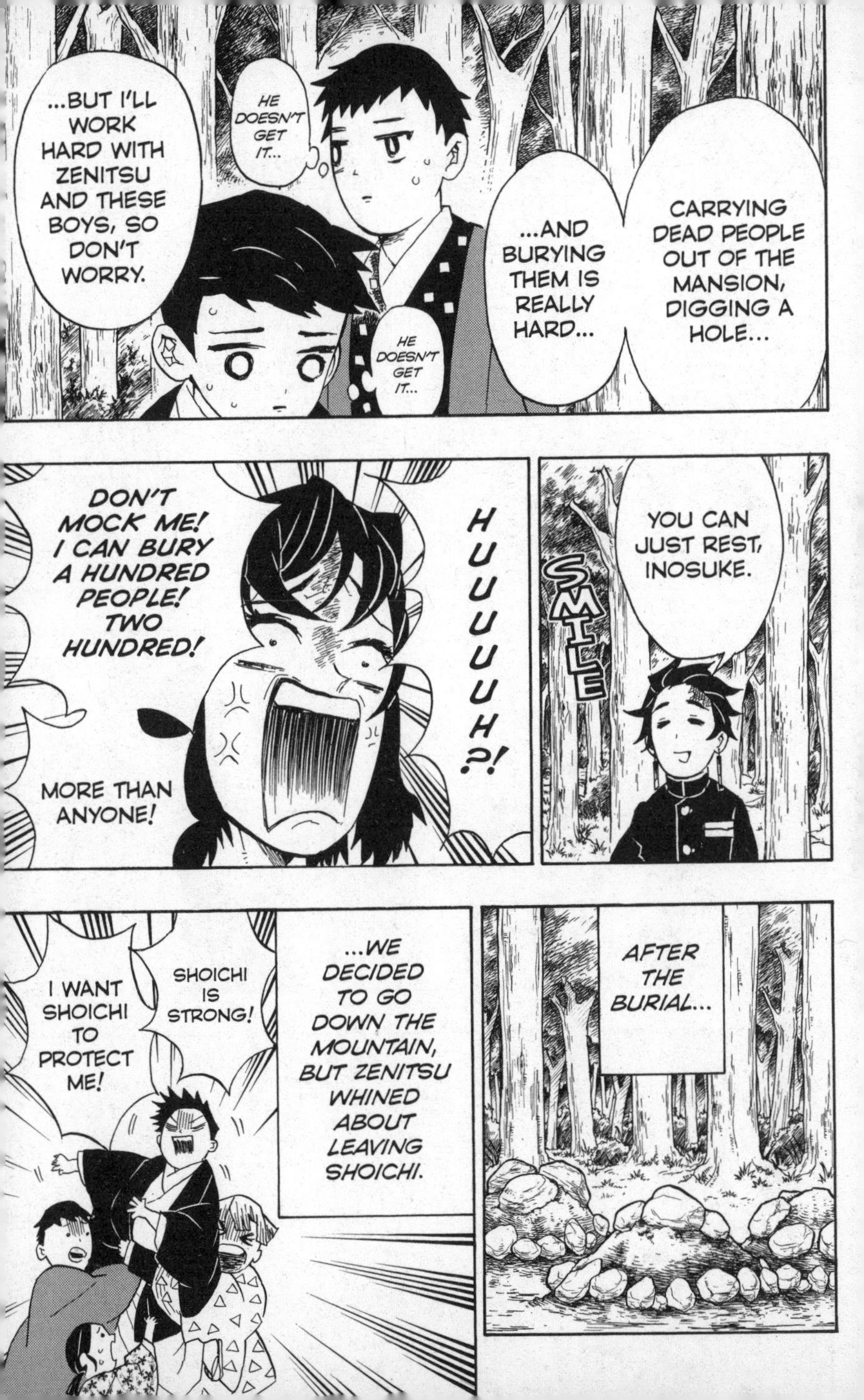

CARRYING DEAD PEOPLE OUT OF THE MANSION, DIGGING A HOLE...
...AND BURYING THEM IS REALLY HARD...
...BUT I'LL WORK HARD WITH ZENITSU AND THESE BOYS, SO DON'T WORRY.
HE DOESN'T GET IT...
HE DOESN'T GET IT...
SMILE
YOU CAN JUST REST, INOSUKE.
HUUUUUH?!
DON'T MOCK ME! I CAN BURY A HUNDRED PEOPLE! TWO HUNDRED!
MORE THAN ANYONE!
AFTER THE BURIAL...
...WE DECIDED TO GO DOWN THE MOUNTAIN, BUT ZENITSU WHINED ABOUT LEAVING SHOICHI.
SHOICHI IS STRONG!
I WANT SHOICHI TO PROTECT ME!

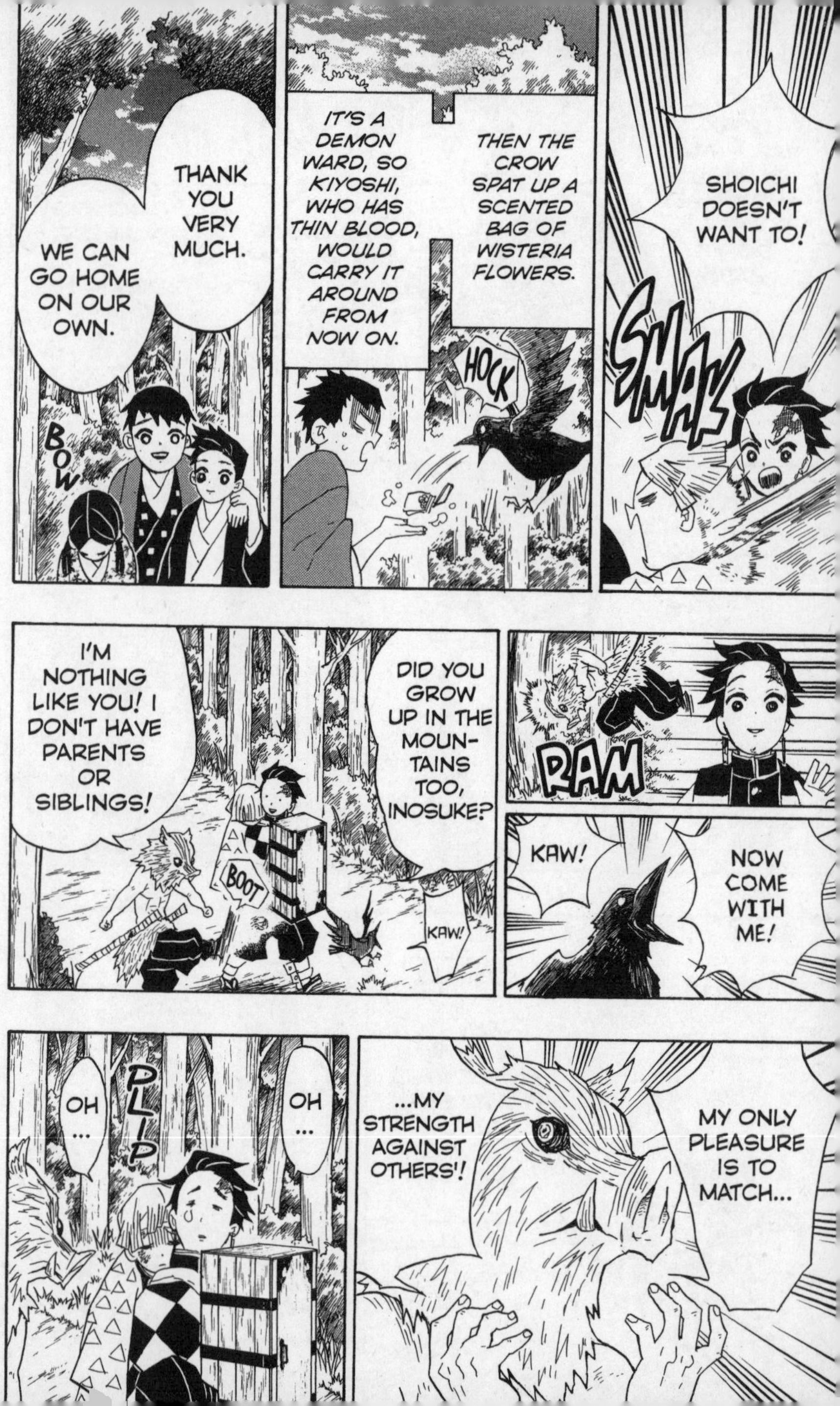
SHOICHI DOESN'T WANT TO!
SMAK
THEN THE CROW SPAT UP A SCENTED BAG OF WISTERIA FLOWERS.
IT'S A DEMON WARD, SO KIYOSHI, WHO HAS THIN BLOOD, WOULD CARRY IT AROUND FROM NOW ON.
HOCK
THANK YOU VERY MUCH.
WE CAN GO HOME ON OUR OWN.
BOW
RAM
NOW COME WITH ME!
KAW!
DID YOU GROW UP IN THE MOUN-TAINS TOO, INOSUKE?
I'M NOTHING LIKE YOU! I DON'T HAVE PARENTS OR SIBLINGS!
BOOT
KAW!
MY ONLY PLEASURE IS TO MATCH...
...MY STRENGTH AGAINST OTHERS!!
OH ...
PLIP
OH ...

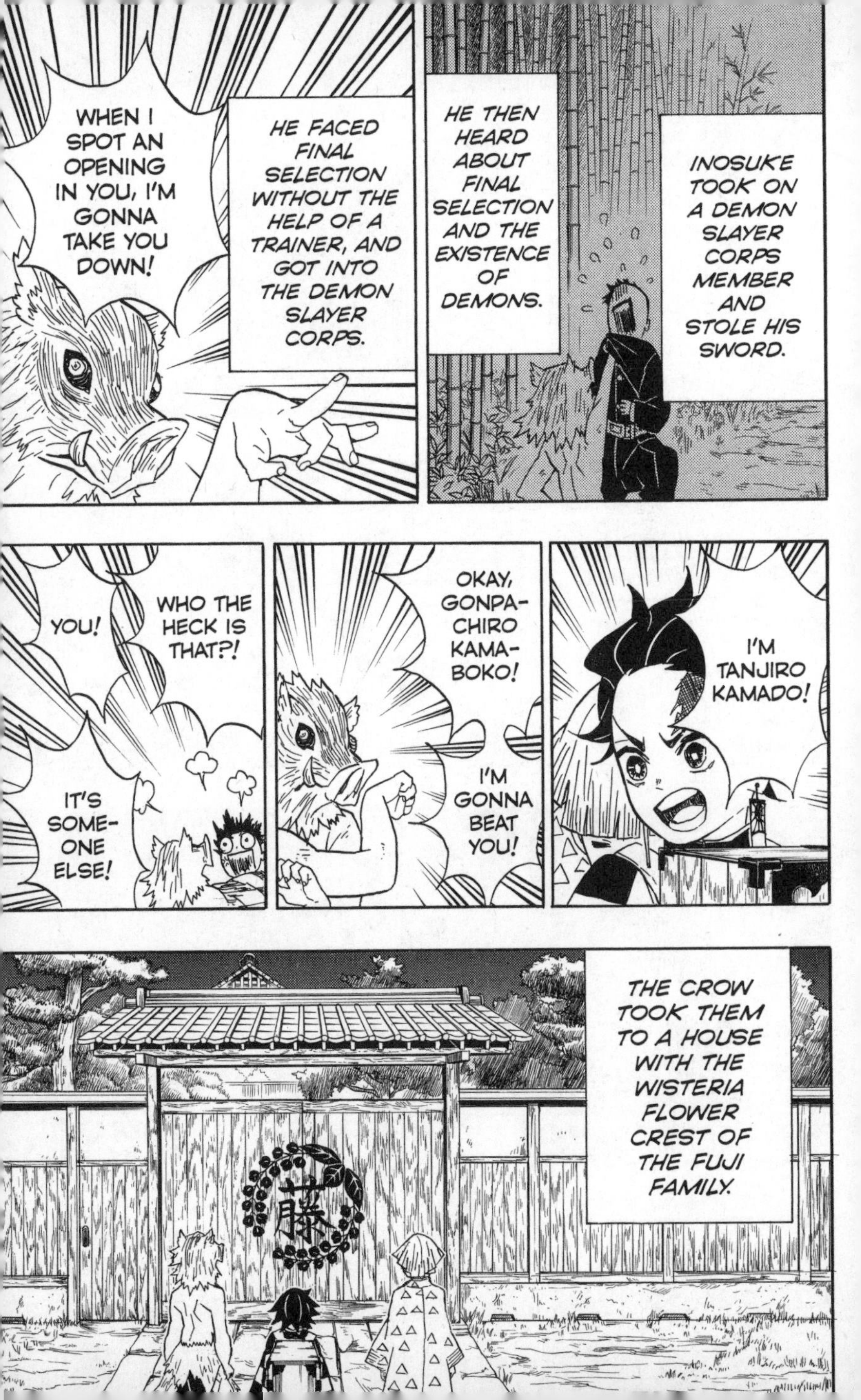
INOSUKE TOOK ON A DEMON SLAYER CORPS MEMBER AND STOLE HIS SWORD.
HE THEN HEARD ABOUT FINAL SELECTION AND THE EXISTENCE OF DEMONS.
HE FACED FINAL SELECTION WITHOUT THE HELP OF A TRAINER, AND GOT INTO THE DEMON SLAYER CORPS.
WHEN I SPOT AN OPENING IN YOU, I'M GONNA TAKE YOU DOWN!
I'M TANJIRO KAMADO!
OKAY, GONPACHIRO KAMABOKO!
I'M GONNA BEAT YOU!
WHO THE HECK IS THAT?!
YOU!
IT'S SOMEONE ELSE!
THE CROW TOOK THEM TO A HOUSE WITH THE WISTERIA FLOWER CREST OF THE FUJI FAMILY.
藤

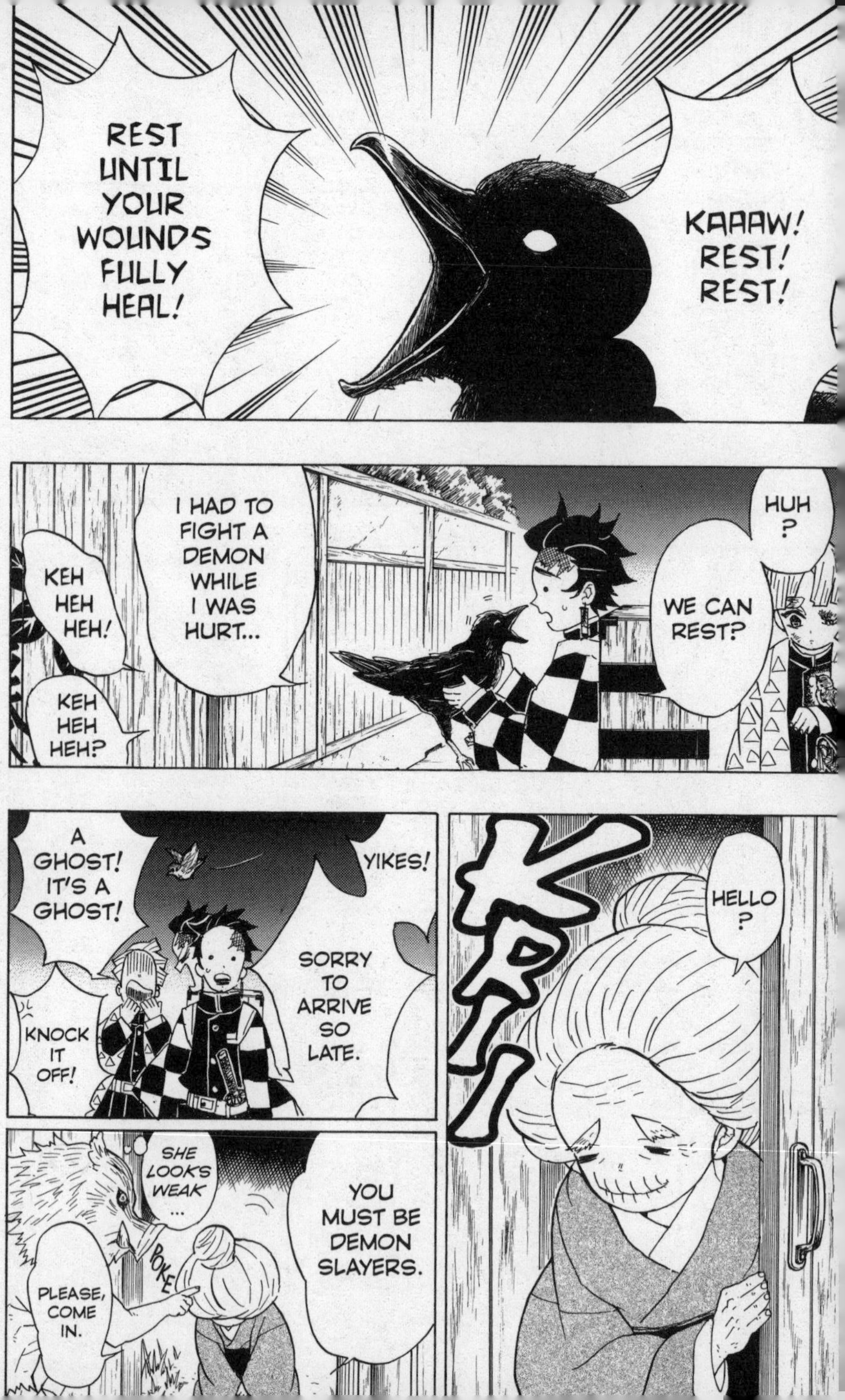
KAAAW! REST! REST!
REST UNTIL YOUR WOUNDS FULLY HEAL!
HUH?
WE CAN REST?
I HAD TO FIGHT A DEMON WHILE I WAS HURT...
KEH HEH HEH!
KEH HEH HEH?
HELLO?
YIKES!
A GHOST! IT'S A GHOST!
SORRY TO ARRIVE SO LATE.
KNOCK IT OFF!
YOU MUST BE DEMON SLAYERS.
SHE LOOKS WEAK...
POKE
PLEASE, COME IN.

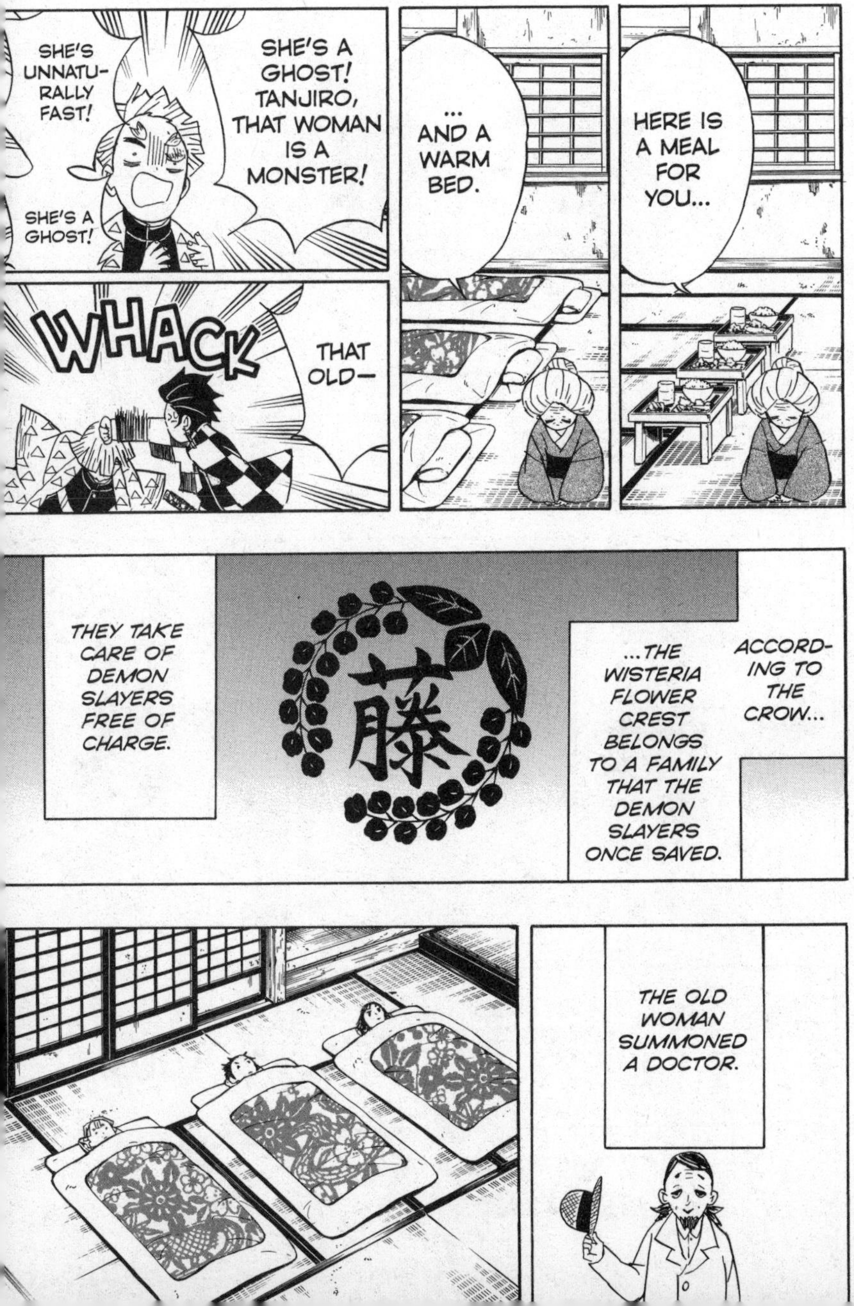
HERE IS A MEAL FOR YOU...
... AND A WARM BED.
SHE'S A GHOST! TANJIRO, THAT WOMAN IS A MONSTER!
SHE'S UNNATU-RALLY FAST!
SHE'S A GHOST!
THAT OLD—
WHACK
ACCORD-ING TO THE CROW...
...THE WISTERIA FLOWER CREST BELONGS TO A FAMILY THAT THE DEMON SLAYERS ONCE SAVED.
藤
THEY TAKE CARE OF DEMON SLAYERS FREE OF CHARGE.
THE OLD WOMAN SUMMONED A DOCTOR.

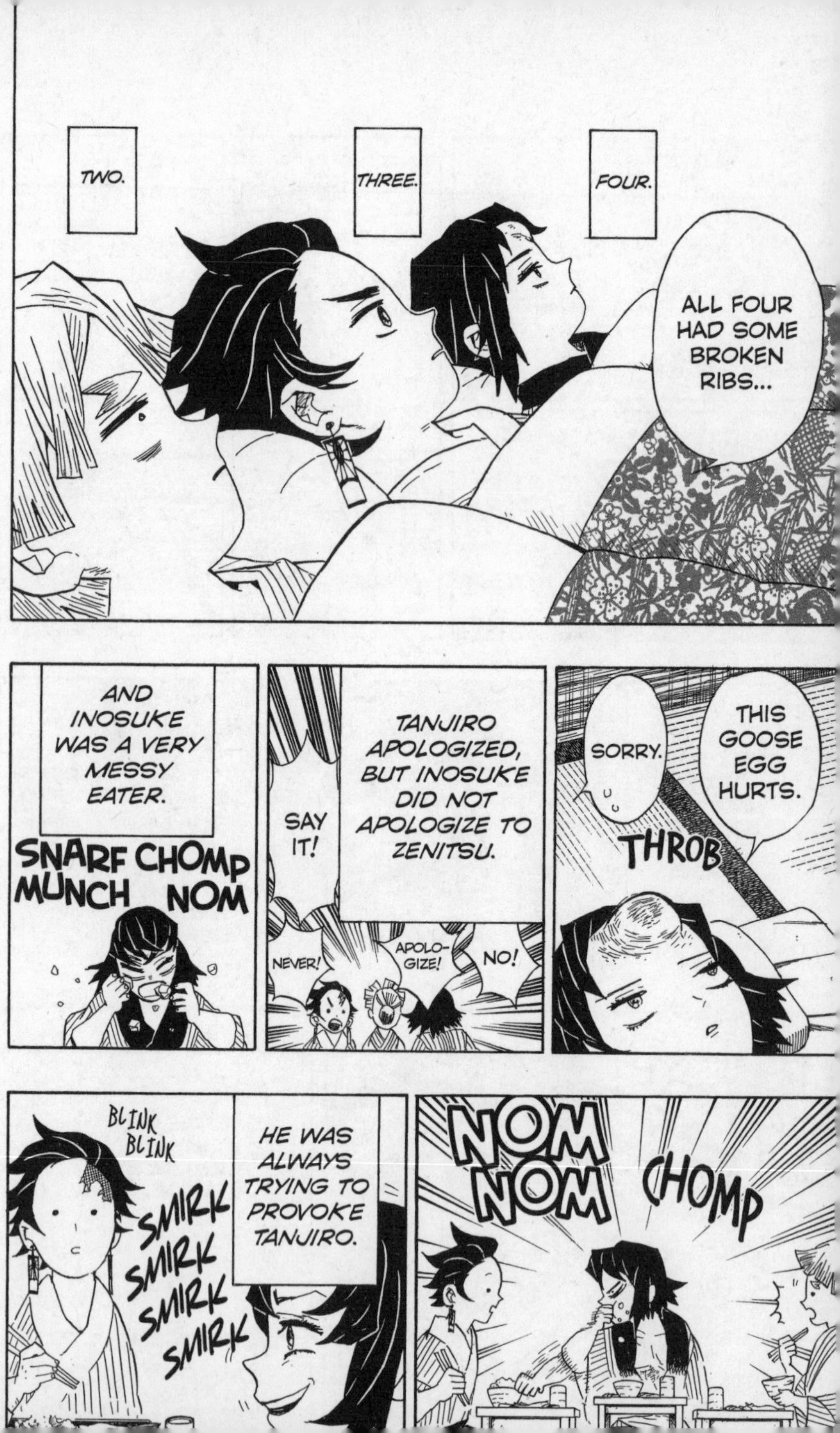
FOUR.
THREE.
TWO.
ALL FOUR HAD SOME BROKEN RIBS...
THIS GOOSE EGG HURTS.
SORRY.
THROB
TANJIRO APOLOGIZED, BUT INOSUKE DID NOT APOLOGIZE TO ZENITSU.
SAY IT!
NO!
APOLO-GIZE!
NEVER!
AND INOSUKE WAS A VERY MESSY EATER.
SNARF CHOMP
MUNCH NOM
NOM NOM
CHOMP
HE WAS ALWAYS TRYING TO PROVOKE TANJIRO.
BLINK BLINK
SMIRK SMIRK SMIRK SMIRK

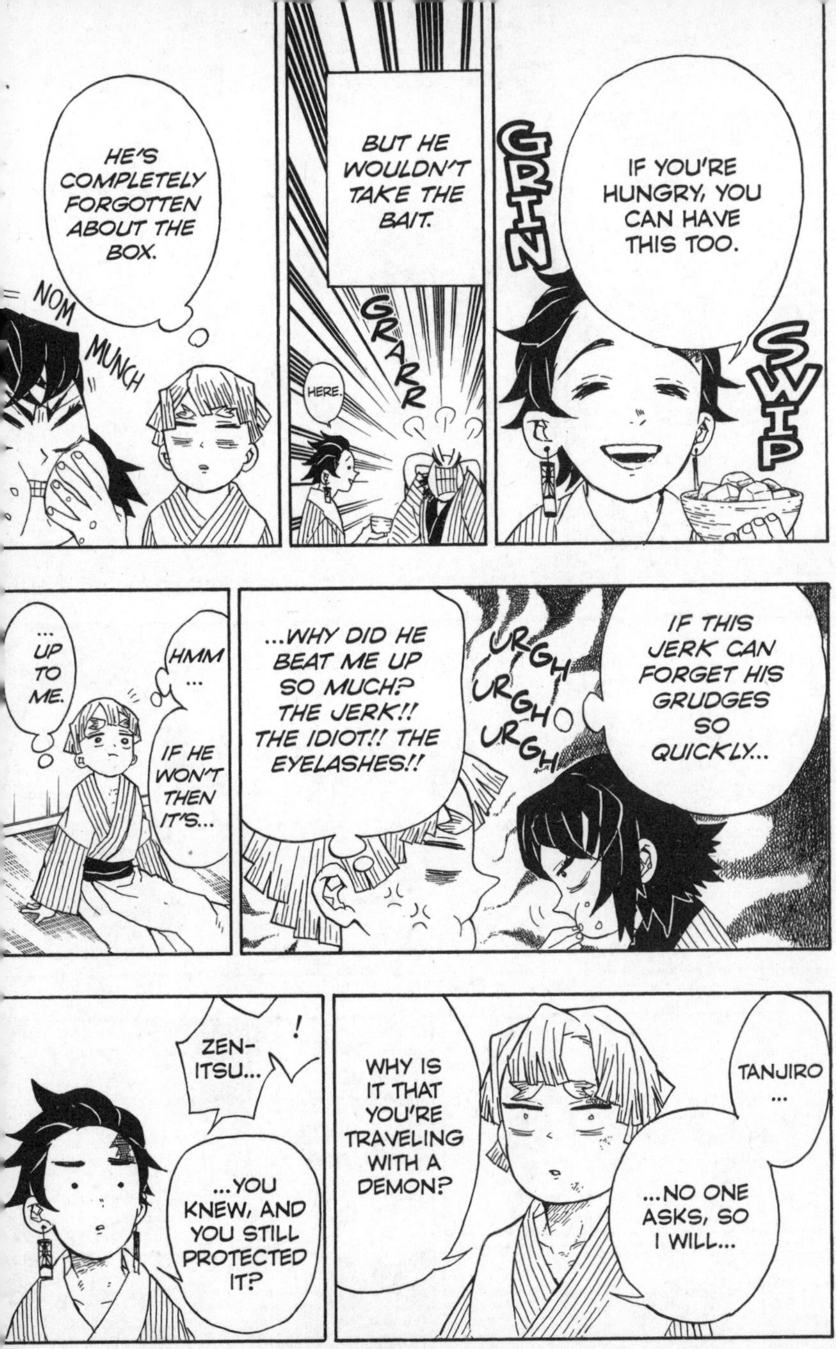
GRIN
IF YOU'RE HUNGRY, YOU CAN HAVE THIS TOO.
SWIP
BUT HE WOULDN'T TAKE THE BAIT.
GRARR
HERE.
HE'S COMPLETELY FORGOTTEN ABOUT THE BOX.
NOM
MUNCH
IF THIS JERK CAN FORGET HIS GRUDGES SO QUICKLY...
URGH
URGH
URGH
...WHY DID HE BEAT ME UP SO MUCH? THE JERK!! THE IDIOT!! THE EYELASHES!!
HMM...
IF HE WON'T THEN IT'S...
...UP TO ME.
TANJIRO...
...NO ONE ASKS, SO I WILL...
WHY IS IT THAT YOU'RE TRAVELING WITH A DEMON?
!
ZEN-ITSU...
...YOU KNEW, AND YOU STILL PROTECTED IT?

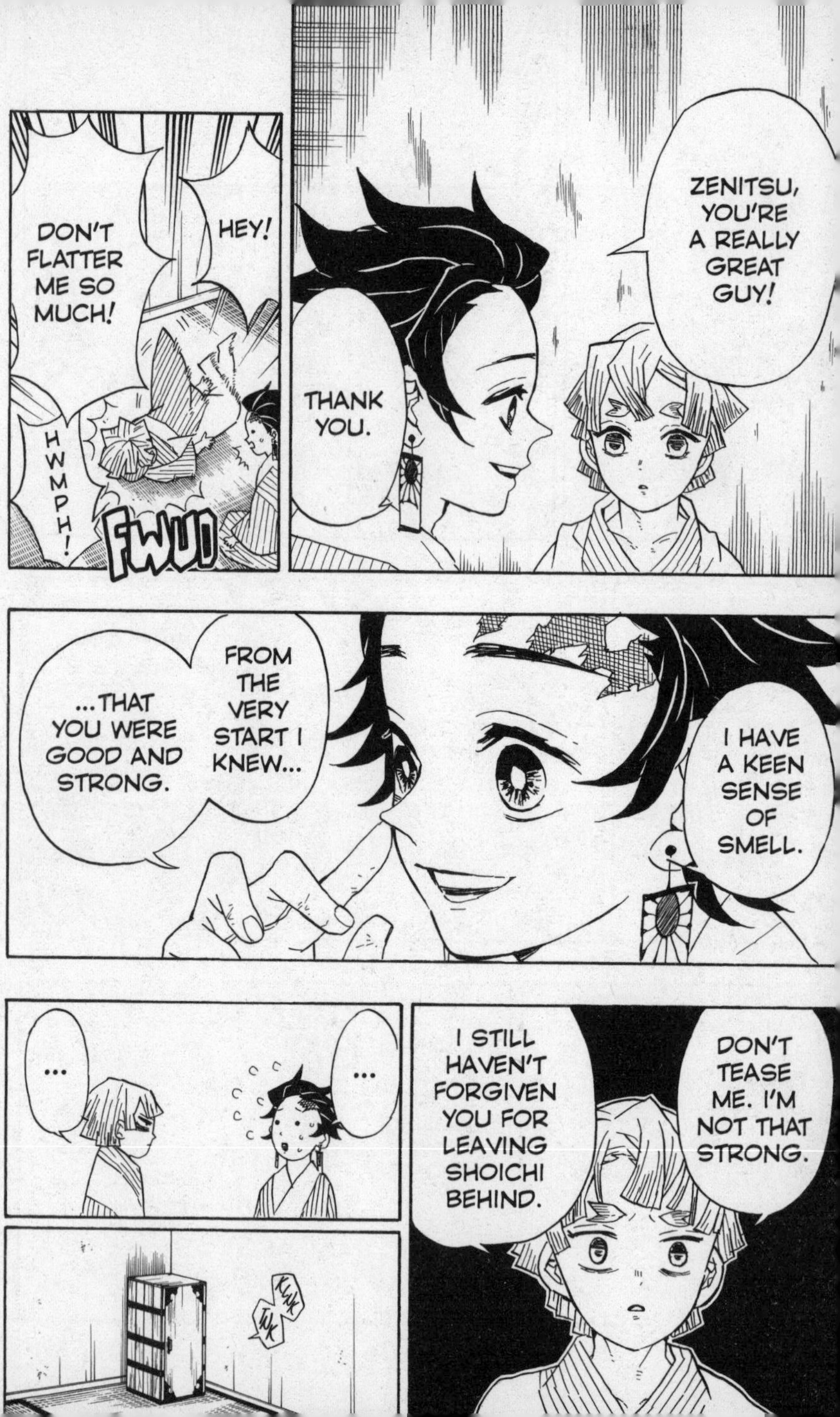

ZENITSU, YOU'RE A REALLY GREAT GUY!
THANK YOU.
HEY!
DON'T FLATTER ME SO MUCH!
HWMPH!
FWUD
I HAVE A KEEN SENSE OF SMELL.
FROM THE VERY START I KNEW...
...THAT YOU WERE GOOD AND STRONG.
DON'T TEASE ME. I'M NOT THAT STRONG.
I STILL HAVEN'T FORGIVEN YOU FOR LEAVING SHOICHI BEHIND.
...
...
KLAK
TUK

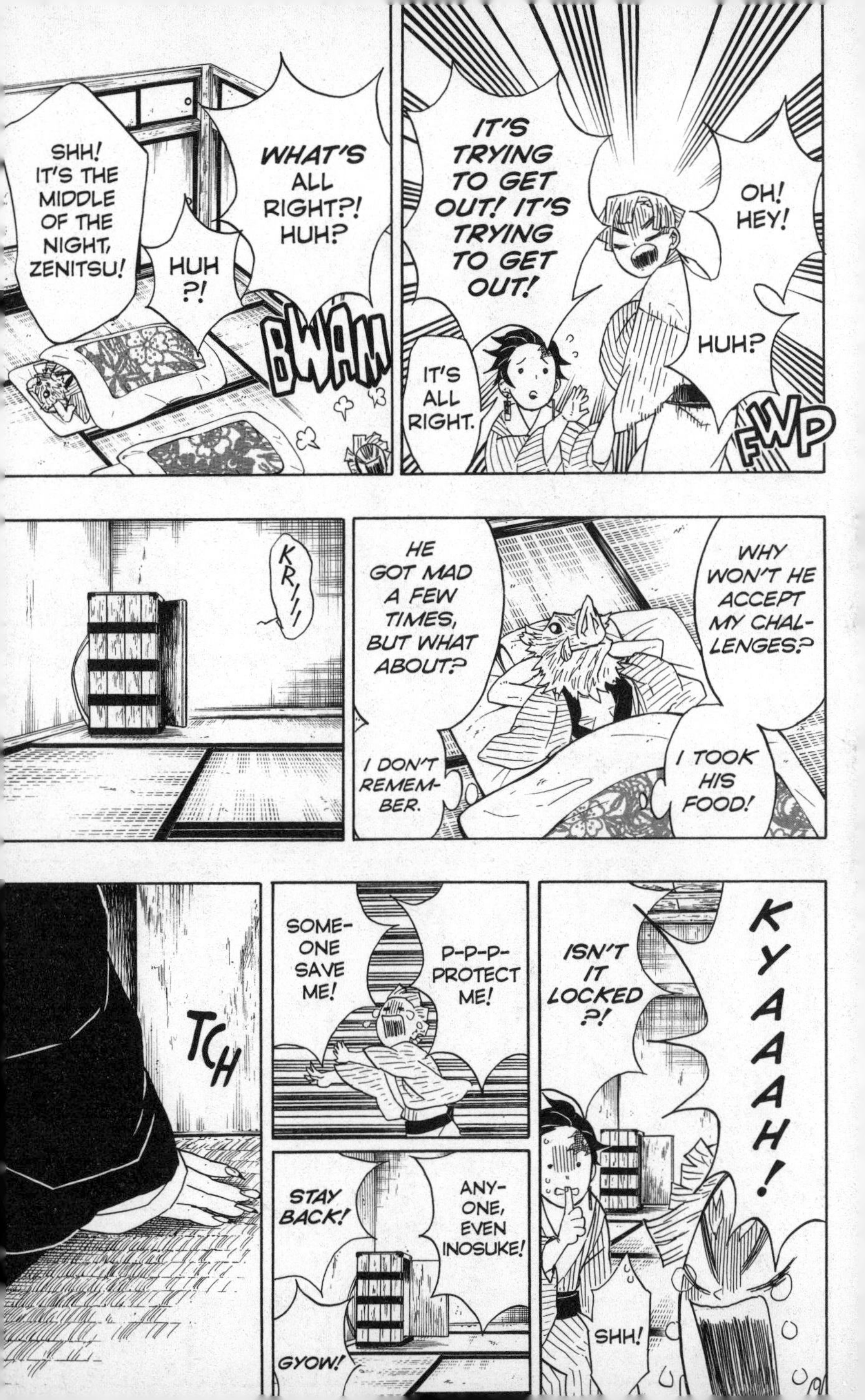
OH! HEY!
IT'S TRYING TO GET OUT! IT'S TRYING TO GET OUT!
HUH?
FWP
IT'S ALL RIGHT.
WHAT'S ALL RIGHT?! HUH?
SHH! IT'S THE MIDDLE OF THE NIGHT, ZENITSU!
HUH ?!
BWAM
WHY WON'T HE ACCEPT MY CHAL-LENGES?
HE GOT MAD A FEW TIMES, BUT WHAT ABOUT?
I TOOK HIS FOOD!
I DON'T REMEM-BER.
KRI
KYAAAAH!
ISN'T IT LOCKED ?!
SHH!
P-P-P-PROTECT ME!
SOME-ONE SAVE ME!
ANY-ONE, EVEN INOSUKE!
STAY BACK!
GYOW!
TCH

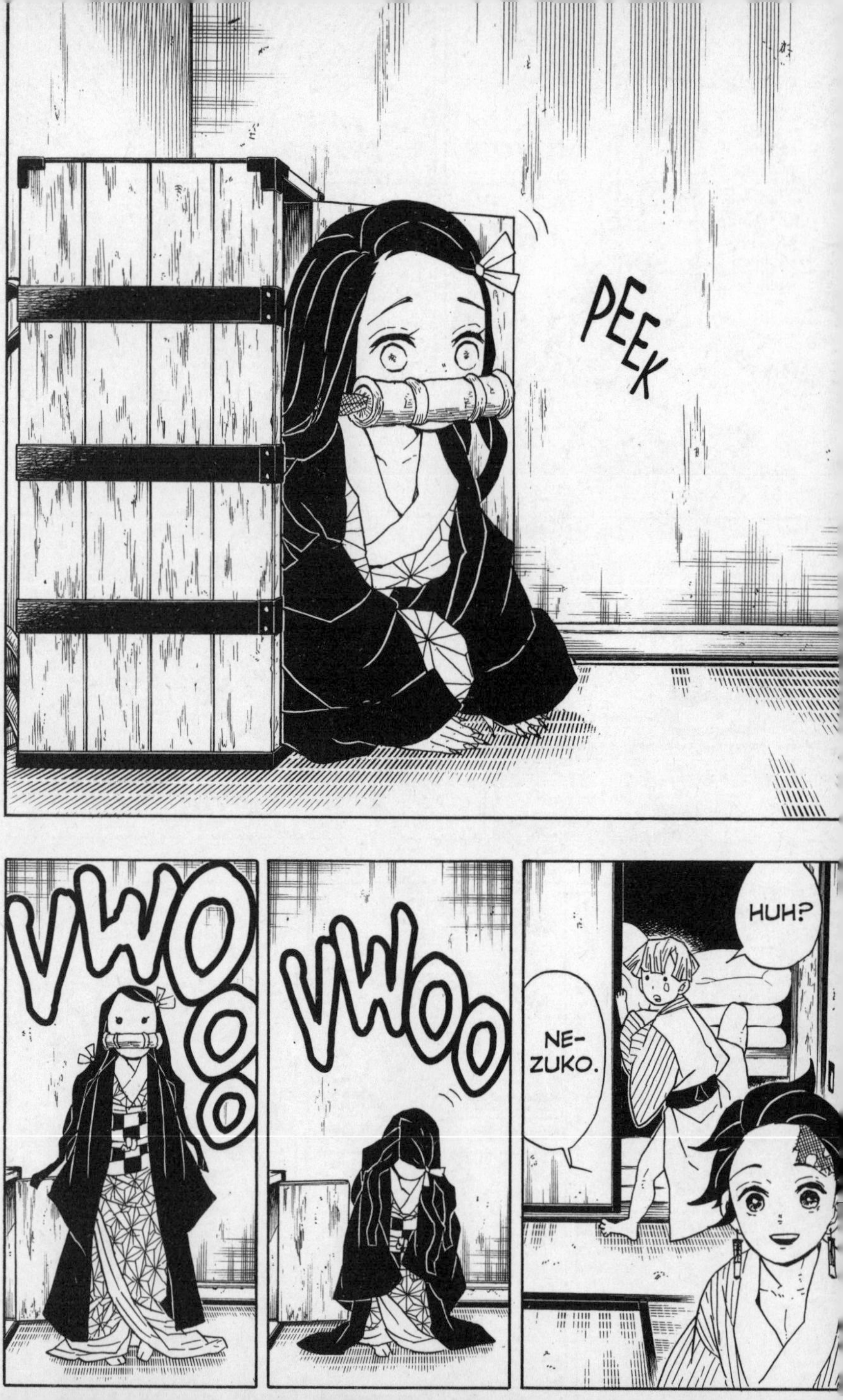
PEEK
HUH?
NE-ZUKO.
VWOO
VWOOOO

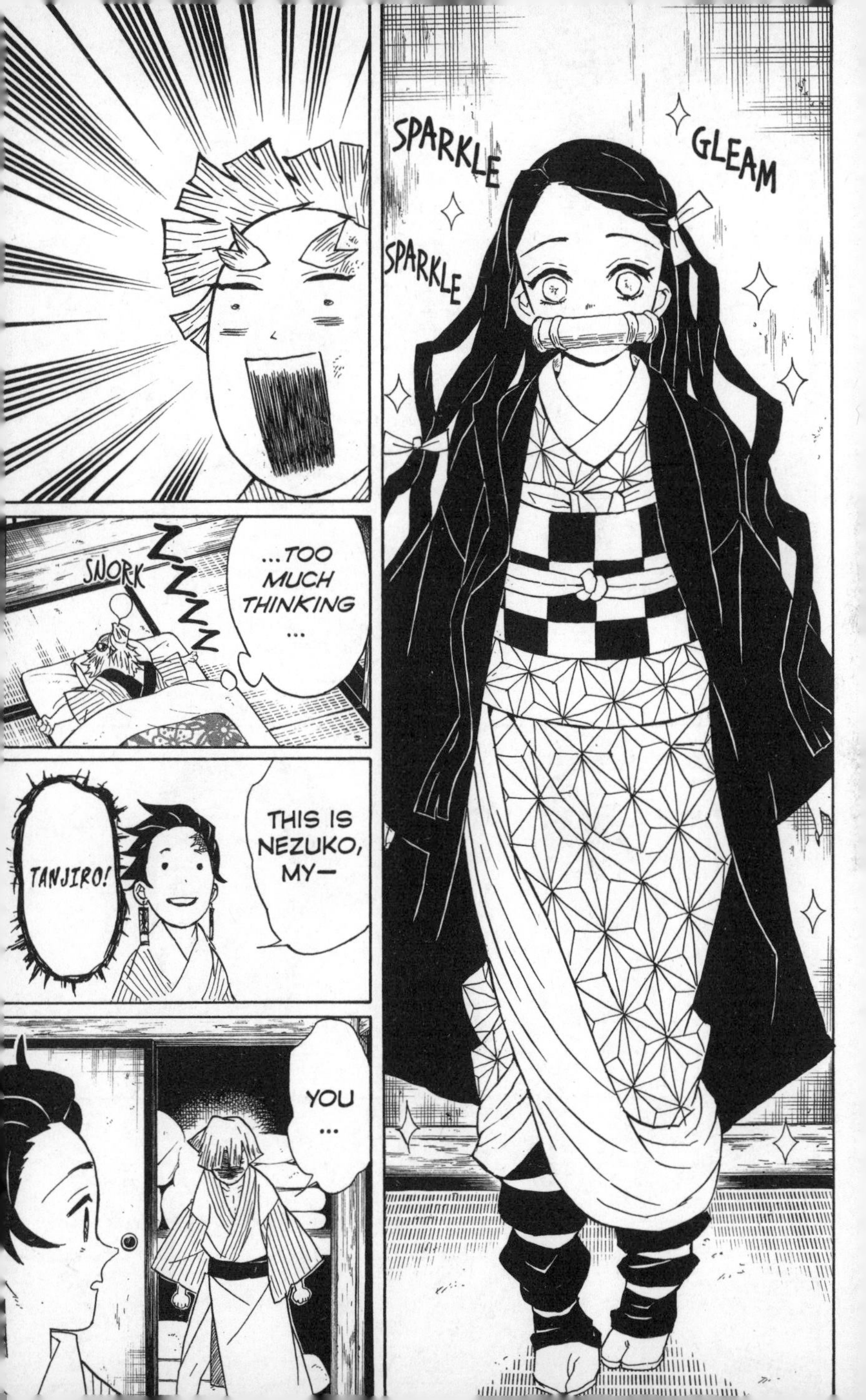
GLEAM
SPARKLE
SPARKLE
...TOO MUCH THINKING ...
ZZZZ
SNORK
THIS IS NEZUKO, MY—
TANJIRO!
YOU ...

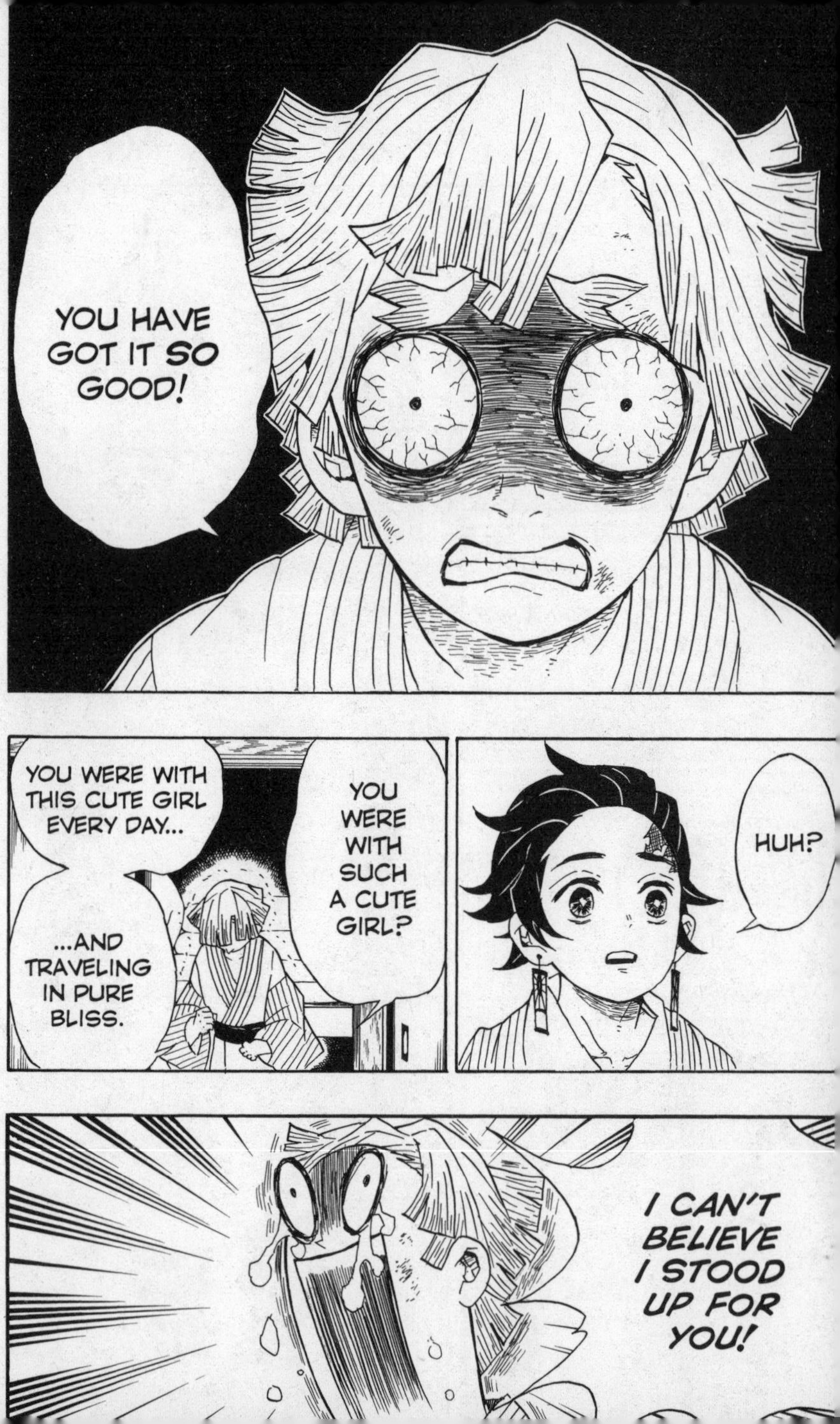
YOU HAVE GOT IT SO GOOD!
HUH?
YOU WERE WITH SUCH A CUTE GIRL?
YOU WERE WITH THIS CUTE GIRL EVERY DAY...
...AND TRAVELING IN PURE BLISS.
I CAN'T BELIEVE I STOOD UP FOR YOU!

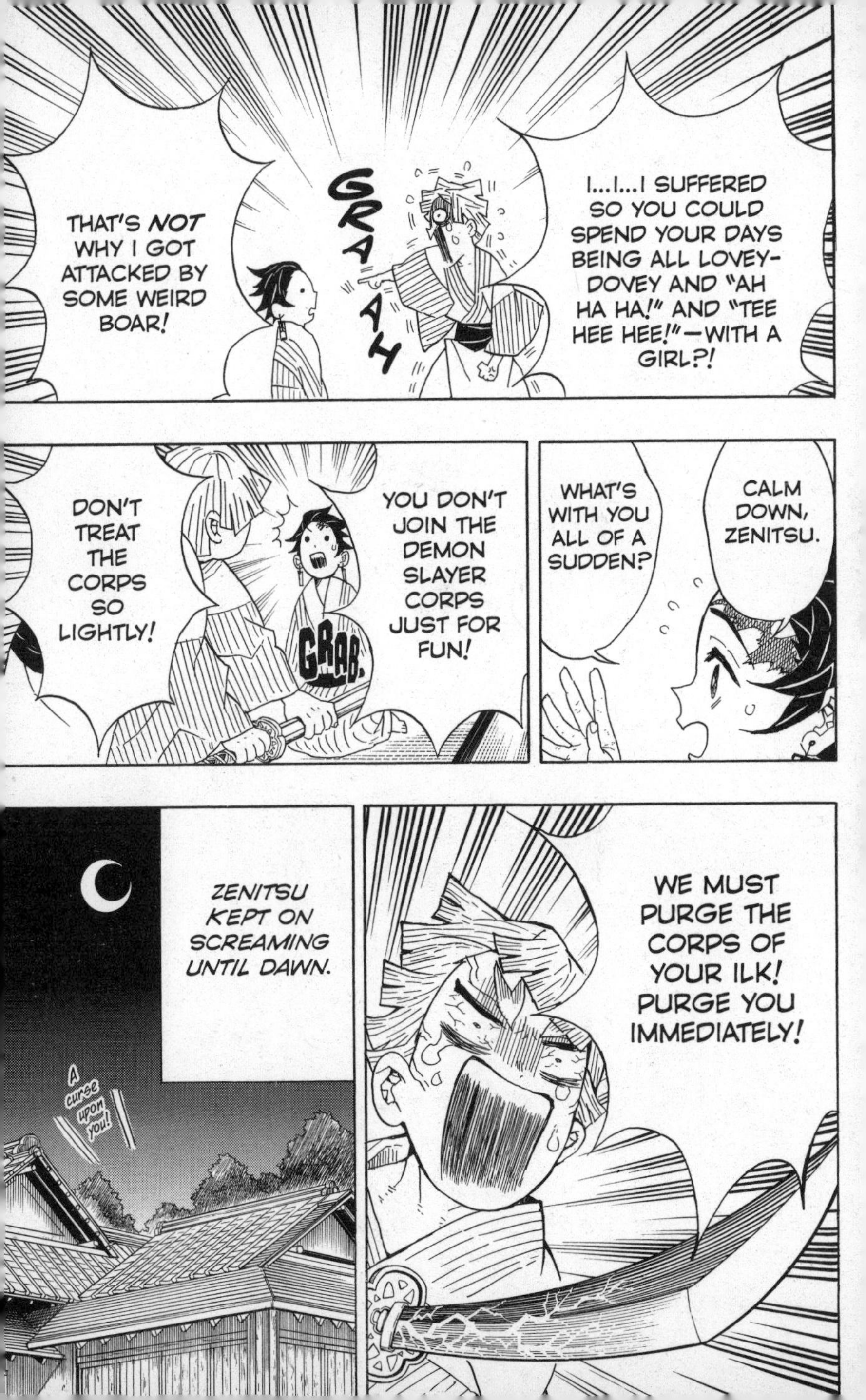
I...I...I SUFFERED SO YOU COULD SPEND YOUR DAYS BEING ALL LOVEY-DOVEY AND "AH HA HA!" AND "TEE HEE HEE!"—WITH A GIRL?!
GRAAAH
THAT'S *NOT* WHY I GOT ATTACKED BY SOME WEIRD BOAR!
CALM DOWN, ZENITSU.
WHAT'S WITH YOU ALL OF A SUDDEN?
YOU DON'T JOIN THE DEMON SLAYER CORPS JUST FOR FUN!
GRAB.
DON'T TREAT THE CORPS SO LIGHTLY!
WE MUST PURGE THE CORPS OF YOUR ILK! PURGE YOU IMMEDIATELY!
ZENITSU KEPT ON SCREAMING UNTIL DAWN.
A curse upon you!

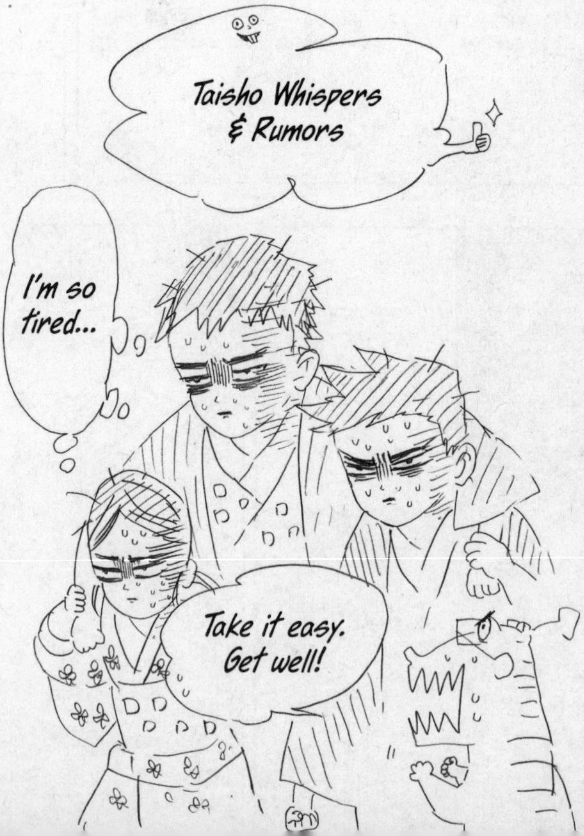
Taisho Whispers
& Rumors
I'm so
tired...
Take it easy.
Get well!

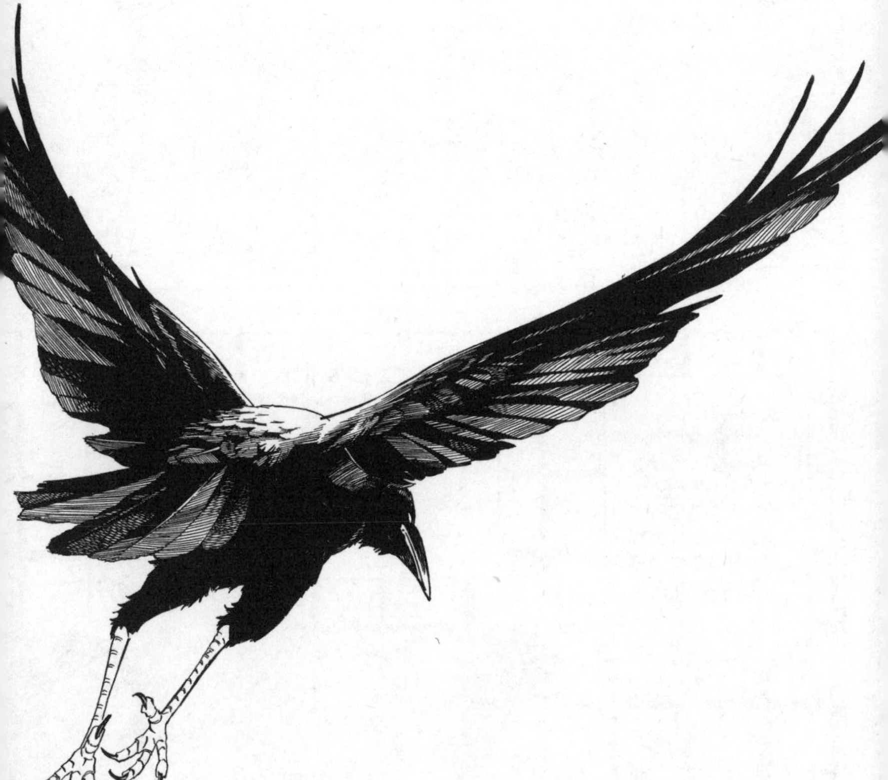

CHAPTER 28: URGENT SUMMONS

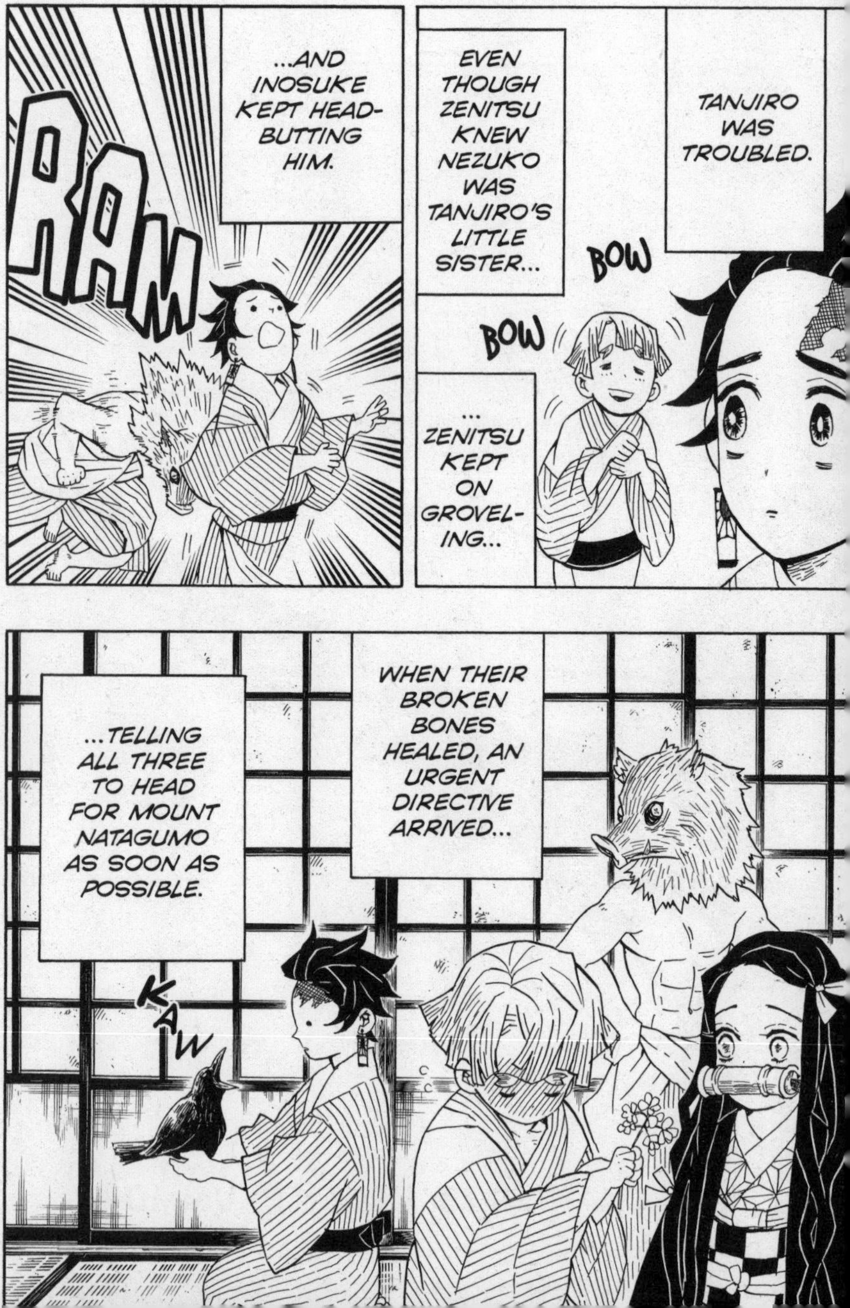
TANJIRO WAS TROUBLED.
EVEN THOUGH ZENITSU KNEW NEZUKO WAS TANJIRO'S LITTLE SISTER...
BOW
BOW
...ZENITSU KEPT ON GROVEL-ING...
...AND INOSUKE KEPT HEAD-BUTTING HIM.
RAM
WHEN THEIR BROKEN BONES HEALED, AN URGENT DIRECTIVE ARRIVED...
...TELLING ALL THREE TO HEAD FOR MOUNT NATAGUMO AS SOON AS POSSIBLE.
KAW

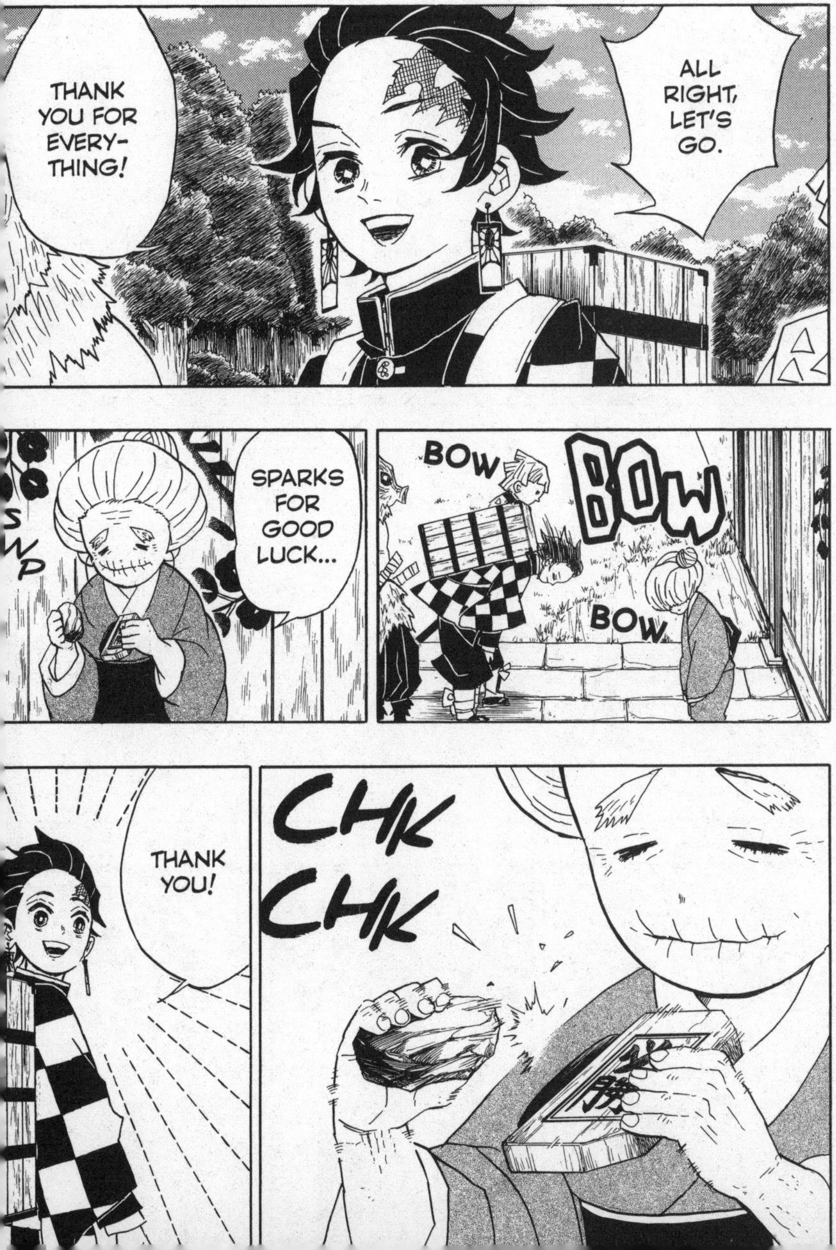
ALL RIGHT, LET'S GO.
THANK YOU FOR EVERY-THING!
BOW
BOW
BOW
SPARKS FOR GOOD LUCK...
SNP
CHK CHK
THANK YOU!

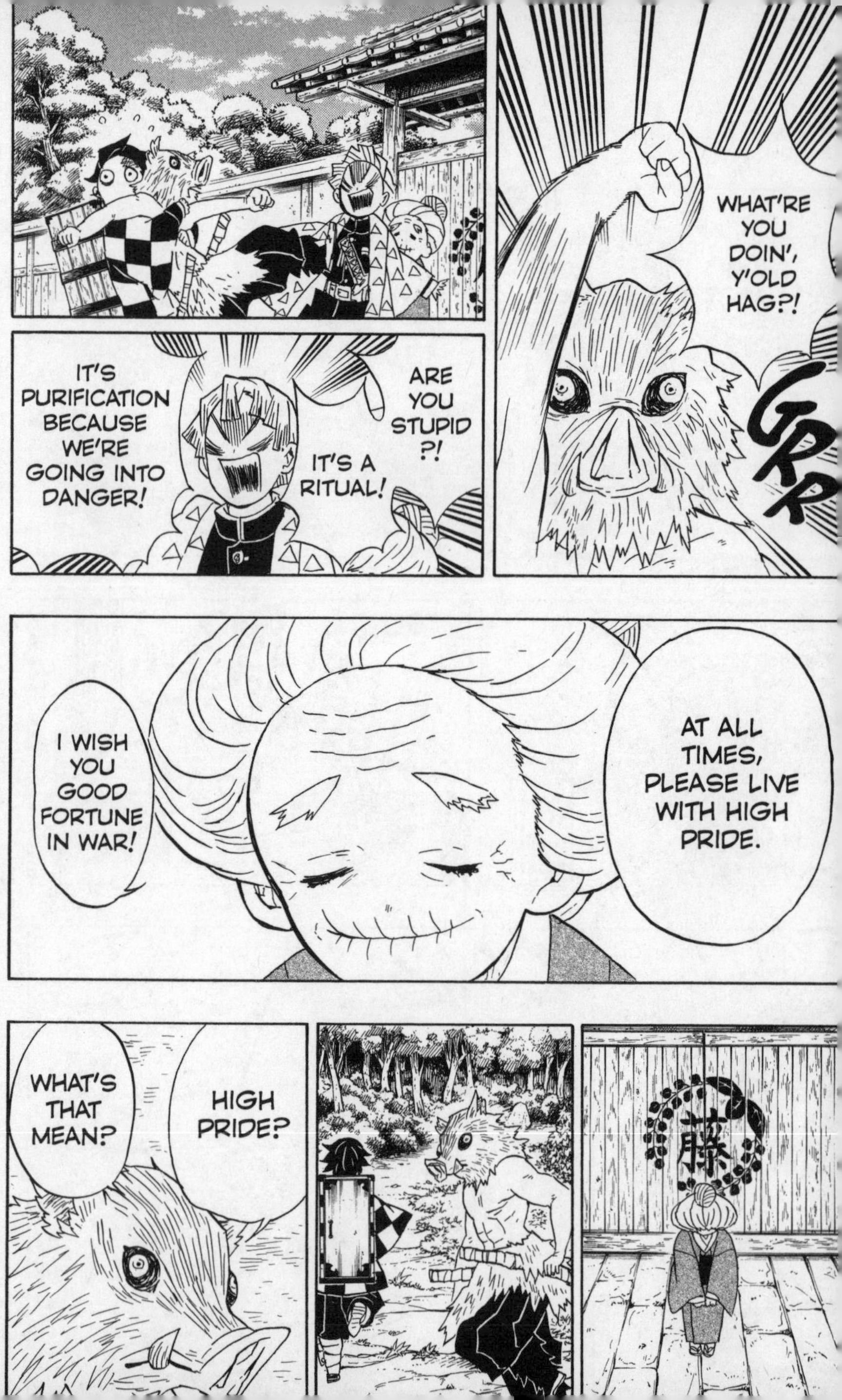
WHAT'RE YOU DOIN', Y'OLD HAG?!
GRR
ARE YOU STUPID?!
IT'S A RITUAL!
IT'S PURIFICATION BECAUSE WE'RE GOING INTO DANGER!
AT ALL TIMES, PLEASE LIVE WITH HIGH PRIDE.
I WISH YOU GOOD FORTUNE IN WAR!
藤
HIGH PRIDE?
WHAT'S THAT MEAN?

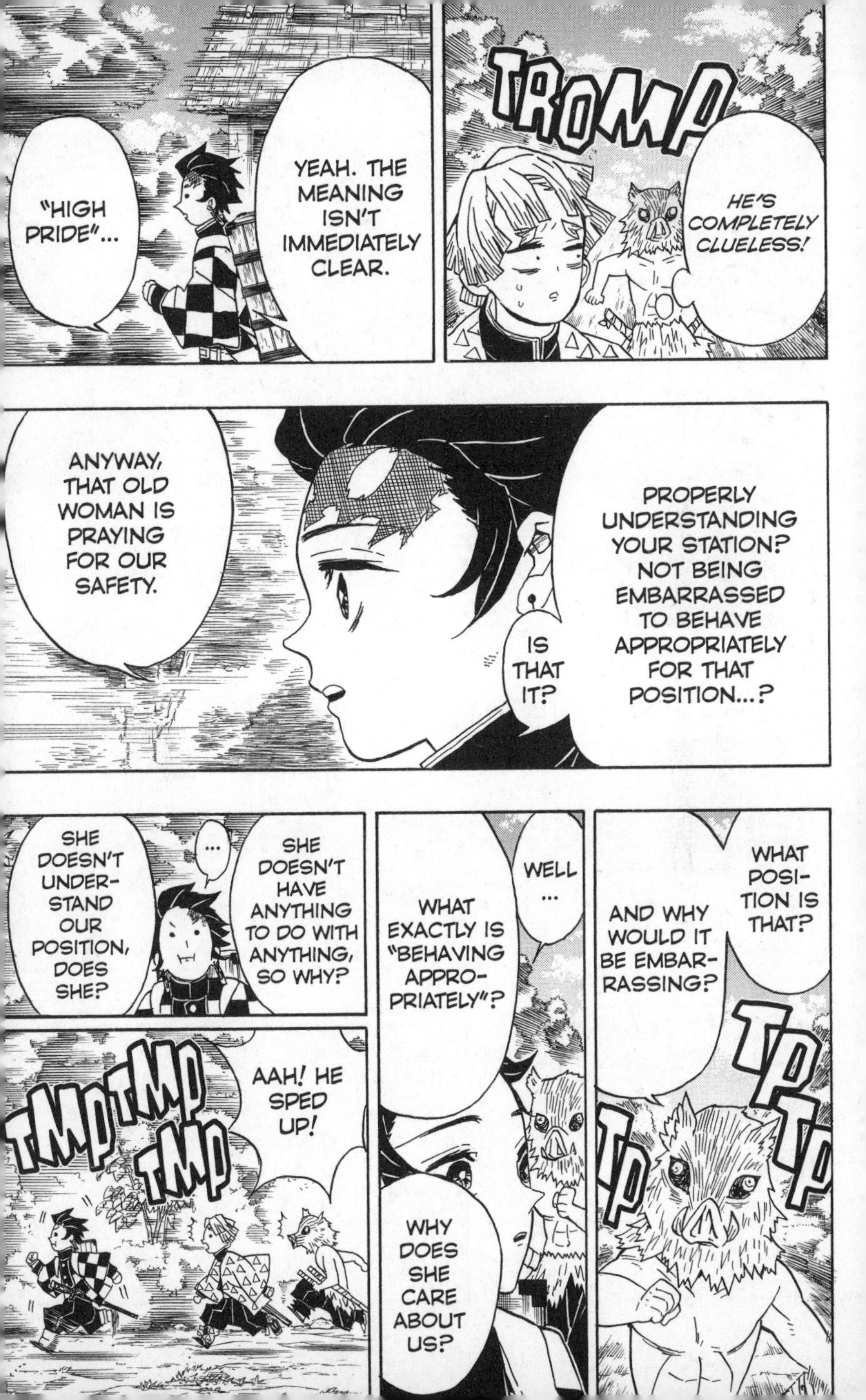
TROMP
HE'S COMPLETELY CLUELESS!
YEAH. THE MEANING ISN'T IMMEDIATELY CLEAR.
"HIGH PRIDE"...
PROPERLY UNDERSTANDING YOUR STATION? NOT BEING EMBARRASSED TO BEHAVE APPROPRIATELY FOR THAT POSITION...?
IS THAT IT?
ANYWAY, THAT OLD WOMAN IS PRAYING FOR OUR SAFETY.
WHAT POSITION IS THAT?
AND WHY WOULD IT BE EMBARRASSING?
TP TP
TP TP
WELL...
WHAT EXACTLY IS "BEHAVING APPROPRIATELY"?
WHY DOES SHE CARE ABOUT US?
SHE DOESN'T HAVE ANYTHING TO DO WITH ANYTHING, SO WHY?
...
SHE DOESN'T UNDERSTAND OUR POSITION, DOES SHE?
AAH! HE SPED UP!
TMP TMP
TMP

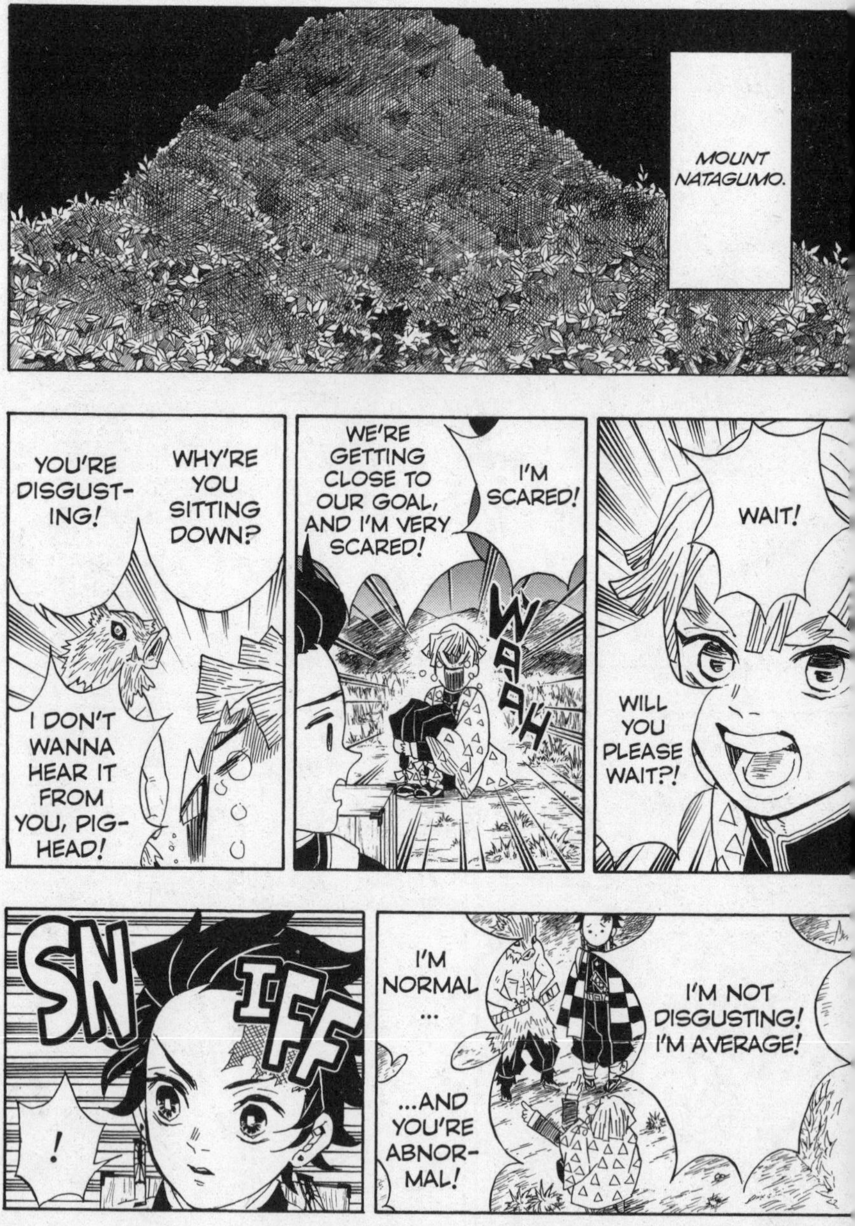
MOUNT NATAGUMO.
WAIT!
WILL YOU PLEASE WAIT?!
I'M SCARED!
WE'RE GETTING CLOSE TO OUR GOAL, AND I'M VERY SCARED!
WAAAH
WHY'RE YOU SITTING DOWN?
YOU'RE DISGUSTING!
I DON'T WANNA HEAR IT FROM YOU, PIG-HEAD!
I'M NOT DISGUSTING! I'M AVERAGE!
I'M NORMAL...
...AND YOU'RE ABNORMAL!
SNIFF
!

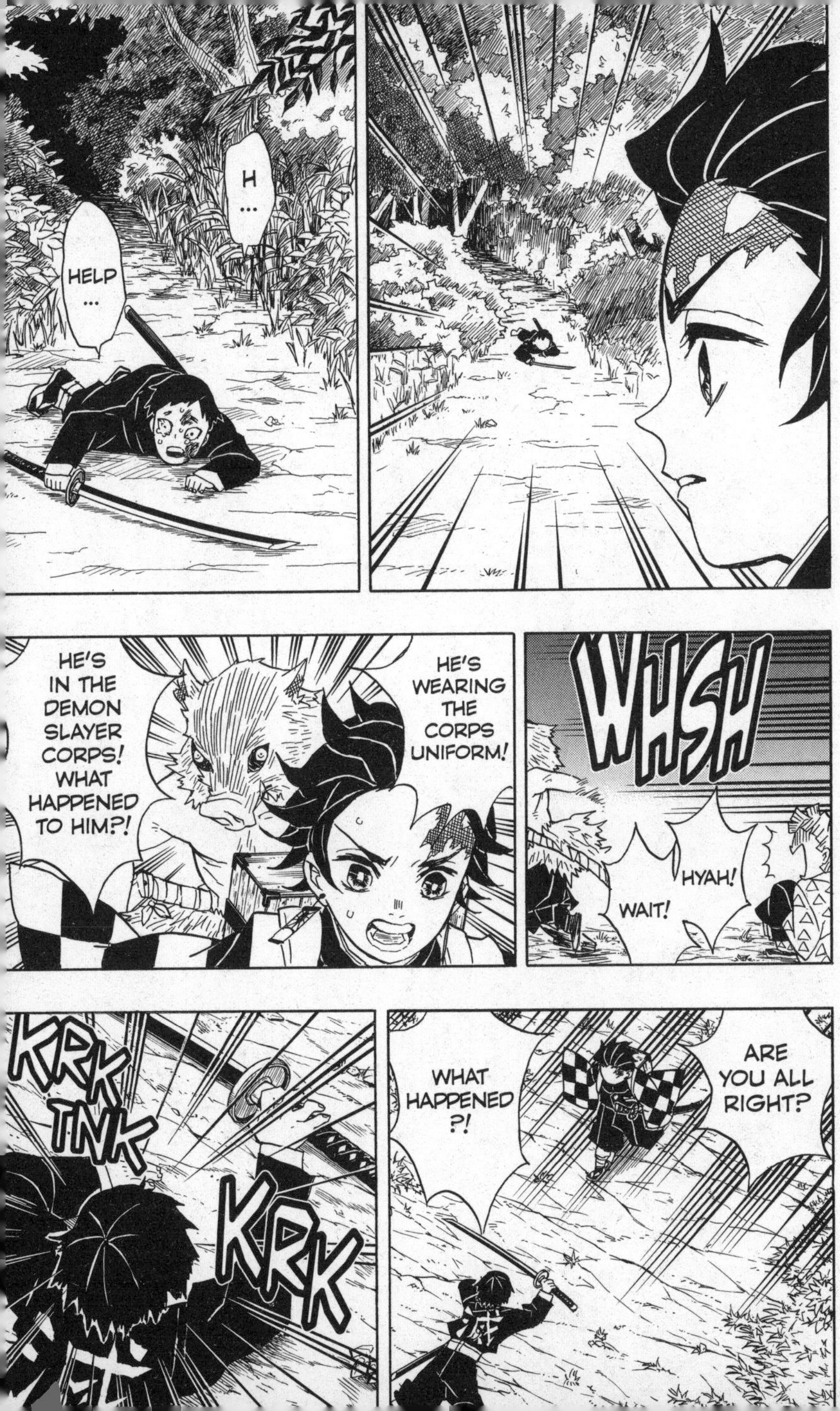
H ...
HELP ...
WHSH
HYAH!
WAIT!
HE'S WEARING THE CORPS UNIFORM!
HE'S IN THE DEMON SLAYER CORPS! WHAT HAPPENED TO HIM?!
ARE YOU ALL RIGHT?
WHAT HAPPENED ?!
KRK TNK
KRK

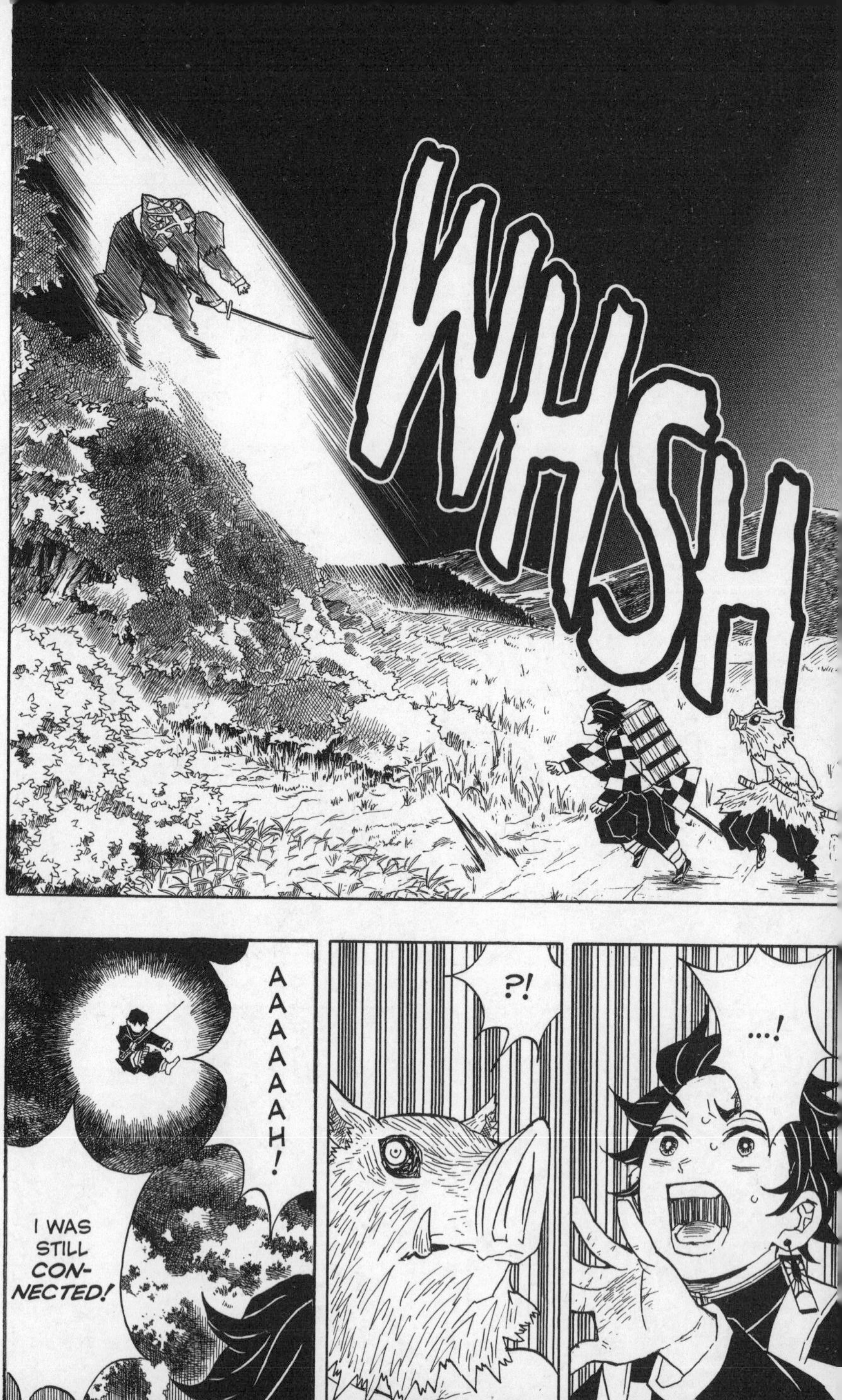
WHSH
...!
?!
AAAAAAAH!
I WAS STILL CON-NECTED!

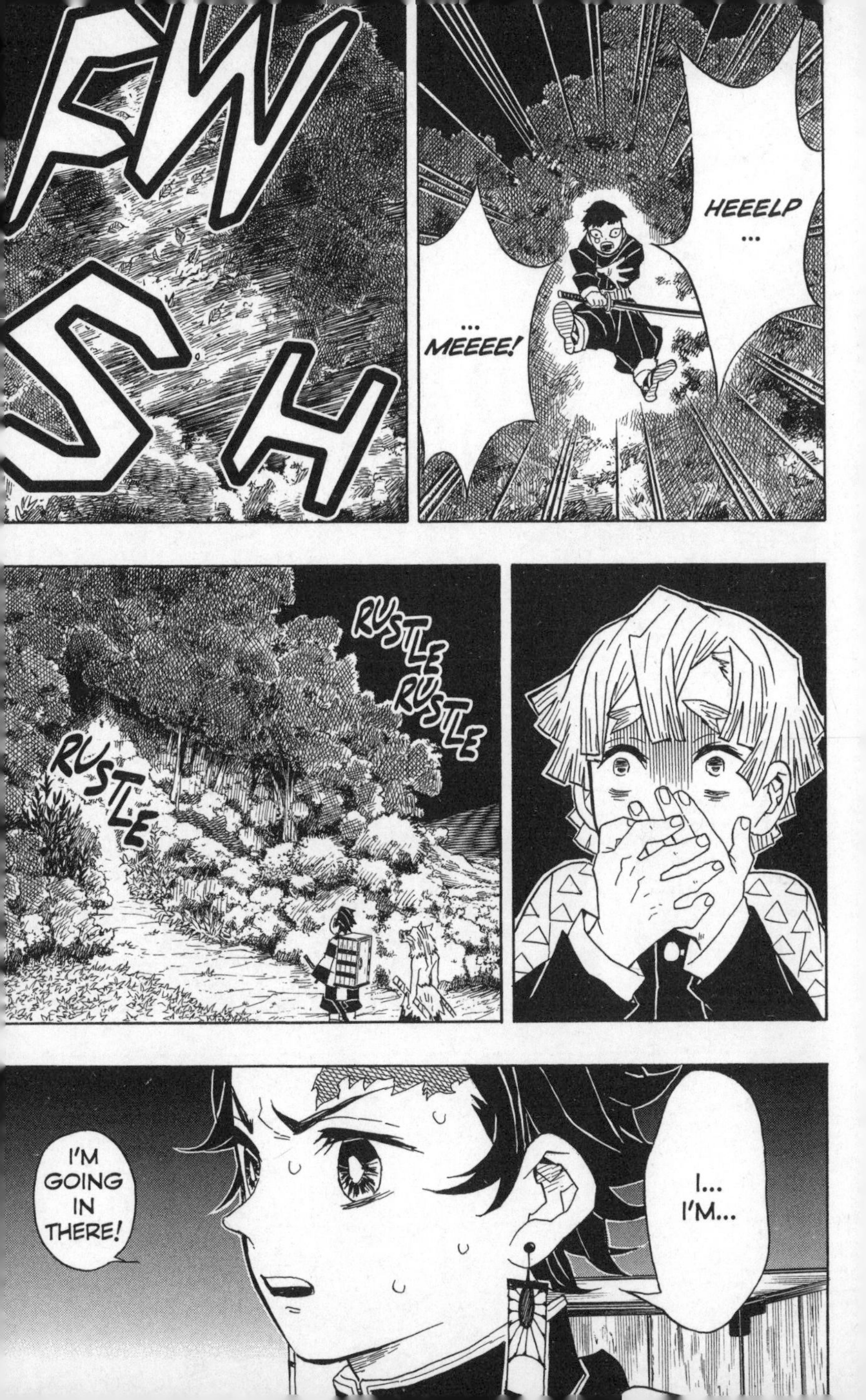
HEEELP ...
... MEEEE!
FWSH
RUSTLE RUSTLE
RUSTLE
I... I'M...
I'M GOING IN THERE!

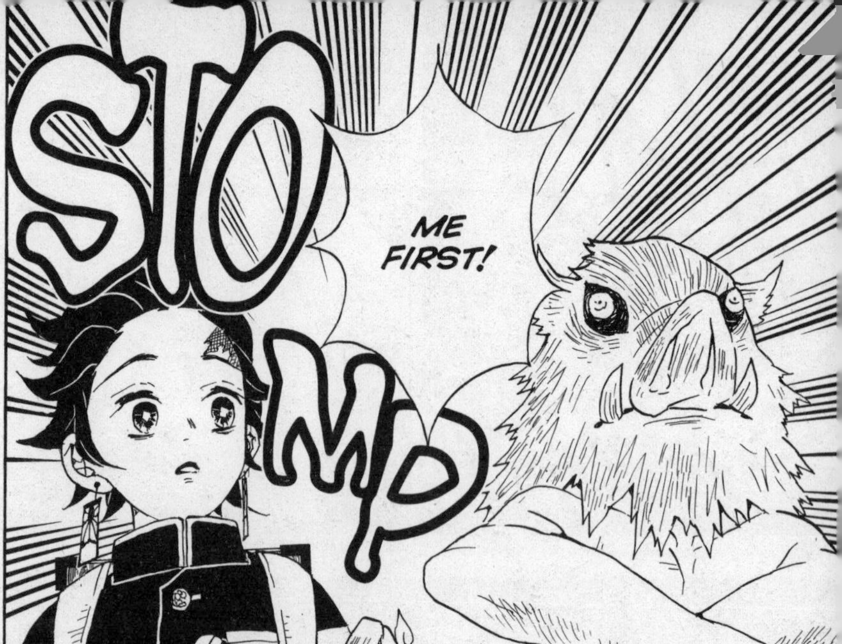
ME FIRST!
STOMP
YOU CAN TREMBLE IN FEAR AND FOLLOW BEHIND!
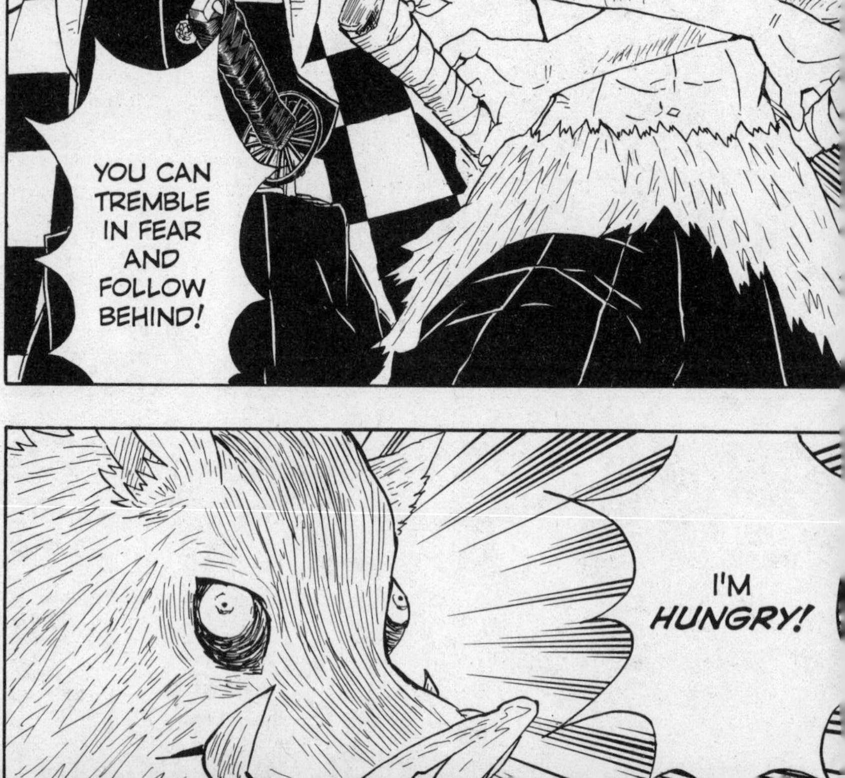
I'M *HUNGRY!*

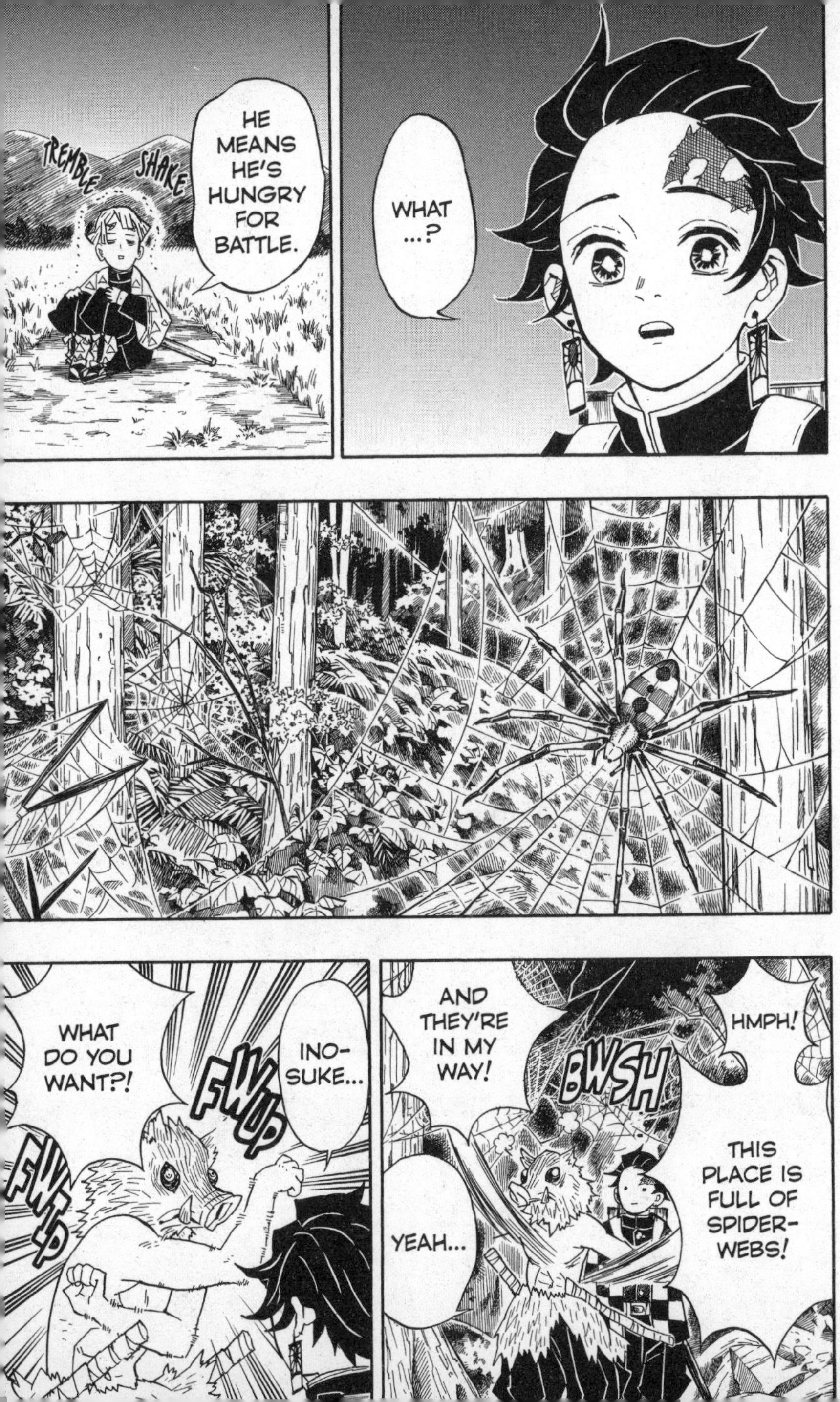
WHAT ...?
HE MEANS HE'S HUNGRY FOR BATTLE.
SHAKE
TREMBLE
HMPH!
THIS PLACE IS FULL OF SPIDER-WEBS!
AND THEY'RE IN MY WAY!
BWSH
YEAH...
INO-SUKE...
WHAT DO YOU WANT?!
FWIP
FWIP

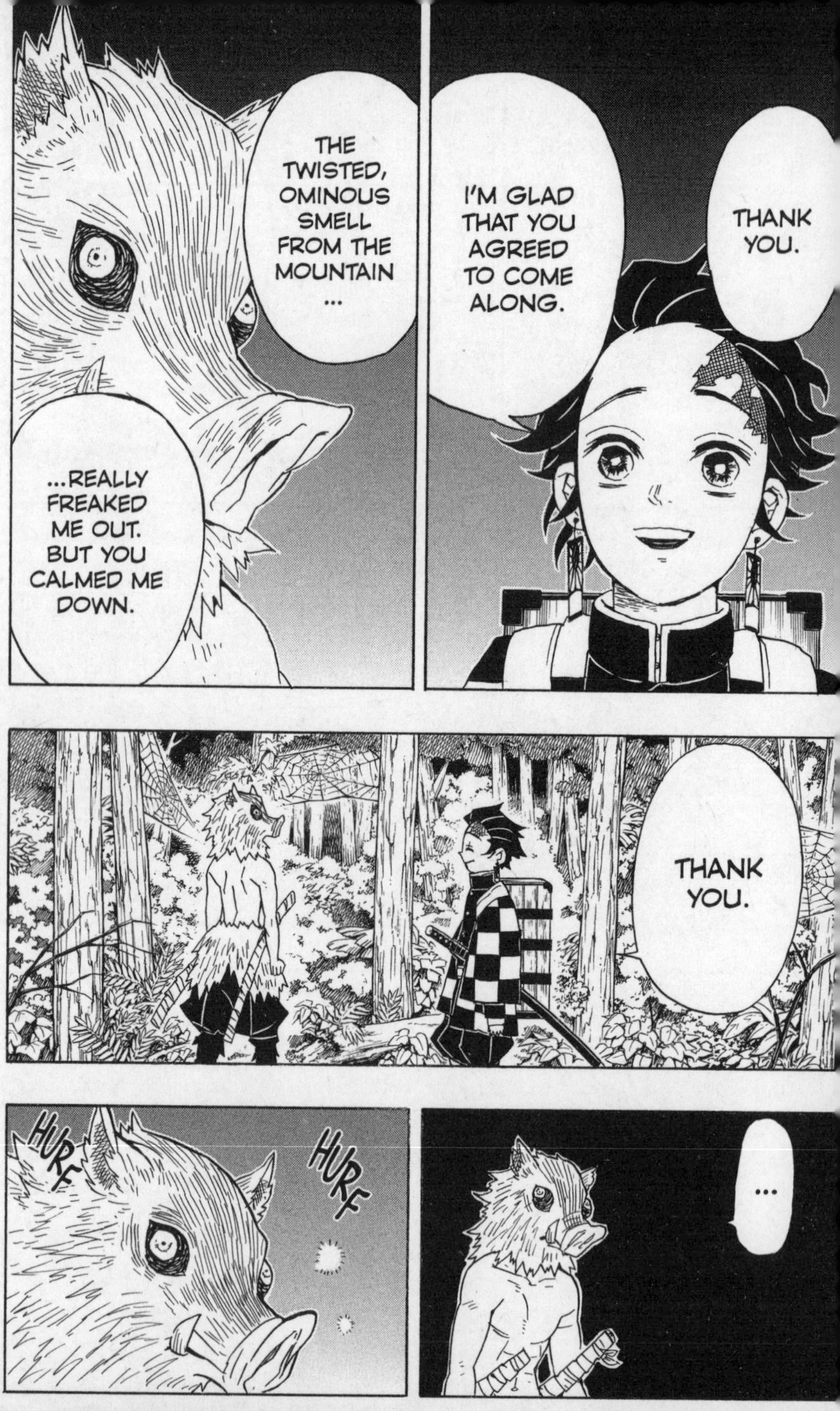
THANK YOU.
I'M GLAD THAT YOU AGREED TO COME ALONG.
THE TWISTED, OMINOUS SMELL FROM THE MOUNTAIN ...
...REALLY FREAKED ME OUT. BUT YOU CALMED ME DOWN.
THANK YOU.
...
HURF
HURF

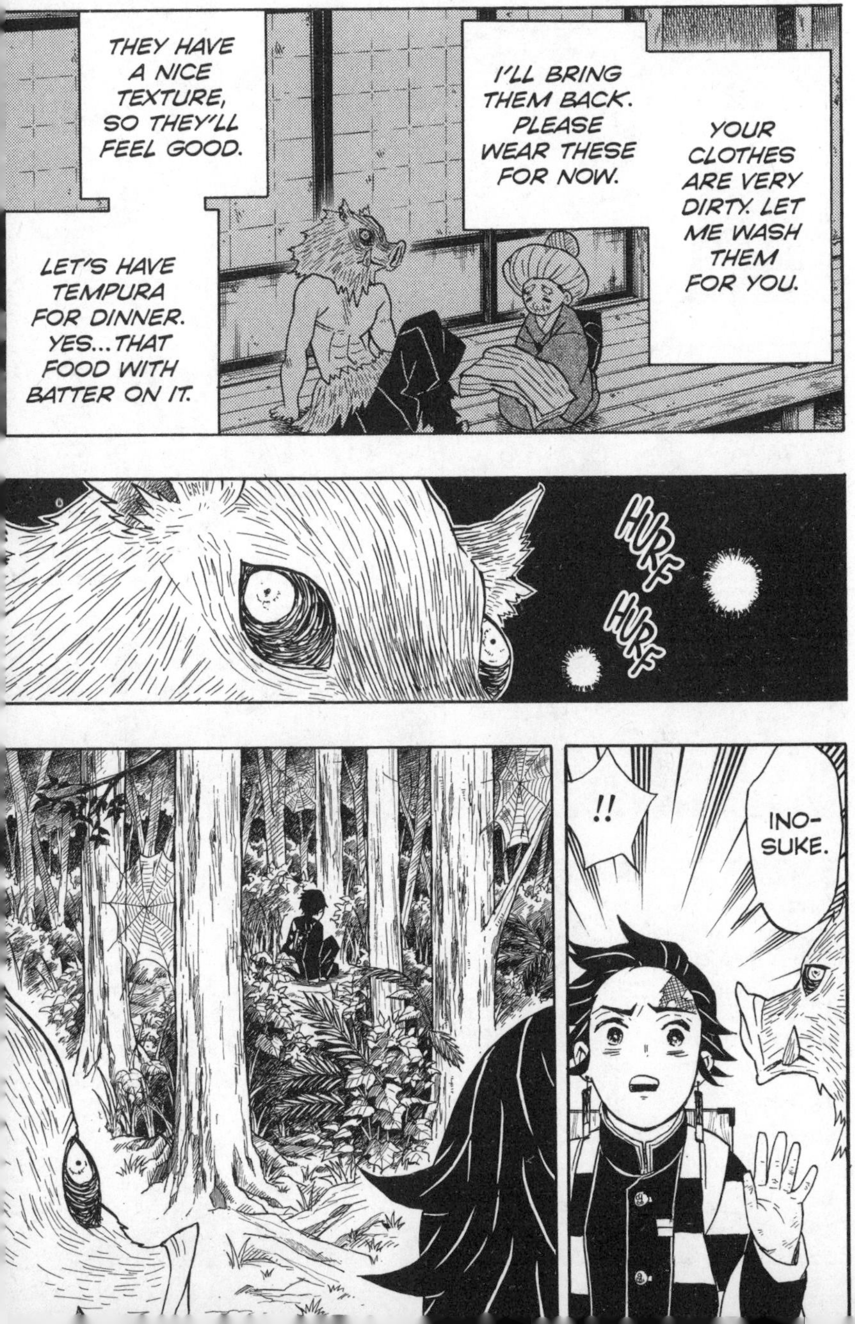
YOUR CLOTHES ARE VERY DIRTY. LET ME WASH THEM FOR YOU.
I'LL BRING THEM BACK. PLEASE WEAR THESE FOR NOW.
THEY HAVE A NICE TEXTURE, SO THEY'LL FEEL GOOD.
LET'S HAVE TEMPURA FOR DINNER. YES...THAT FOOD WITH BATTER ON IT.
HUFF
HUFF
INO-SUKE.
!!

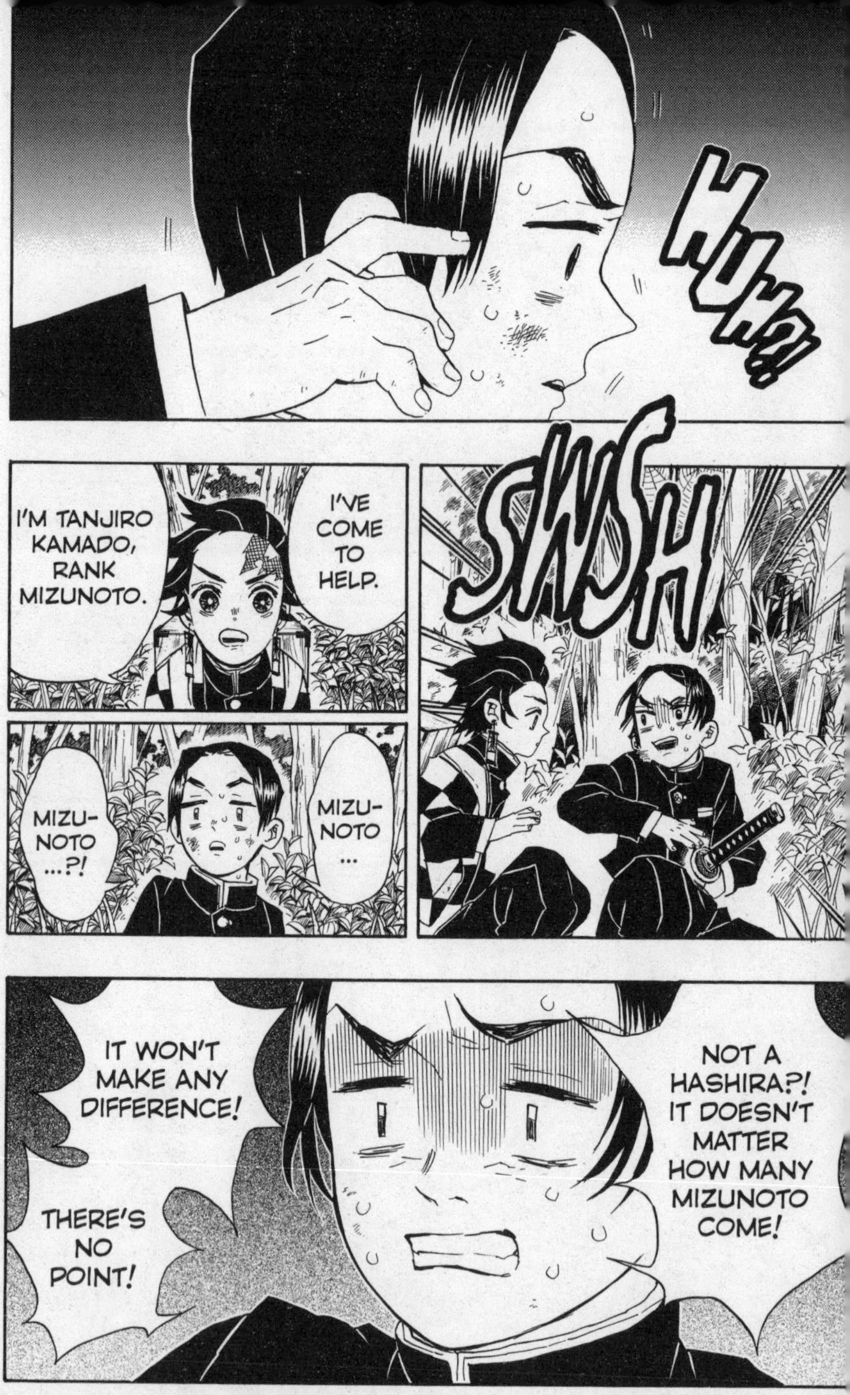
HUH?!
SHSH
I'VE COME TO HELP.
I'M TANJIRO KAMADO, RANK MIZUNOTO.
MIZUNOTO...
MIZUNOTO...?!
NOT A HASHIRA?! IT DOESN'T MATTER HOW MANY MIZUNOTO COME!
IT WON'T MAKE ANY DIFFERENCE!
THERE'S NO POINT!

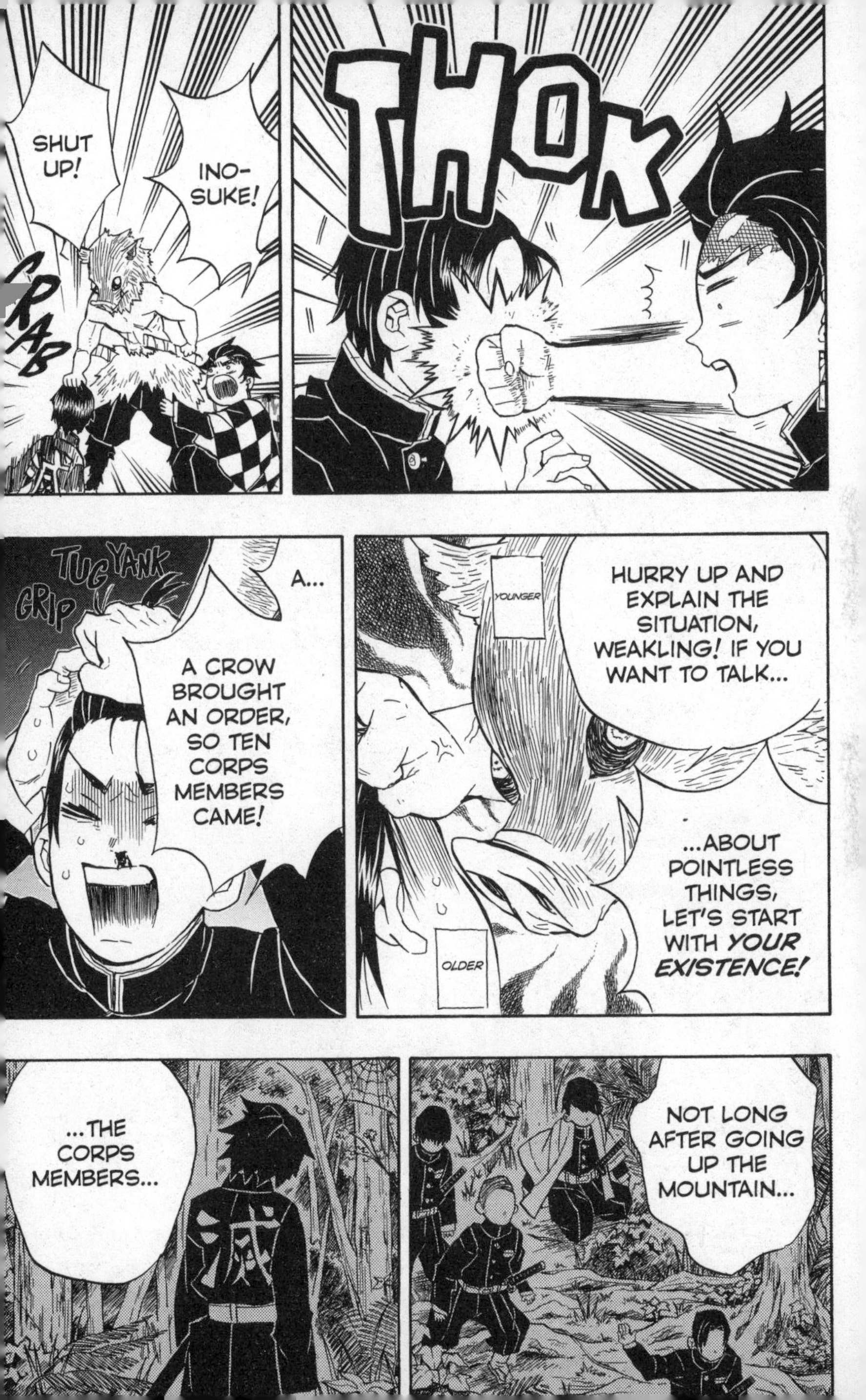
THOK
INO-SUKE!
SHUT UP!
GRAB
HURRY UP AND EXPLAIN THE SITUATION, WEAKLING! IF YOU WANT TO TALK...
YOUNGER
...ABOUT POINTLESS THINGS, LET'S START WITH *YOUR EXISTENCE!*
OLDER
YANK
TUG
GRIP
A...
A CROW BROUGHT AN ORDER, SO TEN CORPS MEMBERS CAME!
NOT LONG AFTER GOING UP THE MOUNTAIN...
...THE CORPS MEMBERS...

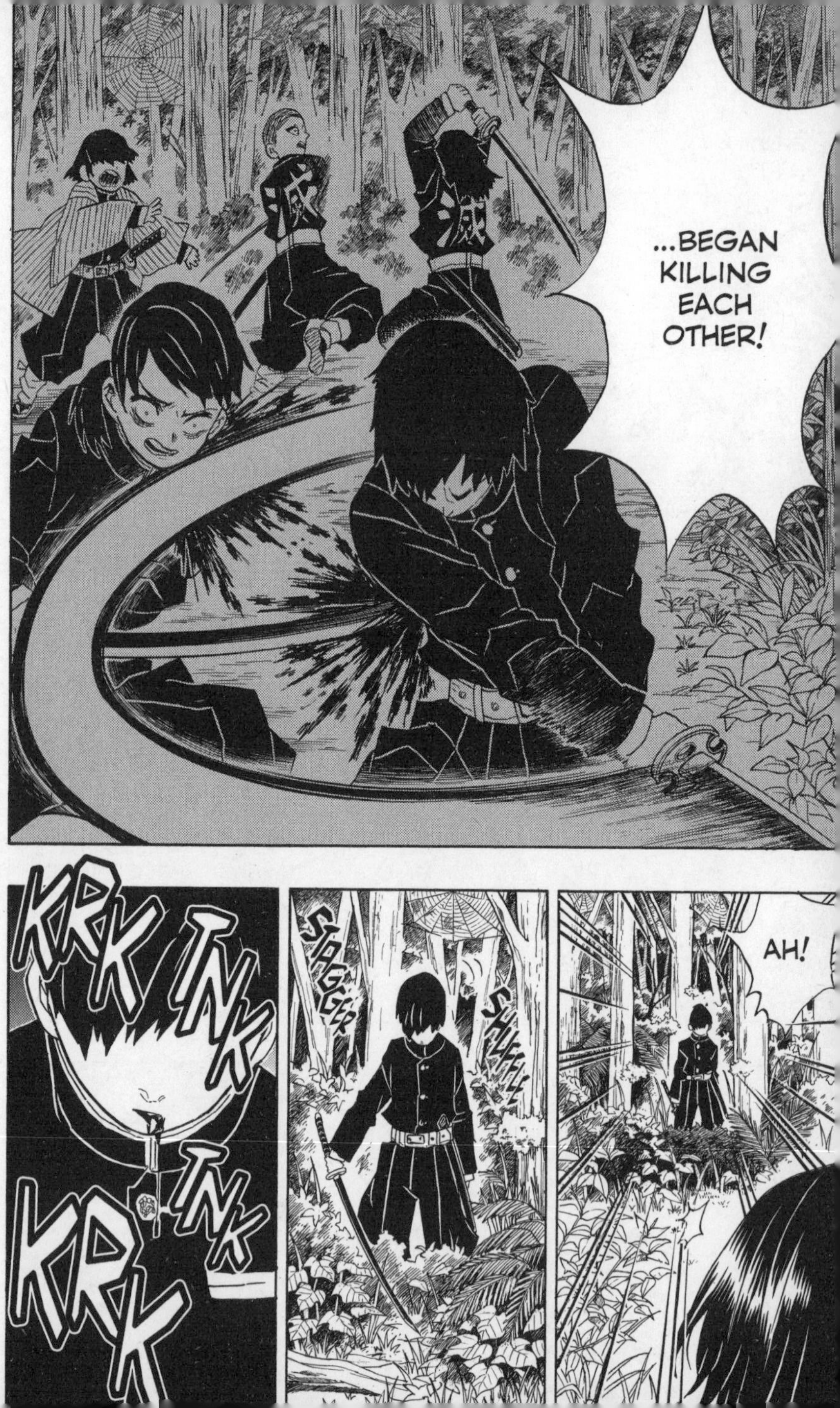
...BEGAN KILLING EACH OTHER!
AH!
STAGGER
SHUFFLE
KRAK
TINK
TINK
KRAK

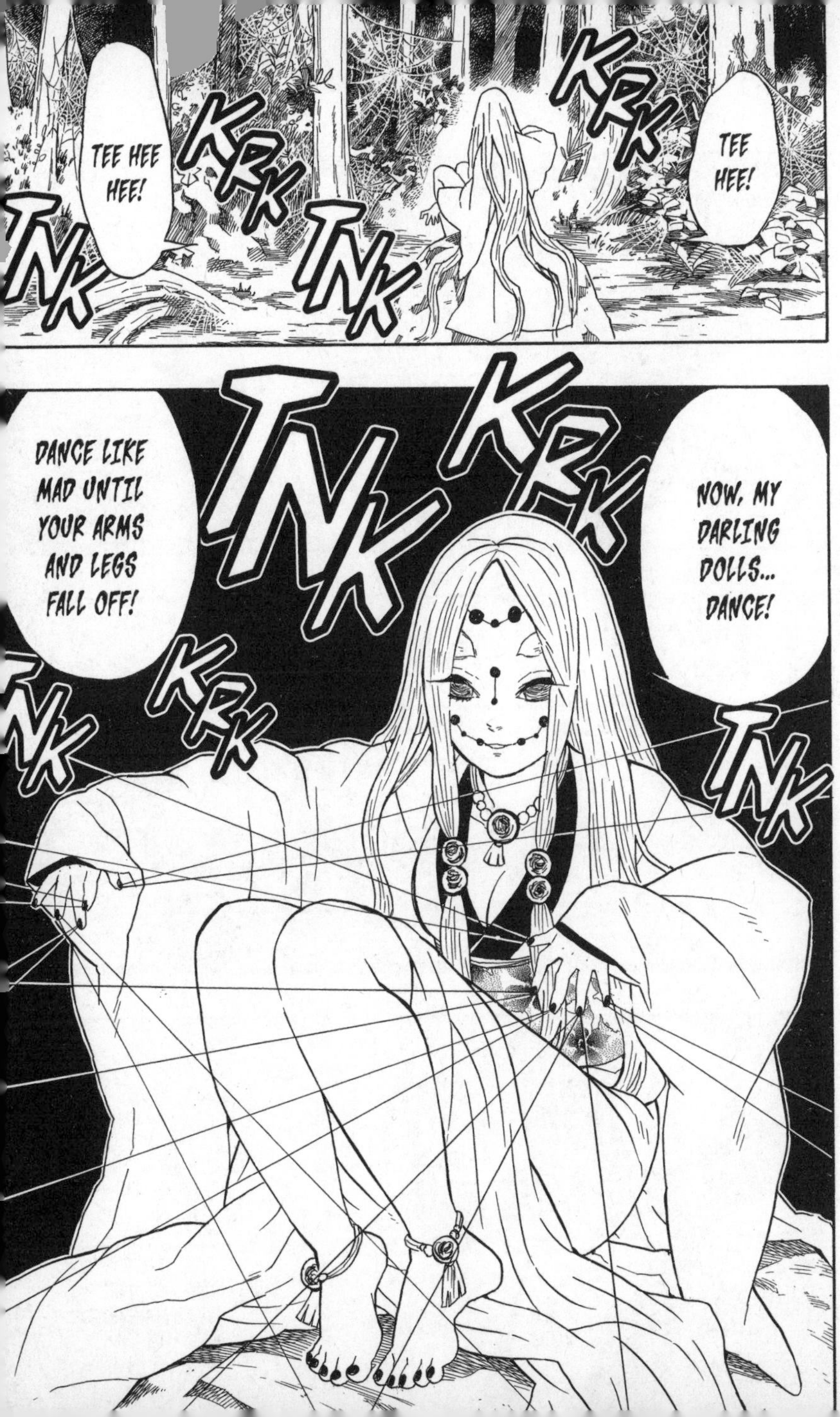
KRK
TEE HEE!
KRK
TEE HEE HEE!
TNK
TNK
NOW, MY DARLING DOLLS... DANCE!
KRK
TNK
DANCE LIKE MAD UNTIL YOUR ARMS AND LEGS FALL OFF!
TNK
KRK
TNK

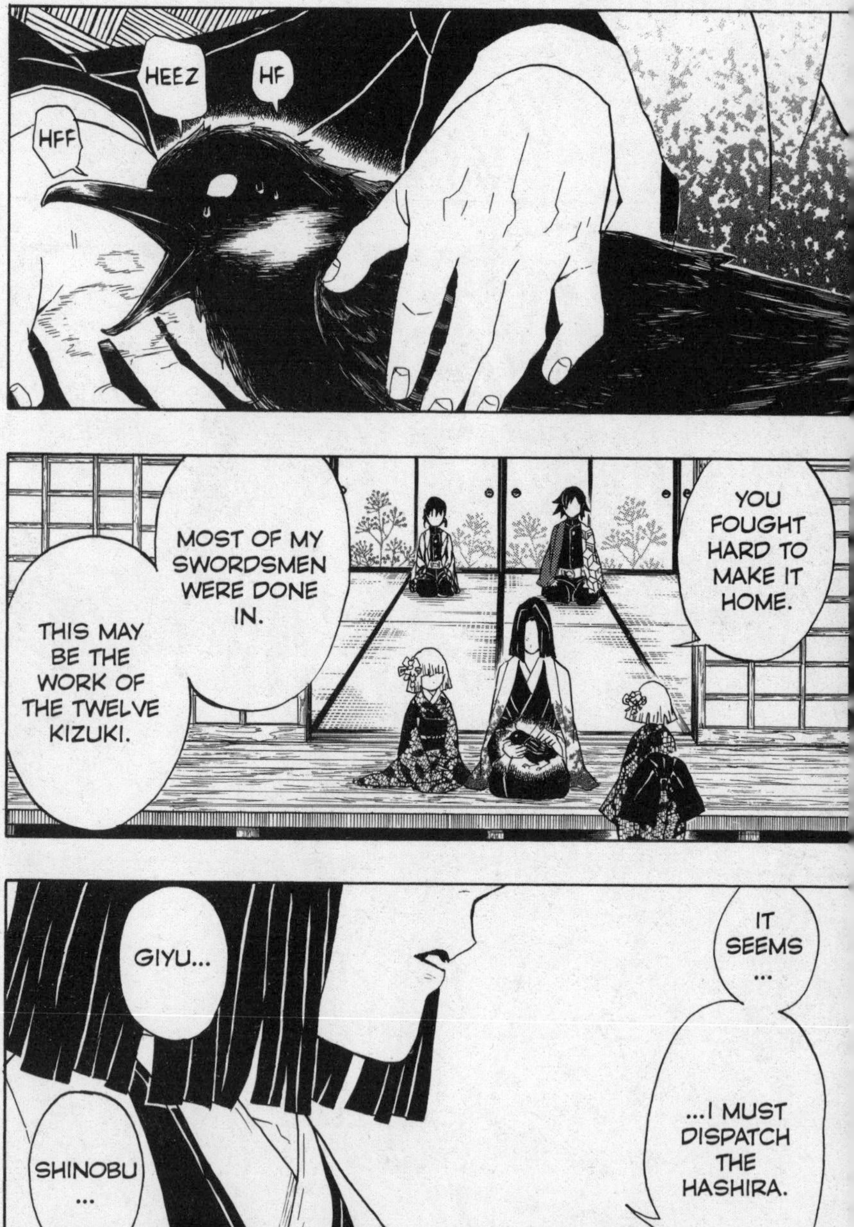
HF
HEEZ
HFF
YOU FOUGHT HARD TO MAKE IT HOME.
MOST OF MY SWORDSMEN WERE DONE IN.
THIS MAY BE THE WORK OF THE TWELVE KIZUKI.
IT SEEMS...
...I MUST DISPATCH THE HASHIRA.
GIYU...
SHINOBU...

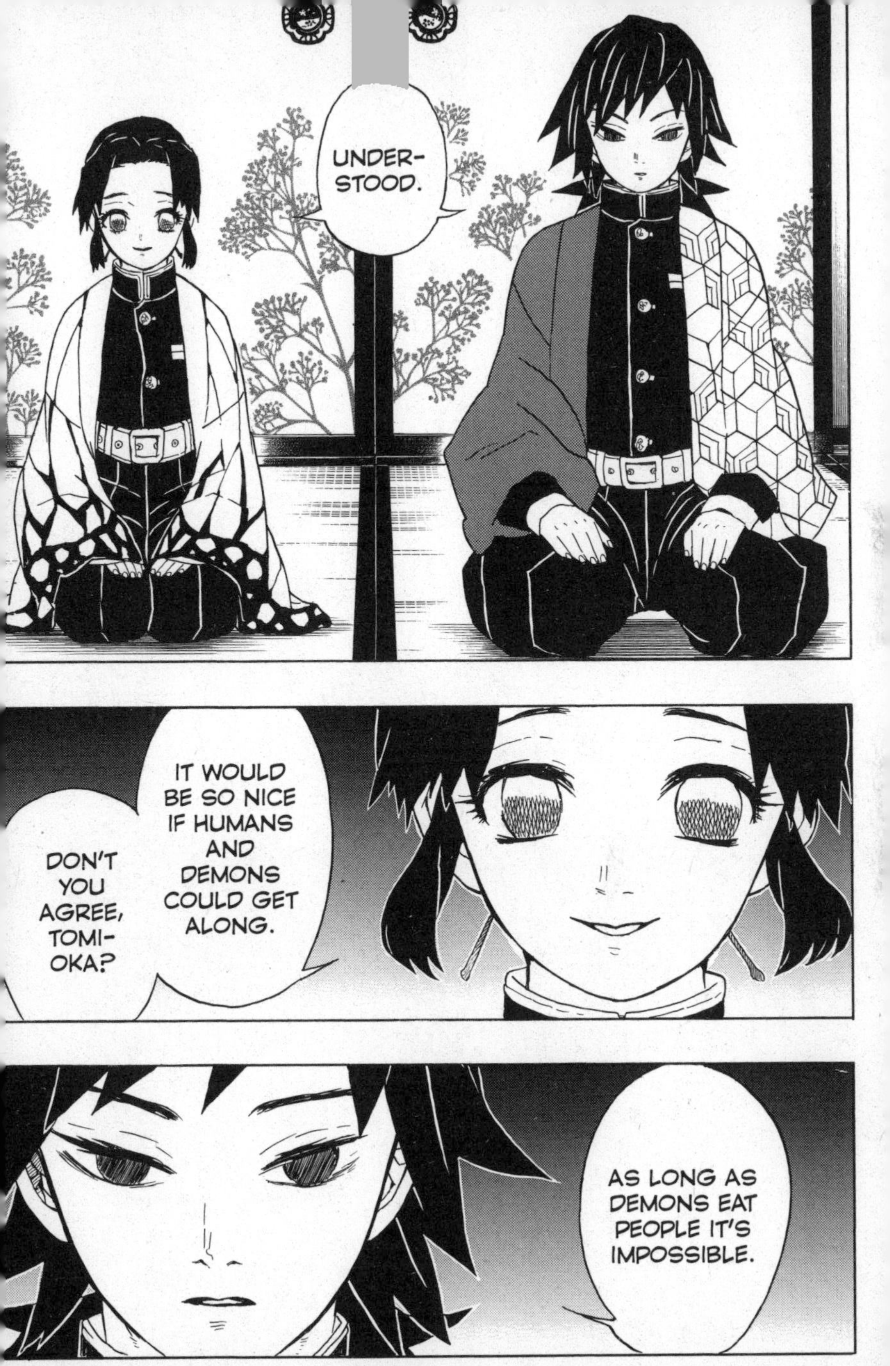
UNDER-STOOD.
IT WOULD BE SO NICE IF HUMANS AND DEMONS COULD GET ALONG.
DON'T YOU AGREE, TOMI-OKA?
AS LONG AS DEMONS EAT PEOPLE IT'S IMPOSSIBLE.

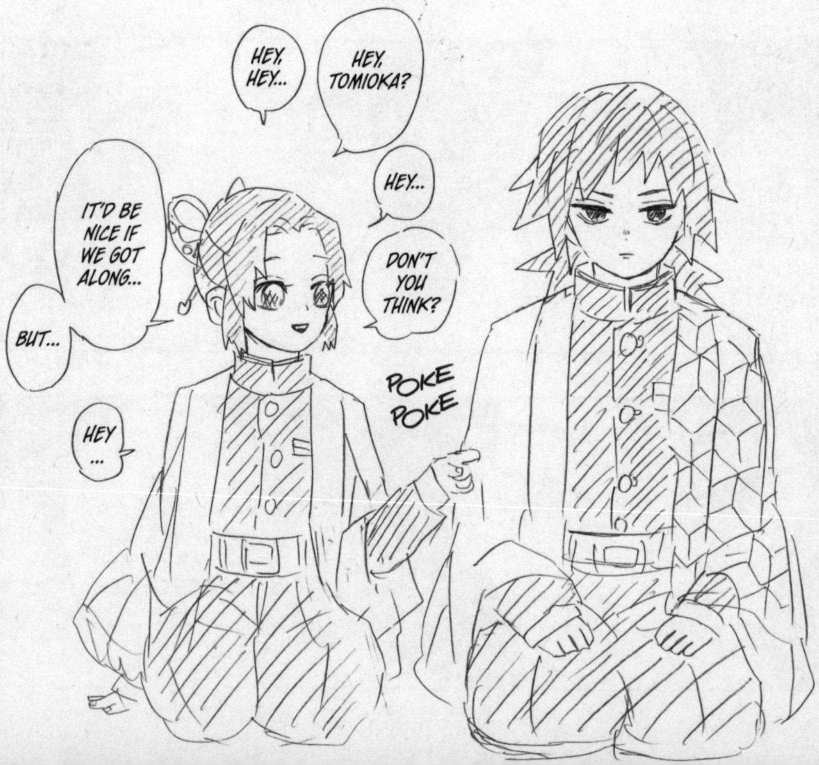
HEY, TOMIOKA?
HEY, HEY...
HEY...
DON'T YOU THINK?
IT'D BE NICE IF WE GOT ALONG...
POKE POKE
BUT...
HEY ...

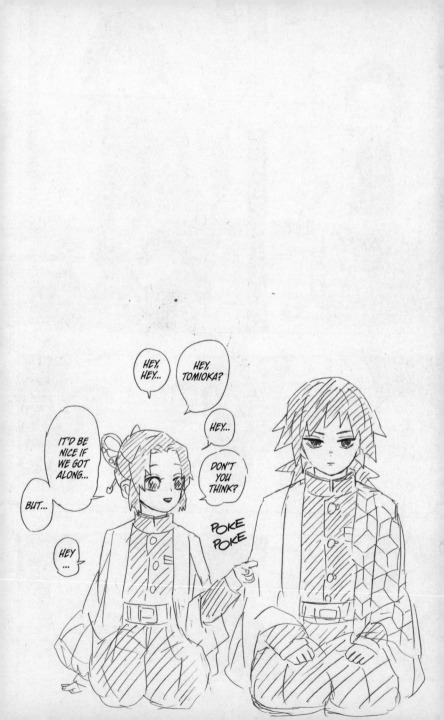

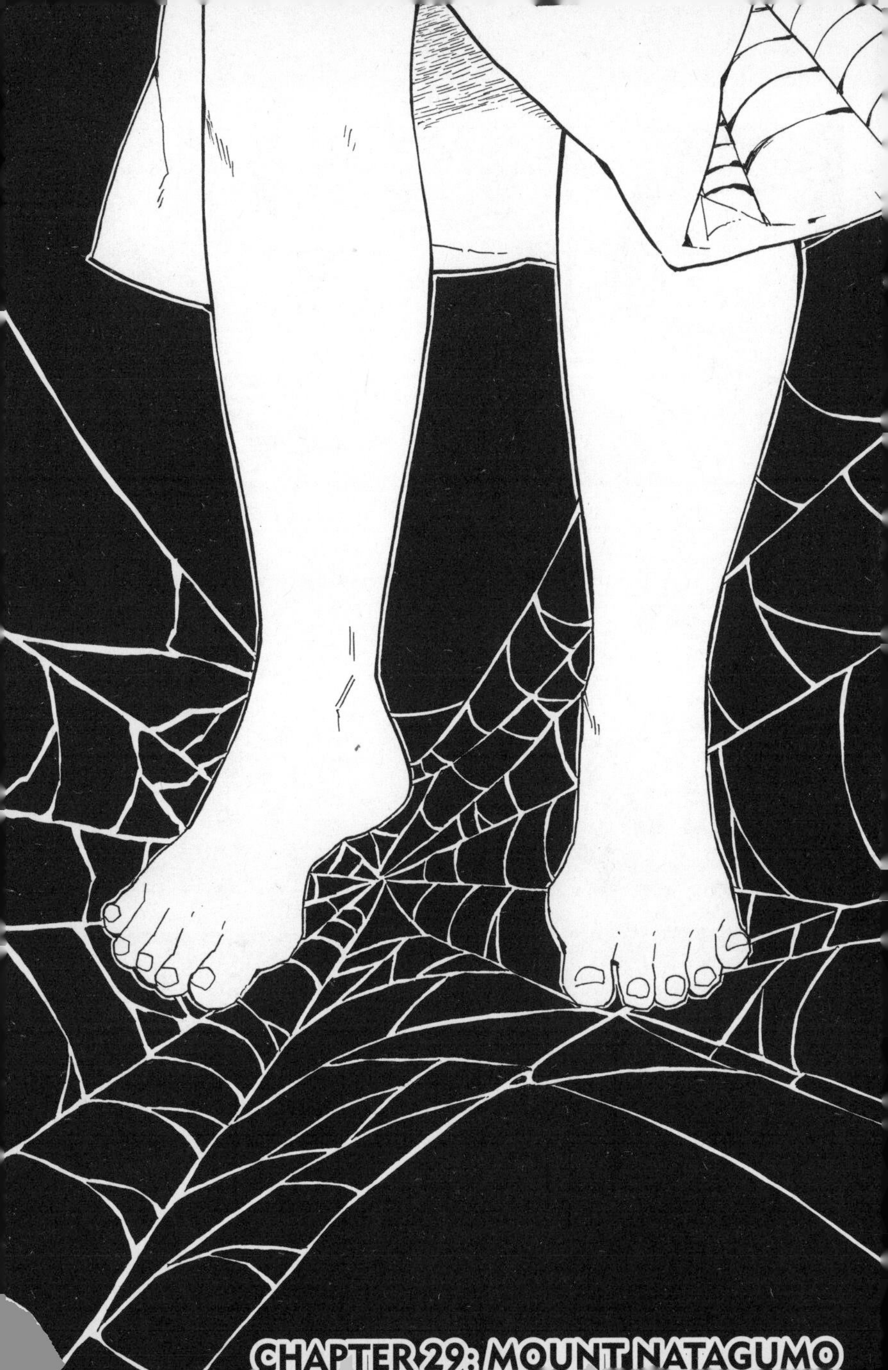

CHAPTER 29: MOUNT NATAGUMO

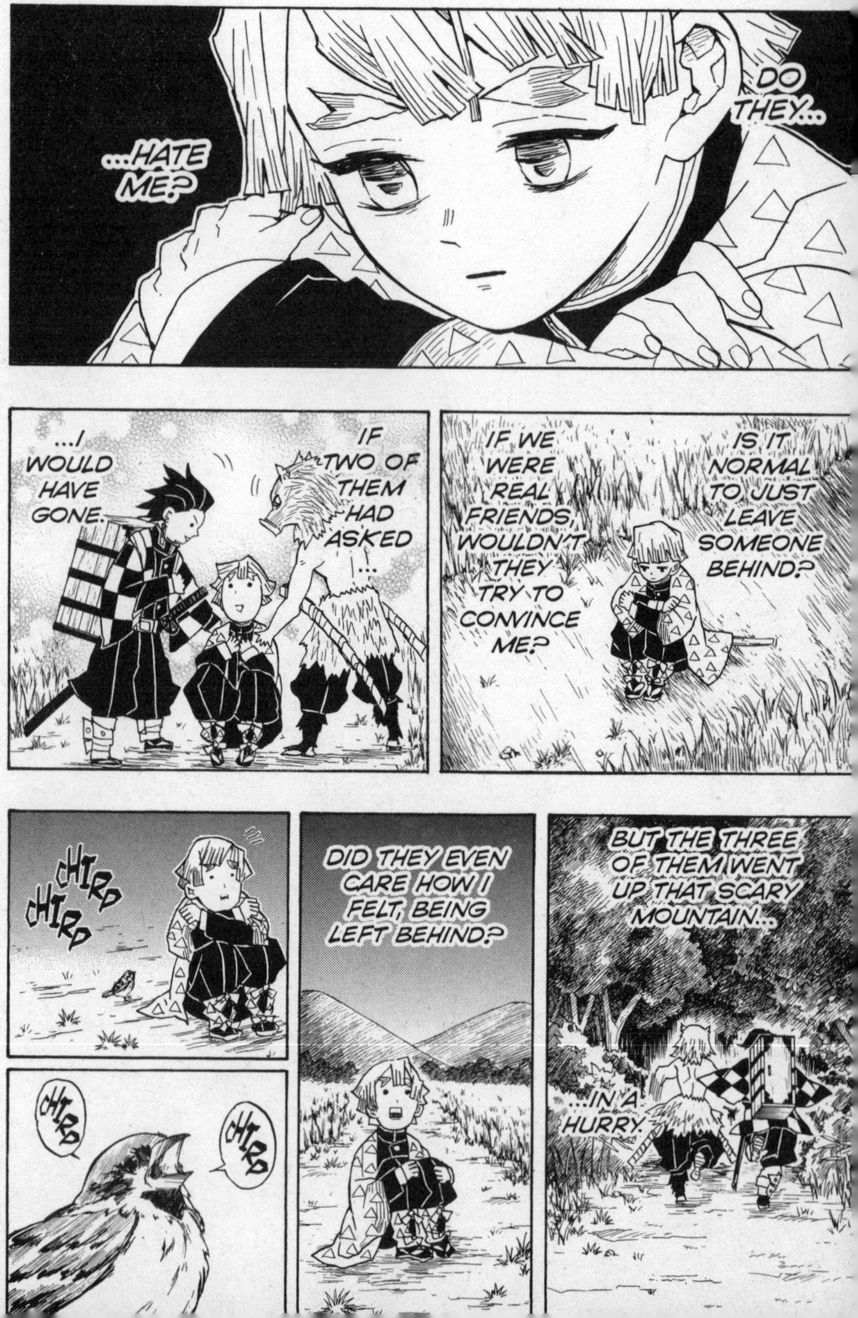
DO THEY...
...HATE ME?
IS IT NORMAL TO JUST LEAVE SOMEONE BEHIND?
IF WE WERE REAL FRIENDS, WOULDN'T THEY TRY TO CONVINCE ME?
IF TWO OF THEM HAD ASKED...
...I WOULD HAVE GONE.
BUT THE THREE OF THEM WENT UP THAT SCARY MOUNTAIN...
...IN A HURRY.
DID THEY EVEN CARE HOW I FELT, BEING LEFT BEHIND?
CHIRP
CHIRP
CHIRP
CHIRP

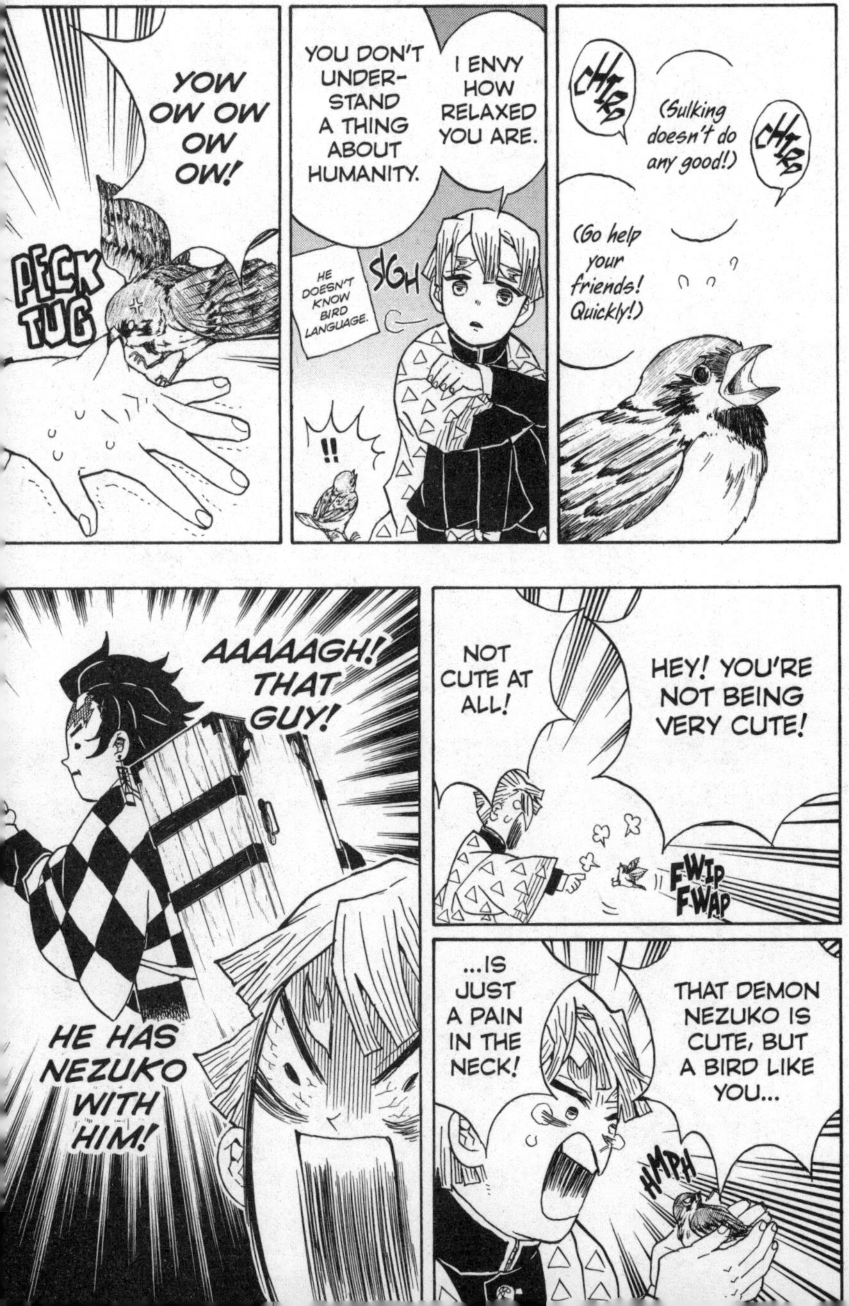
CHIRP
(Sulking doesn't do any good!)
CHIRP
(Go help your friends! Quickly!)
I ENVY HOW RELAXED YOU ARE.
YOU DON'T UNDERSTAND A THING ABOUT HUMANITY.
SIGH
HE DOESN'T KNOW BIRD LANGUAGE.
!!
YOW OW OW OW OW!
PECK TUG
HEY! YOU'RE NOT BEING VERY CUTE!
NOT CUTE AT ALL!
FWIP FWAP
THAT DEMON NEZUKO IS CUTE, BUT A BIRD LIKE YOU...
...IS JUST A PAIN IN THE NECK!
HMPH
AAAAAGH! THAT GUY!
HE HAS NEZUKO WITH HIM!

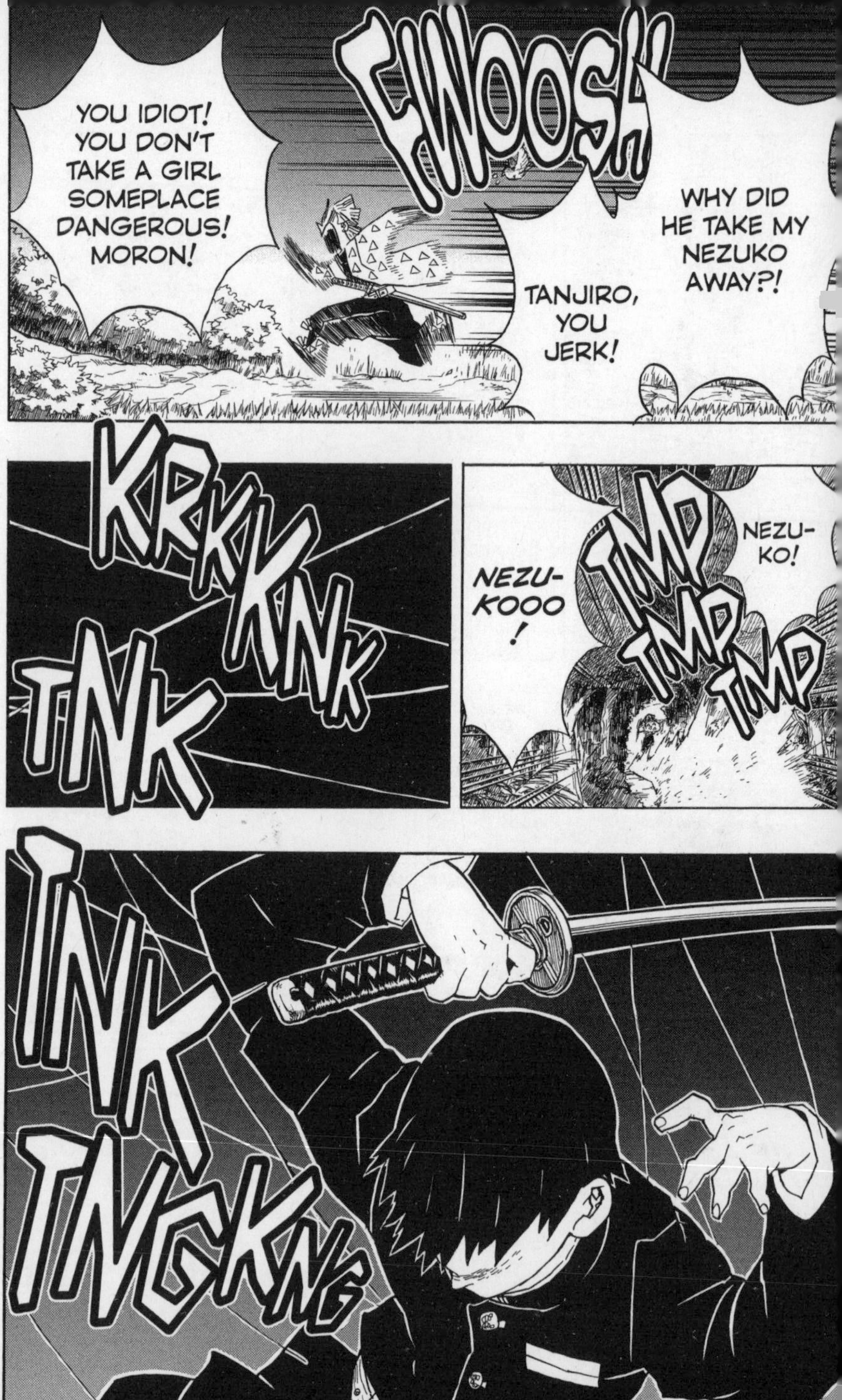
WHY DID HE TAKE MY NEZUKO AWAY?!
TANJIRO, YOU JERK!
WHOOSH
YOU IDIOT! YOU DON'T TAKE A GIRL SOMEPLACE DANGEROUS! MORON!
NEZU-KO!
TMP TMP TMP TMP
NEZU-KOOO!
KRKKNK
TNK
TNK
TNGKNG

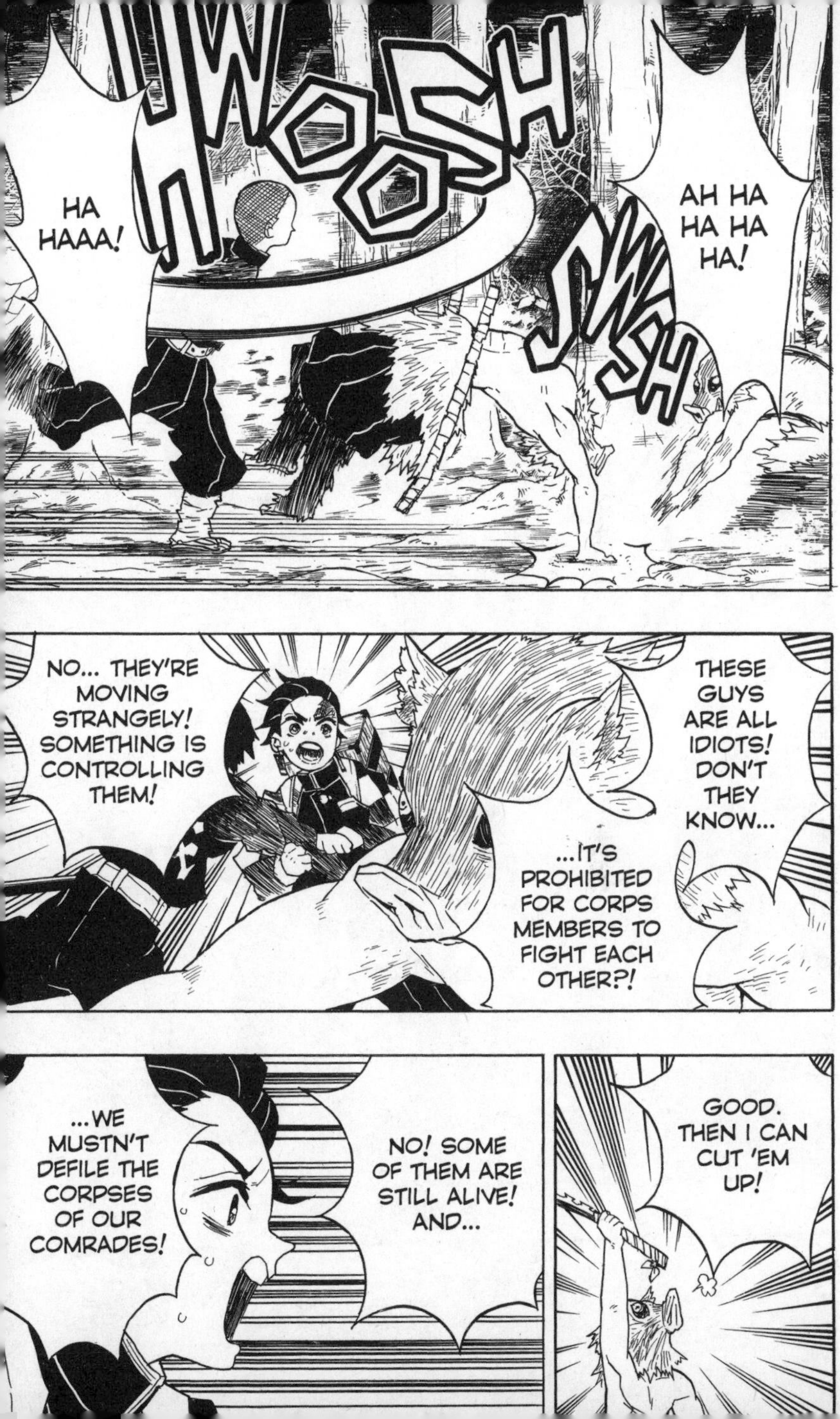
AH HA HA HA HA!
WHOOSH
SWISH
HA HAAA!
THESE GUYS ARE ALL IDIOTS! DON'T THEY KNOW...
...IT'S PROHIBITED FOR CORPS MEMBERS TO FIGHT EACH OTHER?!
NO... THEY'RE MOVING STRANGELY! SOMETHING IS CONTROLLING THEM!
GOOD. THEN I CAN CUT 'EM UP!
NO! SOME OF THEM ARE STILL ALIVE! AND...
...WE MUSTN'T DEFILE THE CORPSES OF OUR COMRADES!

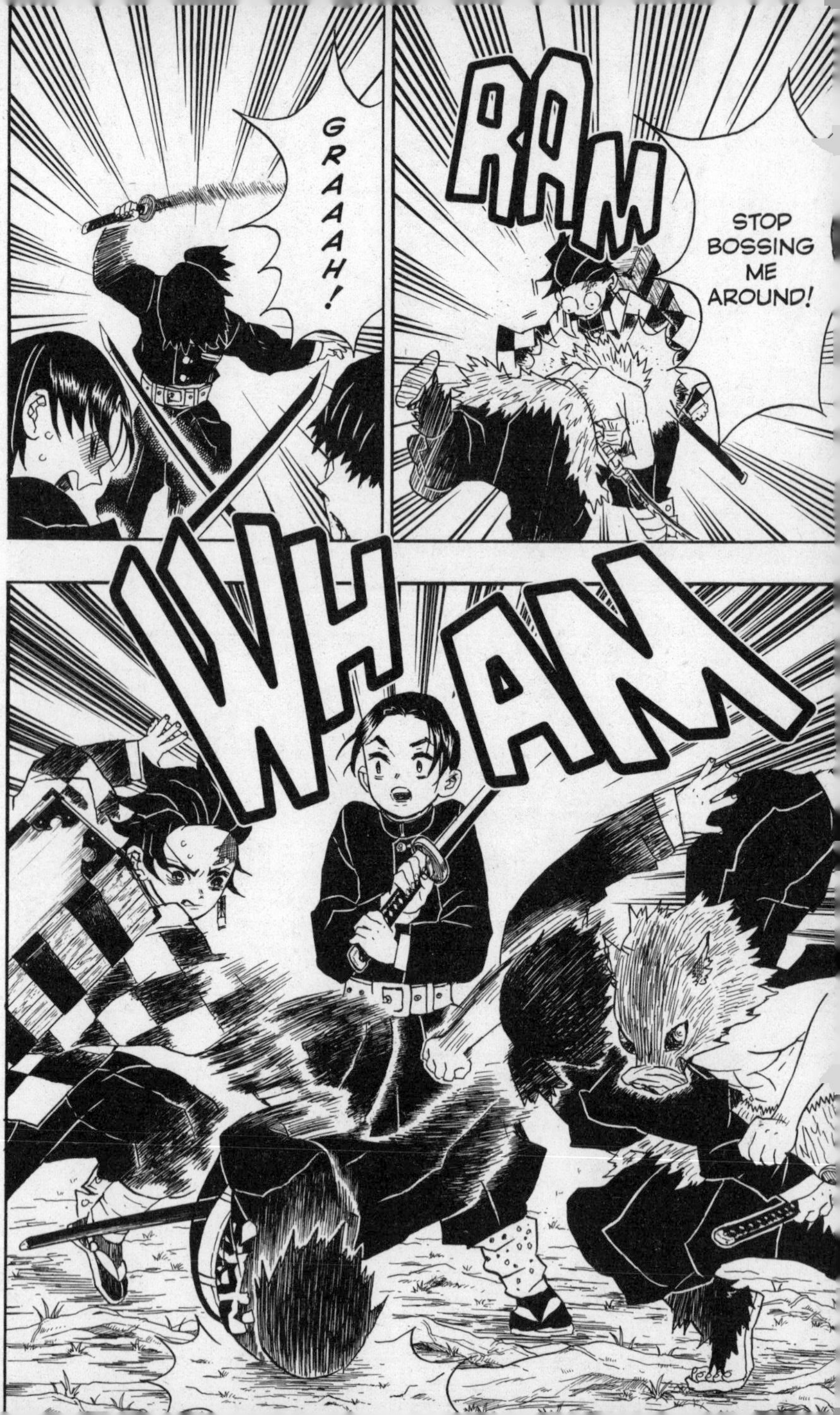
RAM
STOP BOSSING ME AROUND!
GRAAAH!
WHAM

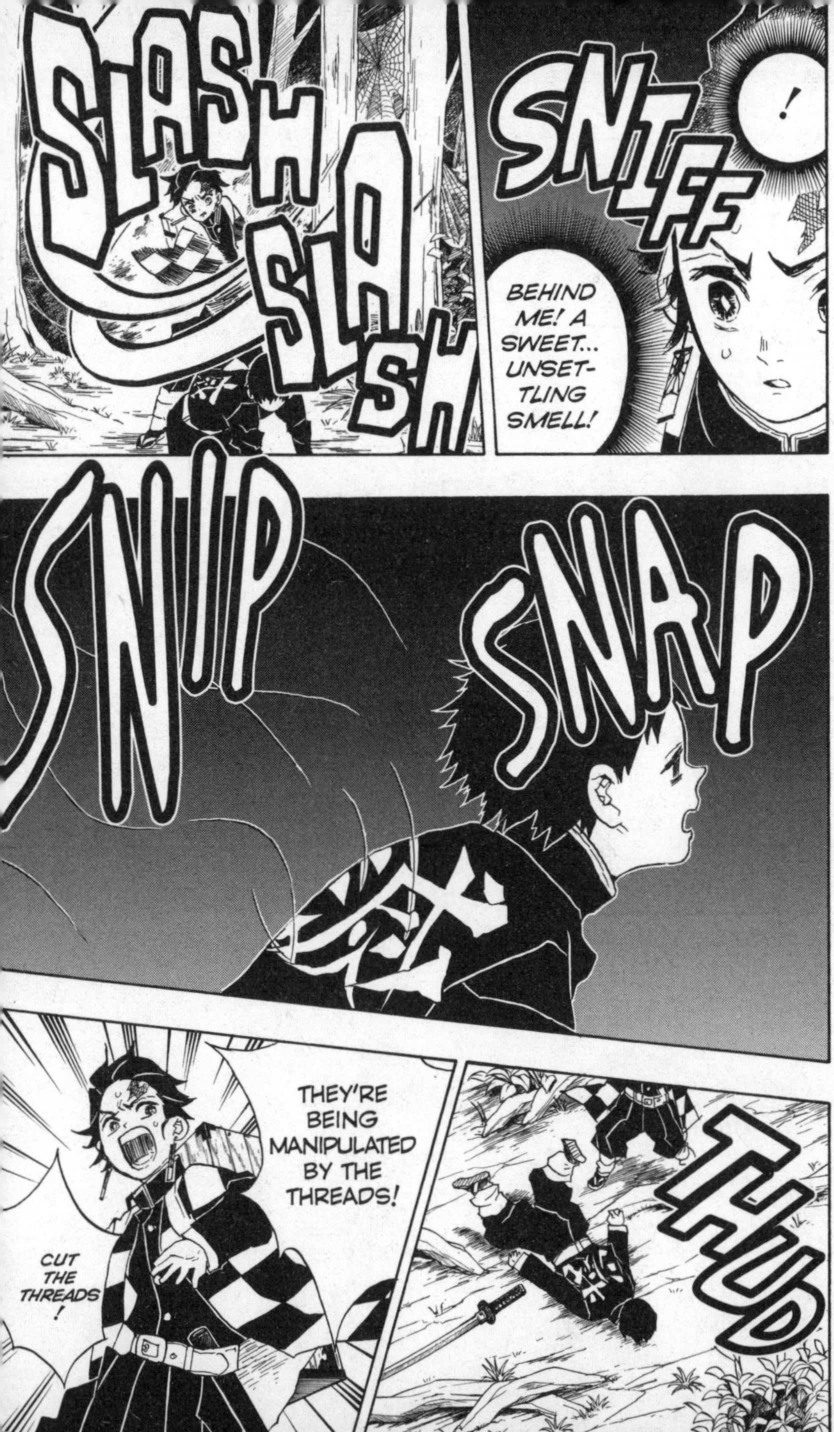
!
SNIFF
BEHIND ME! A SWEET... UNSETTLING SMELL!
SLASH
SLASH
SNAP
SNIP
THUD
THEY'RE BEING MANIPULATED BY THE THREADS!
CUT THE THREADS!

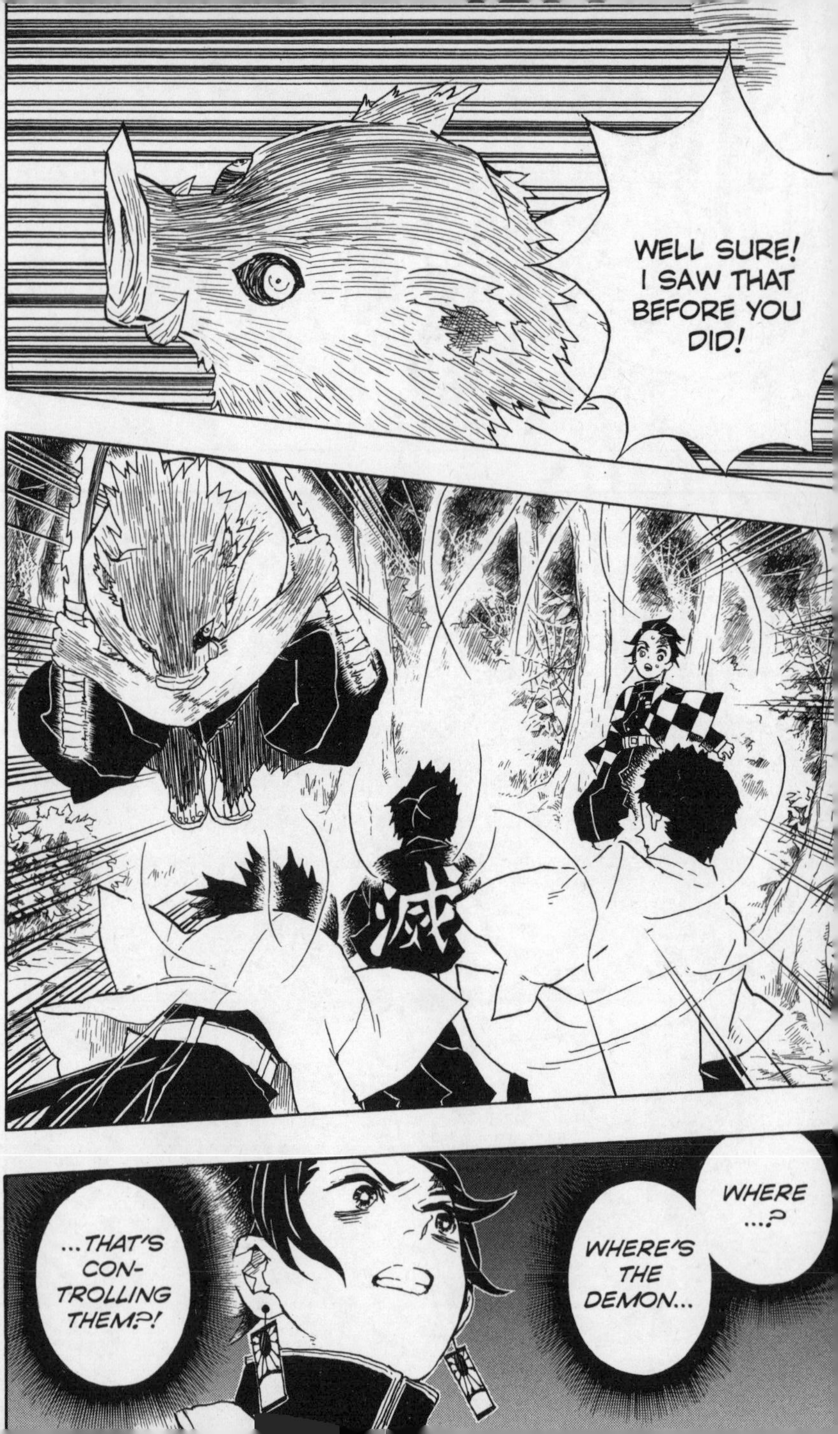
WELL SURE! I SAW THAT BEFORE YOU DID!
WHERE ...?
WHERE'S THE DEMON...
...THAT'S CON-TROLLING THEM?!

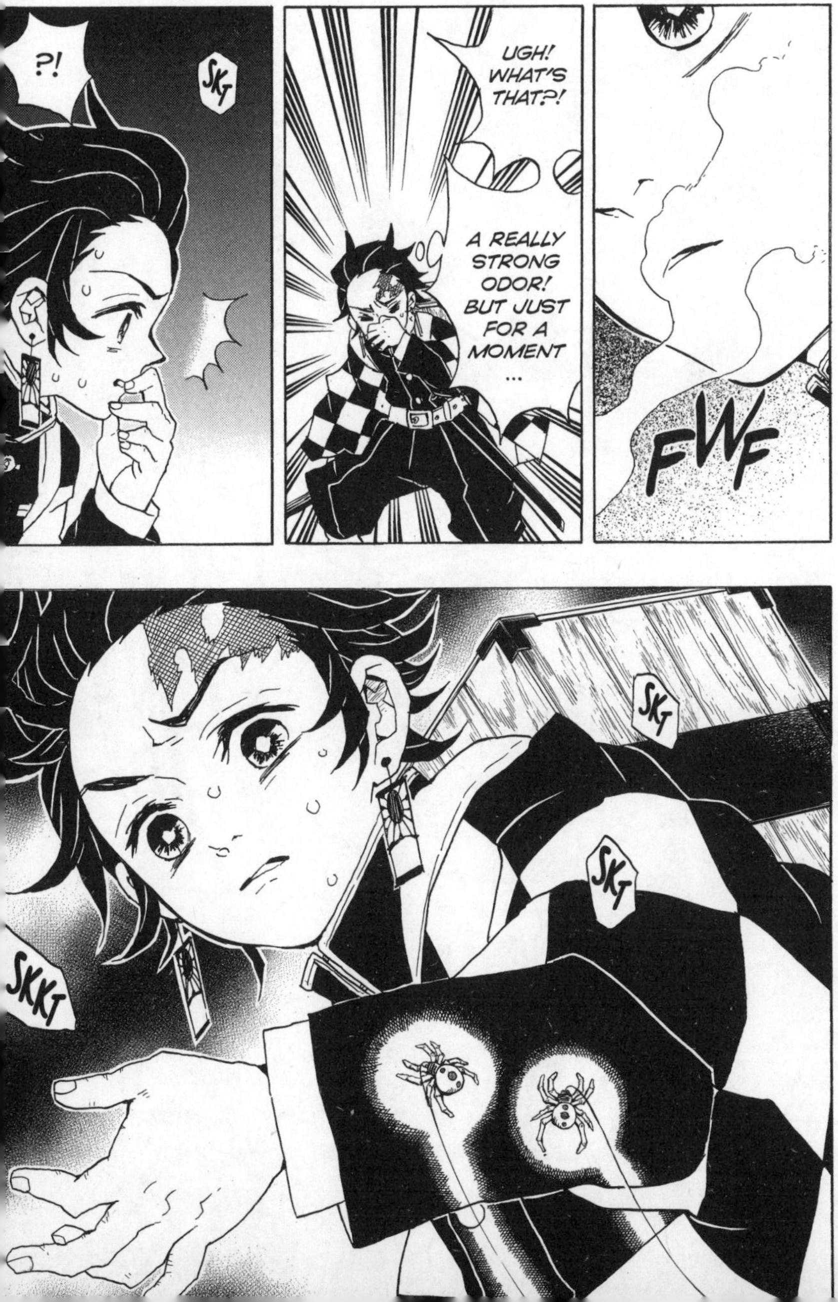
FWF
UGH! WHAT'S THAT?!
A REALLY STRONG ODOR! BUT JUST FOR A MOMENT ...
?!
SKT
SKT
SKT
SKKT

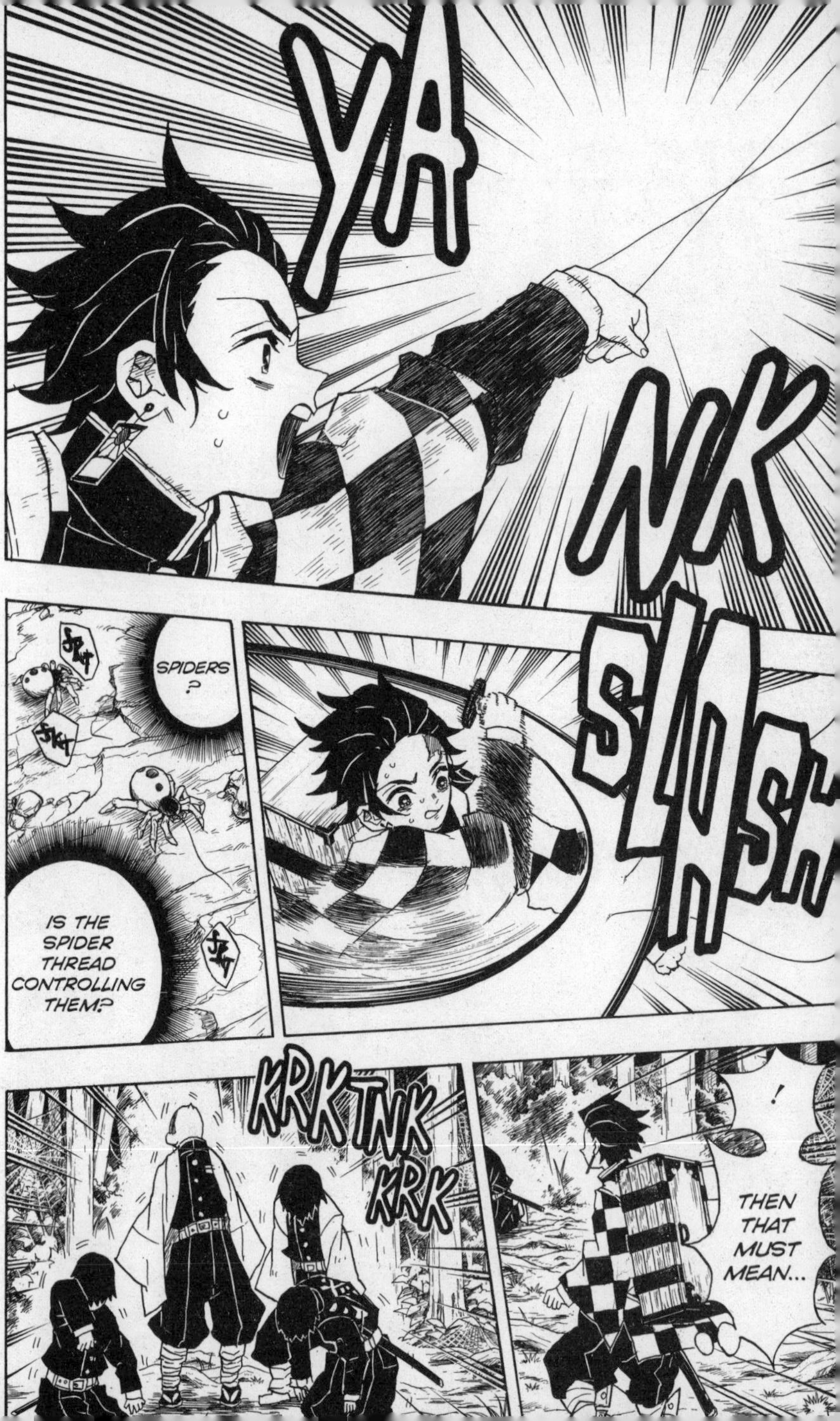
YANK
SLASH
SPIDERS?
IS THE SPIDER THREAD CONTROLLING THEM?
!
THEN THAT MUST MEAN...
KRKTNK KRK

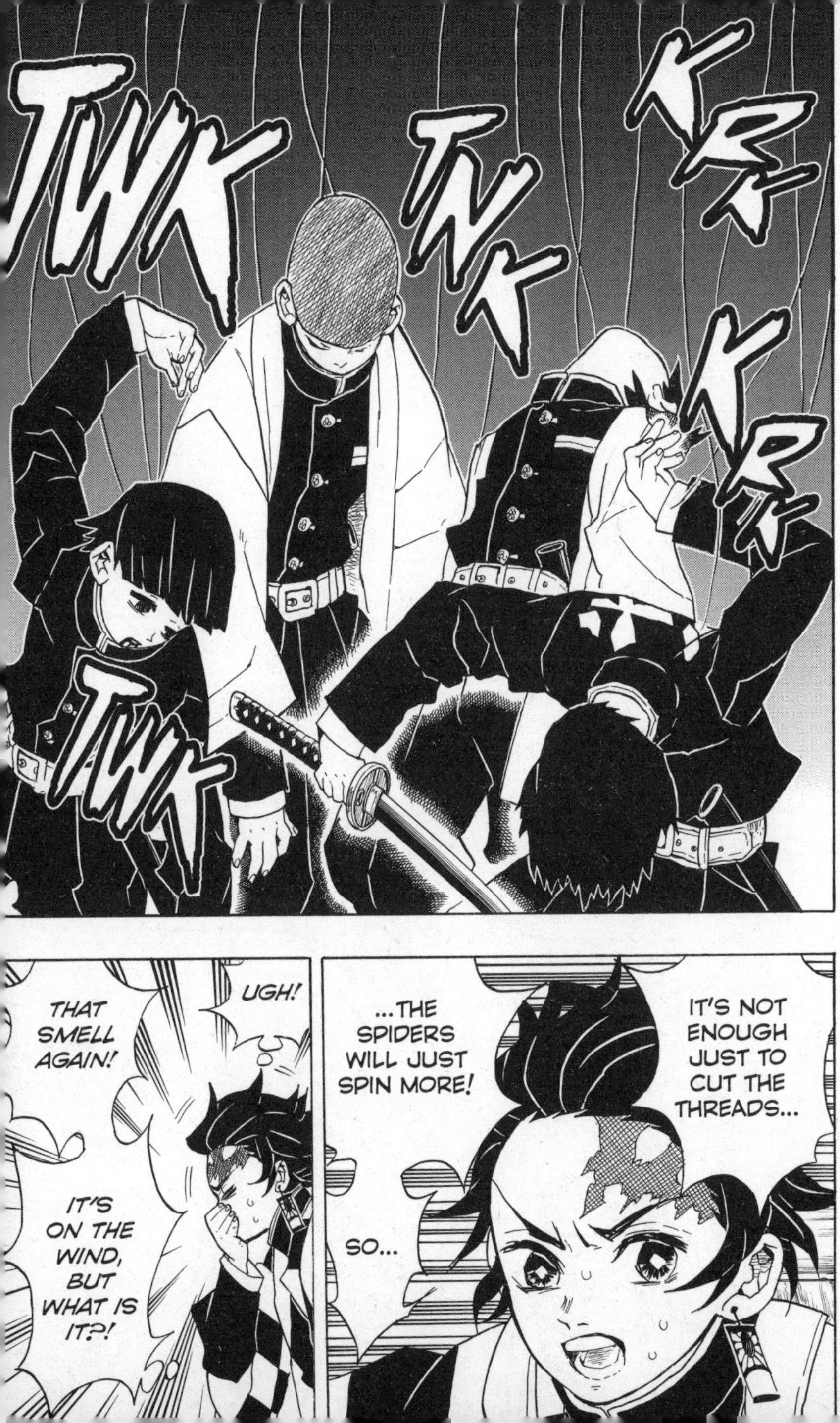

KRK
KRK
TWK
TWK
TWK
IT'S NOT ENOUGH JUST TO CUT THE THREADS...
...THE SPIDERS WILL JUST SPIN MORE!
SO...
UGH!
THAT SMELL AGAIN!
IT'S ON THE WIND, BUT WHAT IS IT?!

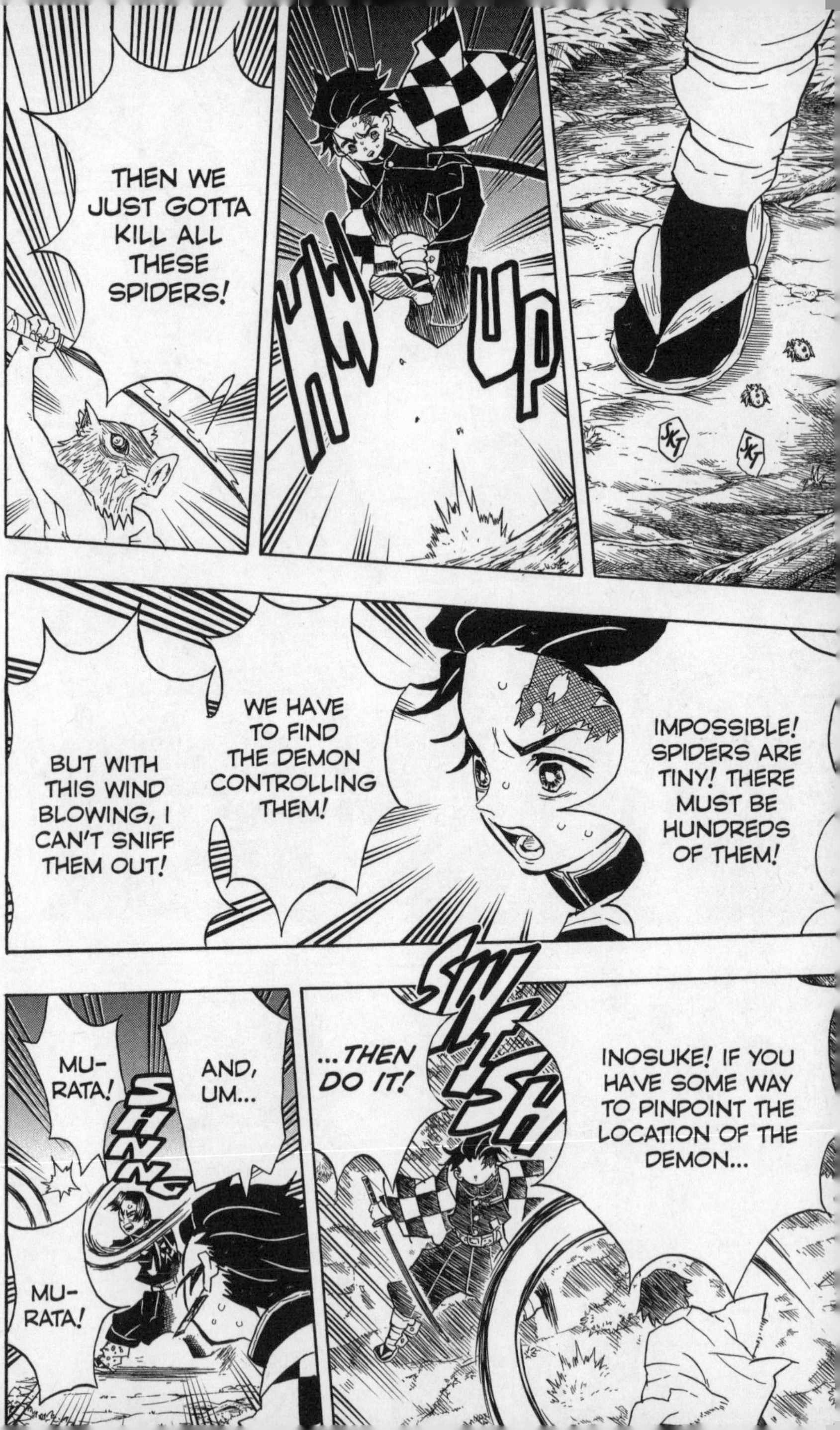
SKT
SKT
WHUP
THEN WE JUST GOTTA KILL ALL THESE SPIDERS!
IMPOSSIBLE! SPIDERS ARE TINY! THERE MUST BE HUNDREDS OF THEM!
WE HAVE TO FIND THE DEMON CONTROLLING THEM!
BUT WITH THIS WIND BLOWING, I CAN'T SNIFF THEM OUT!
SWISH
INOSUKE! IF YOU HAVE SOME WAY TO PINPOINT THE LOCATION OF THE DEMON...
...THEN DO IT!
AND, UM...
MU-RATA!
SHING
MU-RATA!

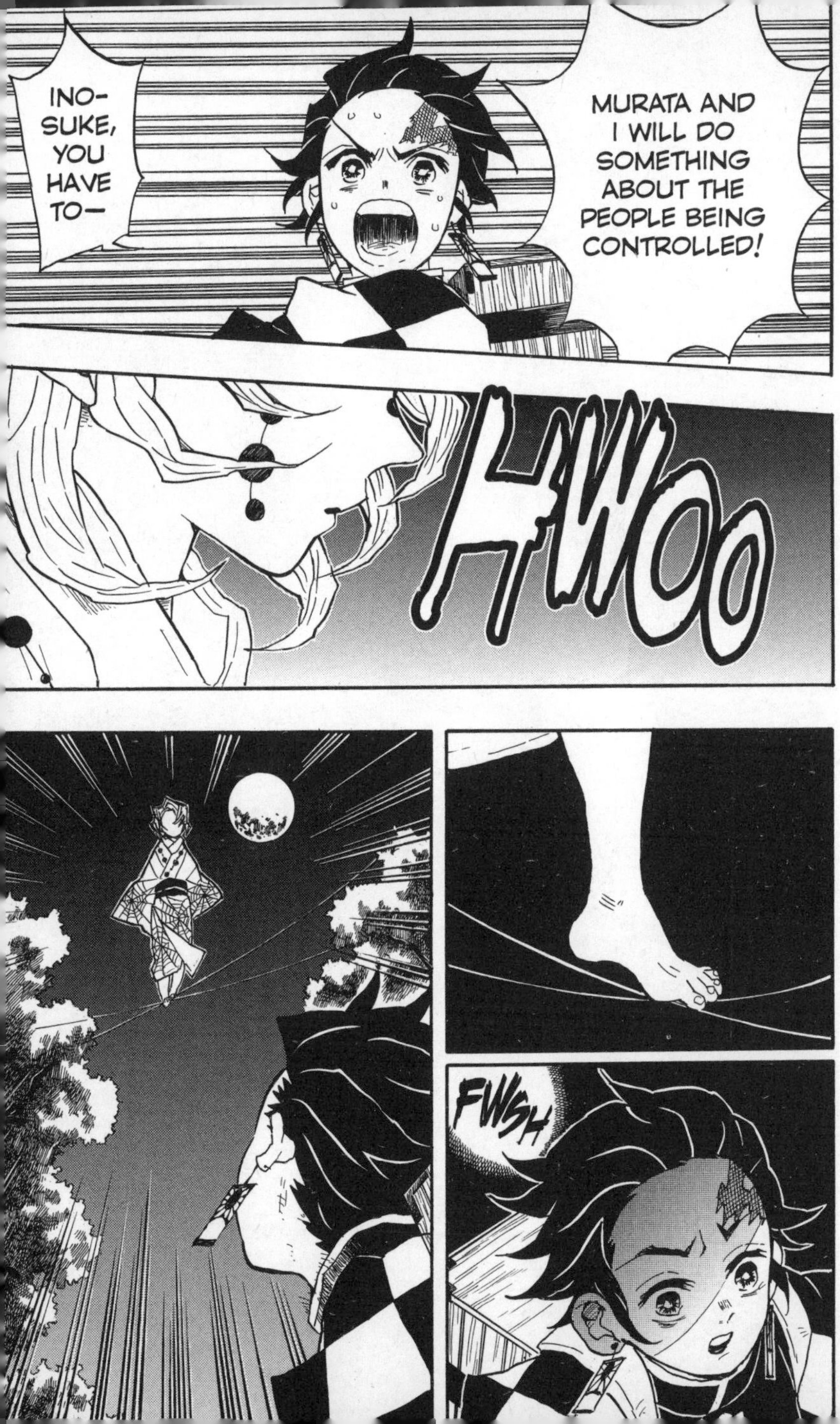
MURATA AND I WILL DO SOMETHING ABOUT THE PEOPLE BEING CONTROLLED!
INO-SUKE, YOU HAVE TO—
HWOO
FWSH

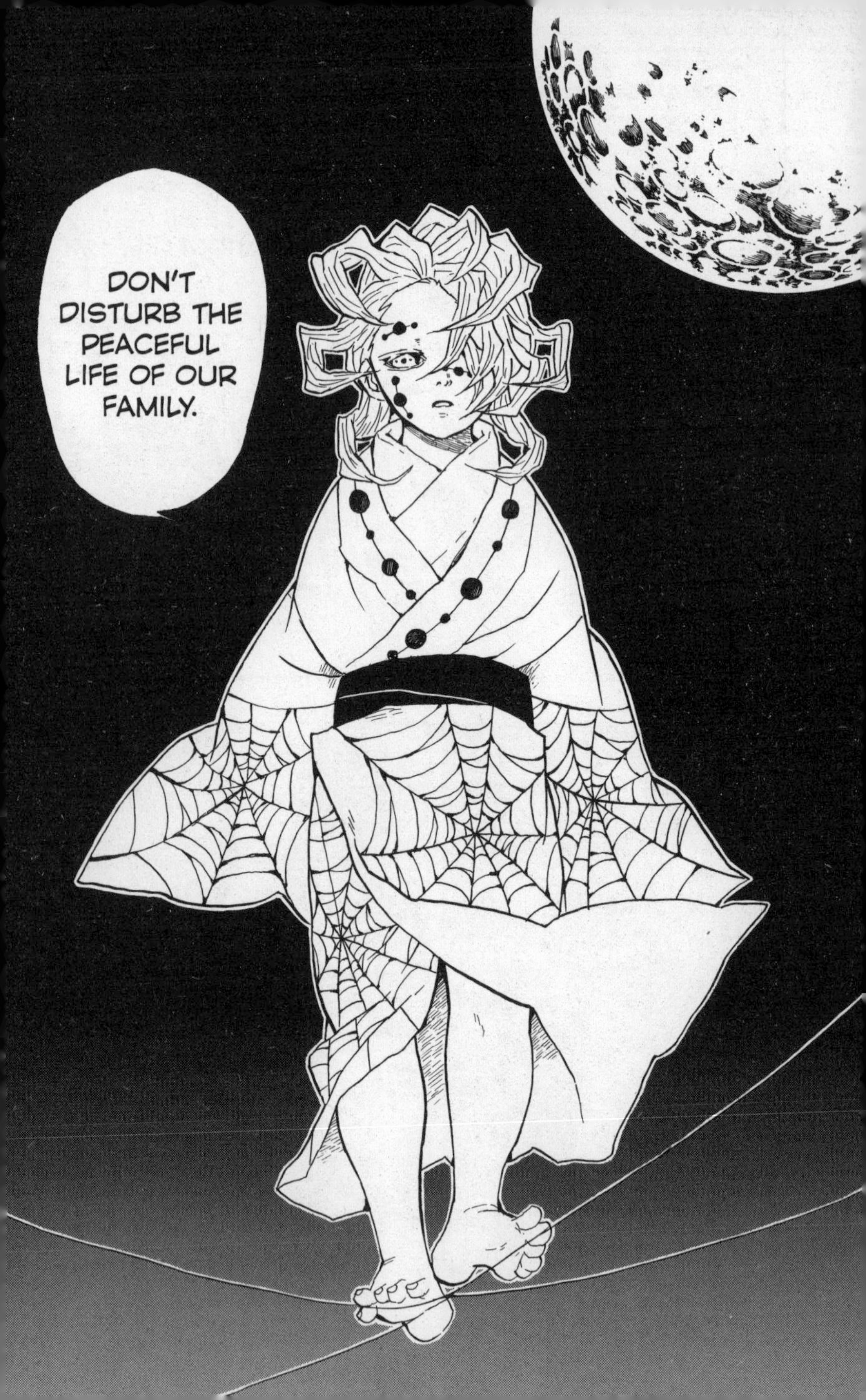
DON'T DISTURB THE PEACEFUL LIFE OF OUR FAMILY.

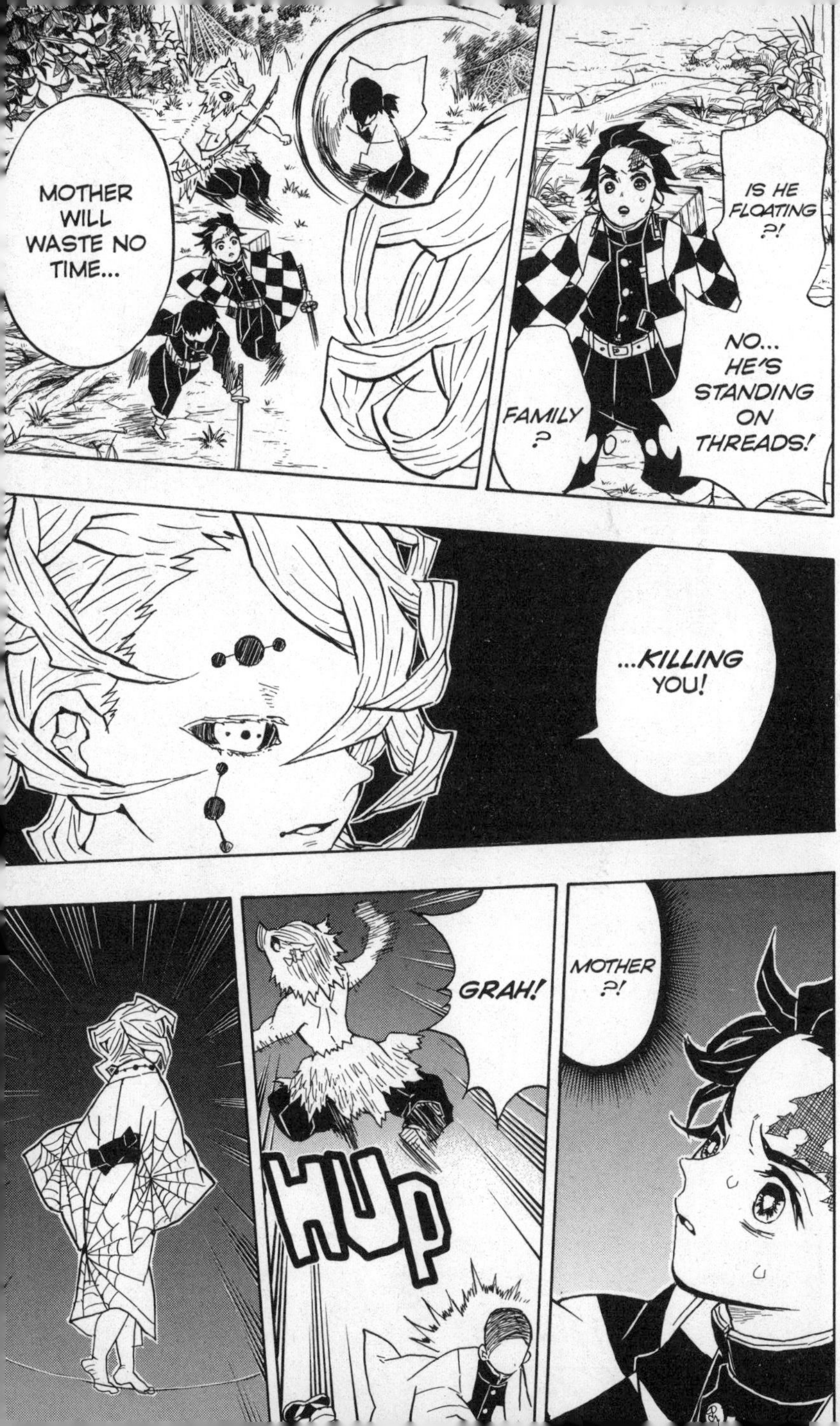
IS HE FLOATING ?!
NO... HE'S STANDING ON THREADS!
FAMILY ?
MOTHER WILL WASTE NO TIME...
...KILLING YOU!
MOTHER ?!
GRAH!
HUP

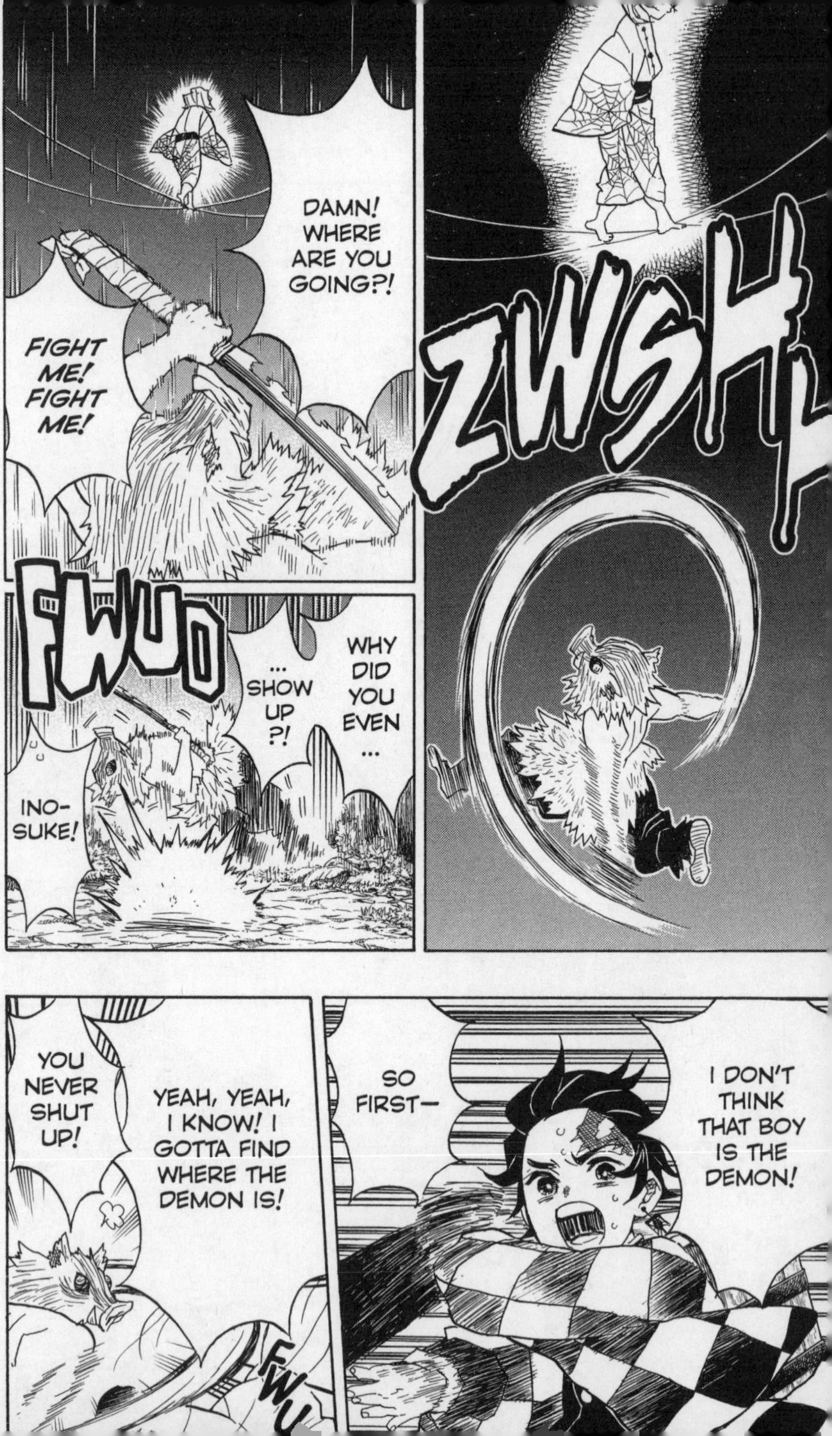
ZWSH
DAMN! WHERE ARE YOU GOING?!
FIGHT ME! FIGHT ME!
WHY DID YOU EVEN ...
... SHOW UP ?!
INO-SUKE!
FWUD
I DON'T THINK THAT BOY IS THE DEMON!
SO FIRST—
YEAH, YEAH, I KNOW! I GOTTA FIND WHERE THE DEMON IS!
YOU NEVER SHUT UP!
FWU

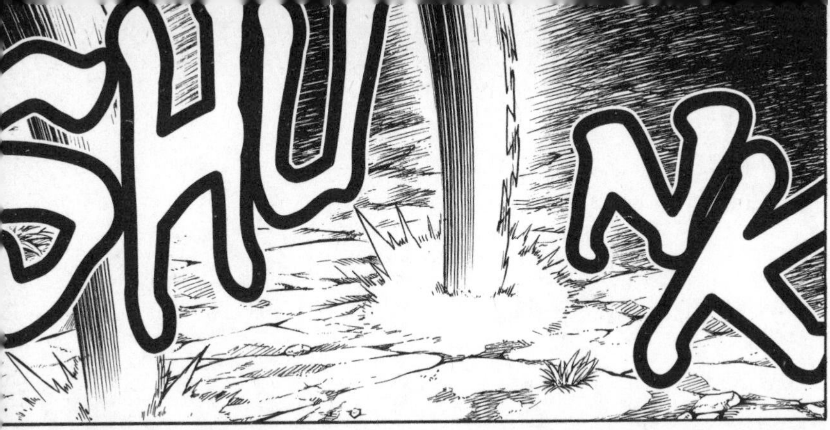
SHUNK
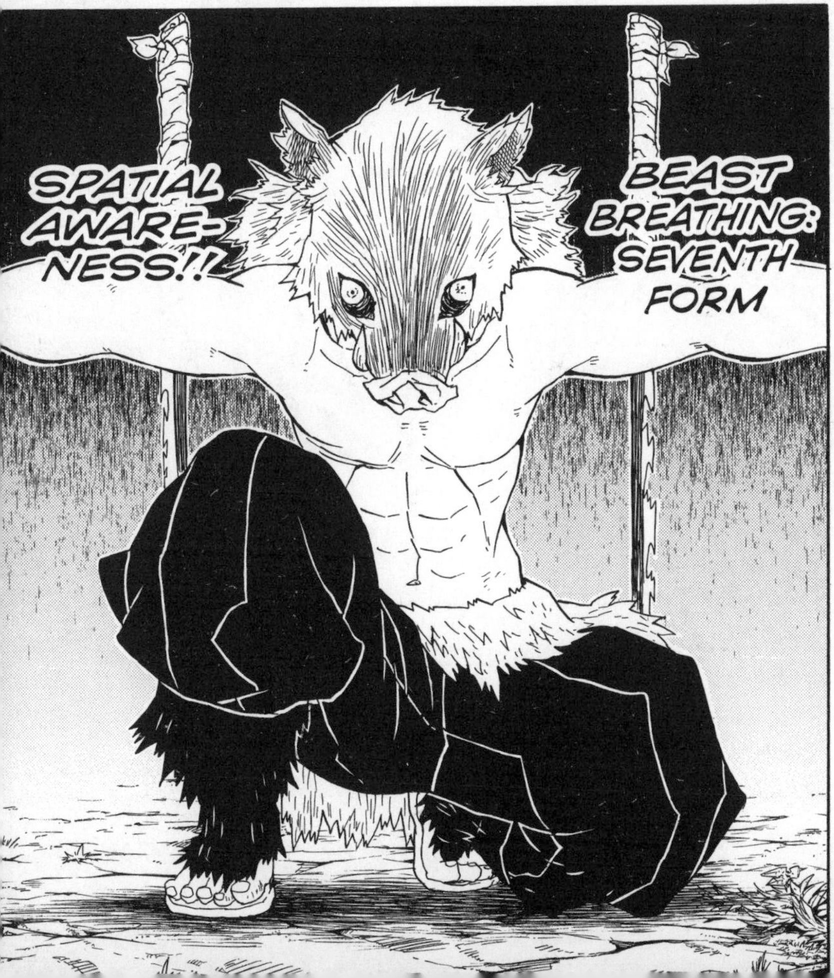
BEAST BREATHING: SEVENTH FORM
SPATIAL AWARENESS!!

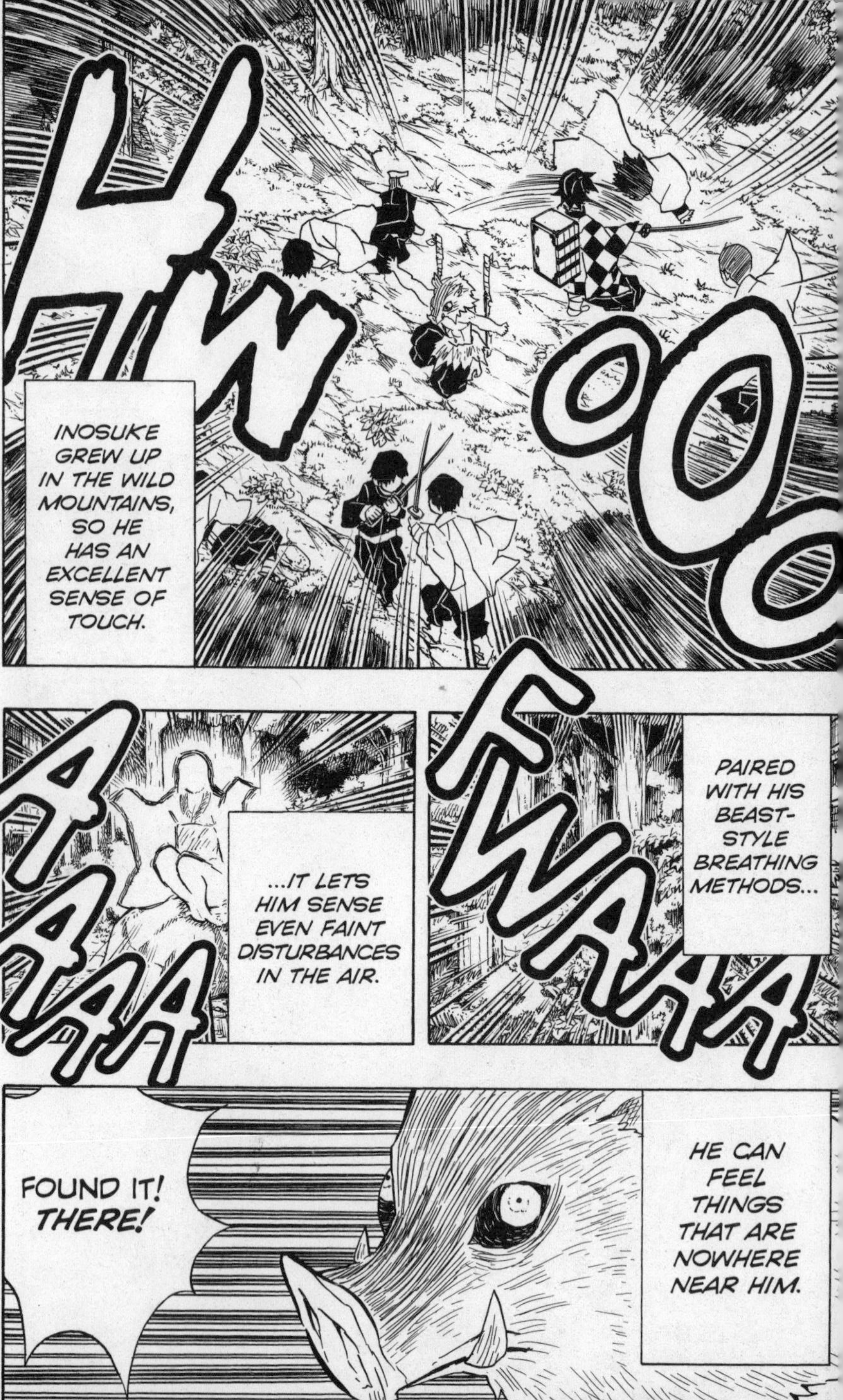
HWOOO
INOSUKE GREW UP IN THE WILD MOUNTAINS, SO HE HAS AN EXCELLENT SENSE OF TOUCH.
PAIRED WITH HIS BEAST-STYLE BREATHING METHODS...
FWAHA
...IT LETS HIM SENSE EVEN FAINT DISTURBANCES IN THE AIR.
AAAA
HE CAN FEEL THINGS THAT ARE NOWHERE NEAR HIM.
FOUND IT! THERE!

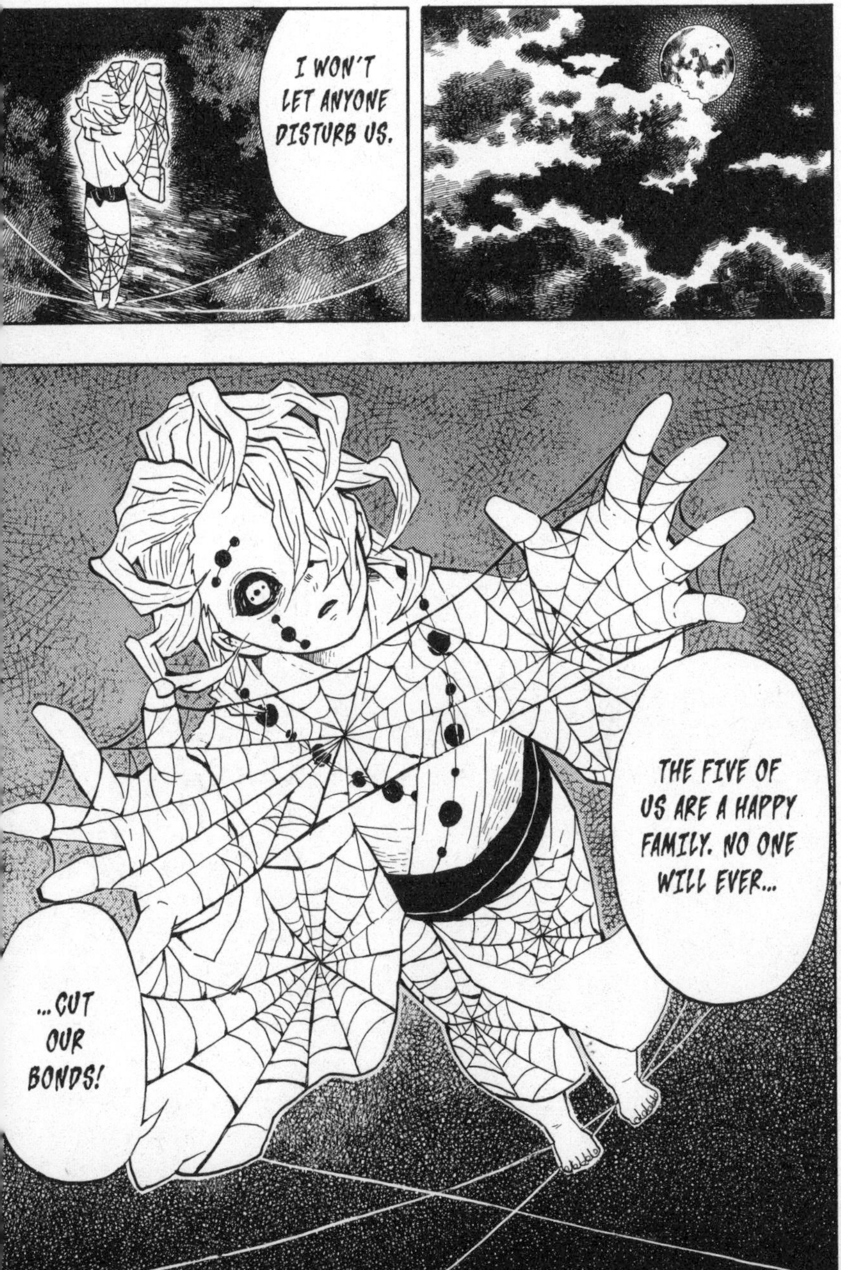
I WON'T LET ANYONE DISTURB US.
THE FIVE OF US ARE A HAPPY FAMILY. NO ONE WILL EVER...
...CUT OUR BONDS!

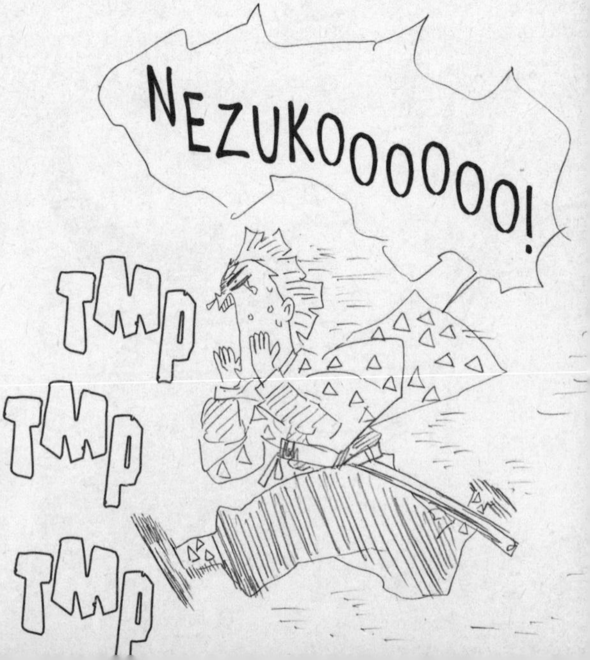
NEZUKOOOOOOO!
TMP TMP TMP

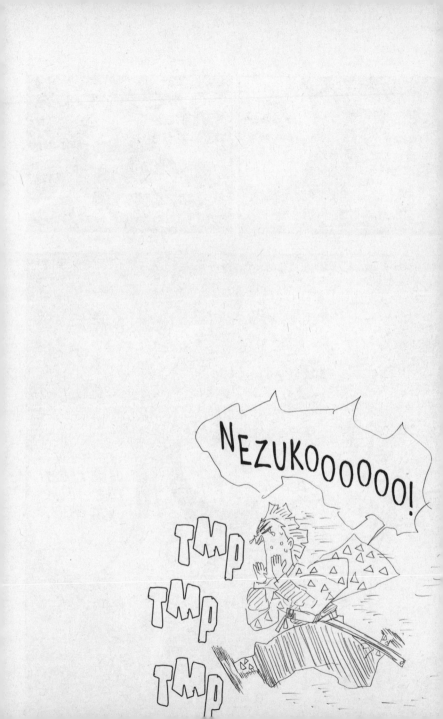

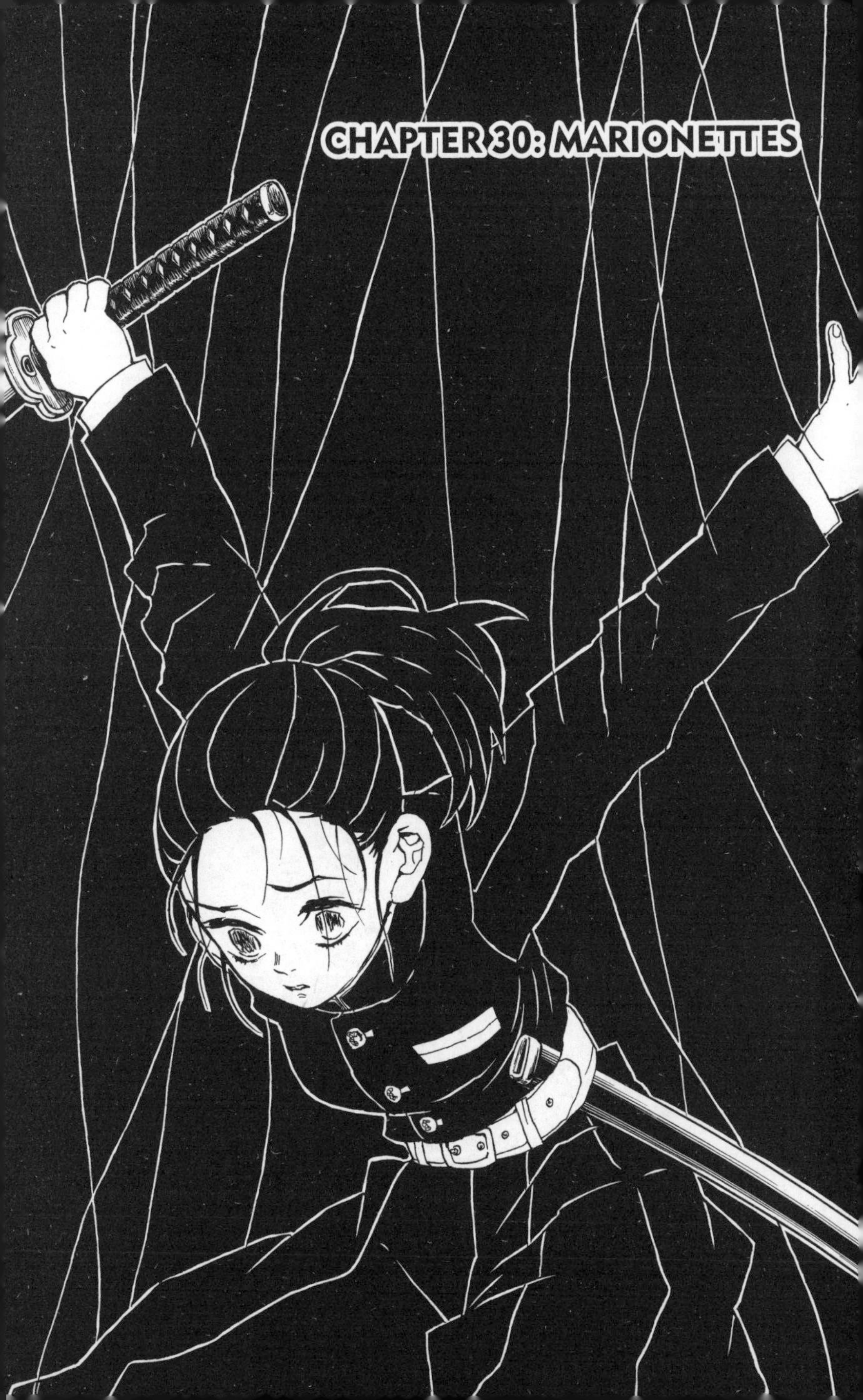
CHAPTER 30: MARIONETTES

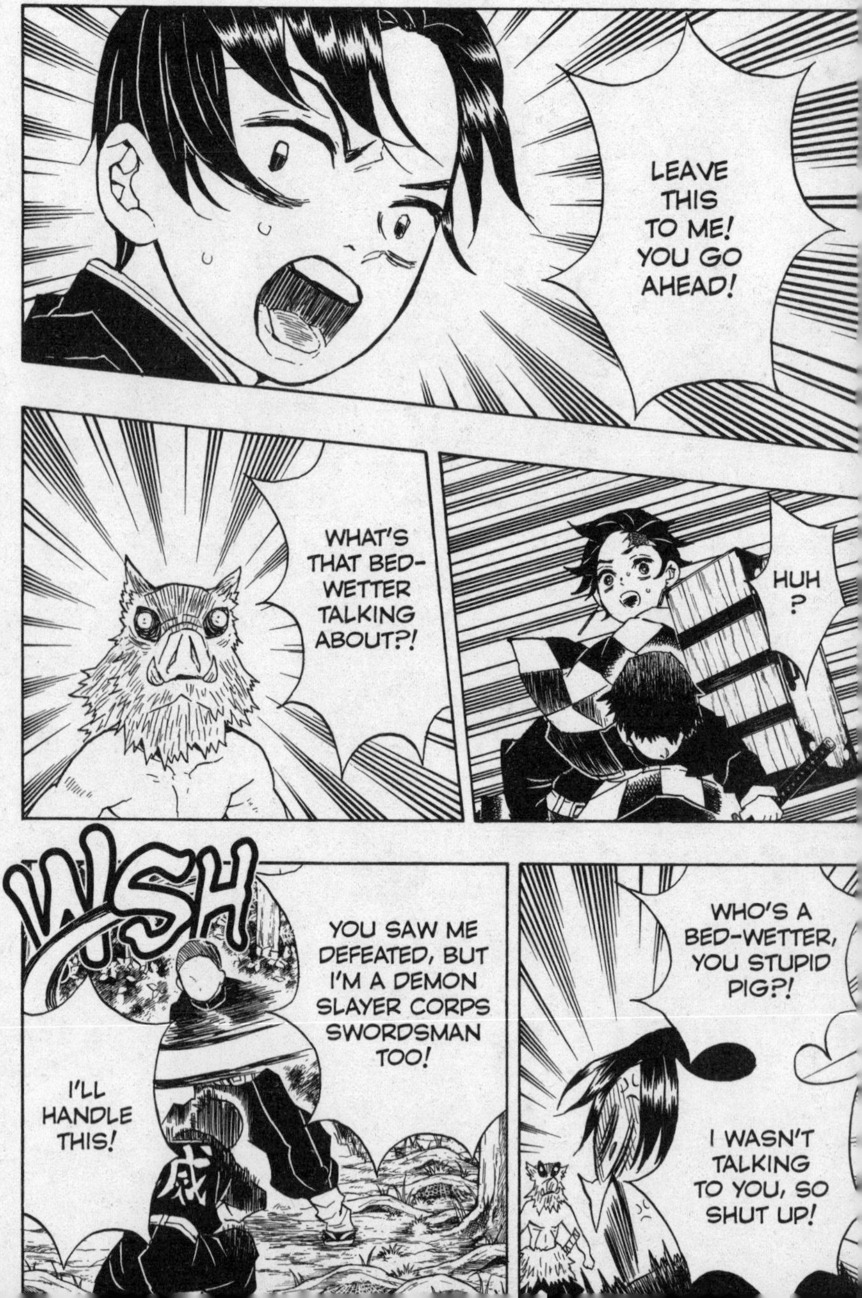
LEAVE THIS TO ME! YOU GO AHEAD!
HUH?
WHAT'S THAT BED-WETTER TALKING ABOUT?!
WHO'S A BED-WETTER, YOU STUPID PIG?!
I WASN'T TALKING TO YOU, SO SHUT UP!
WSH
YOU SAW ME DEFEATED, BUT I'M A DEMON SLAYER CORPS SWORDSMAN TOO!
I'LL HANDLE THIS!

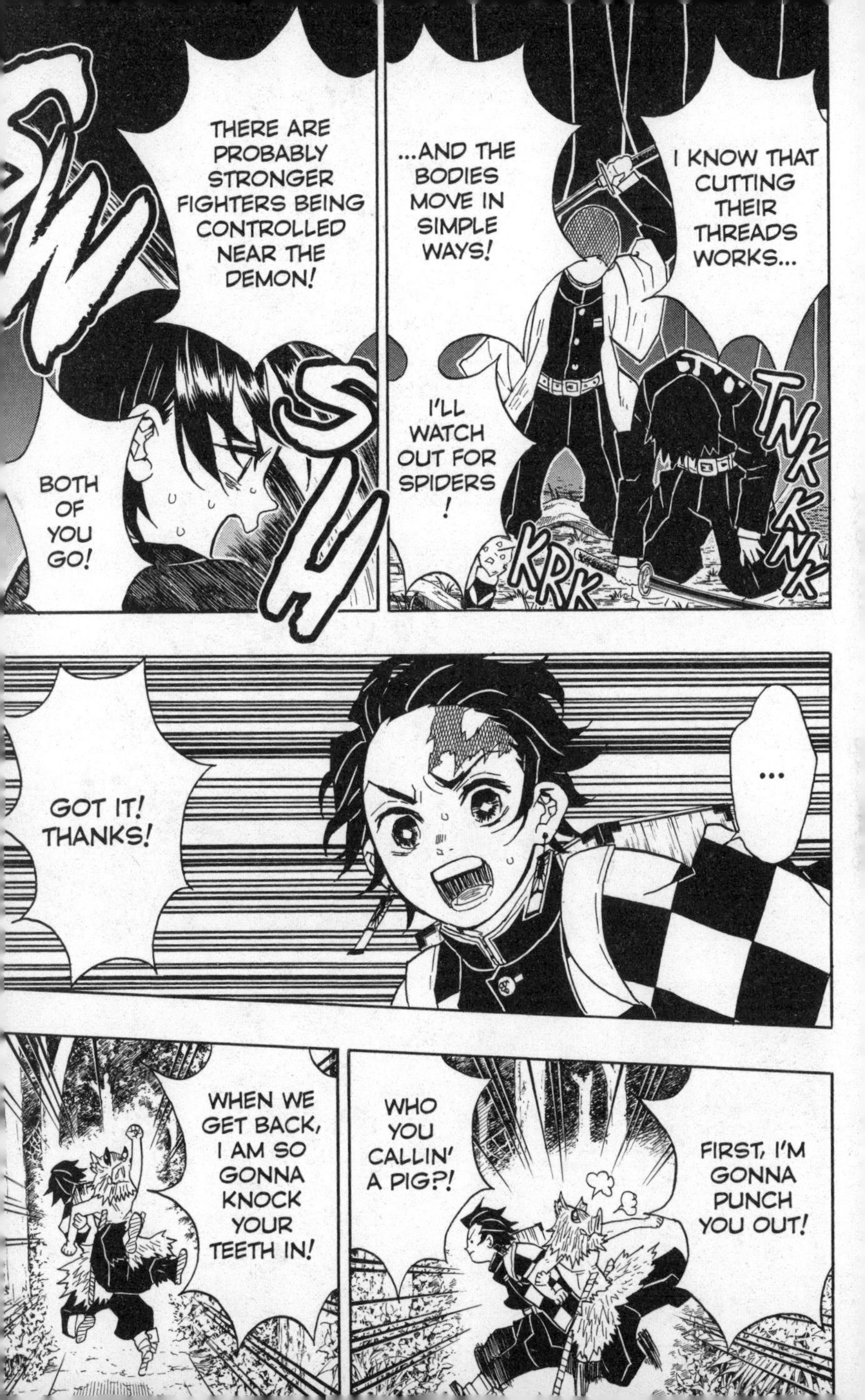
I KNOW THAT CUTTING THEIR THREADS WORKS...
...AND THE BODIES MOVE IN SIMPLE WAYS!
TNK KNK KNK
KRK
I'LL WATCH OUT FOR SPIDERS!
THERE ARE PROBABLY STRONGER FIGHTERS BEING CONTROLLED NEAR THE DEMON!
BOTH OF YOU GO!
...
GOT IT! THANKS!
FIRST, I'M GONNA PUNCH YOU OUT!
WHO YOU CALLIN' A PIG?!
WHEN WE GET BACK, I AM SO GONNA KNOCK YOUR TEETH IN!

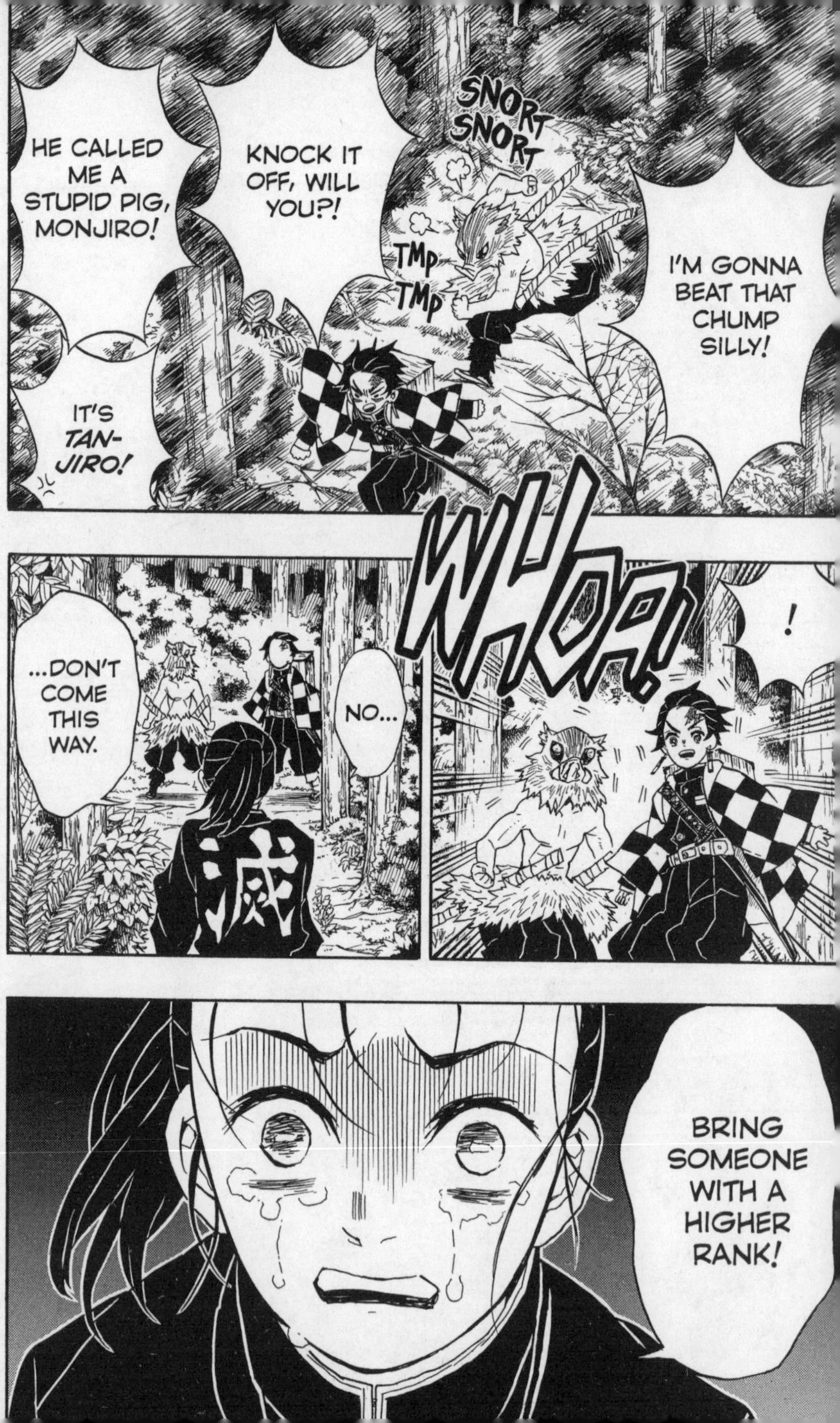
I'M GONNA BEAT THAT CHUMP SILLY!
SNORT SNORT
TMP TMP
KNOCK IT OFF, WILL YOU?!
HE CALLED ME A STUPID PIG, MONJIRO!
IT'S *TANJIRO!*
!
WHOA!
NO...
...DON'T COME THIS WAY.
BRING SOMEONE WITH A HIGHER RANK!

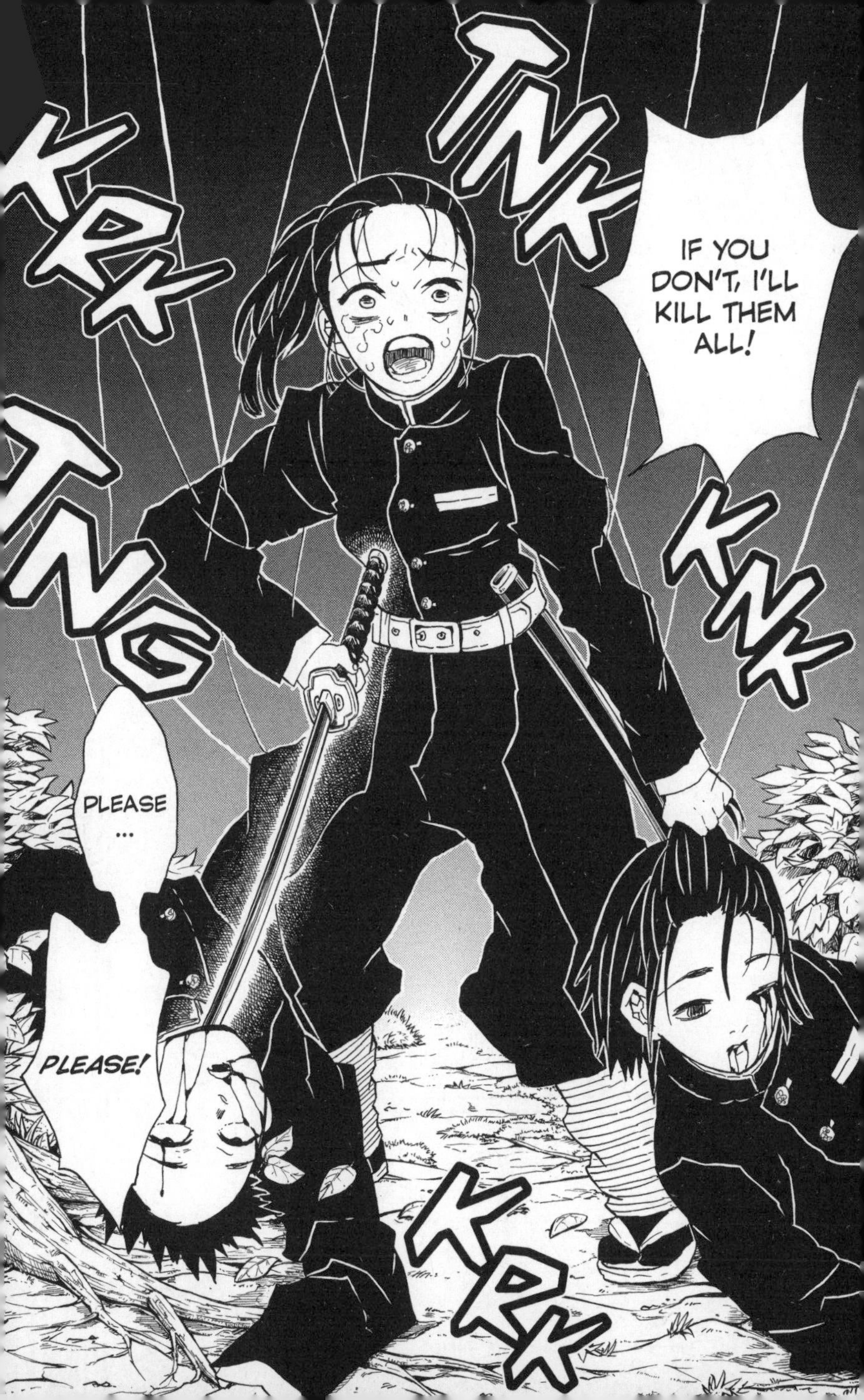
TNK
IF YOU DON'T, I'LL KILL THEM ALL!
KRK
KNK
TNG
PLEASE ...
PLEASE!
KRK

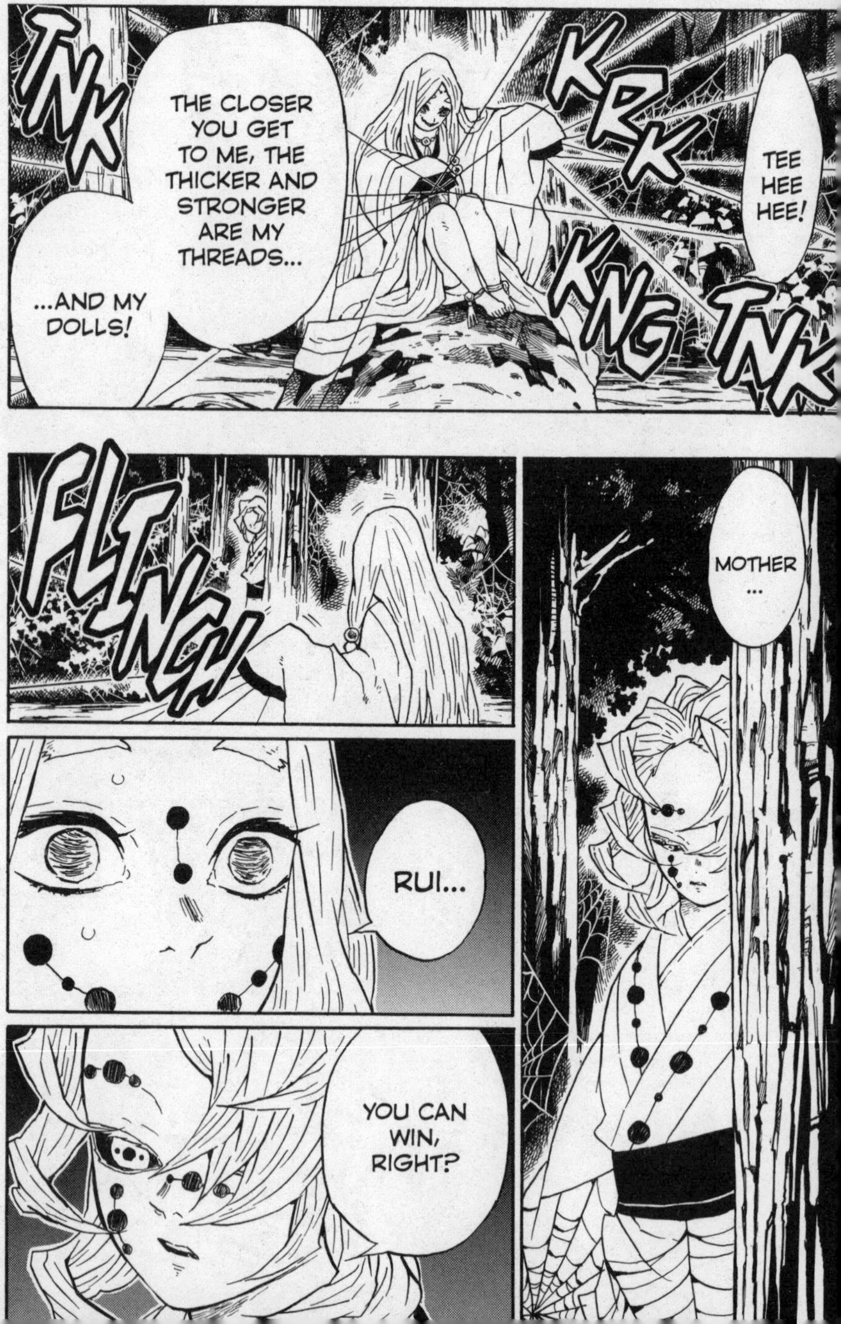
KRK
TEE HEE HEE!
KNG
TNK
TNK
THE CLOSER YOU GET TO ME, THE THICKER AND STRONGER ARE MY THREADS...
...AND MY DOLLS!
MOTHER ...
FLINCH
RUI...
YOU CAN WIN, RIGHT?

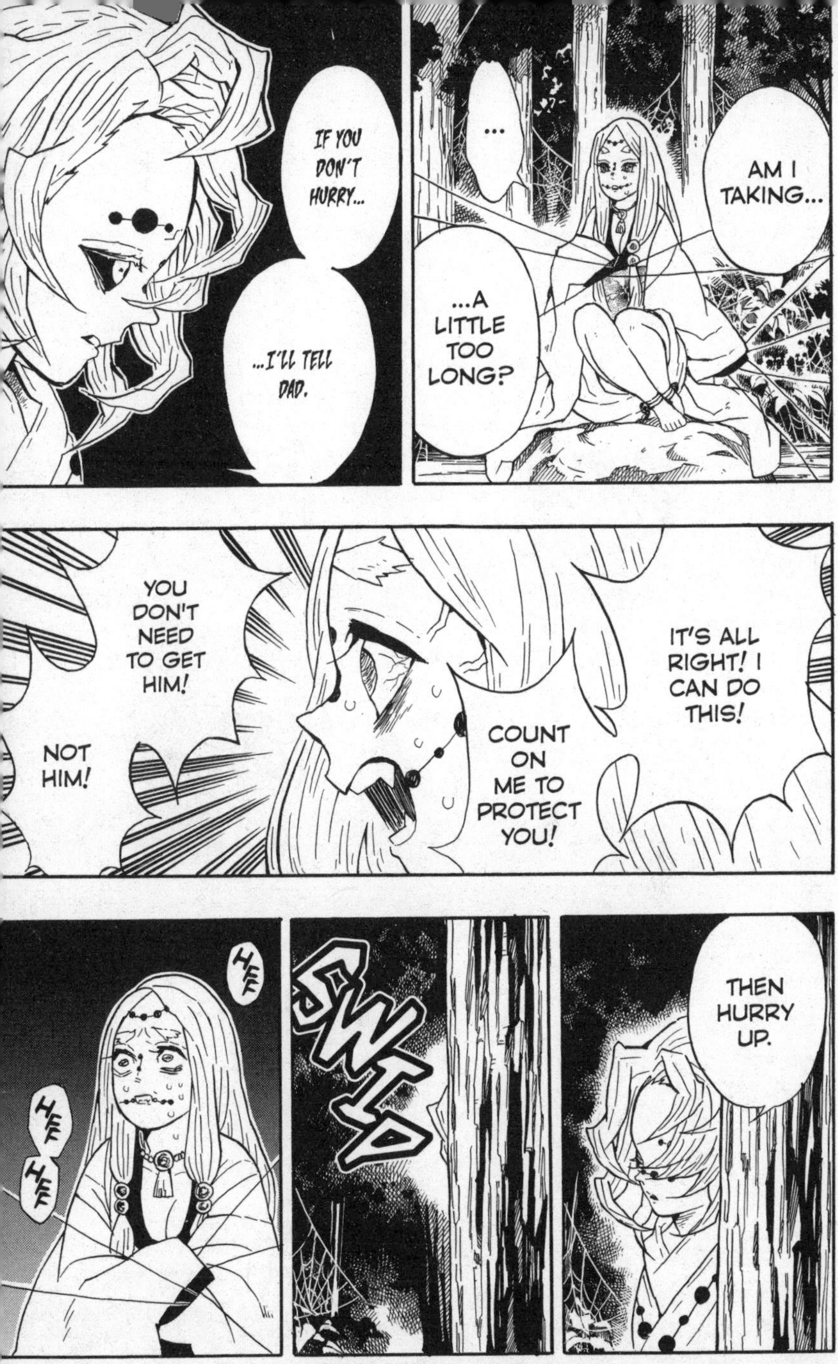
AM I TAKING...
...
...A LITTLE TOO LONG?
IF YOU DON'T HURRY...
...I'LL TELL DAD.
IT'S ALL RIGHT! I CAN DO THIS!
COUNT ON ME TO PROTECT YOU!
YOU DON'T NEED TO GET HIM!
NOT HIM!
THEN HURRY UP.
SWIP
HEF
HEF HEF

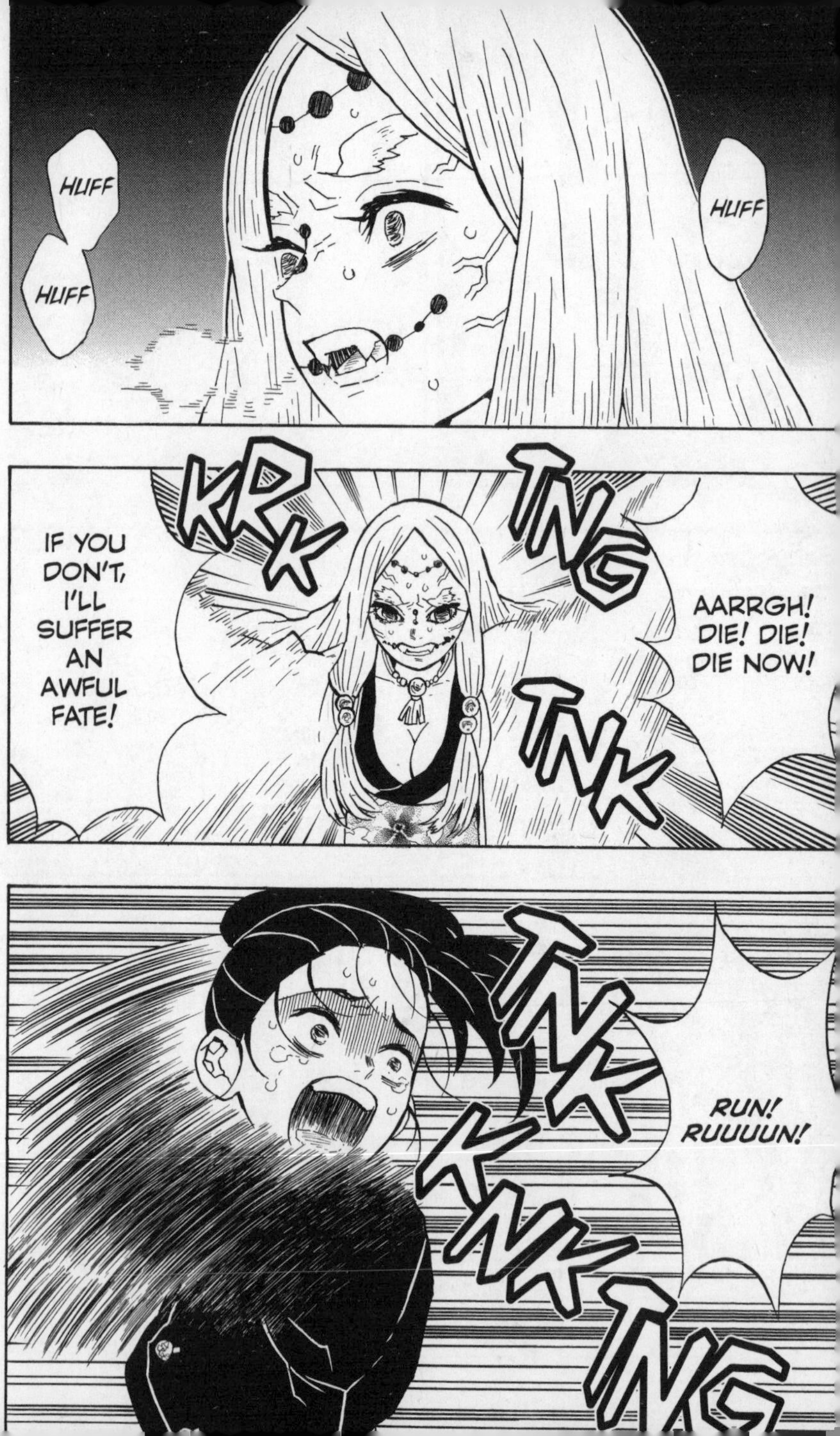
HUFF
HUFF
HUFF
TNG
KRK
AARRGH! DIE! DIE! DIE NOW!
TNK
IF YOU DON'T, I'LL SUFFER AN AWFUL FATE!
RUN! RUUUUN!
TNK
KNK
TNG

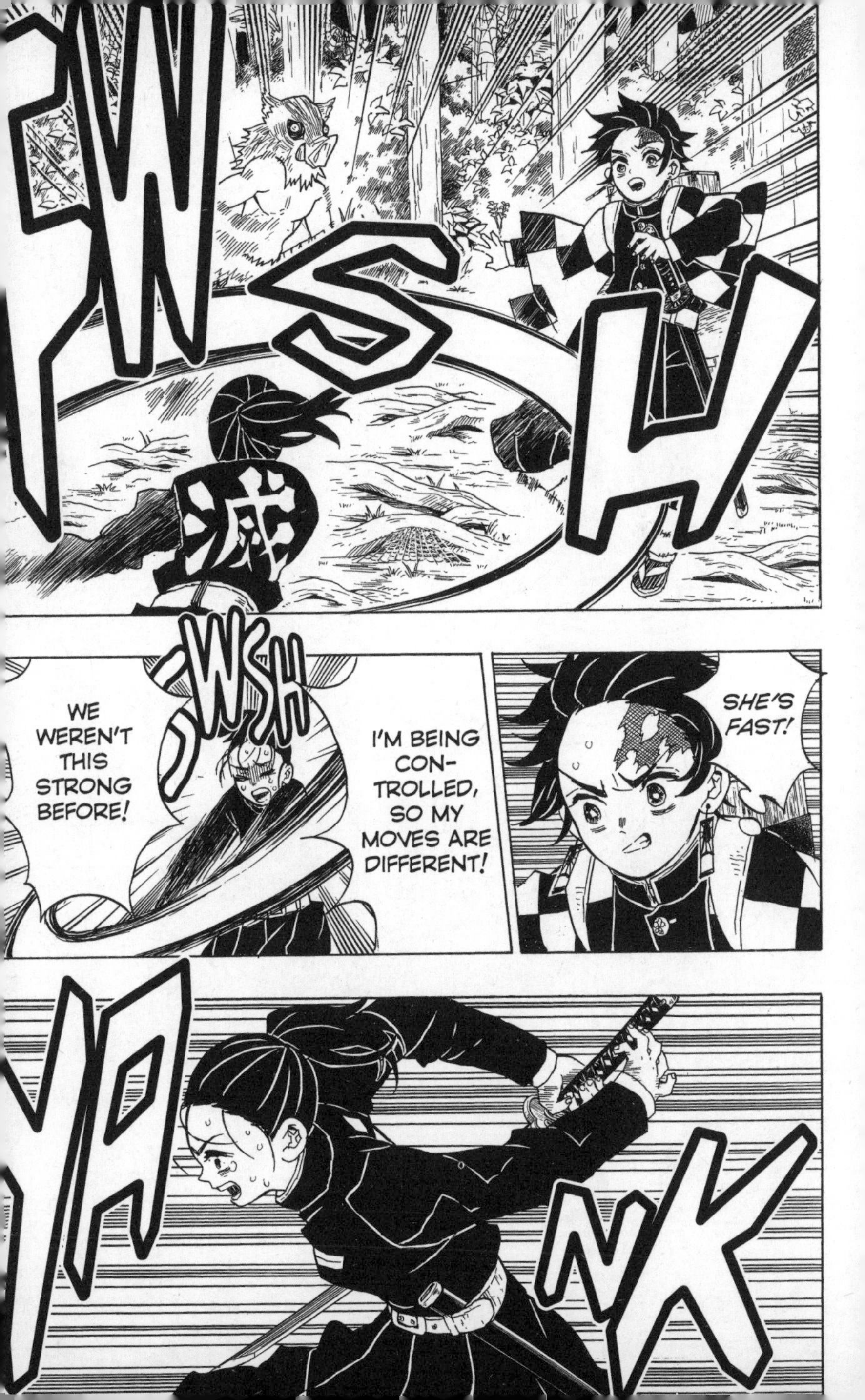
SWSH
SHE'S FAST!
SWSH
I'M BEING CON-TROLLED, SO MY MOVES ARE DIFFERENT!
WE WEREN'T THIS STRONG BEFORE!
YANK

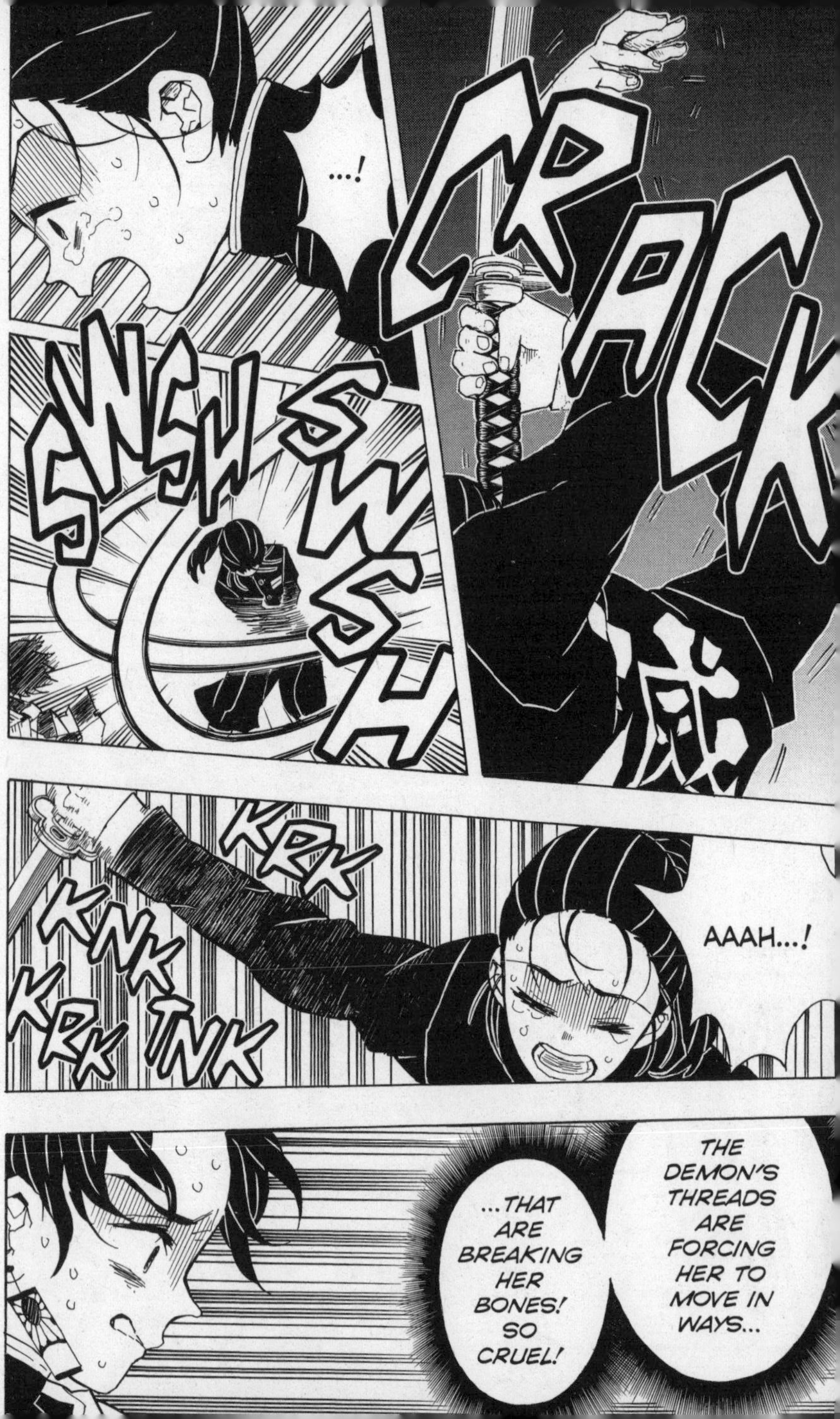
CRACK
...!
SWSH
SWSH
AAAH...!
KRK
KNK
KRK TNK
THE DEMON'S THREADS ARE FORCING HER TO MOVE IN WAYS...
...THAT ARE BREAKING HER BONES! SO CRUEL!

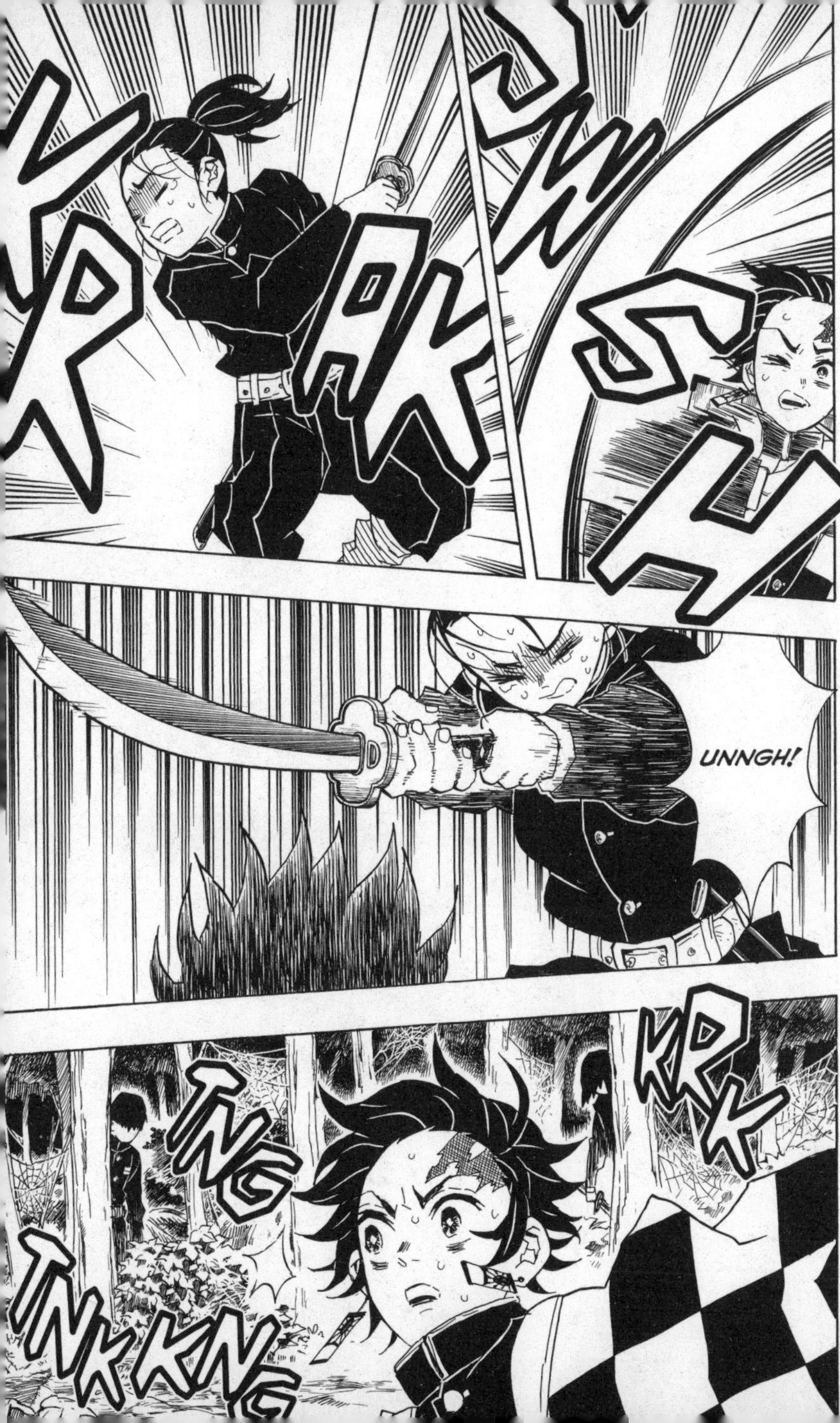
KRAK
UNNGH!
KRK
TNG
TNK KNG

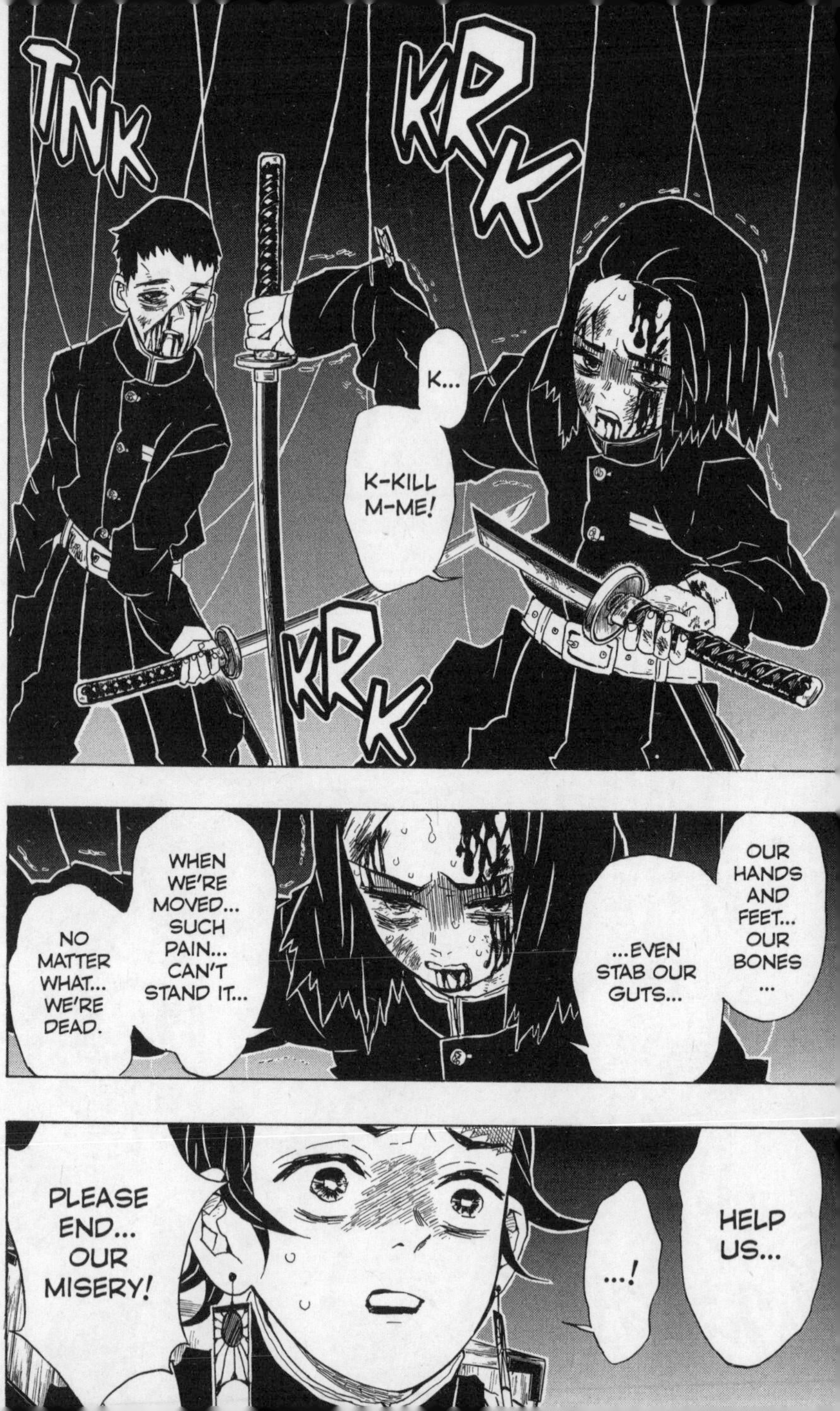
KRK
TNK
K...
K-KILL M-ME!
KRK
OUR HANDS AND FEET... OUR BONES ...
...EVEN STAB OUR GUTS...
WHEN WE'RE MOVED... SUCH PAIN... CAN'T STAND IT...
NO MATTER WHAT... WE'RE DEAD.
HELP US...
...!
PLEASE END... OUR MISERY!

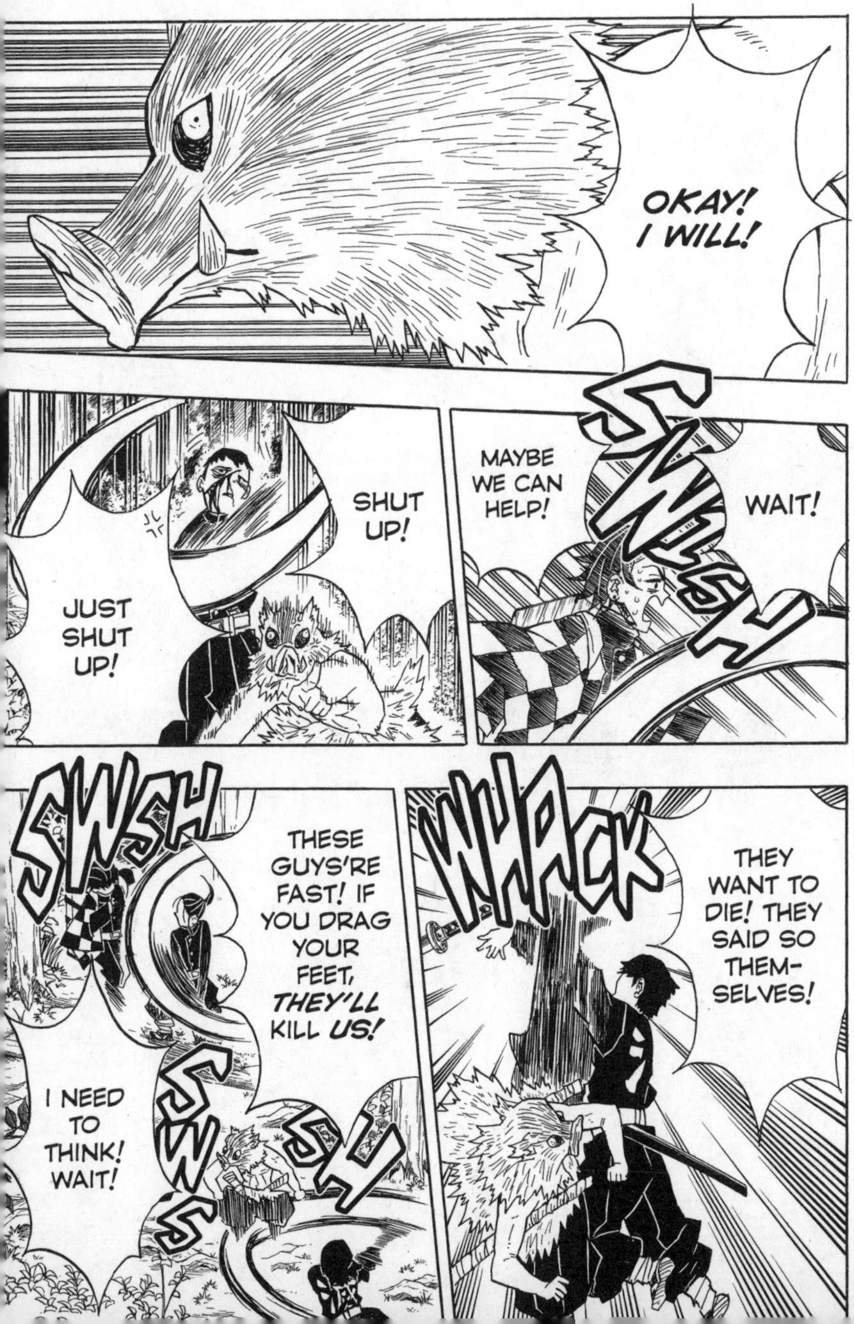
OKAY! I WILL!
WAIT!
SWISH
MAYBE WE CAN HELP!
SHUT UP!
JUST SHUT UP!
THEY WANT TO DIE! THEY SAID SO THEM-SELVES!
WHACK
THESE GUYS'RE FAST! IF YOU DRAG YOUR FEET, THEY'LL KILL US!
SWSH
I NEED TO THINK! WAIT!
SWSH

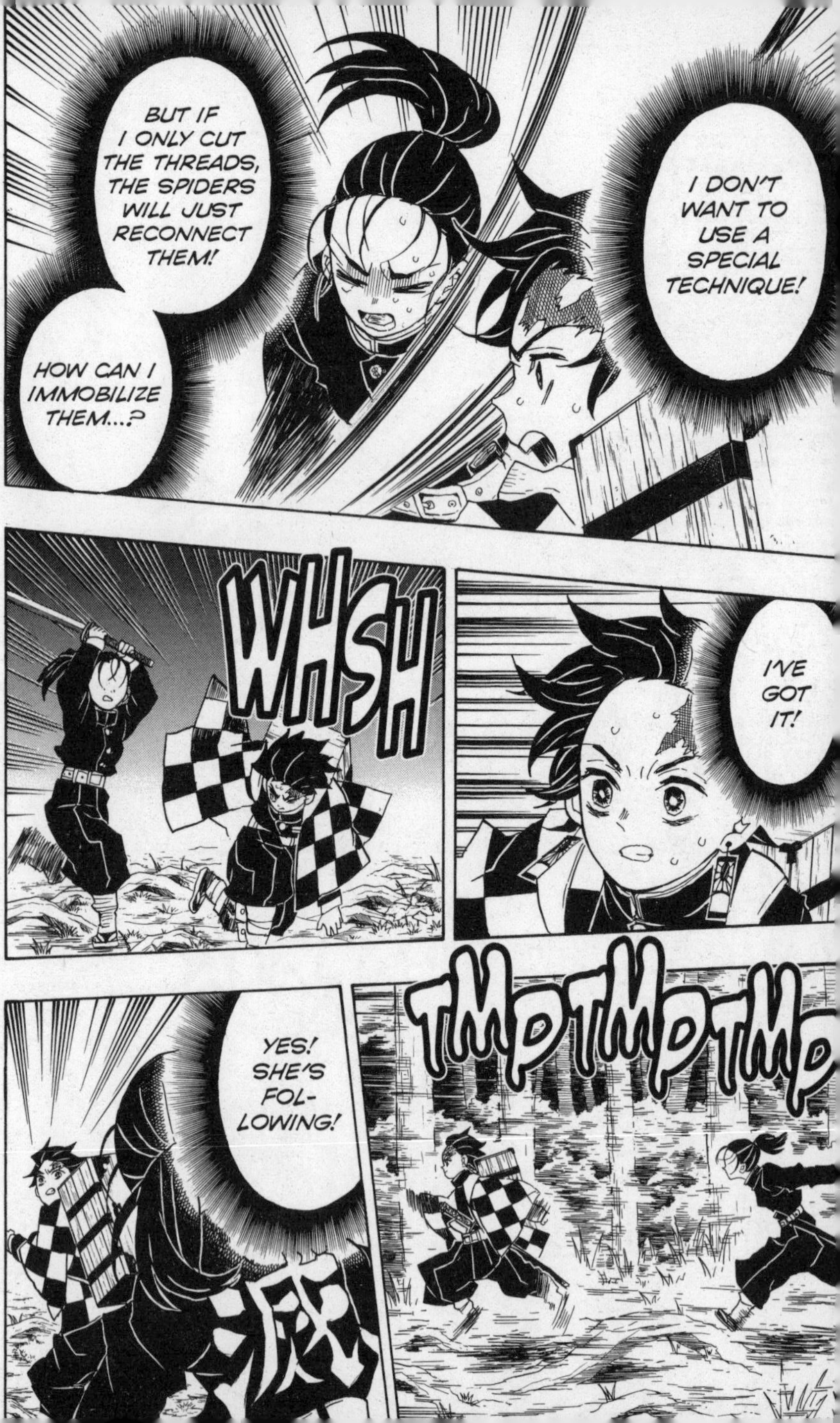
I DON'T WANT TO USE A SPECIAL TECHNIQUE!
BUT IF I ONLY CUT THE THREADS, THE SPIDERS WILL JUST RECONNECT THEM!
HOW CAN I IMMOBILIZE THEM...?
I'VE GOT IT!
WHSH
TMP TMP TMP
YES! SHE'S FOL-LOWING!

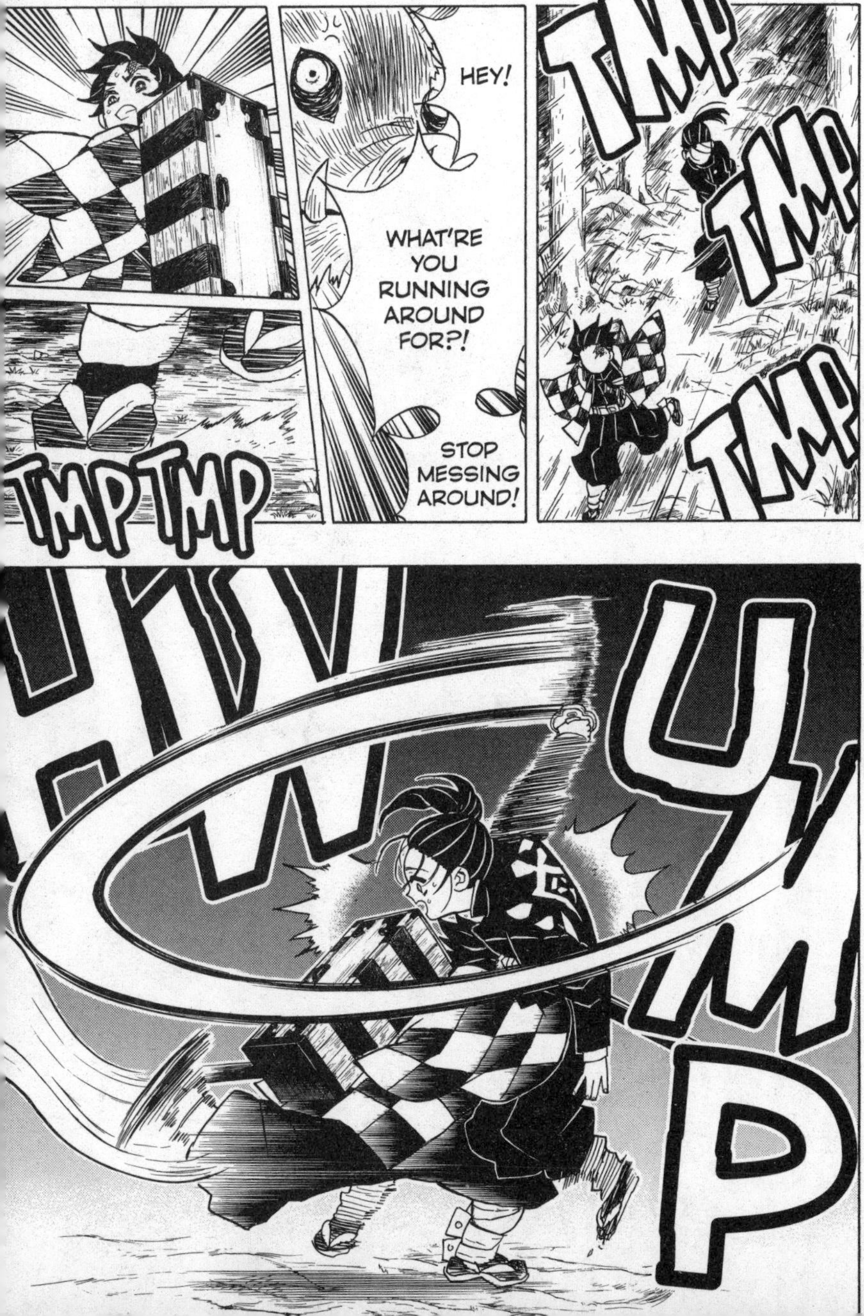
TMP
TMP
TMP
HEY!
WHAT'RE YOU RUNNING AROUND FOR?!
STOP MESSING AROUND!
TMP TMP

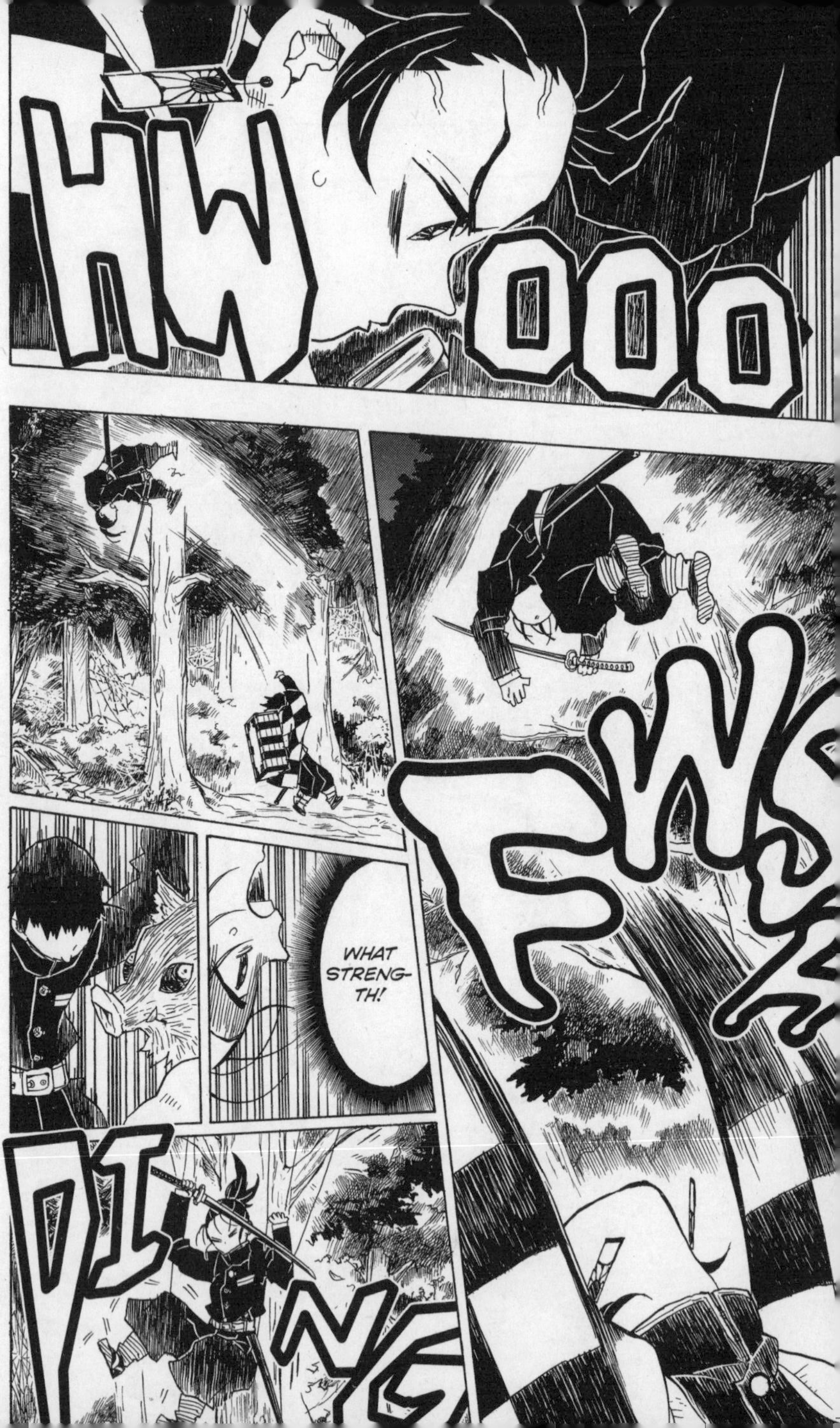
HWOOO
WHAT STRENG-TH!

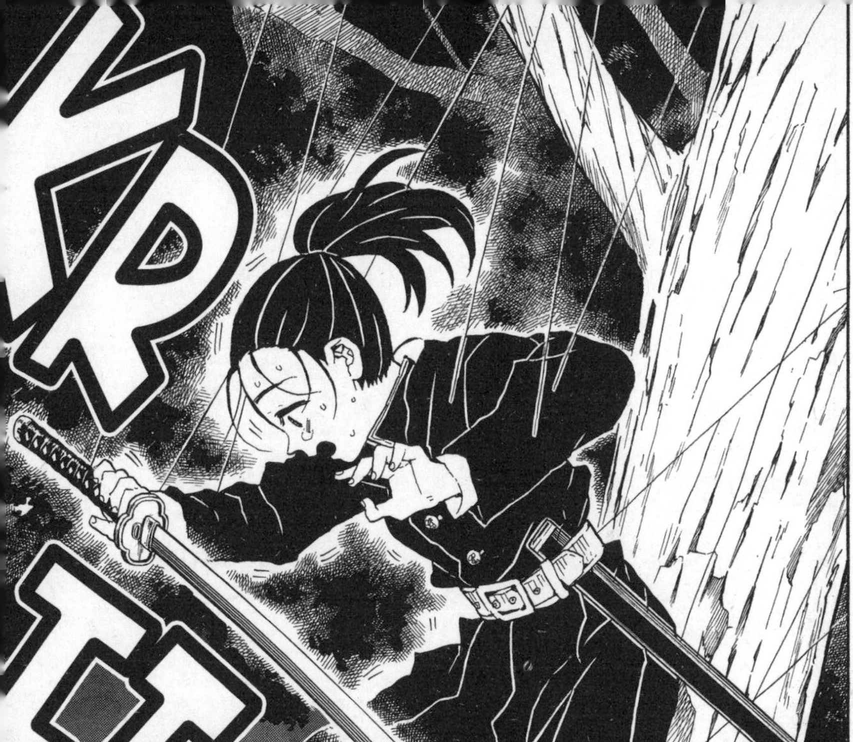

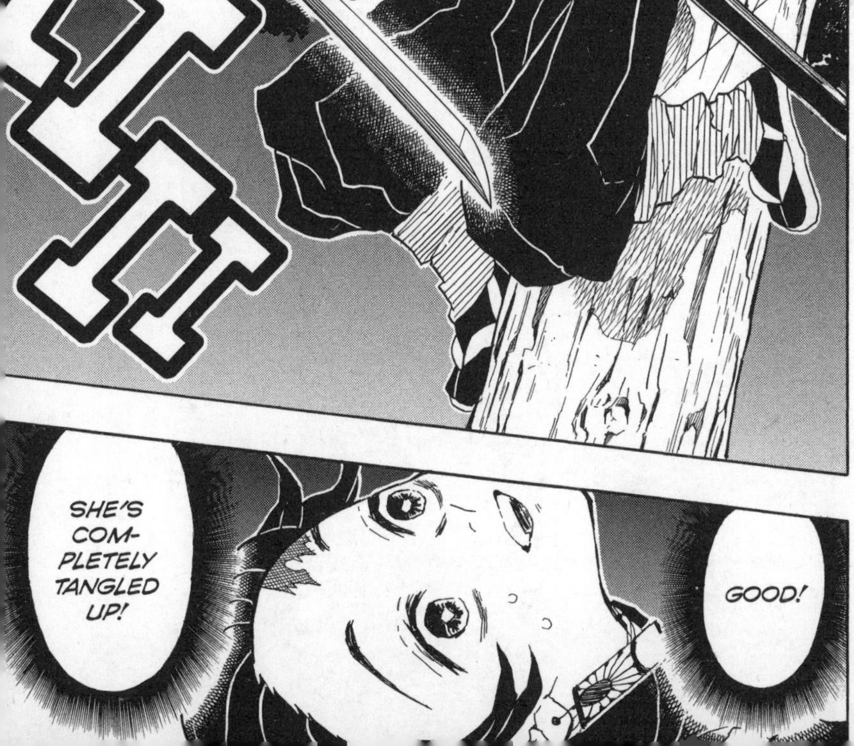
SHE'S COM-PLETELY TANGLED UP!
GOOD!

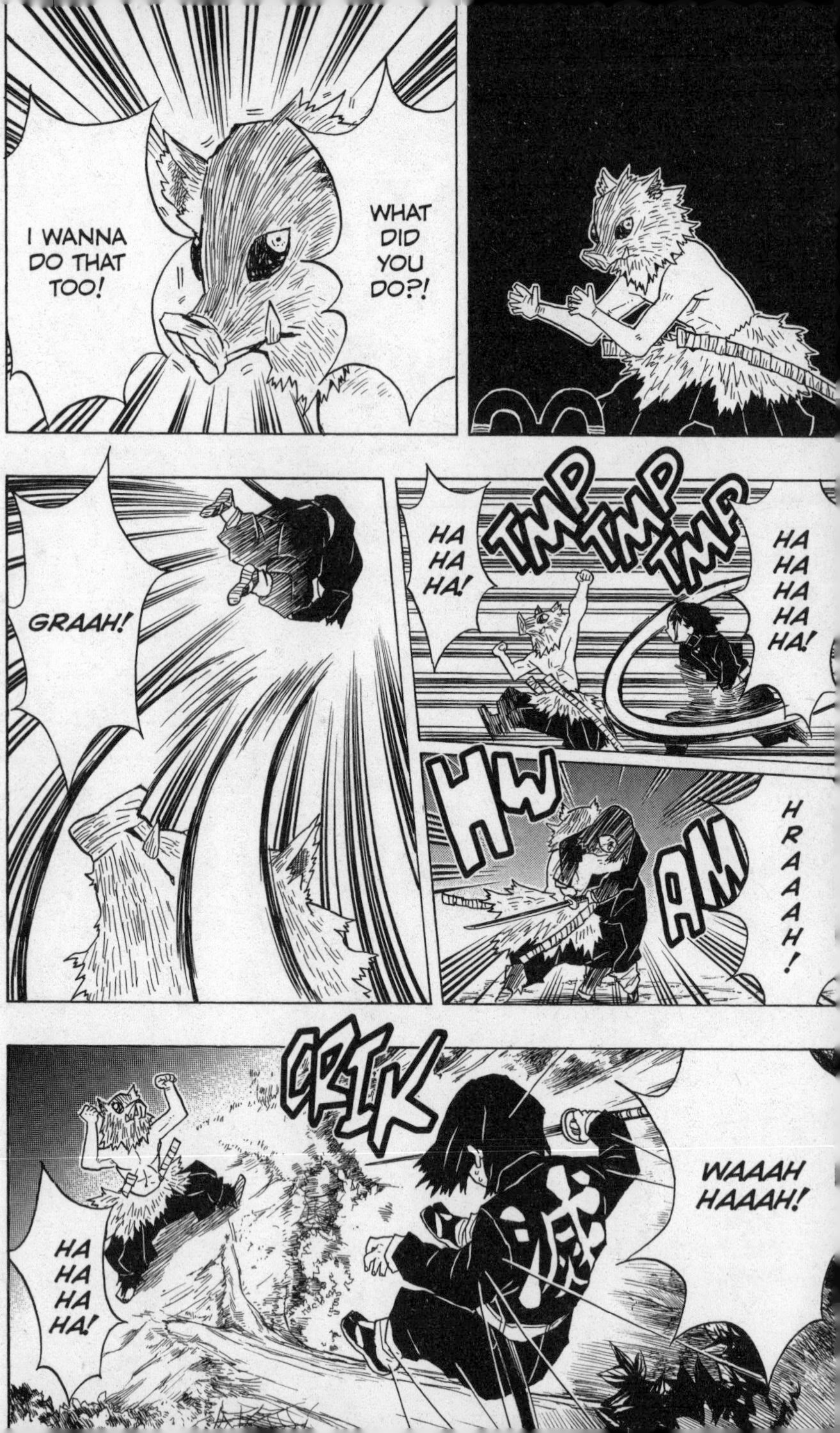
WHAT DID YOU DO?!
I WANNA DO THAT TOO!
HA HA HA HA HA!
TMP TMP TMP
HA HA HA!
HRAAAAH!
HWAM
GRAAH!
WAAAH HAAAH!
CRIK
HA HA HA HA!

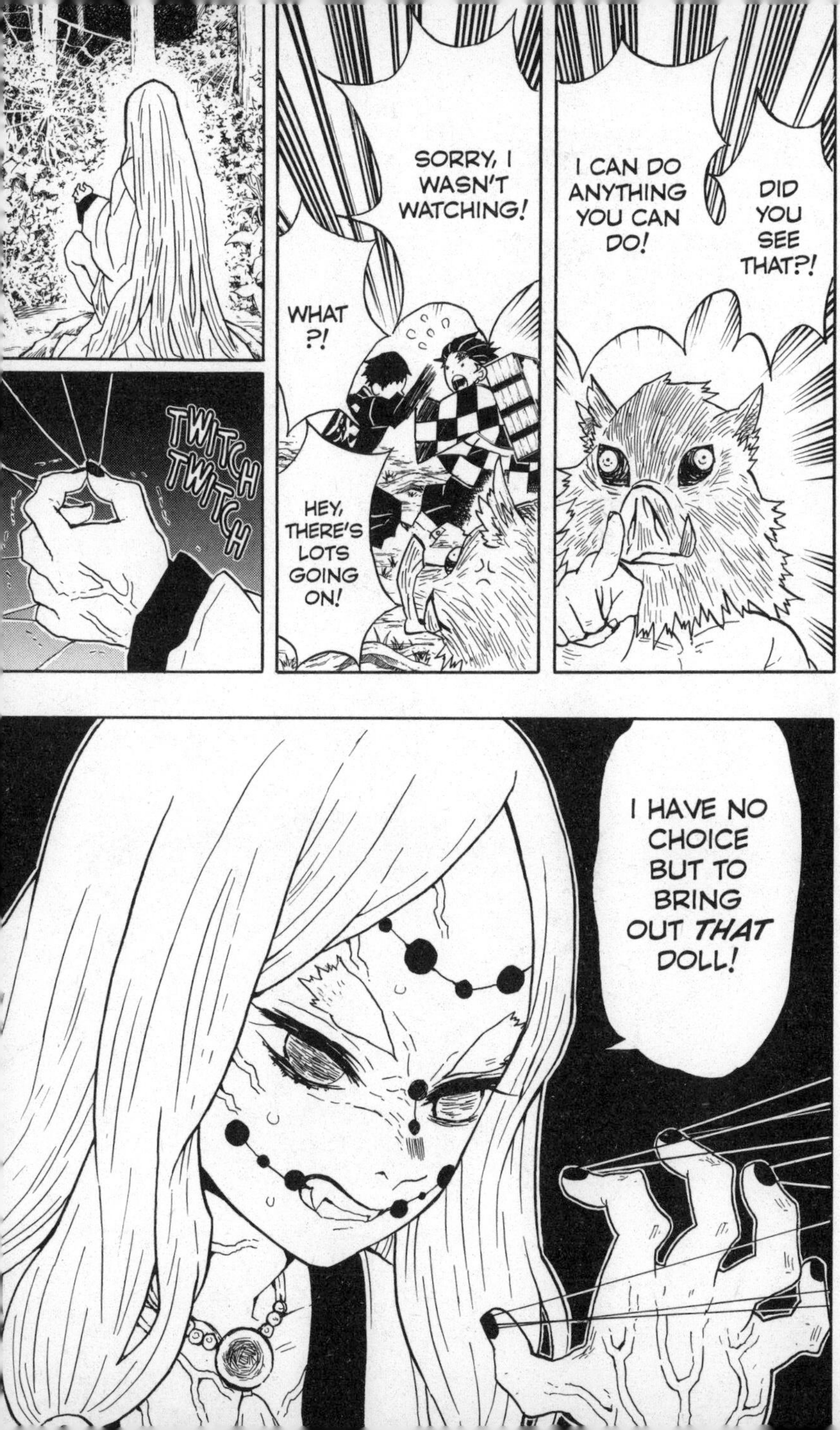
DID YOU SEE THAT?!
I CAN DO ANYTHING YOU CAN DO!
SORRY, I WASN'T WATCHING!
WHAT?!
HEY, THERE'S LOTS GOING ON!
TWITCH TWITCH
I HAVE NO CHOICE BUT TO BRING OUT *THAT* DOLL!

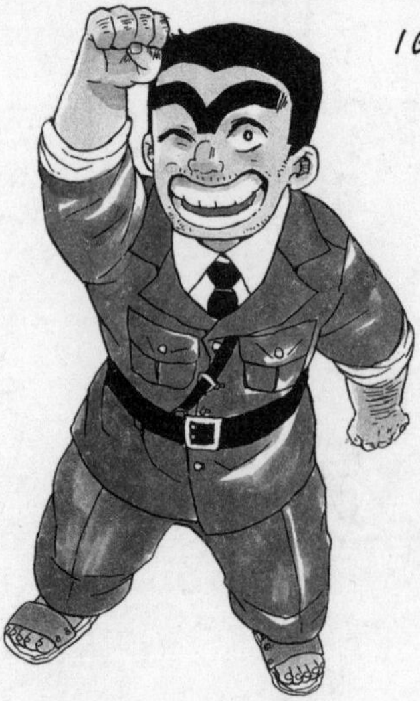

2016, ISSUE NO. 42 OF JUMP.
I GOT TO DRAW RYO FOR THE ISSUE WITH
THE FINAL CHAPTER OF KOCHIKAME.

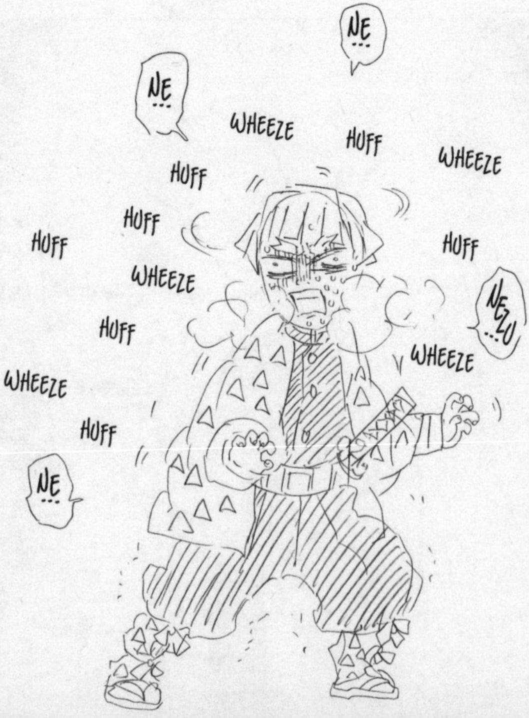

NE...
NE...
WHEEZE
HUFF
WHEEZE
HUFF
HUFF
HUFF
HUFF
WHEEZE
NEZU...
WHEEZE
HUFF
WHEEZE
HUFF
NE...

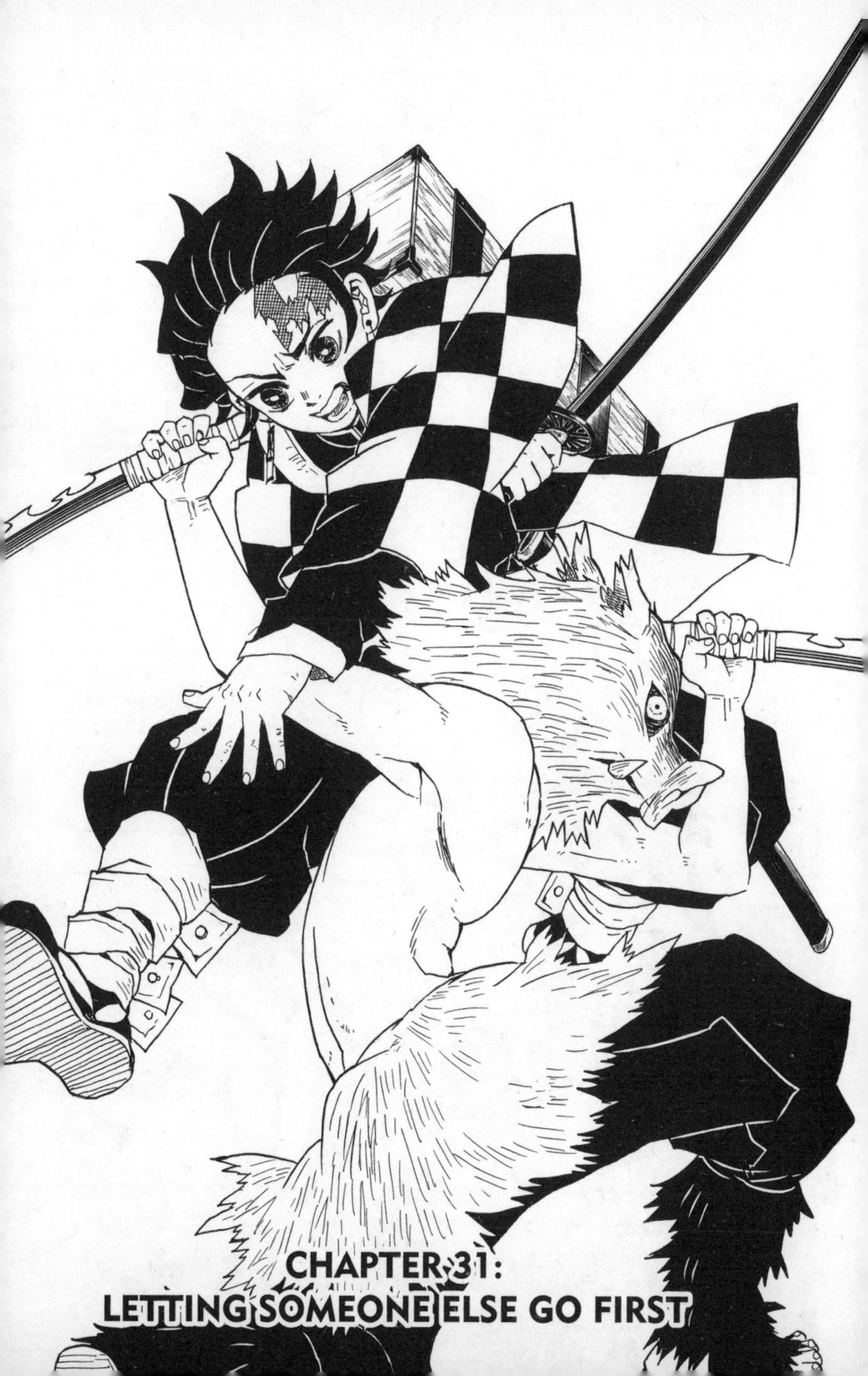
CHAPTER 31:
LETTING SOMEONE ELSE GO FIRST

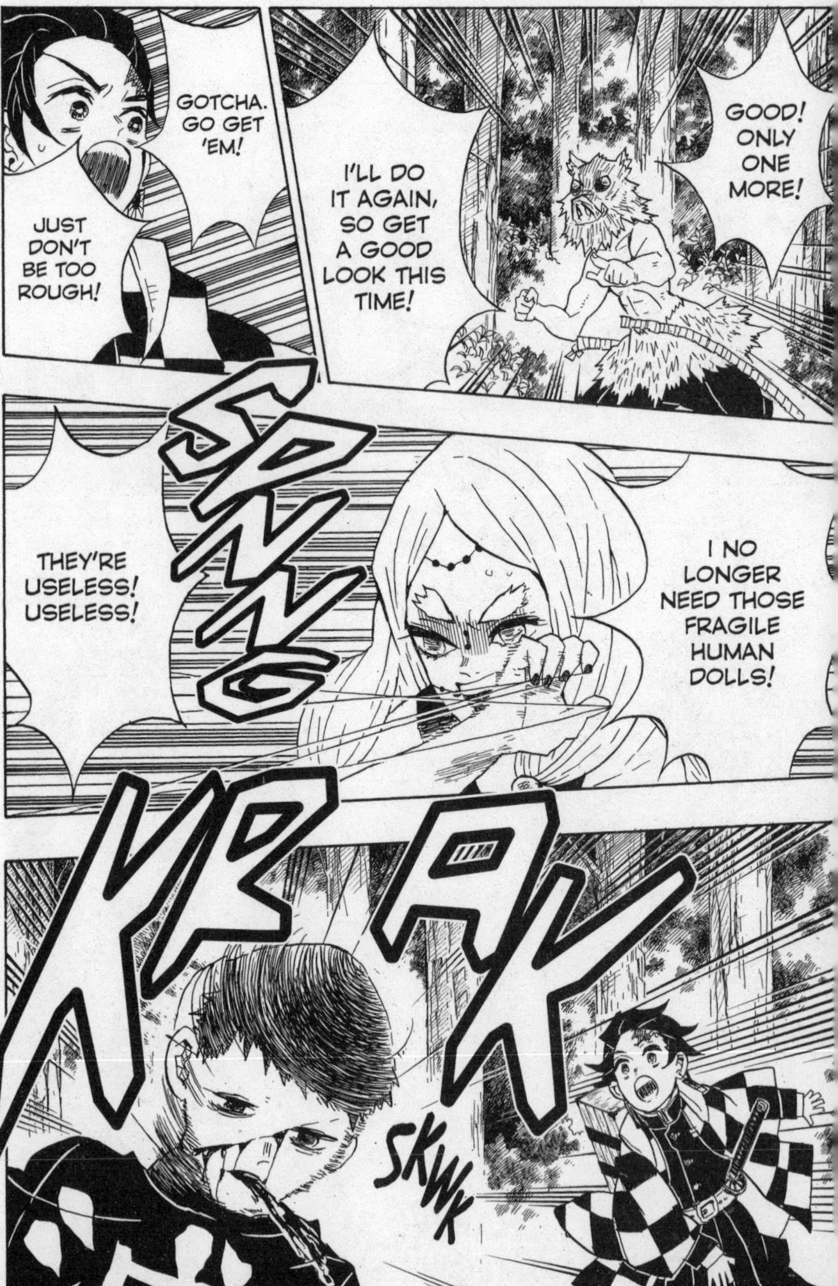
GOOD! ONLY ONE MORE!
I'LL DO IT AGAIN, SO GET A GOOD LOOK THIS TIME!
GOTCHA. GO GET 'EM!
JUST DON'T BE TOO ROUGH!
SPNNG
I NO LONGER NEED THOSE FRAGILE HUMAN DOLLS!
THEY'RE USELESS! USELESS!
KRAK
SKWK

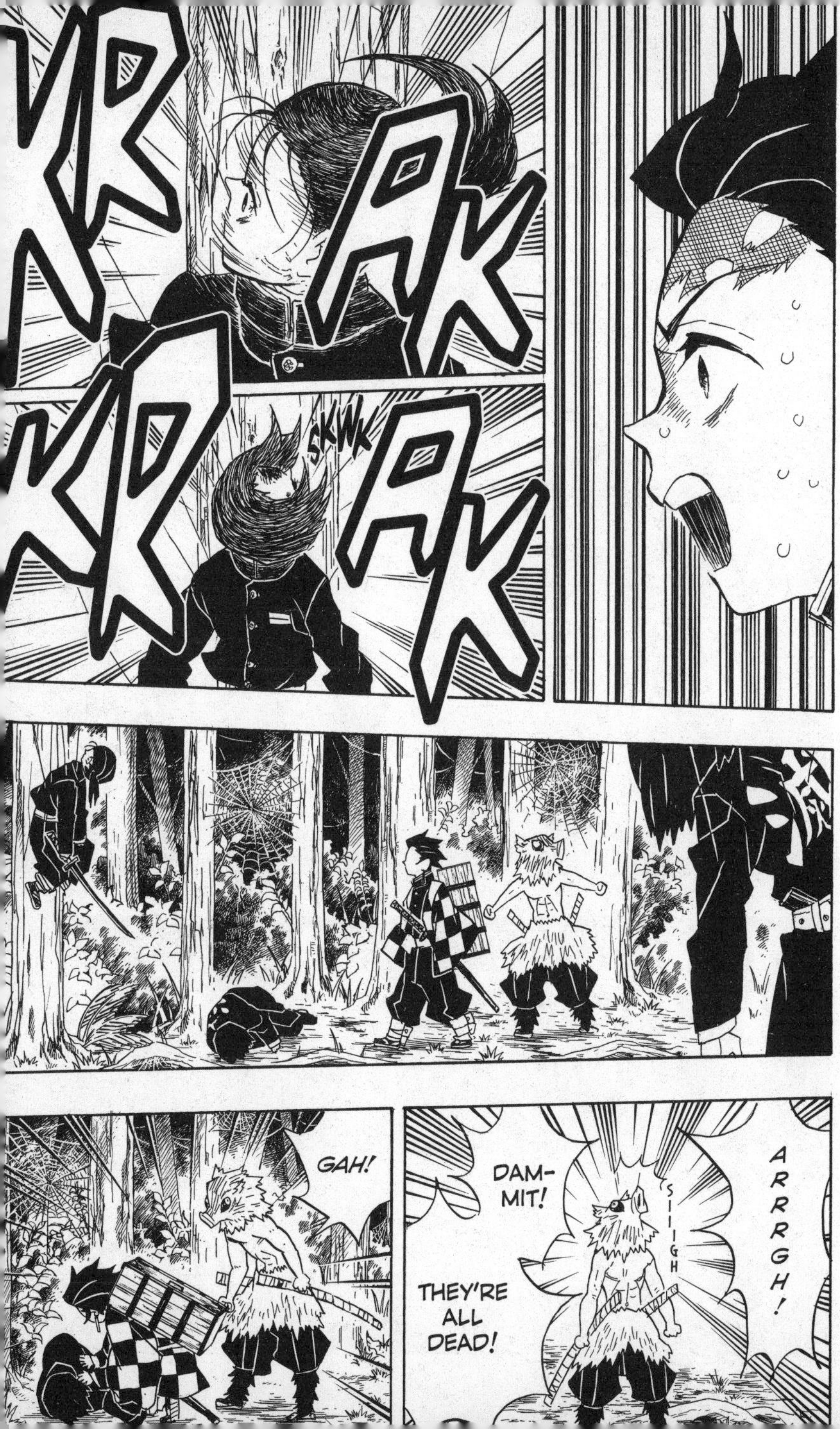
KRAK
KRAK
SKWK
ARRRGH!
DAM-
MIT!
SIIIGH
THEY'RE
ALL
DEAD!
GAH!

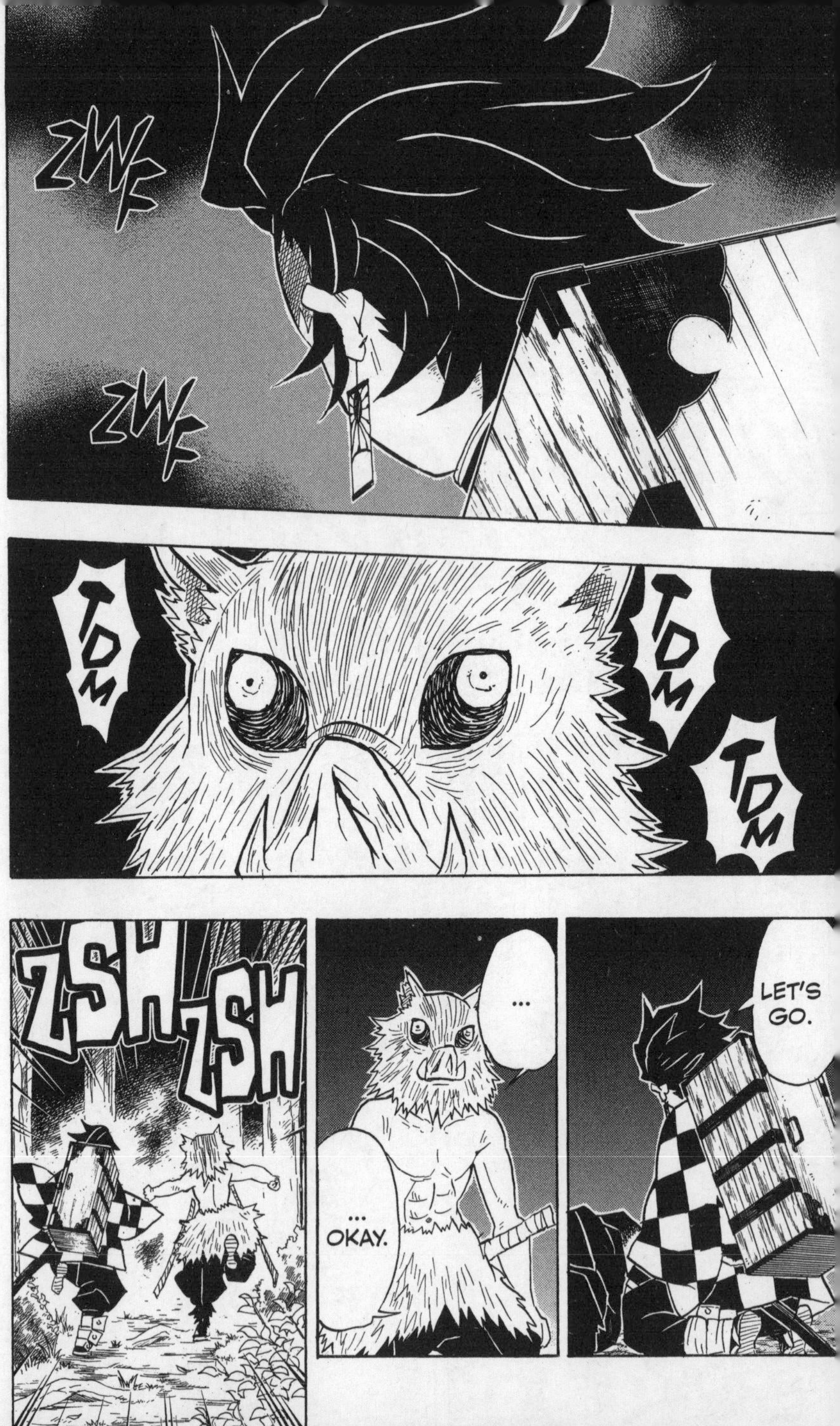

ZWF
ZWF
TOM
TOM
TOM
LET'S GO.
...
... OKAY.
ZSH ZSH

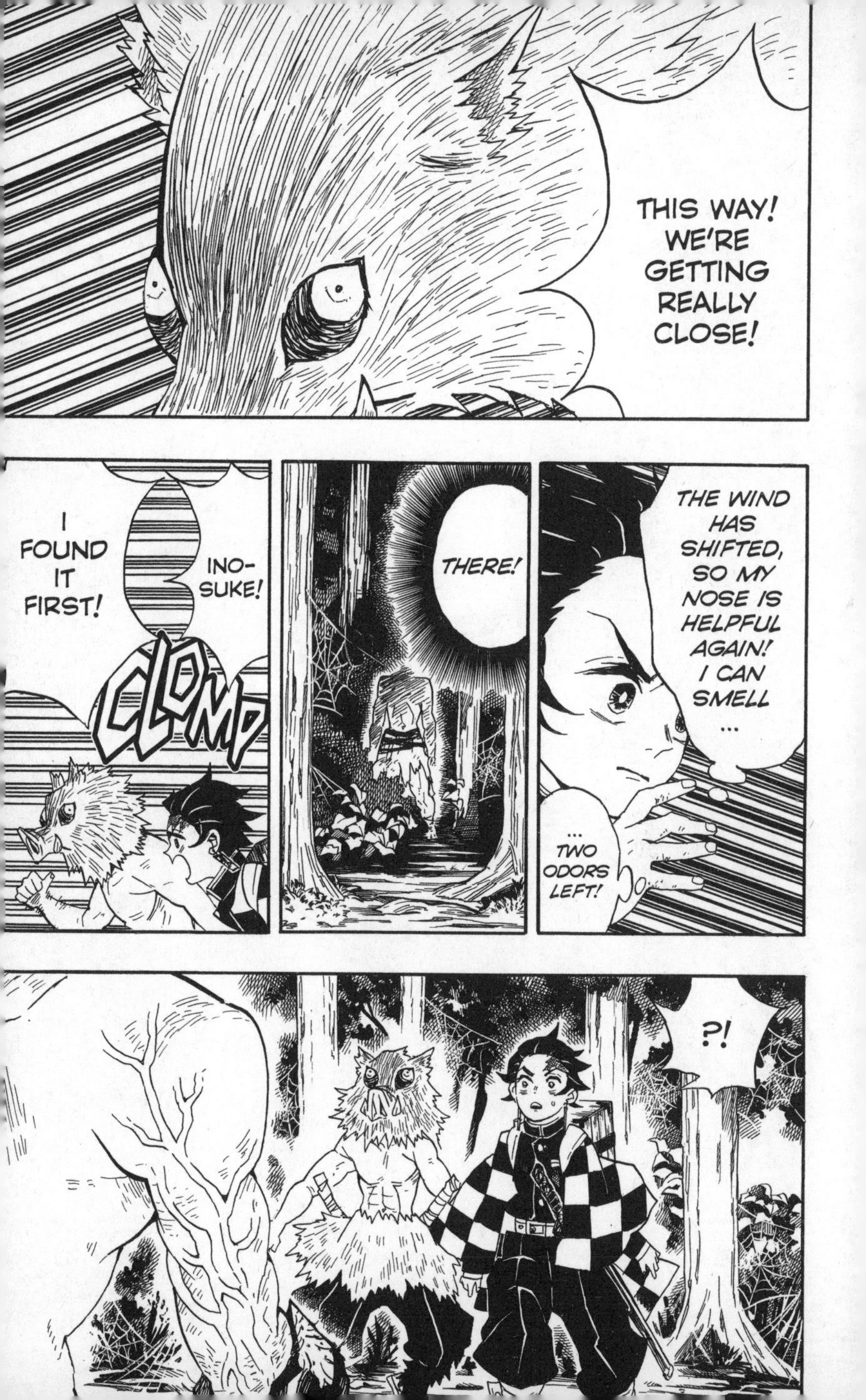
THIS WAY! WE'RE GETTING REALLY CLOSE!
THE WIND HAS SHIFTED, SO MY NOSE IS HELPFUL AGAIN! I CAN SMELL ...
... TWO ODORS LEFT!
THERE!
INO-SUKE!
I FOUND IT FIRST!
CLOMP
?!

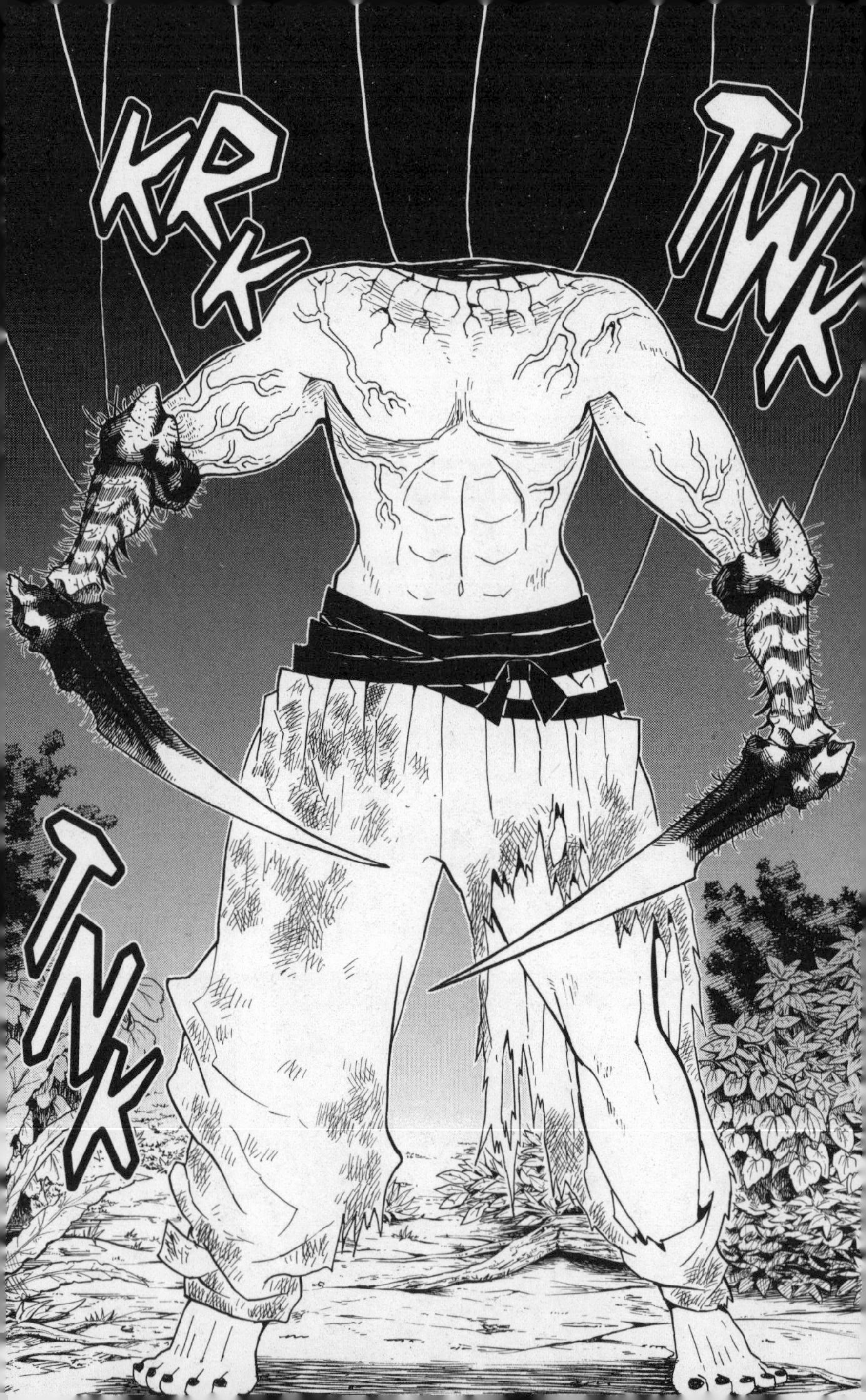
TWNK
KRK
TINK

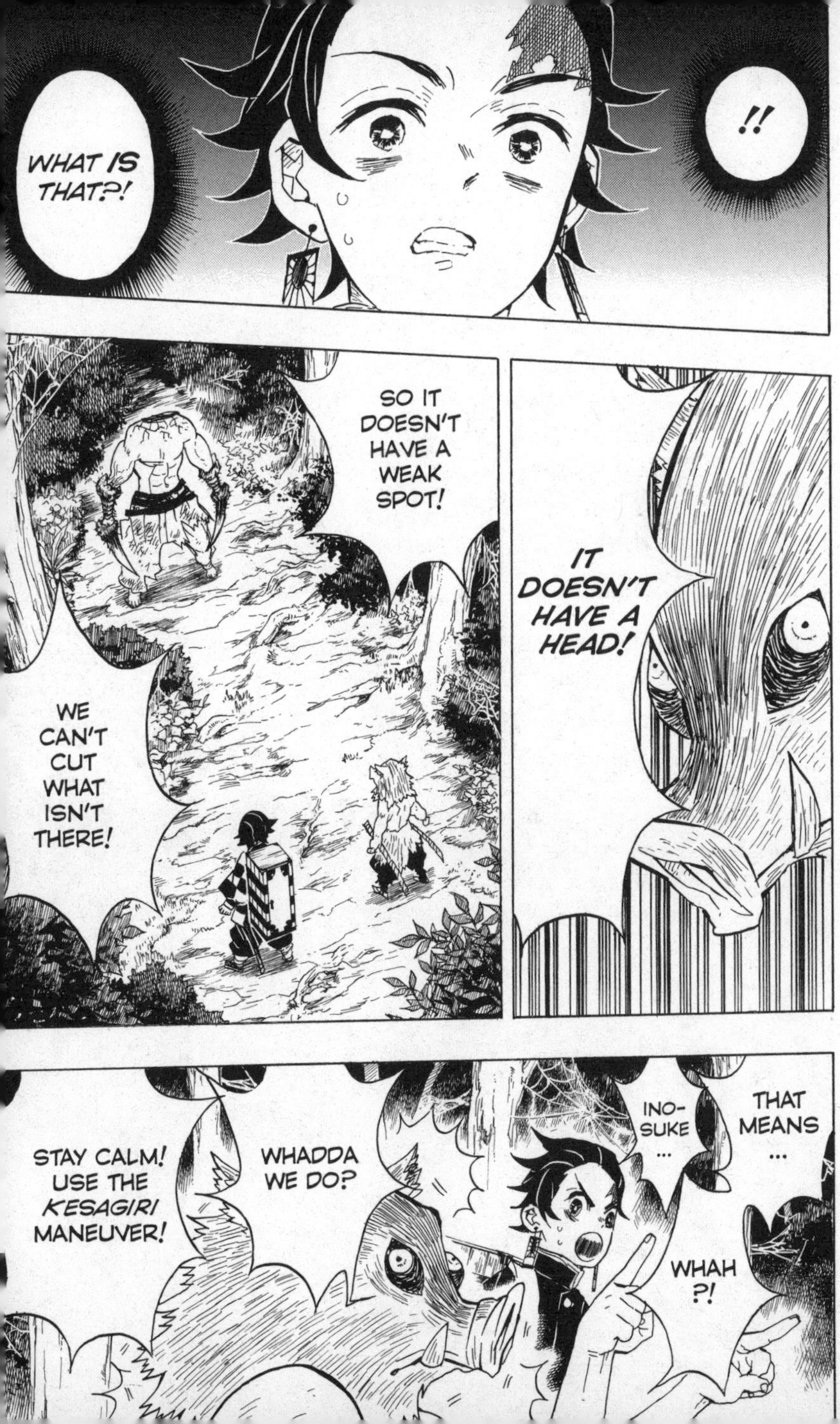
!!
WHAT *IS* THAT?!
IT DOESN'T HAVE A HEAD!
SO IT DOESN'T HAVE A WEAK SPOT!
WE CAN'T CUT WHAT ISN'T THERE!
THAT MEANS ...
INO-SUKE ...
WHAH ?!
WHADDA WE DO?
STAY CALM! USE THE *KESAGIRI* MANEUVER!

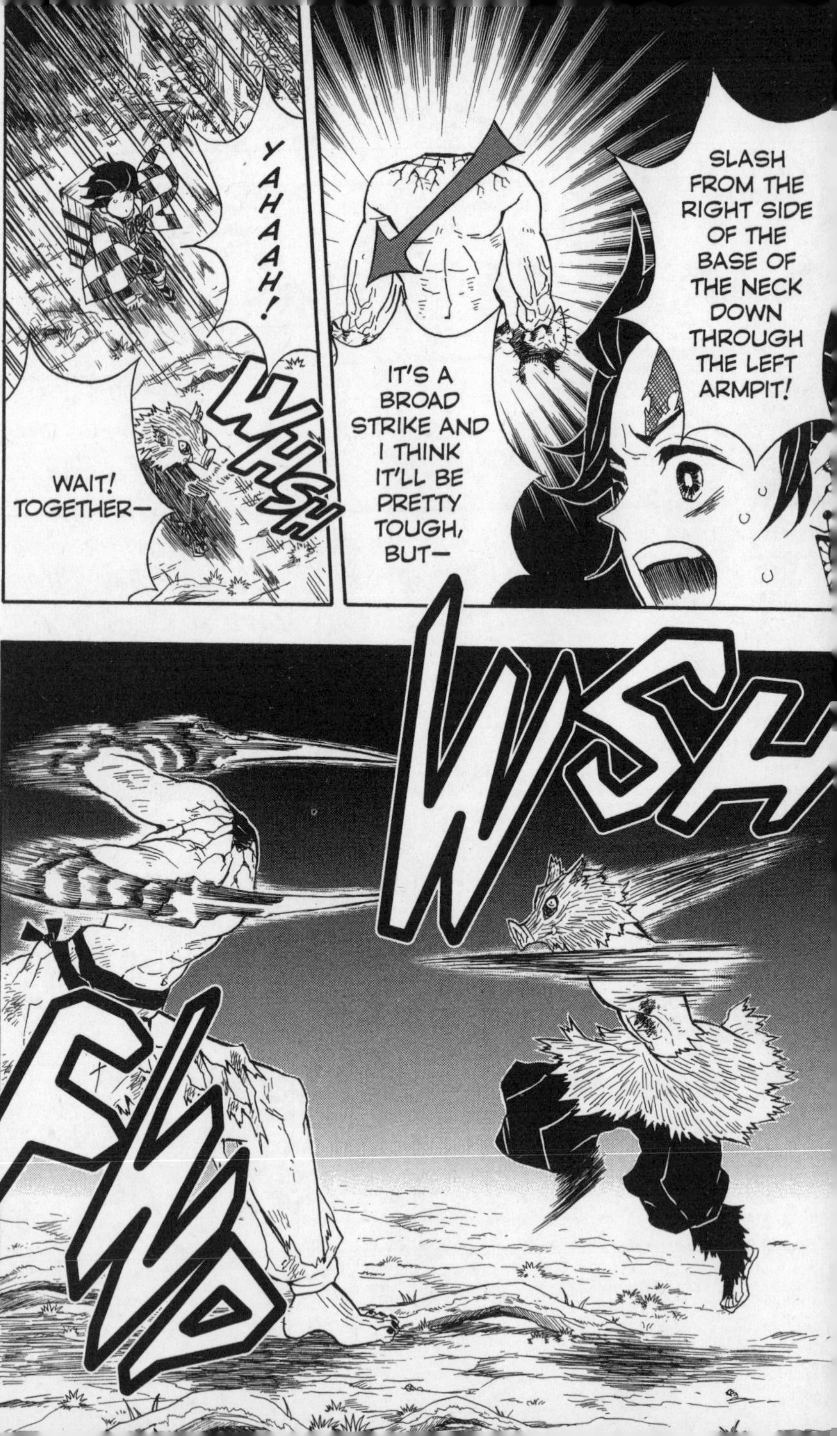
SLASH FROM THE RIGHT SIDE OF THE BASE OF THE NECK DOWN THROUGH THE LEFT ARMPIT!
IT'S A BROAD STRIKE AND I THINK IT'LL BE PRETTY TOUGH, BUT—
YAHAAAAH!
WHSH
WAIT! TOGETHER—
WSH

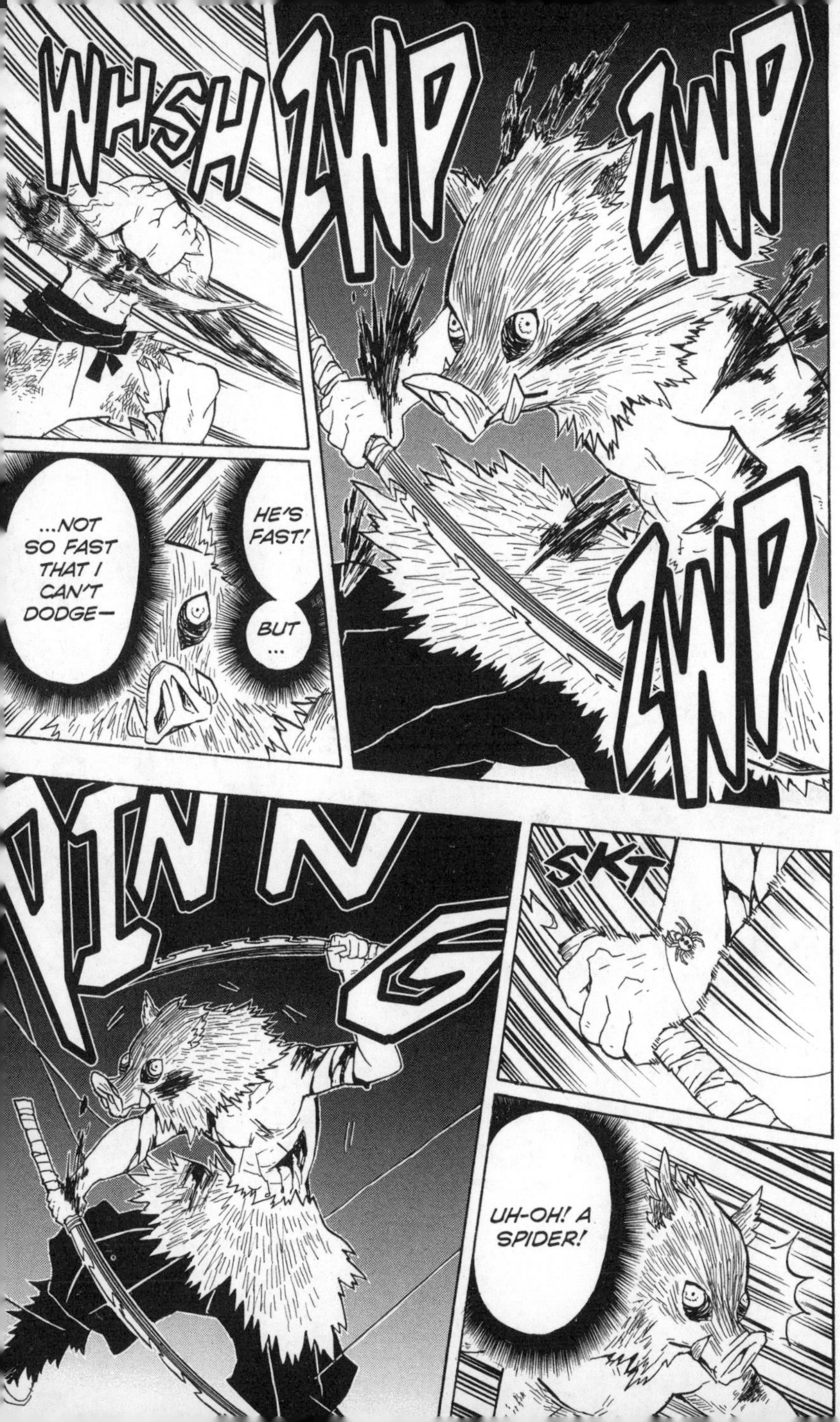
ZWP
ZWP
ZWP
WHSH
HE'S FAST!
BUT ...
...NOT SO FAST THAT I CAN'T DODGE—
SKT
UH-OH! A SPIDER!
INNG

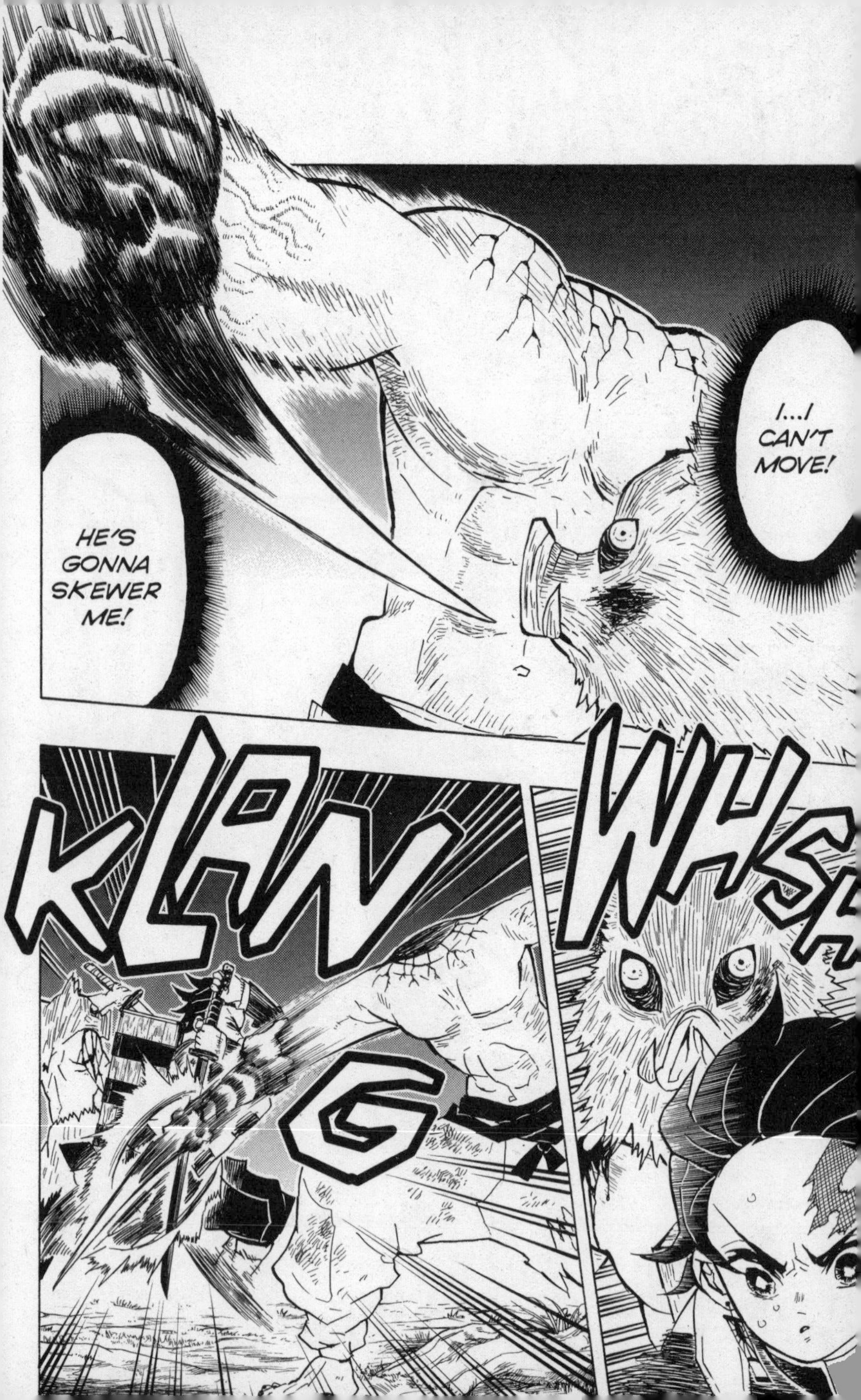
I...I CAN'T MOVE!
HE'S GONNA SKEWER ME!
WHS
KLAN
G

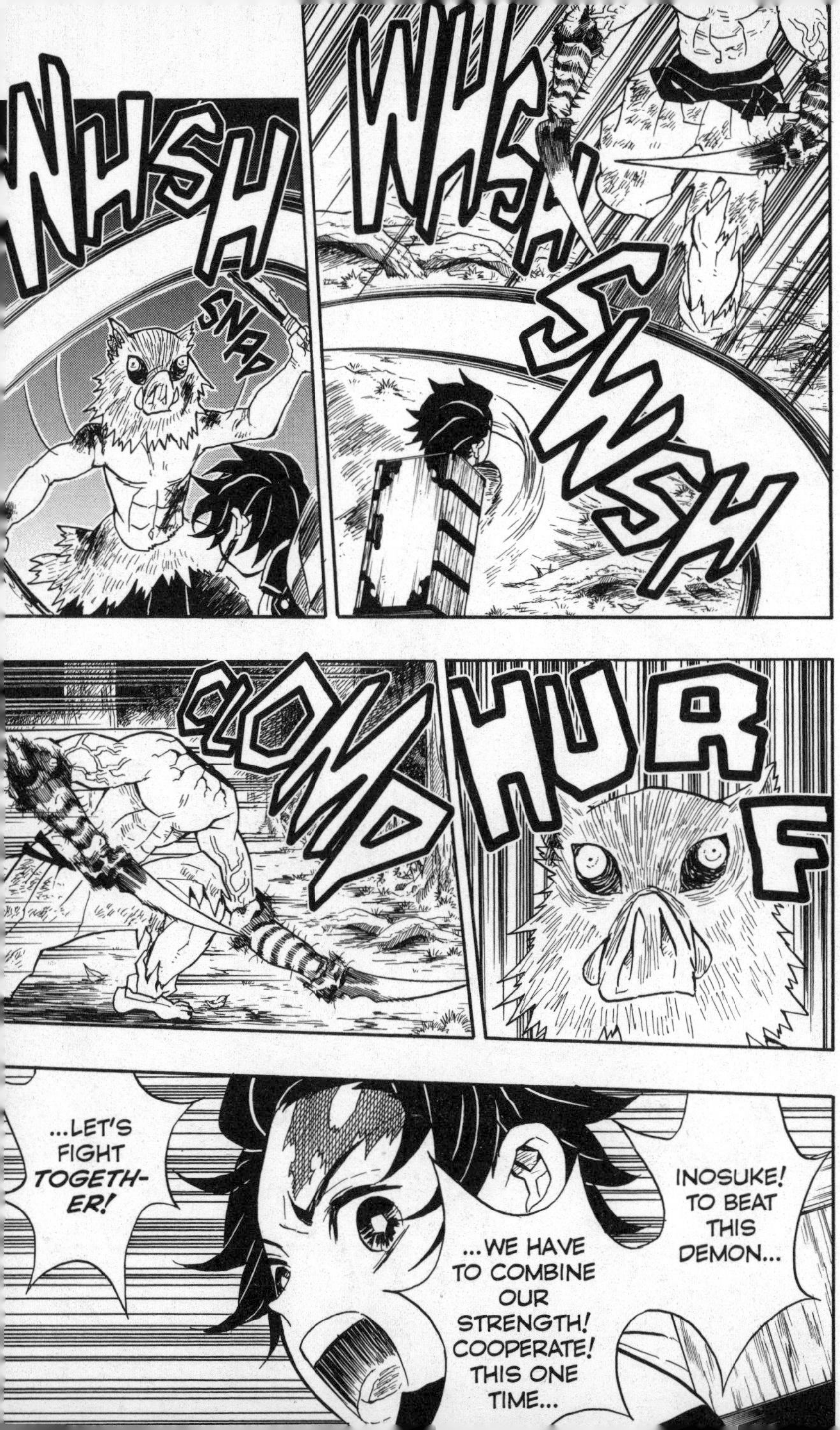
WHSH
SWSH
WHSH
SNAP
HURF
CLOMP
INOSUKE! TO BEAT THIS DEMON...
...WE HAVE TO COMBINE OUR STRENGTH! COOPERATE! THIS ONE TIME...
...LET'S FIGHT *TOGETHER!*

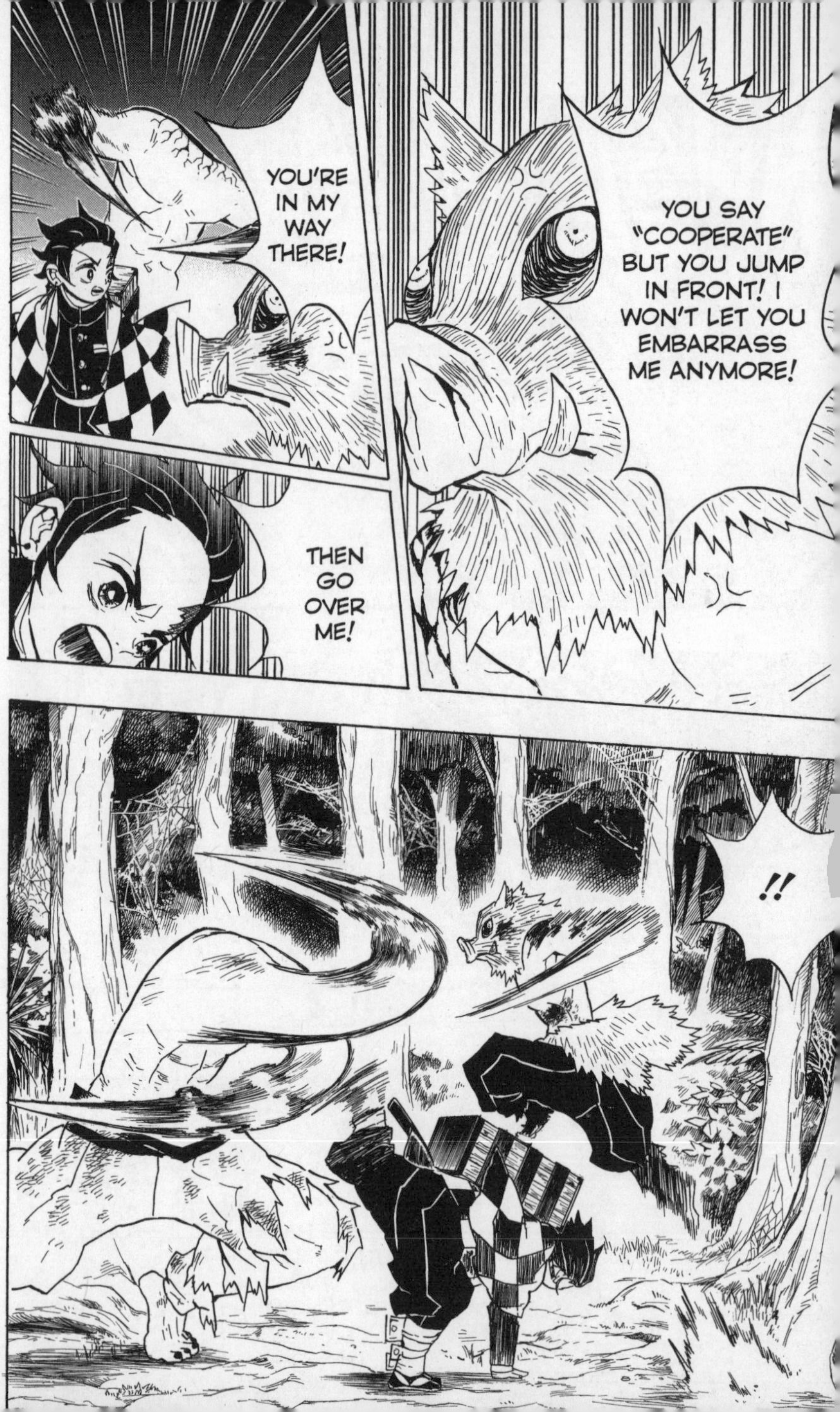
YOU SAY "COOPERATE" BUT YOU JUMP IN FRONT! I WON'T LET YOU EMBARRASS ME ANYMORE!
YOU'RE IN MY WAY THERE!
THEN GO OVER ME!
!!

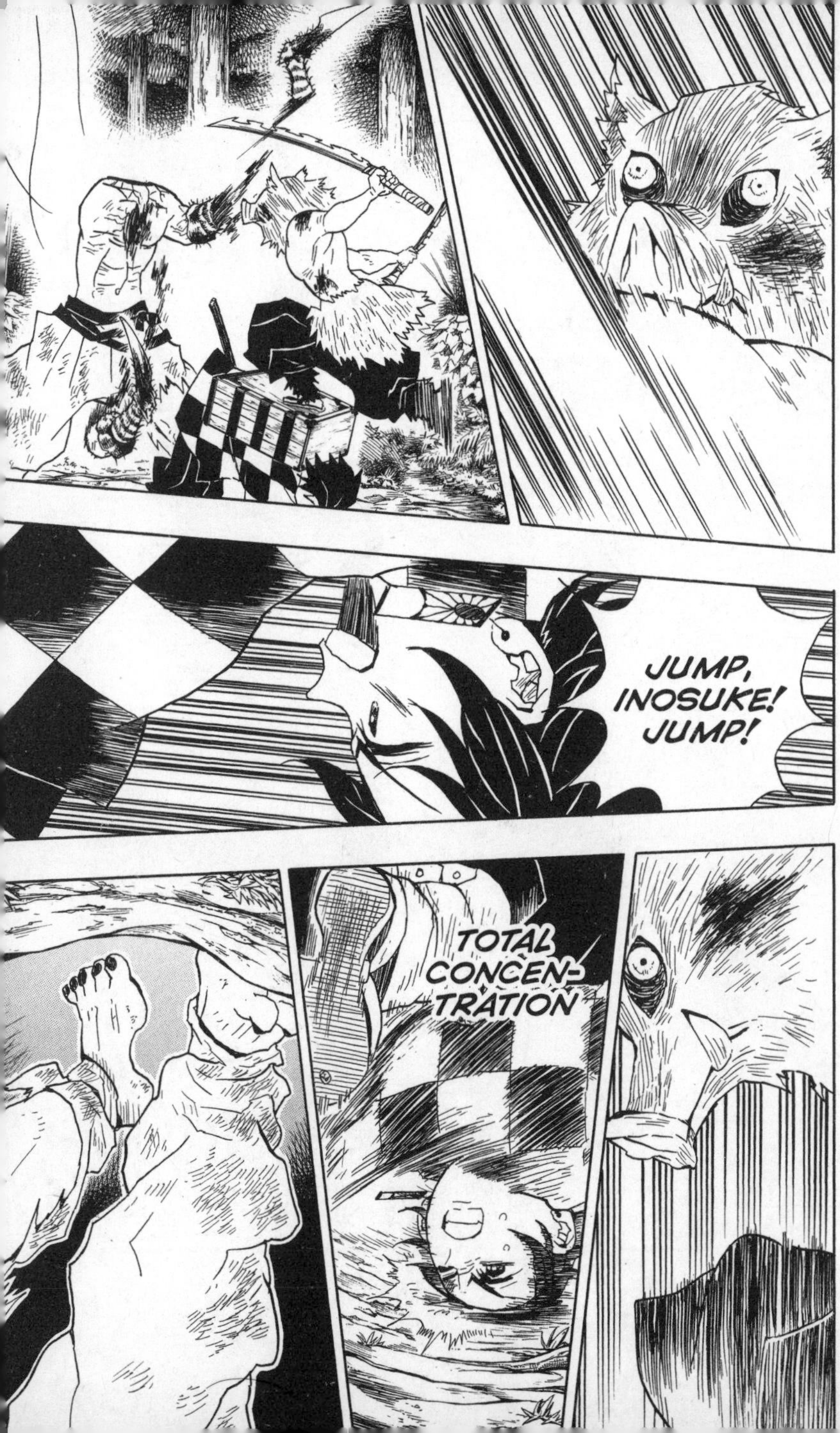
JUMP, INOSUKE! JUMP!
TOTAL CONCEN-TRATION

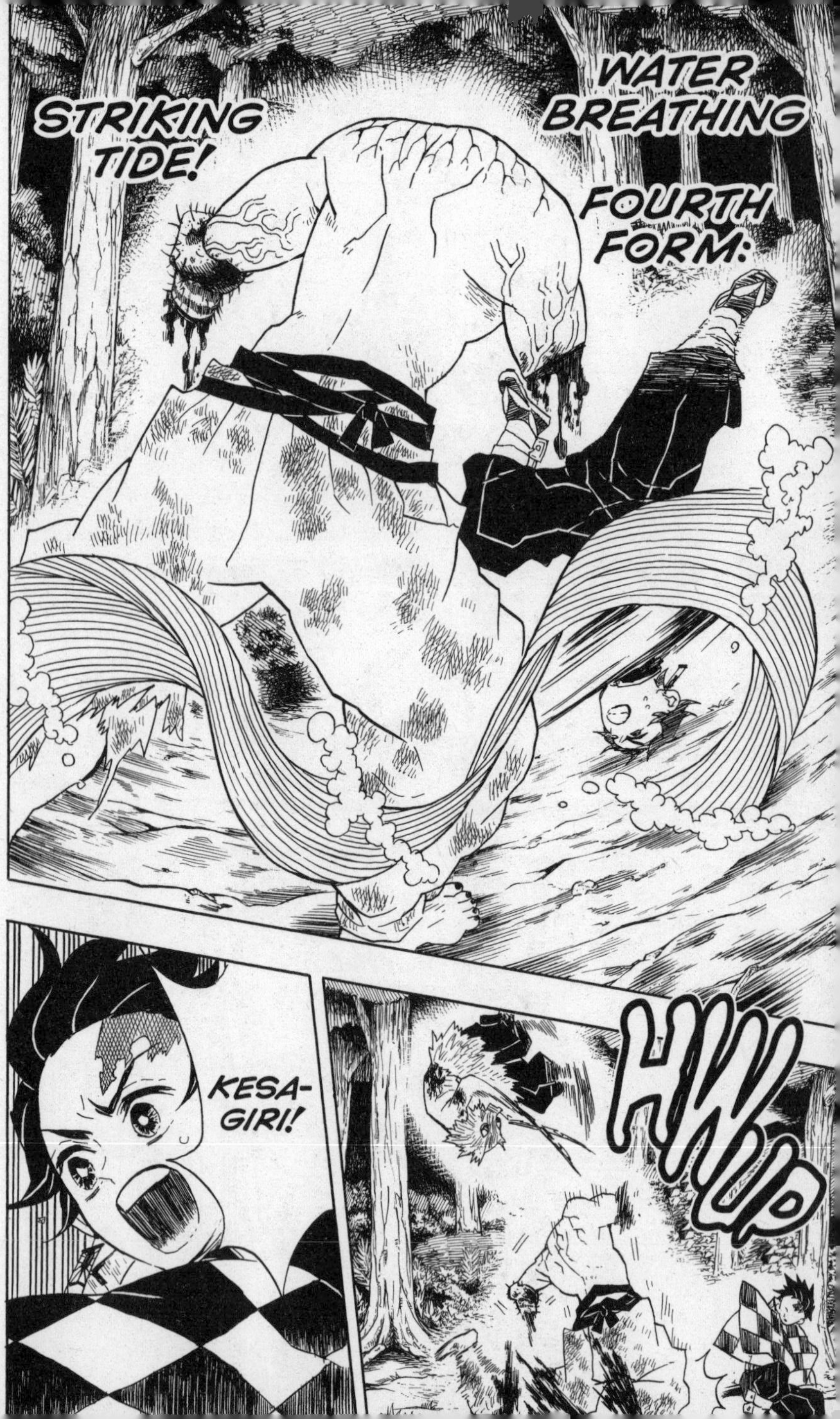
WATER BREATHING
FOURTH FORM:
STRIKING TIDE!
HWIP
KESA-GIRI!

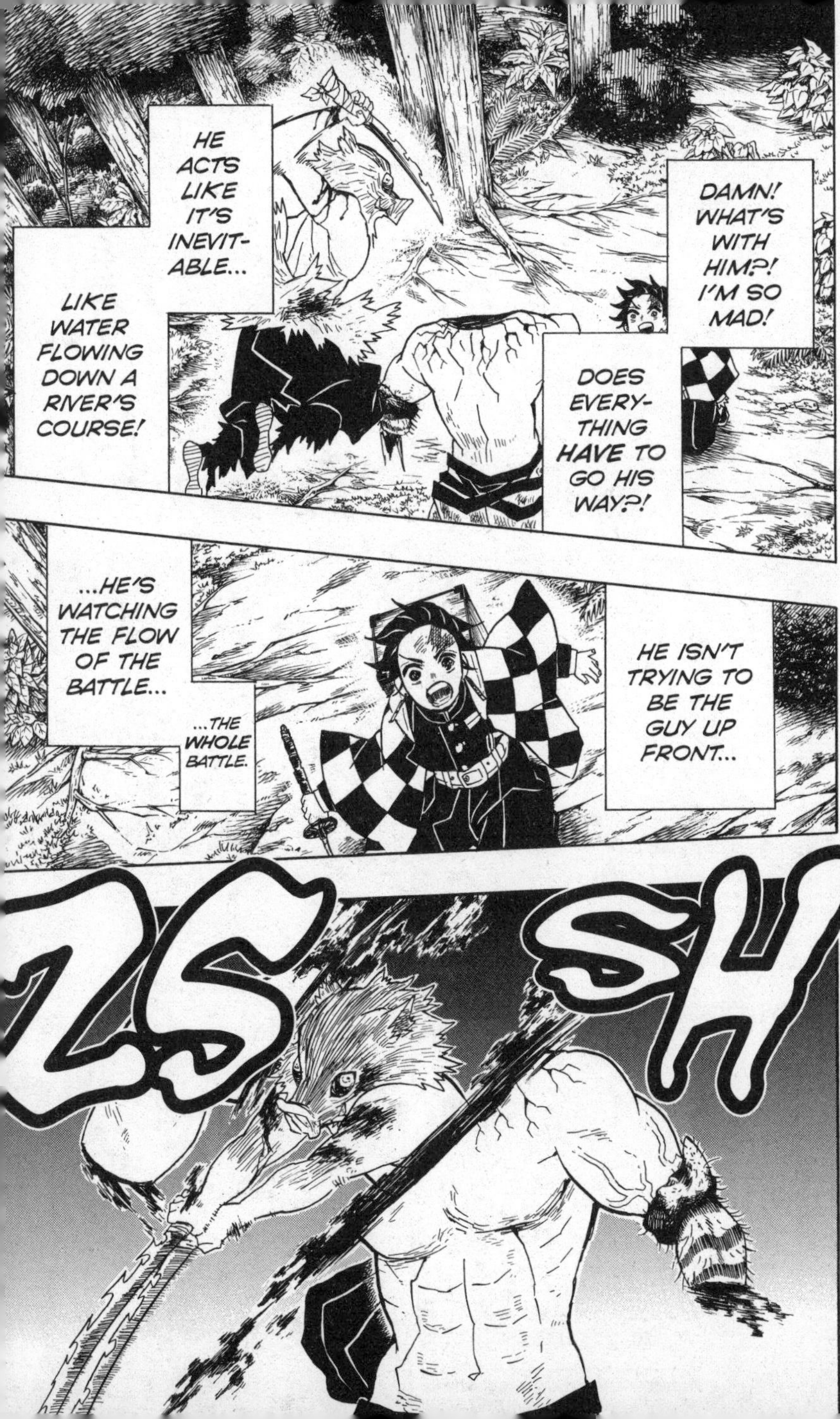
DAMN! WHAT'S WITH HIM?! I'M SO MAD!
DOES EVERYTHING HAVE TO GO HIS WAY?!
HE ACTS LIKE IT'S INEVITABLE...
LIKE WATER FLOWING DOWN A RIVER'S COURSE!
HE ISN'T TRYING TO BE THE GUY UP FRONT...
...HE'S WATCHING THE FLOW OF THE BATTLE...
...THE WHOLE BATTLE.
ZSSH

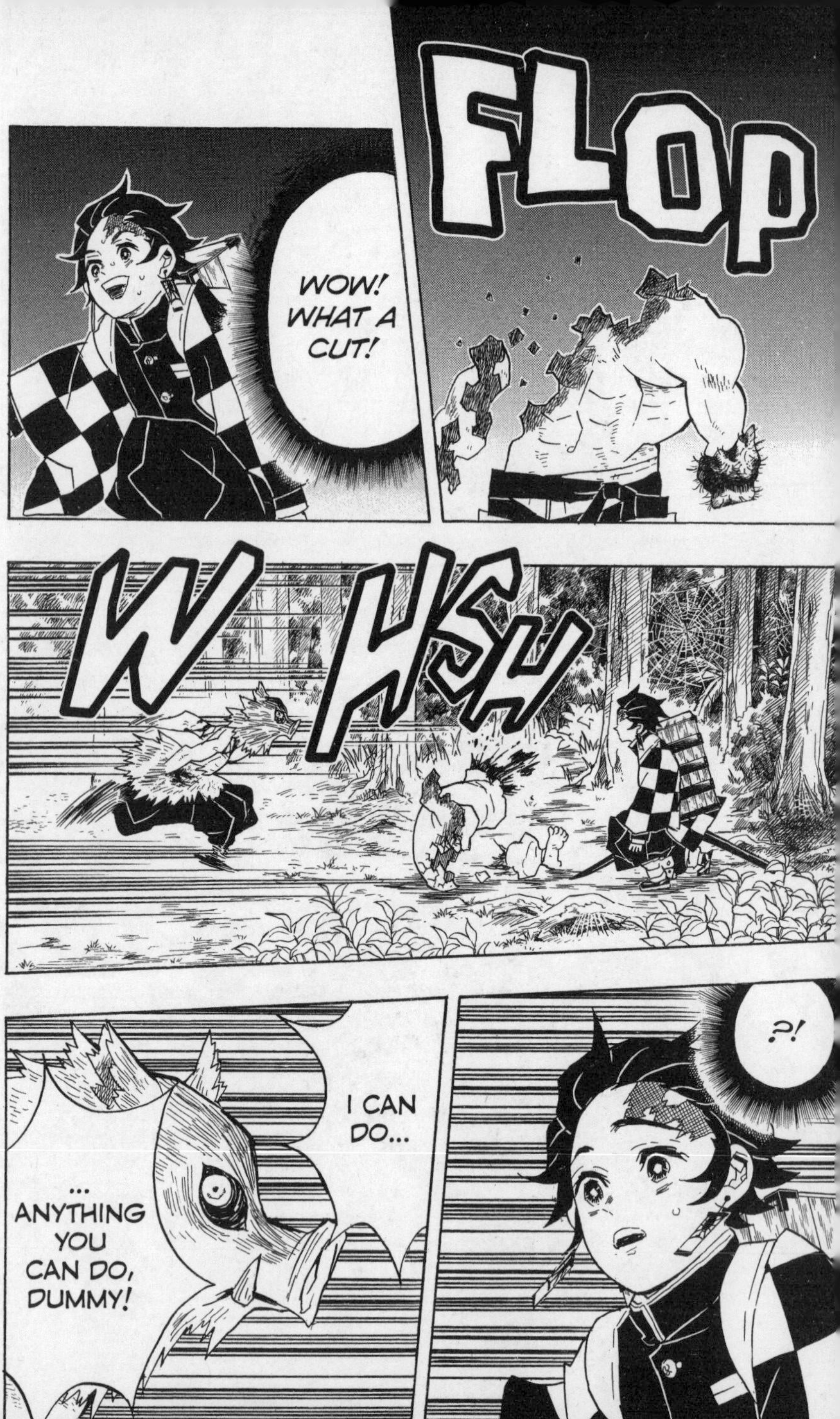
FLOP
WOW! WHAT A CUT!
WHSH
?!
I CAN DO...
... ANYTHING YOU CAN DO, DUMMY!

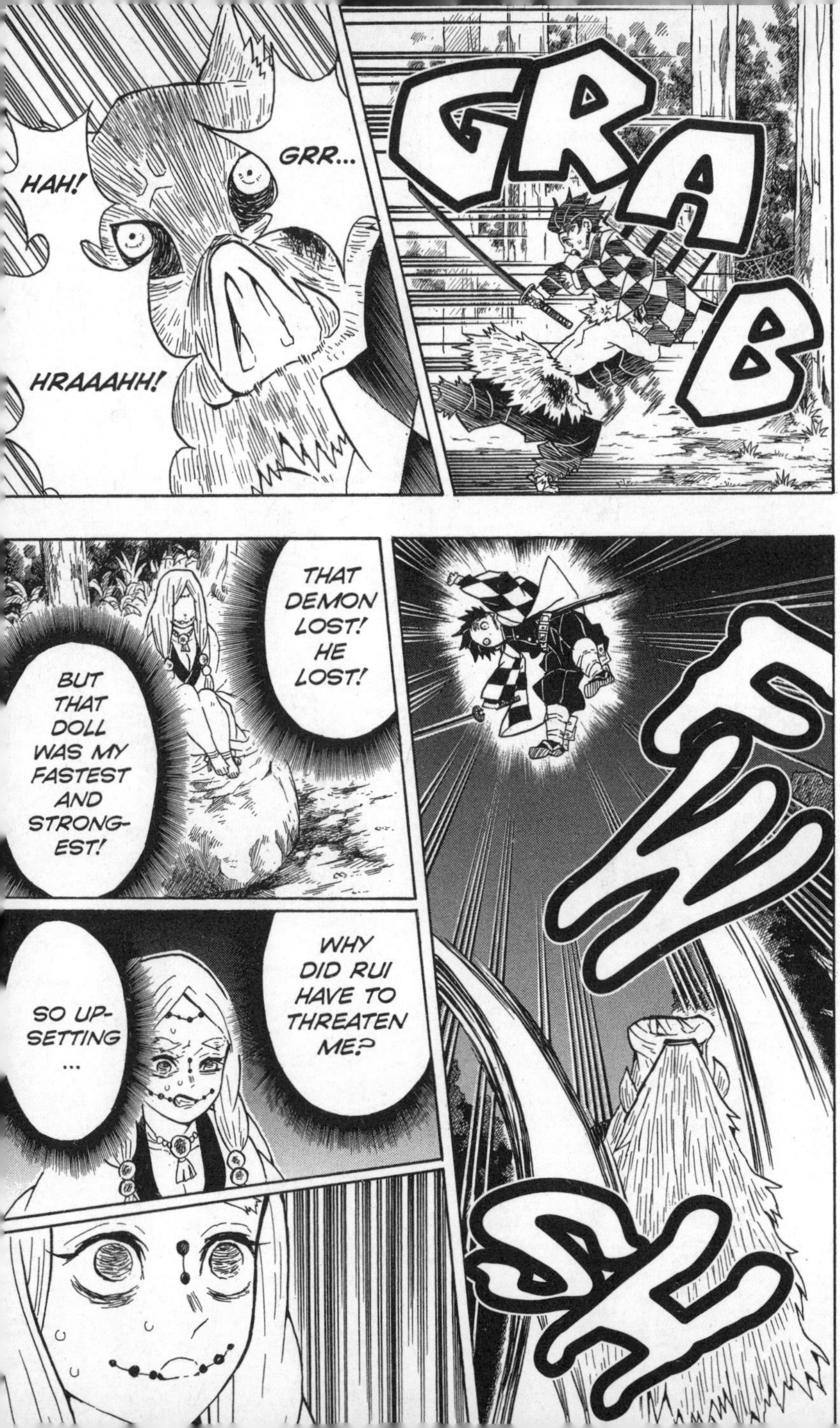
GRAB
GRR...
HAH!
HRAAAHH!
THAT DEMON LOST! HE LOST!
BUT THAT DOLL WAS MY FASTEST AND STRONG-EST!
WHY DID RUI HAVE TO THREATEN ME?
SO UP-SETTING ...

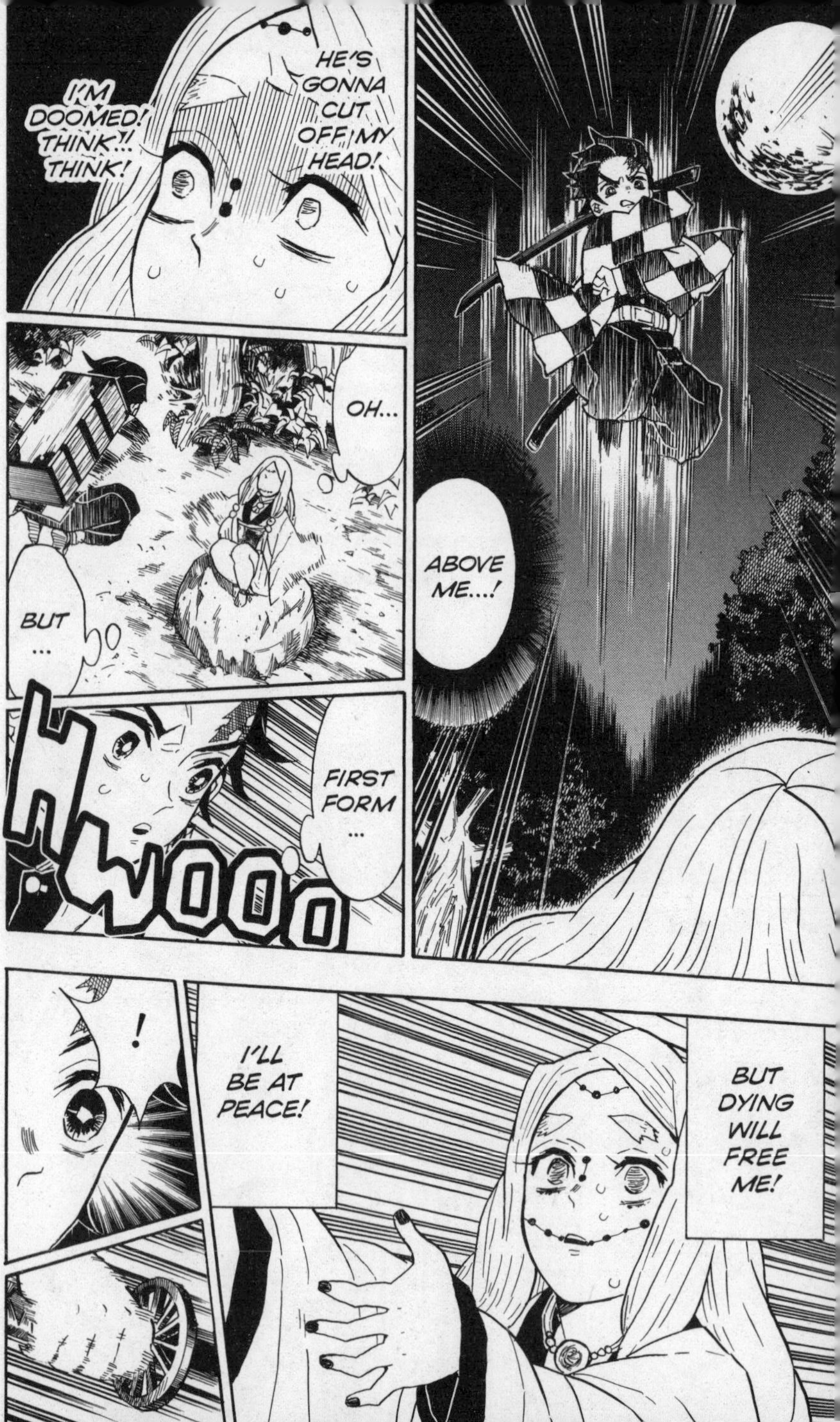
ABOVE ME...!
HE'S GONNA CUT OFF MY HEAD!
I'M DOOMED! THINK!! THINK!
OH...
BUT...
FIRST FORM...
HWOOO
BUT DYING WILL FREE ME!
I'LL BE AT PEACE!
!

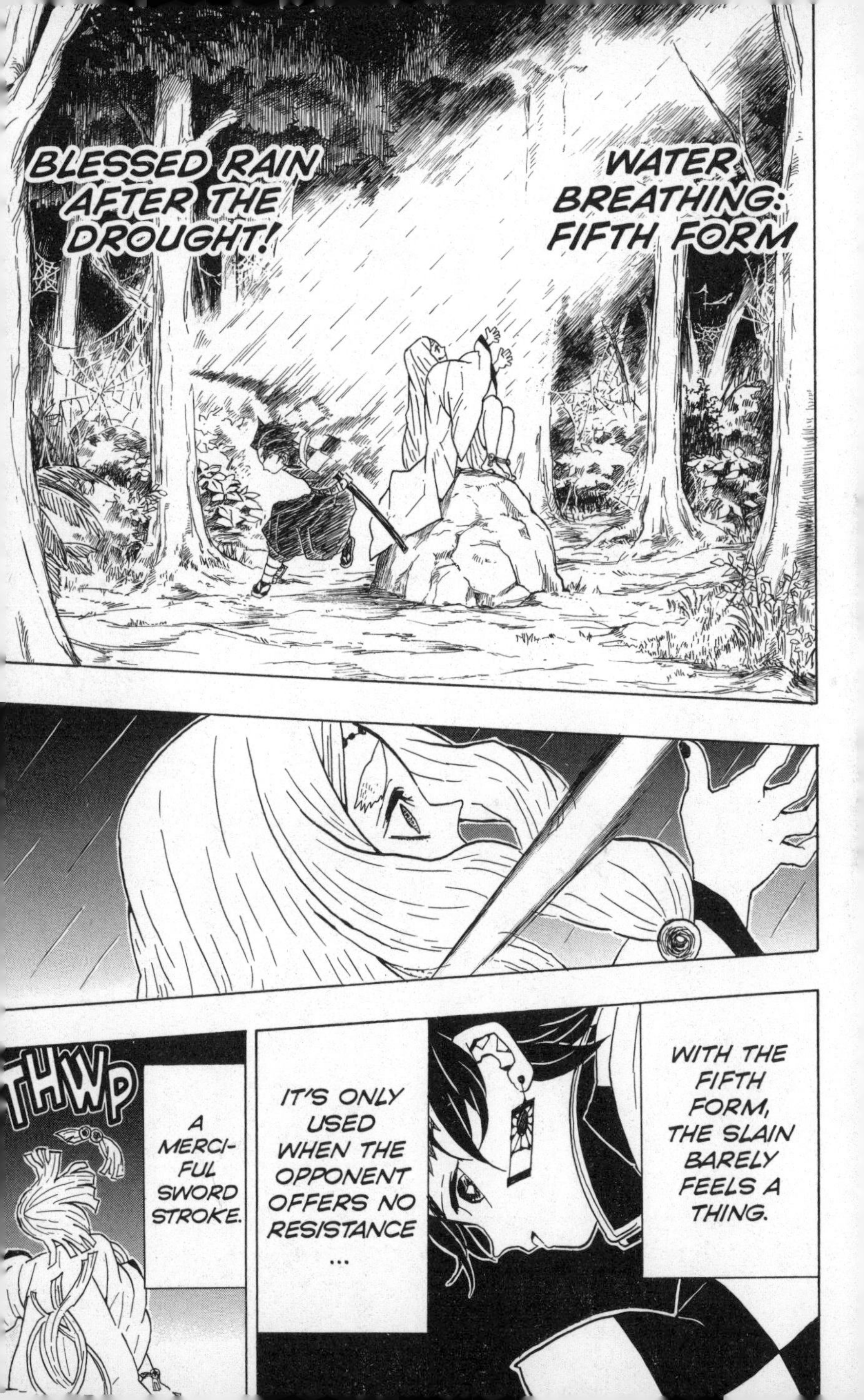
WATER BREATHING: FIFTH FORM
BLESSED RAIN AFTER THE DROUGHT!
WITH THE FIFTH FORM, THE SLAIN BARELY FEELS A THING.
IT'S ONLY USED WHEN THE OPPONENT OFFERS NO RESISTANCE ...
A MERCIFUL SWORD STROKE.
THWP

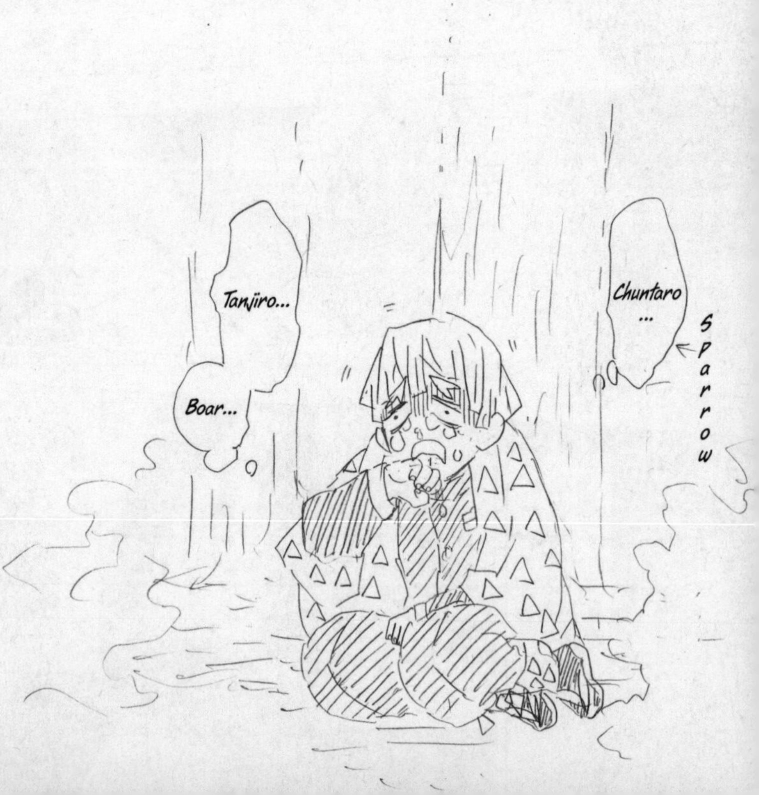
Chuntaro ...
Sparrow
Tanjiro...
Boar...

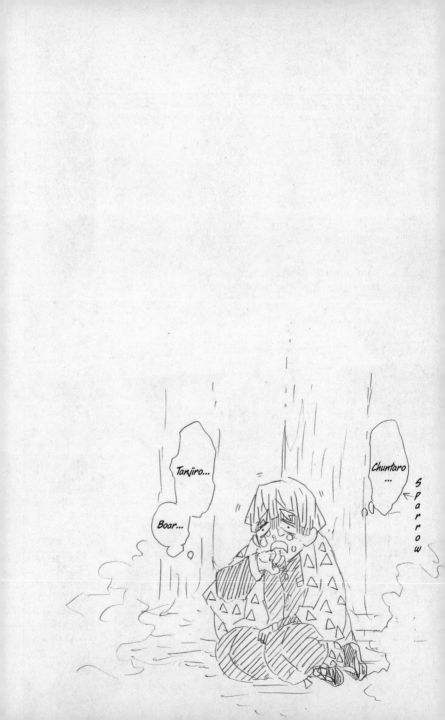

CHAPTER 32: PUNGENT ODOR

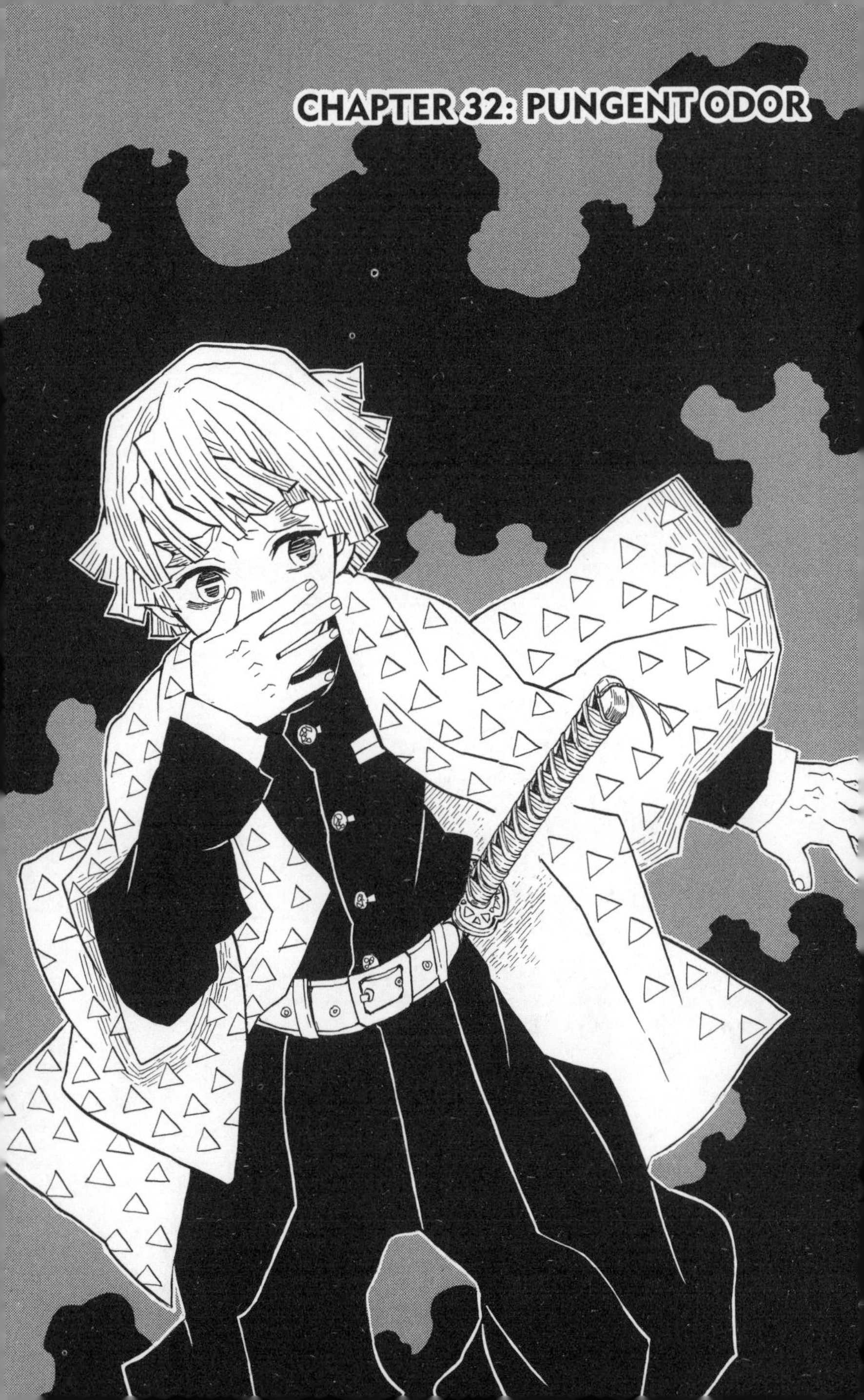

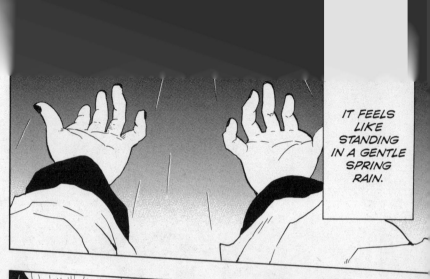

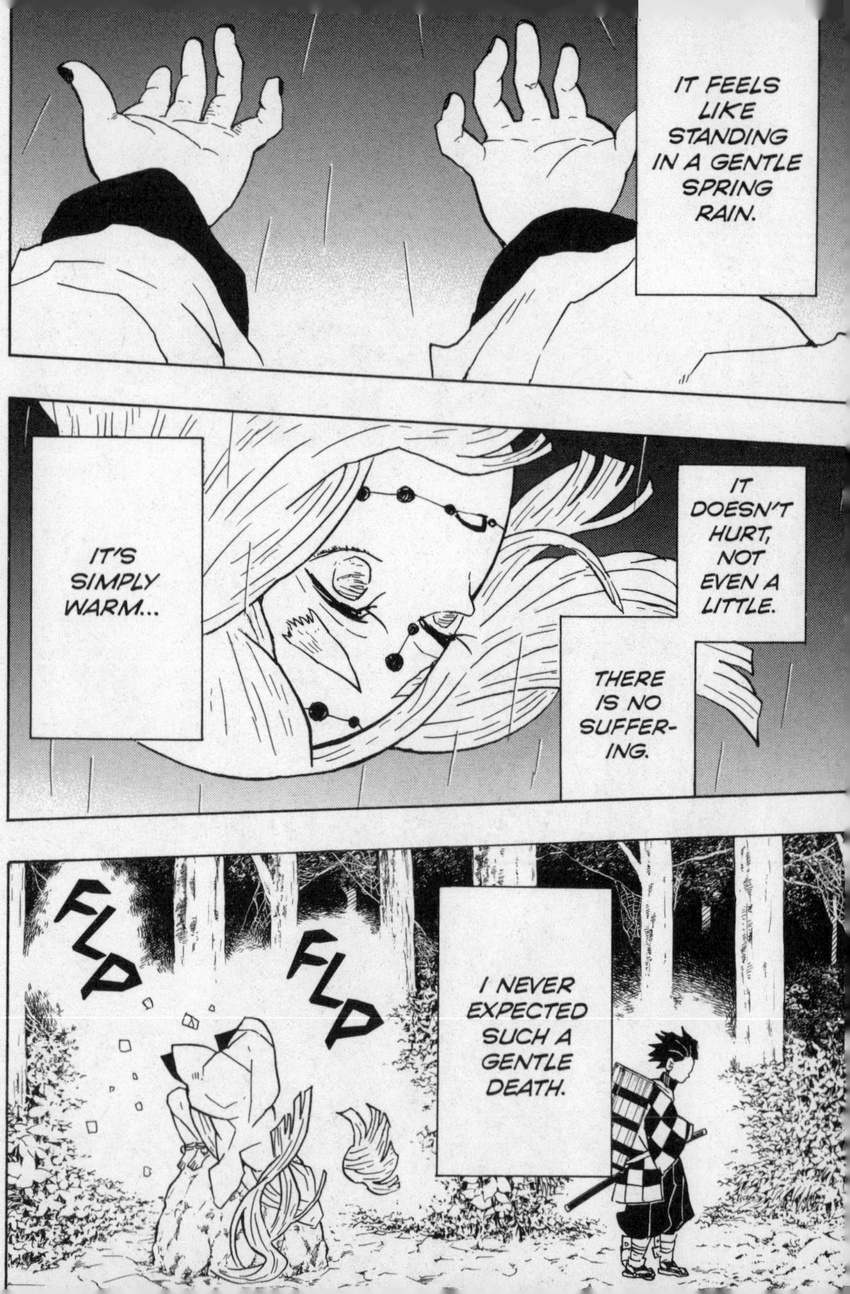
IT FEELS LIKE STANDING IN A GENTLE SPRING RAIN.
IT DOESN'T HURT, NOT EVEN A LITTLE.
THERE IS NO SUFFER-ING.
IT'S SIMPLY WARM...
I NEVER EXPECTED SUCH A GENTLE DEATH.
FLP
FLP

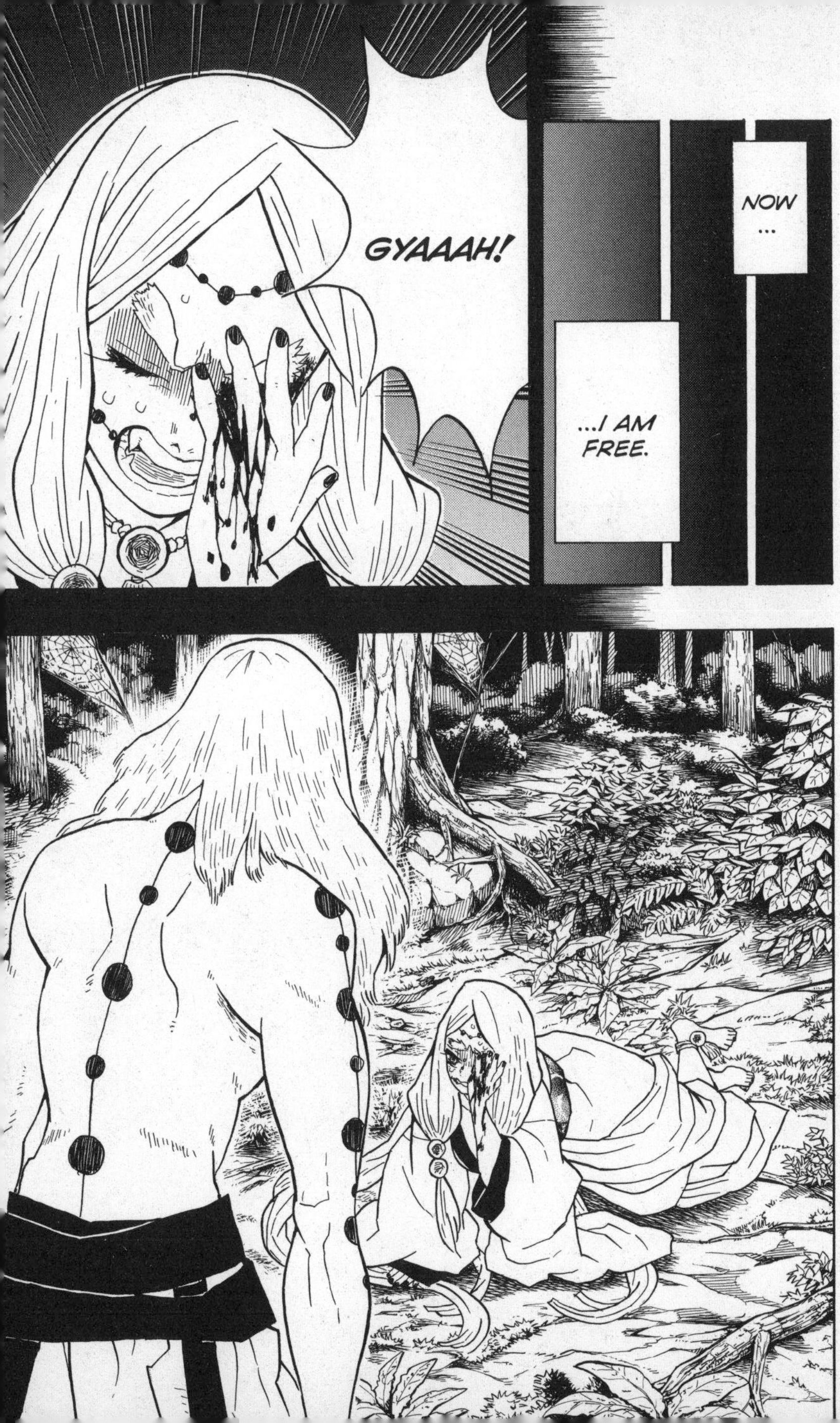
NOW ...
...I AM FREE.
GYAAAH!

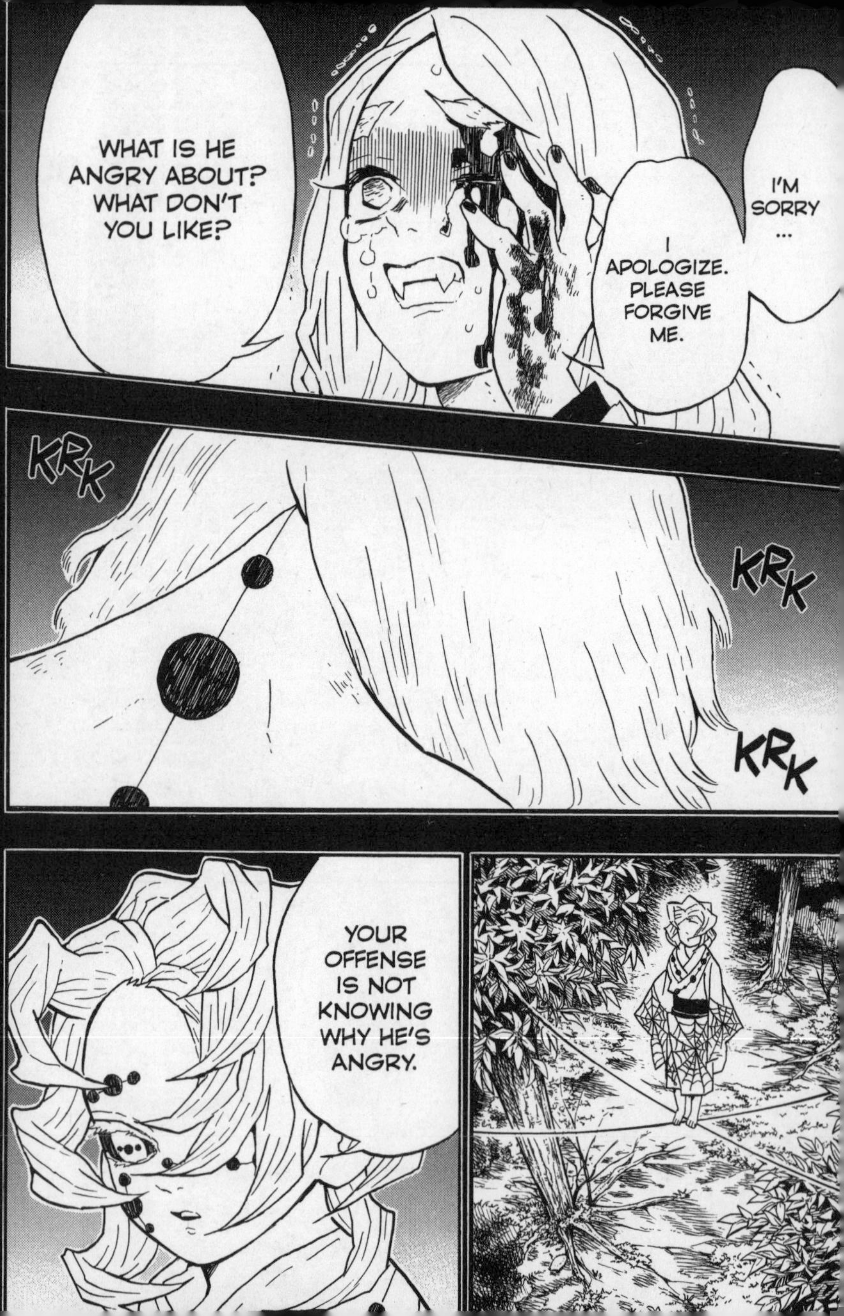
I'M SORRY ...
I APOLOGIZE. PLEASE FORGIVE ME.
WHAT IS HE ANGRY ABOUT? WHAT DON'T YOU LIKE?
KRK
KRK
KRK
YOUR OFFENSE IS NOT KNOWING WHY HE'S ANGRY.

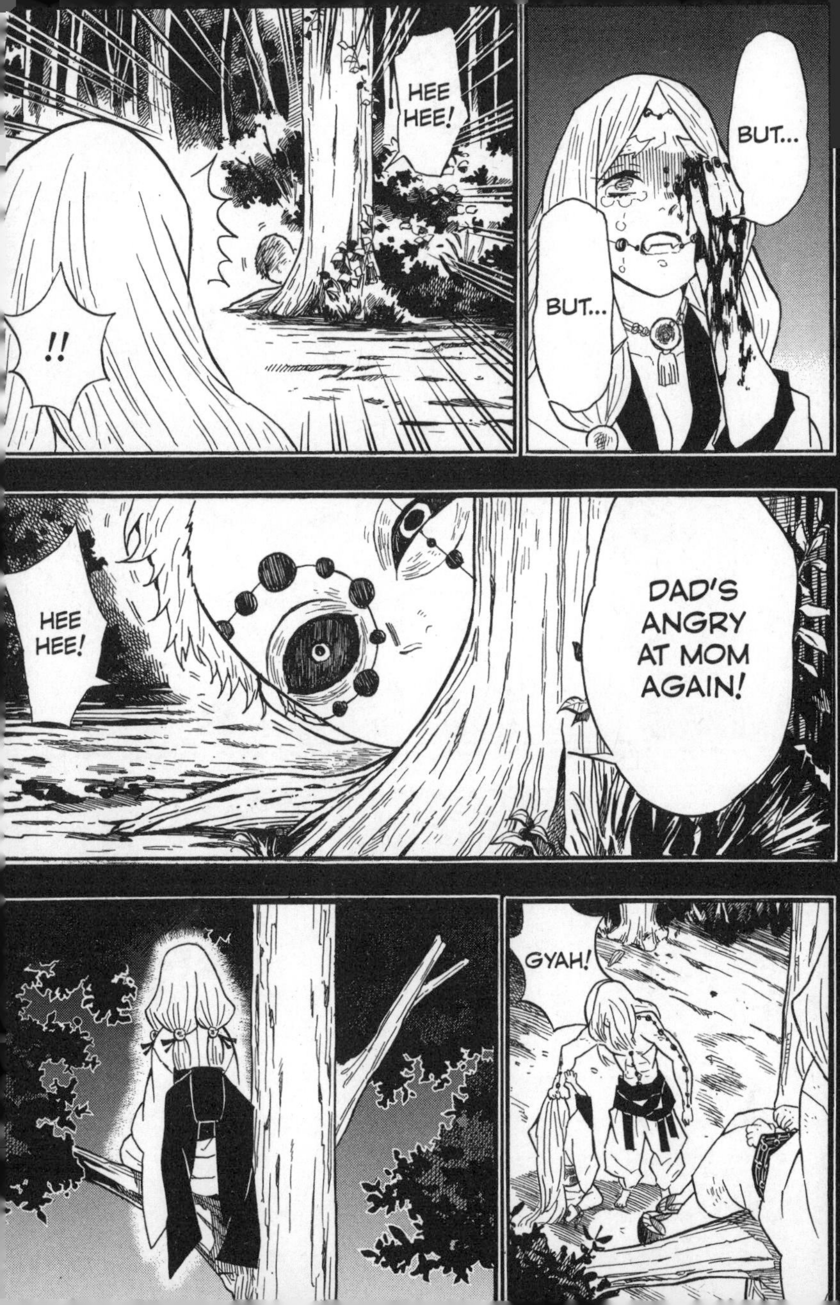
BUT...
BUT...
HEE HEE!
!!
DAD'S ANGRY AT MOM AGAIN!
HEE HEE!
GYAH!

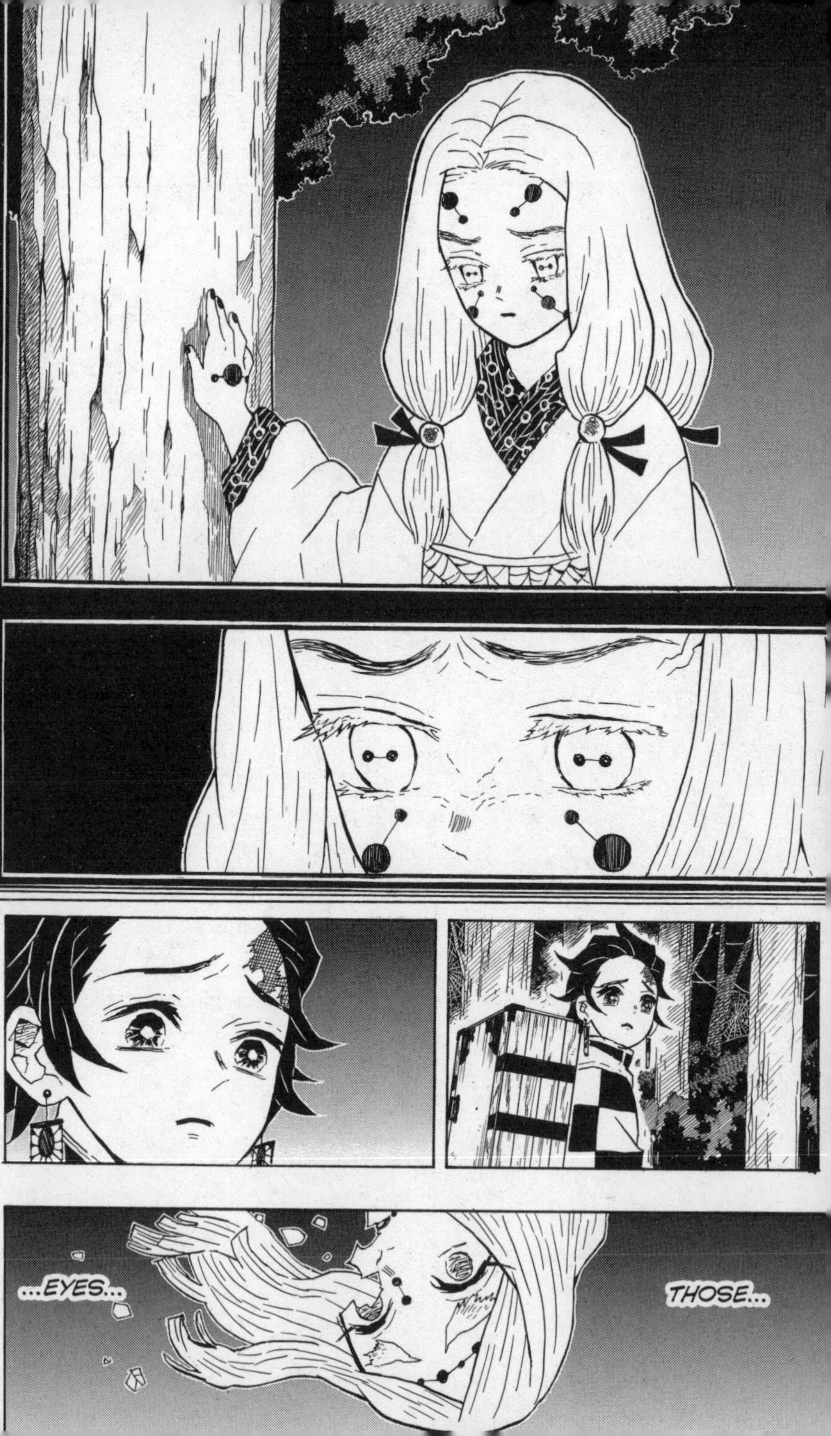
THOSE...
...EYES...

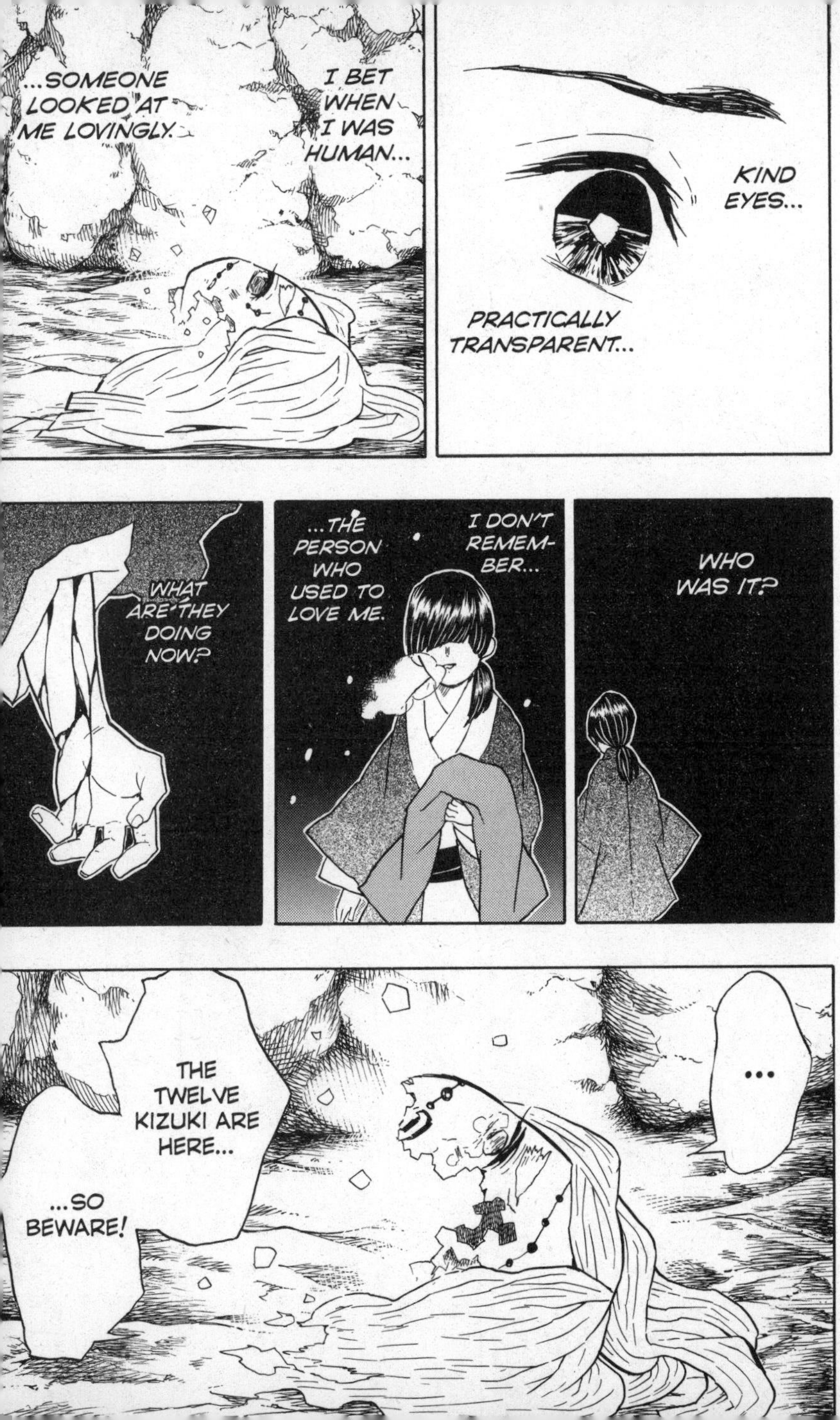
KIND EYES...
PRACTICALLY TRANSPARENT...
I BET WHEN I WAS HUMAN...
...SOMEONE LOOKED AT ME LOVINGLY.
WHO WAS IT?
I DON'T REMEMBER...
...THE PERSON WHO USED TO LOVE ME.
WHAT ARE THEY DOING NOW?
...
THE TWELVE KIZUKI ARE HERE...
...SO BEWARE!

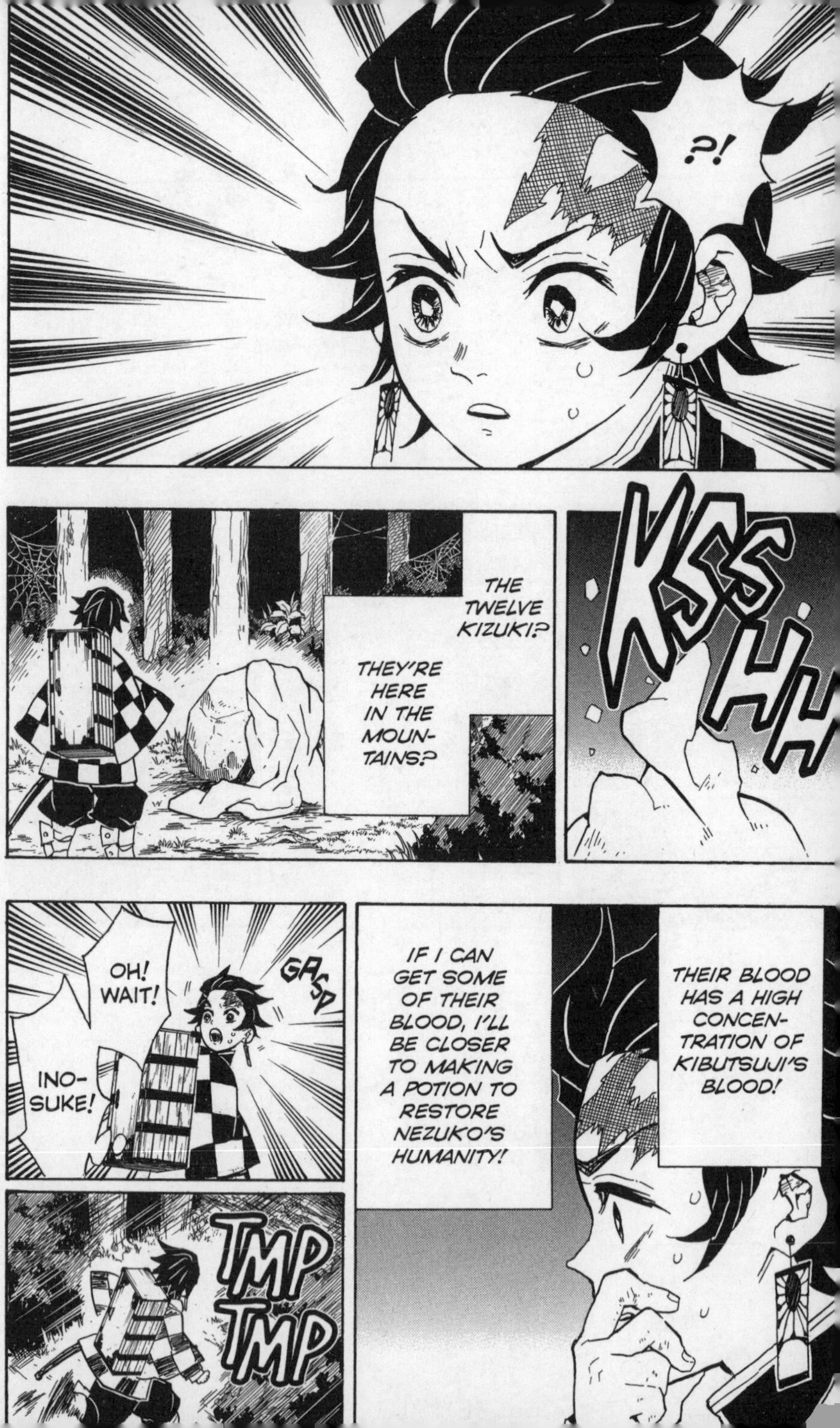
?!
KSSHHH
THE TWELVE KIZUKI?
THEY'RE HERE IN THE MOUN-TAINS?
THEIR BLOOD HAS A HIGH CONCEN-TRATION OF KIBUTSUJI'S BLOOD!
IF I CAN GET SOME OF THEIR BLOOD, I'LL BE CLOSER TO MAKING A POTION TO RESTORE NEZUKO'S HUMANITY!
GASP
OH! WAIT!
INO-SUKE!
TMP TMP

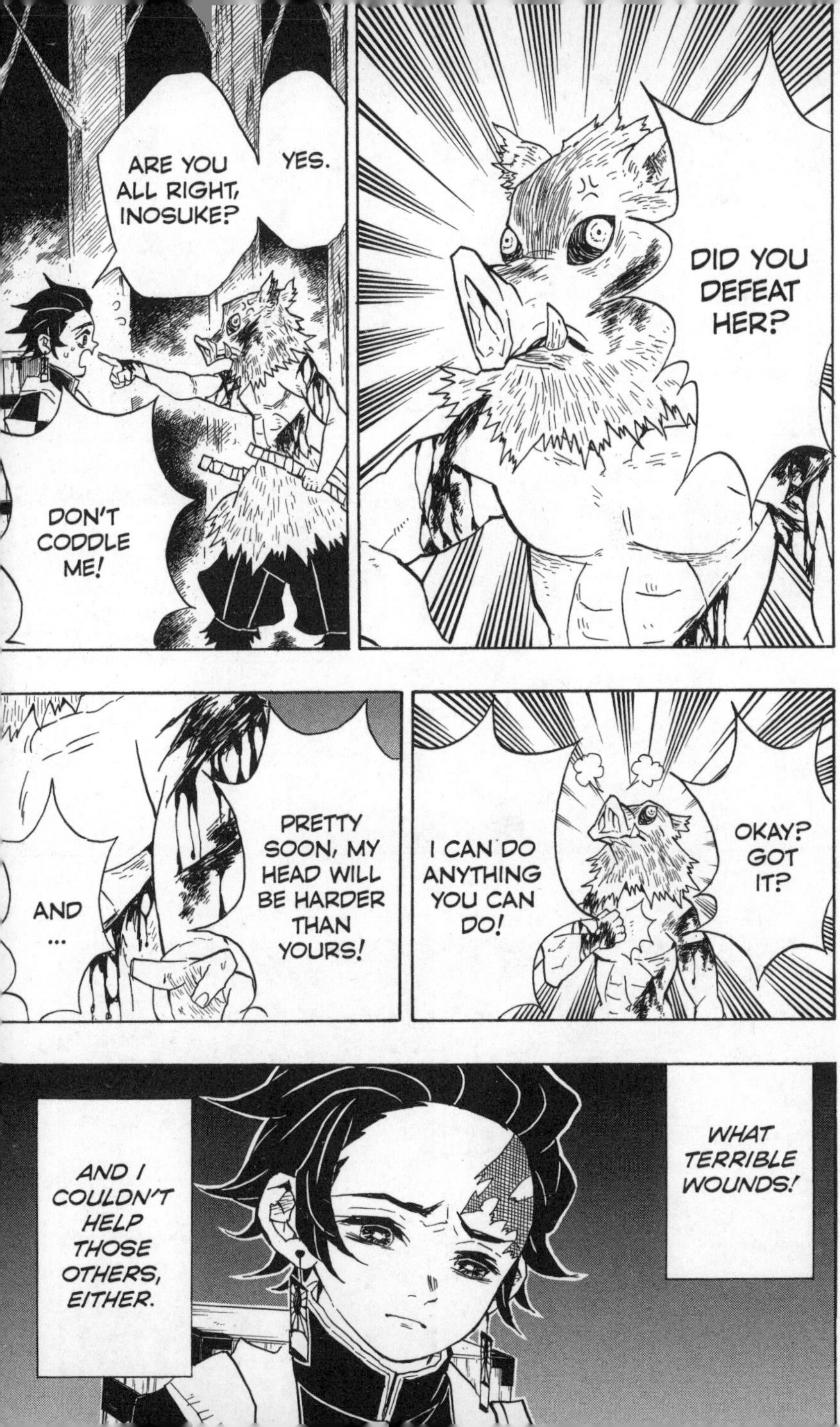
DID YOU DEFEAT HER?
YES.
ARE YOU ALL RIGHT, INOSUKE?
DON'T CODDLE ME!
OKAY? GOT IT?
I CAN DO ANYTHING YOU CAN DO!
PRETTY SOON, MY HEAD WILL BE HARDER THAN YOURS!
AND ...
WHAT TERRIBLE WOUNDS!
AND I COULDN'T HELP THOSE OTHERS, EITHER.

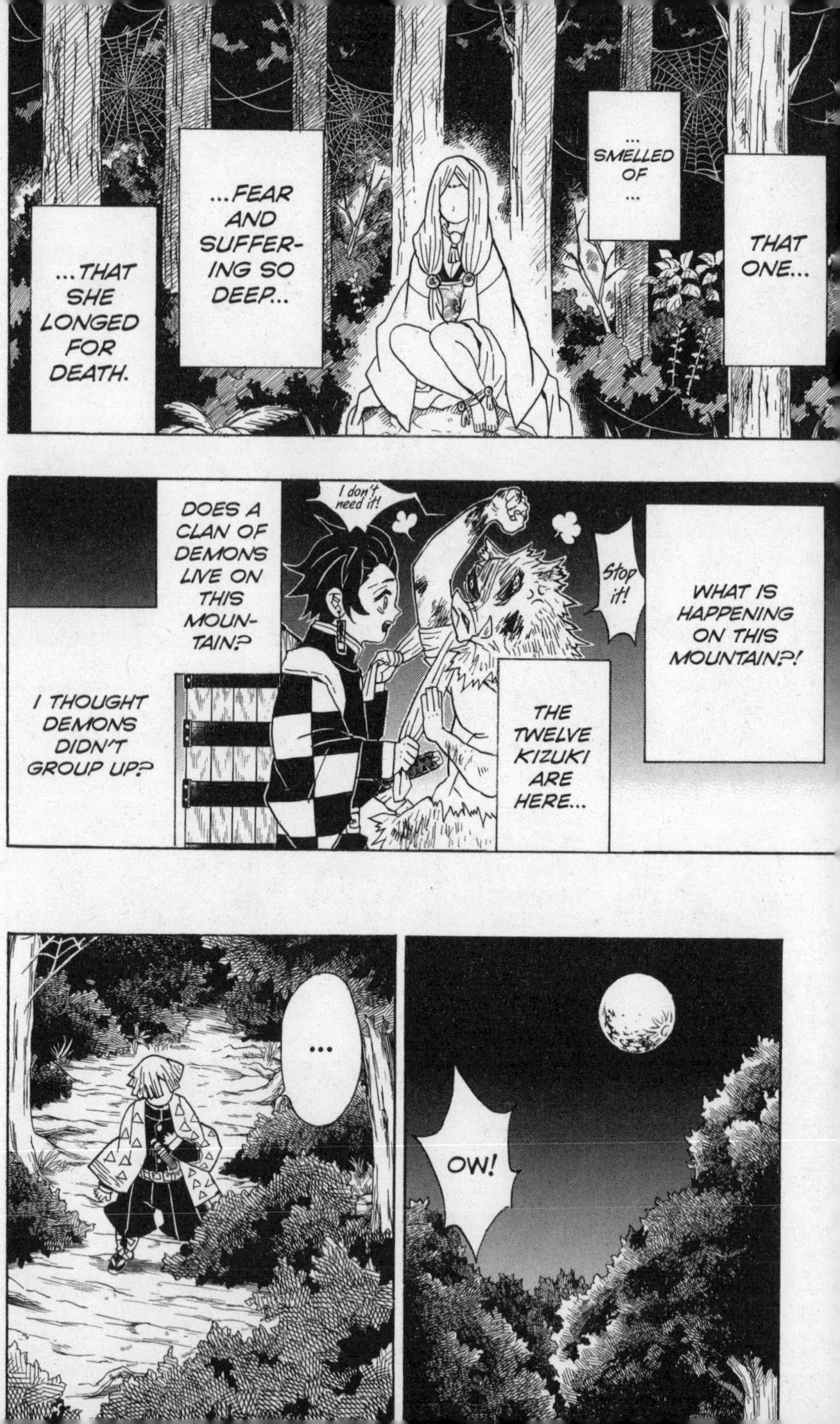
THAT ONE...
...SMELLED OF ...
...FEAR AND SUFFERING SO DEEP...
...THAT SHE LONGED FOR DEATH.
WHAT IS HAPPENING ON THIS MOUNTAIN?!
Stop it!
I don't need it!
THE TWELVE KIZUKI ARE HERE...
DOES A CLAN OF DEMONS LIVE ON THIS MOUNTAIN?
I THOUGHT DEMONS DIDN'T GROUP UP?
OW!
...

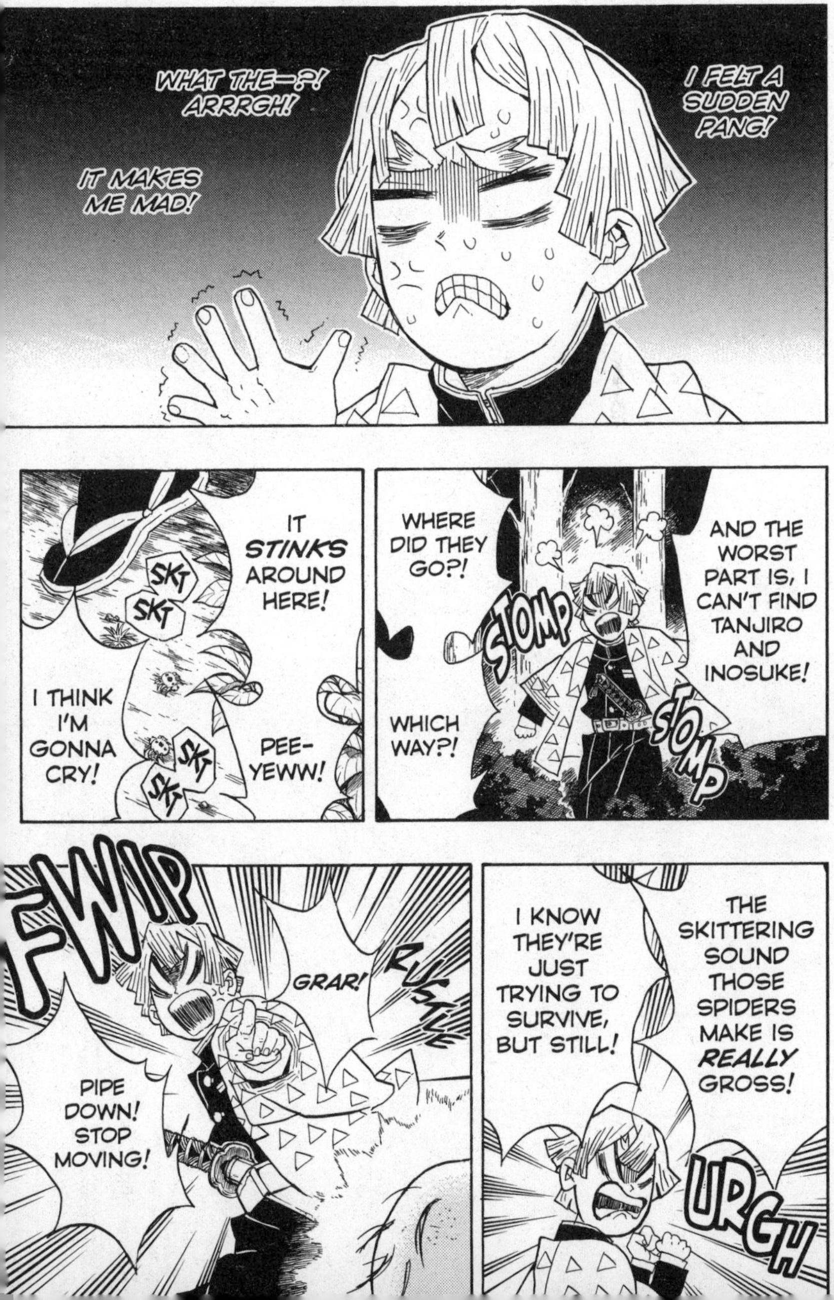
I FELT A SUDDEN PANG!
WHAT THE—?! ARRRGH!
IT MAKES ME MAD!
AND THE WORST PART IS, I CAN'T FIND TANJIRO AND INOSUKE!
WHERE DID THEY GO?!
STOMP
STOMP
WHICH WAY?!
IT STINKS AROUND HERE!
SKT
SKT
PEE-YEWW!
SKT
SKT
I THINK I'M GONNA CRY!
THE SKITTERING SOUND THOSE SPIDERS MAKE IS REALLY GROSS!
I KNOW THEY'RE JUST TRYING TO SURVIVE, BUT STILL!
URCH
RUSTLE
GRAR!
FWIP
PIPE DOWN! STOP MOVING!

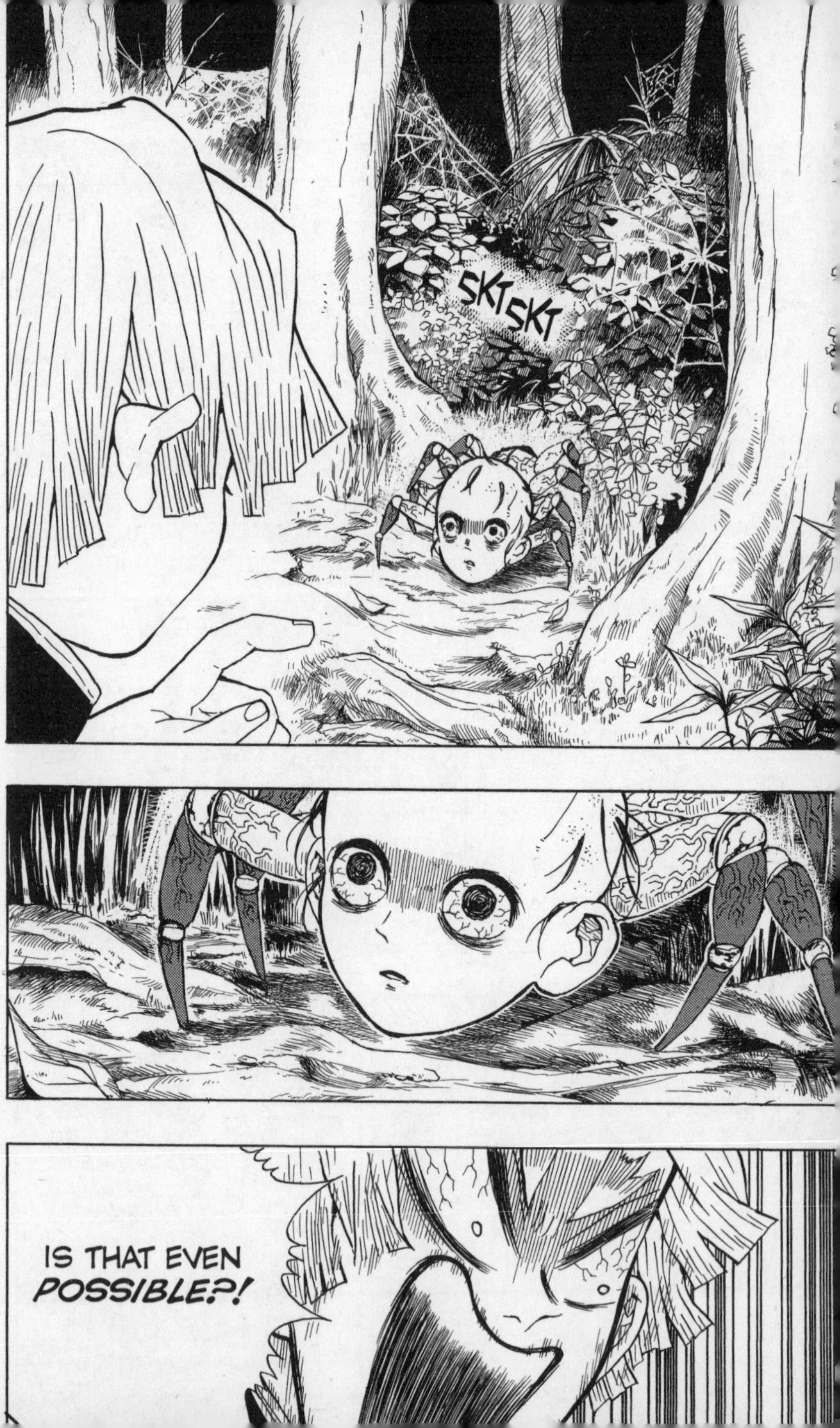
SKT SKT
IS THAT EVEN POSSIBLE?!

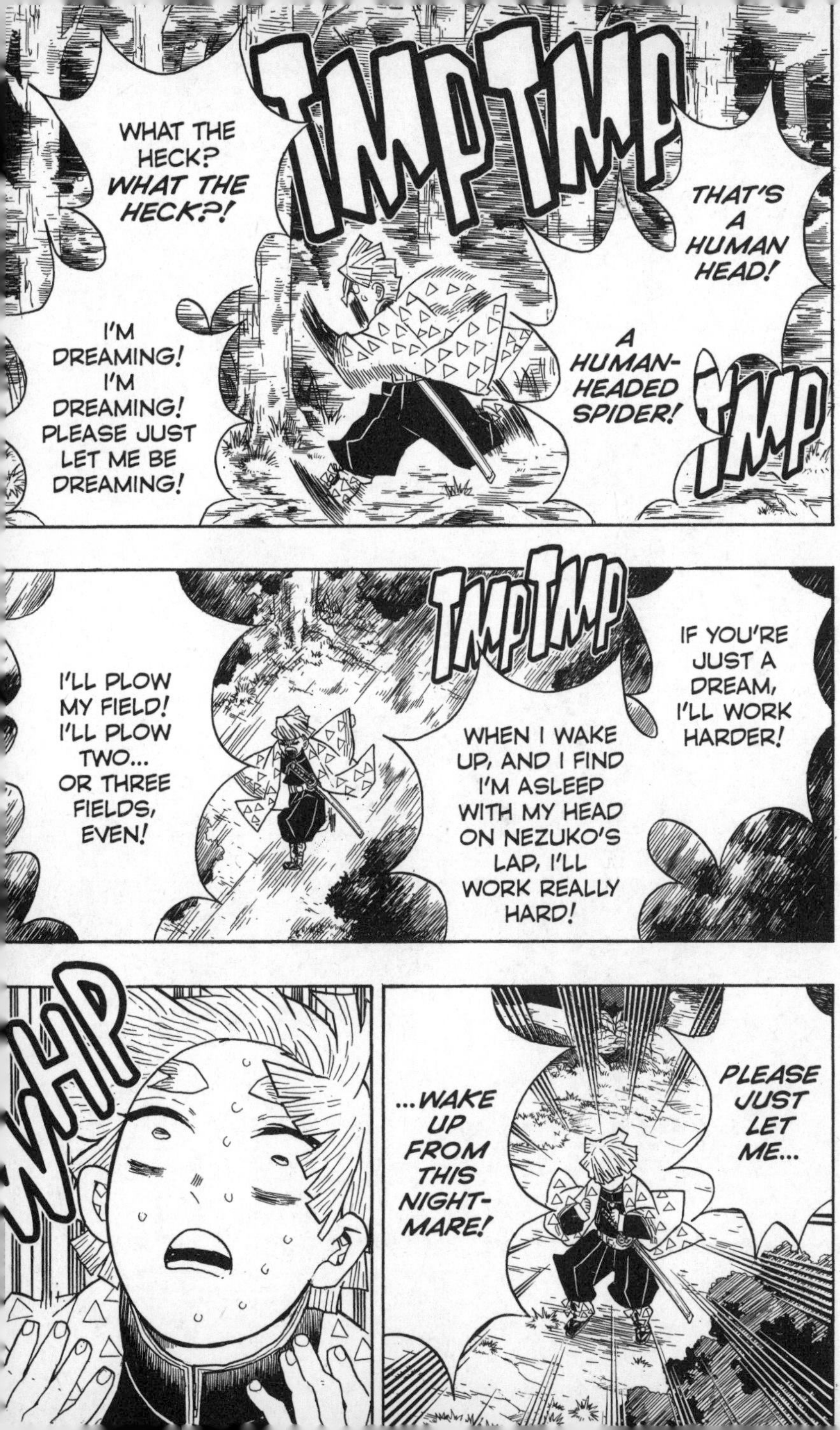
TMP TMP
THAT'S A HUMAN HEAD!
WHAT THE HECK? WHAT THE HECK?!
A HUMAN-HEADED SPIDER!
TMP
I'M DREAMING! I'M DREAMING! PLEASE JUST LET ME BE DREAMING!
TMP TMP
IF YOU'RE JUST A DREAM, I'LL WORK HARDER!
WHEN I WAKE UP, AND I FIND I'M ASLEEP WITH MY HEAD ON NEZUKO'S LAP, I'LL WORK REALLY HARD!
I'LL PLOW MY FIELD! I'LL PLOW TWO... OR THREE FIELDS, EVEN!
PLEASE JUST LET ME...
...WAKE UP FROM THIS NIGHT-MARE!
WHP

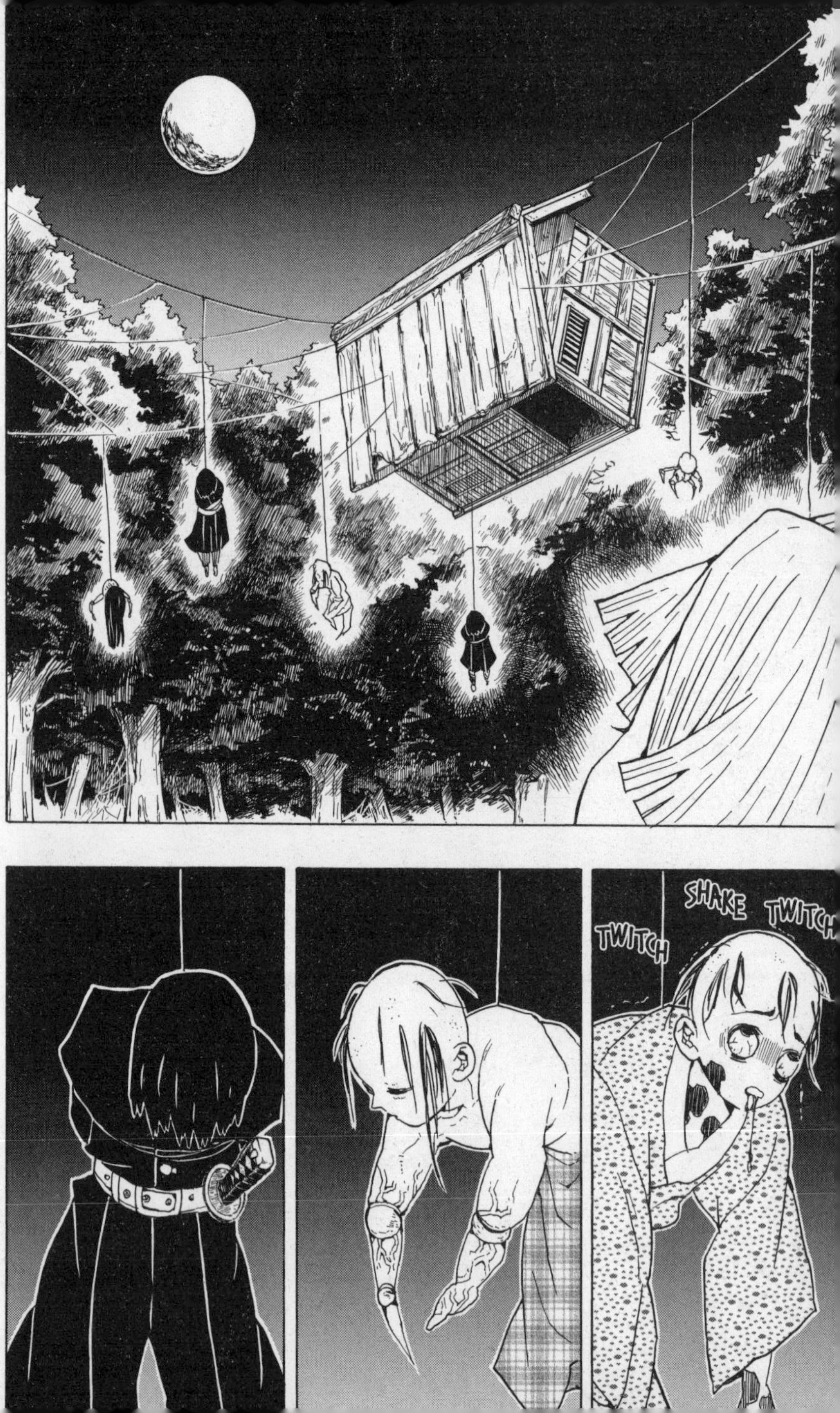
SHAKE
TWITCH
TWITCH

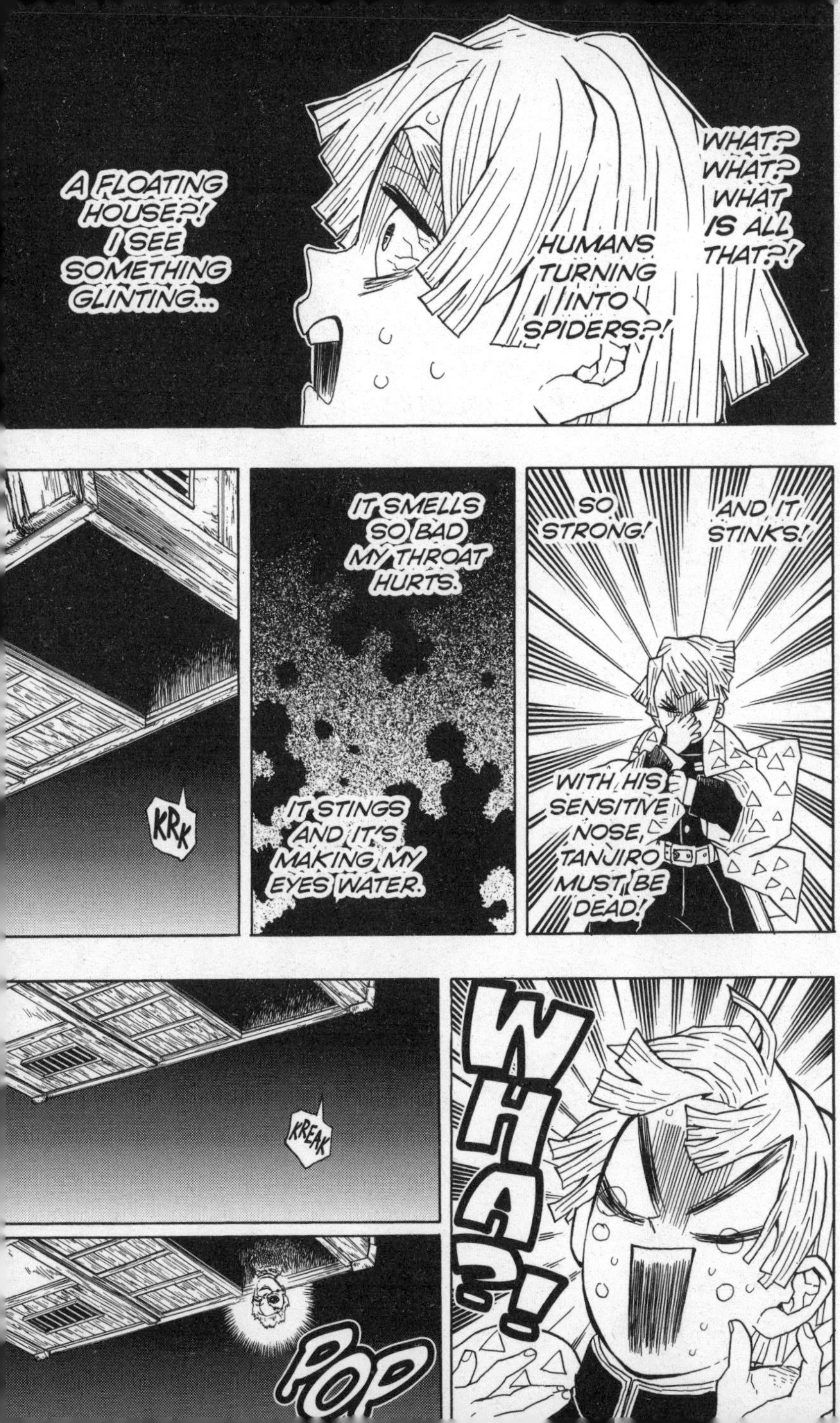
WHAT? WHAT? WHAT IS ALL THAT?!
HUMANS TURNING INTO SPIDERS?!
A FLOATING HOUSE?! I SEE SOMETHING GLINTING...
AND IT STINKS!
SO STRONG!
WITH HIS SENSITIVE NOSE, TANJIRO MUST BE DEAD!
IT SMELLS SO BAD MY THROAT HURTS.
IT STINGS AND IT'S MAKING MY EYES WATER.
KRK
WHA?!
KREAK
POP

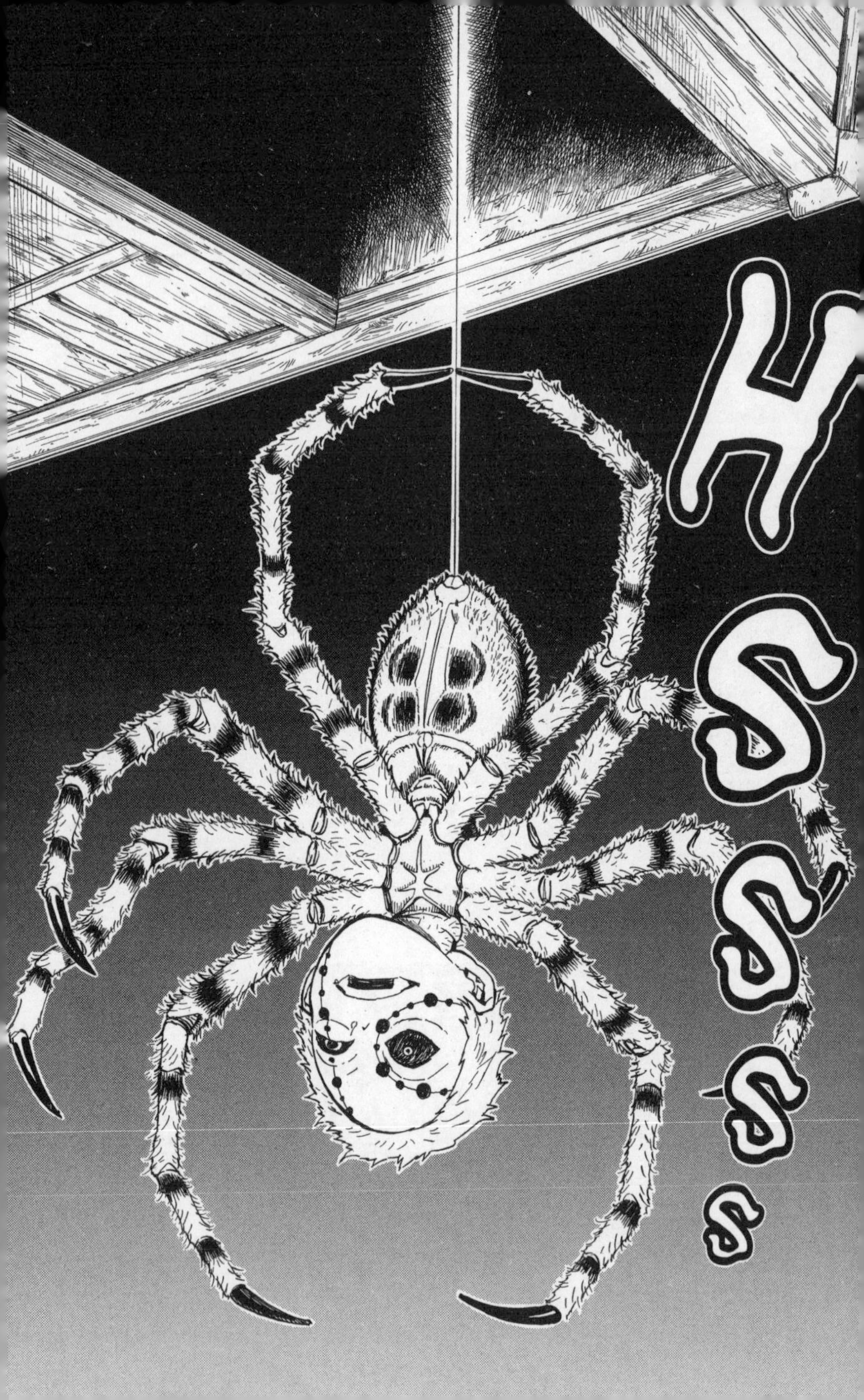
HSSSS

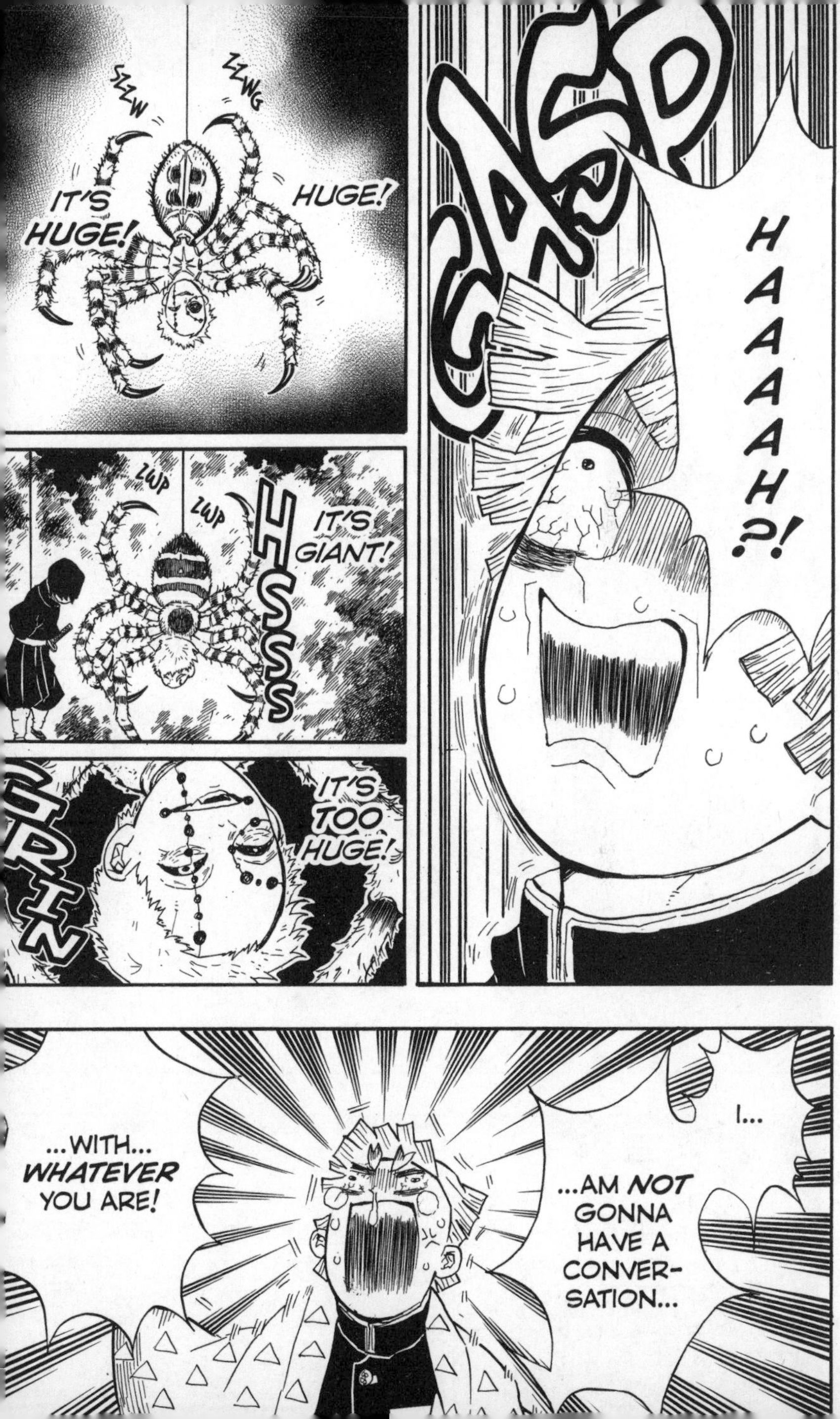
GASP
HAAAAAH?!
ZZWG
HUGE!
SZZW
IT'S HUGE!
ZWP
ZWP
IT'S GIANT!
HSSS
IT'S TOO HUGE!
I...
...AM NOT GONNA HAVE A CONVER-SATION...
...WITH... WHATEVER YOU ARE!

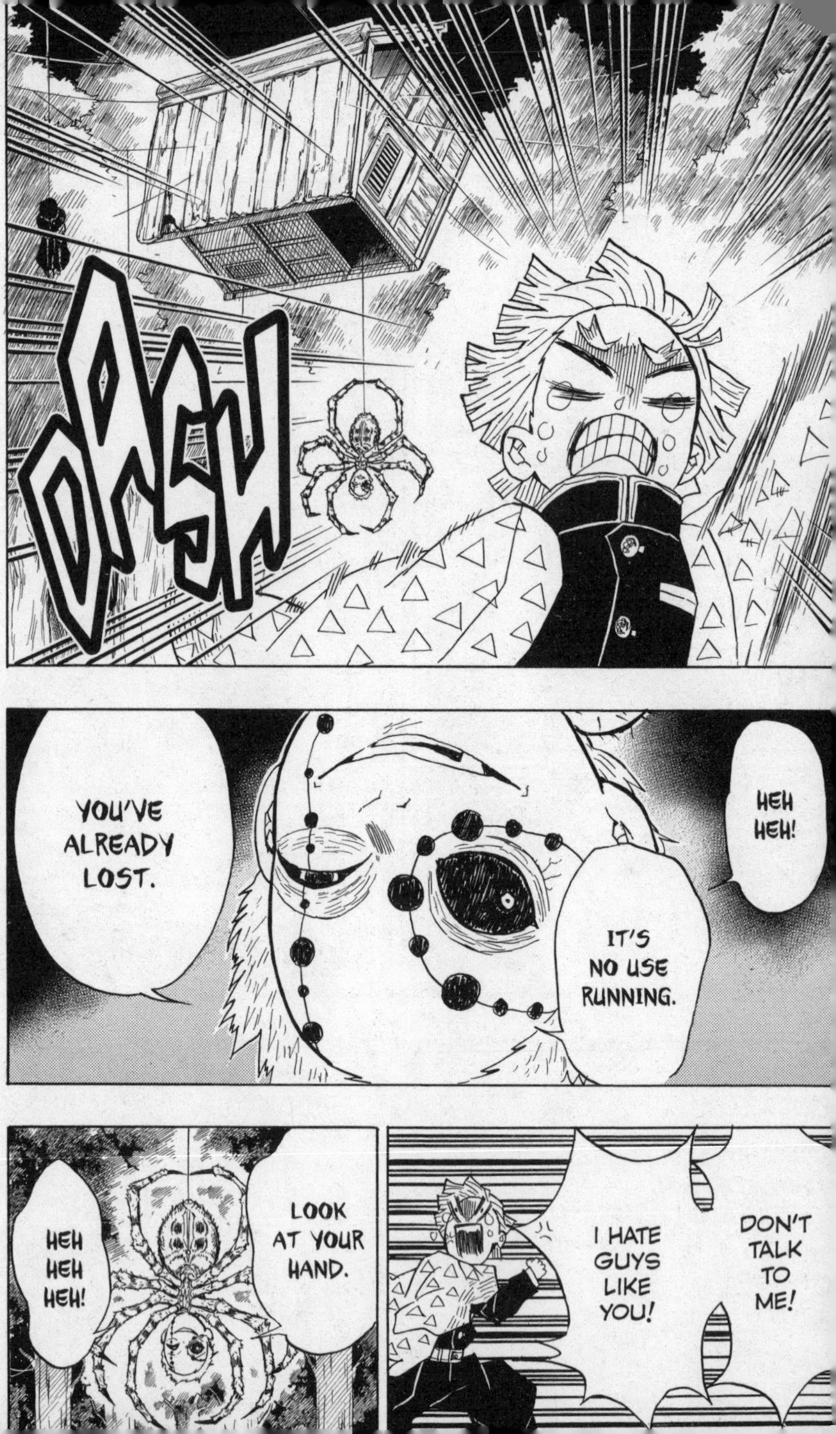
DASH
HEH HEH!
IT'S NO USE RUNNING.
YOU'VE ALREADY LOST.
DON'T TALK TO ME!
I HATE GUYS LIKE YOU!
LOOK AT YOUR HAND.
HEH HEH HEH!

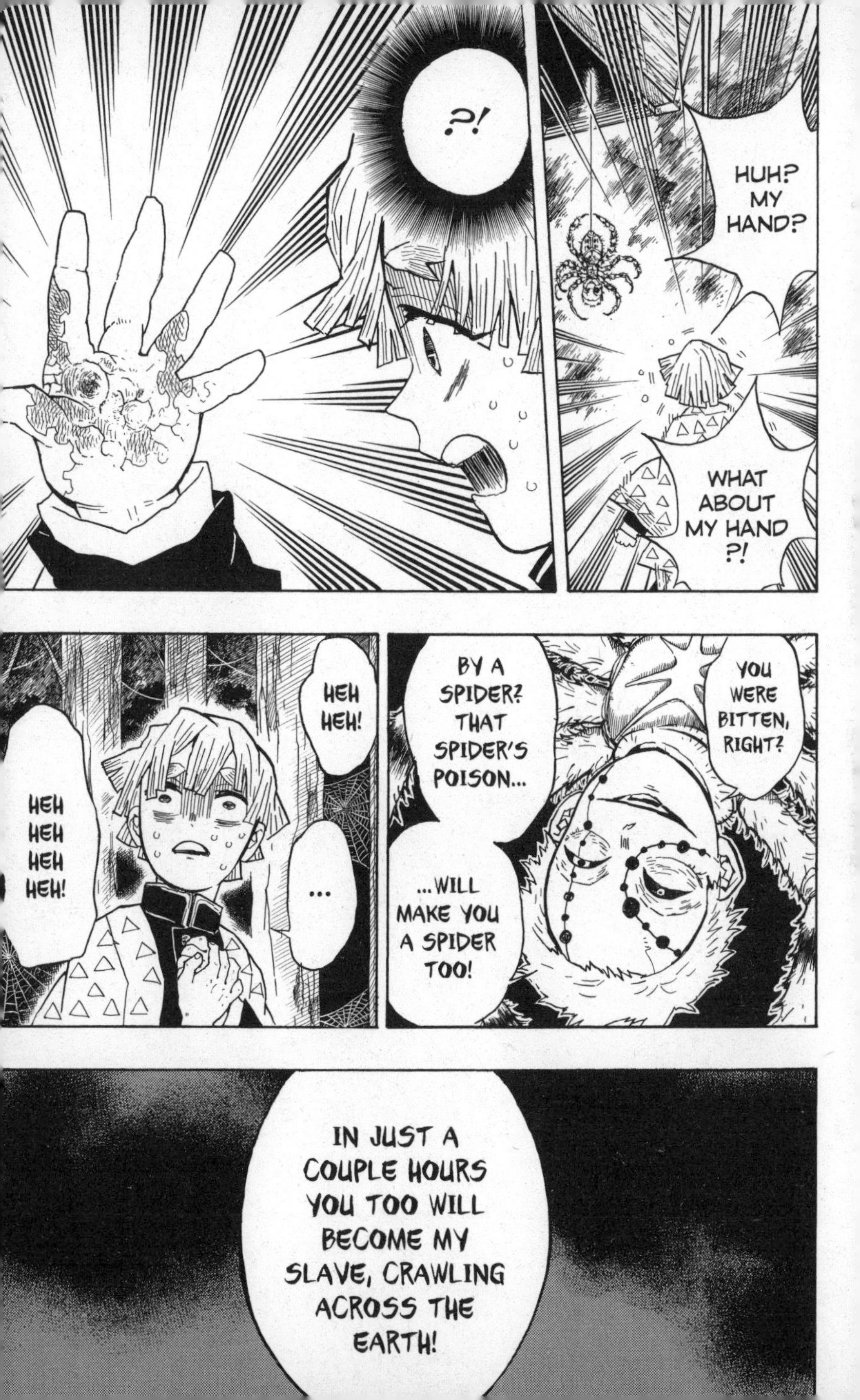
HUH? MY HAND?
WHAT ABOUT MY HAND ?!
?!
YOU WERE BITTEN, RIGHT?
BY A SPIDER? THAT SPIDER'S POISON...
...WILL MAKE YOU A SPIDER TOO!
HEH HEH!
HEH HEH HEH HEH!
...
IN JUST A COUPLE HOURS YOU TOO WILL BECOME MY SLAVE, CRAWLING ACROSS THE EARTH!

Stinks.
Hee hee hee!

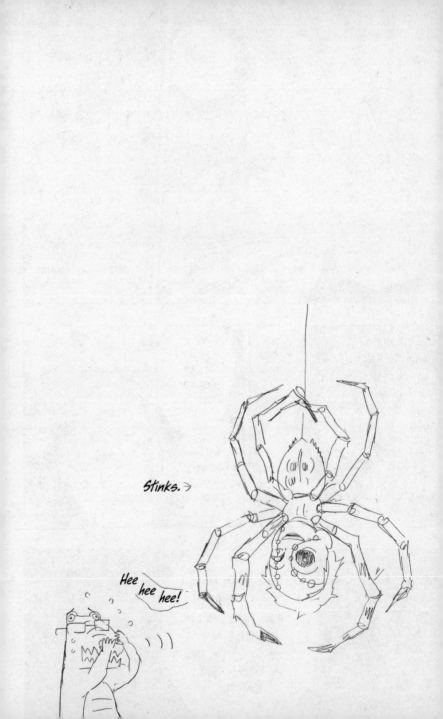

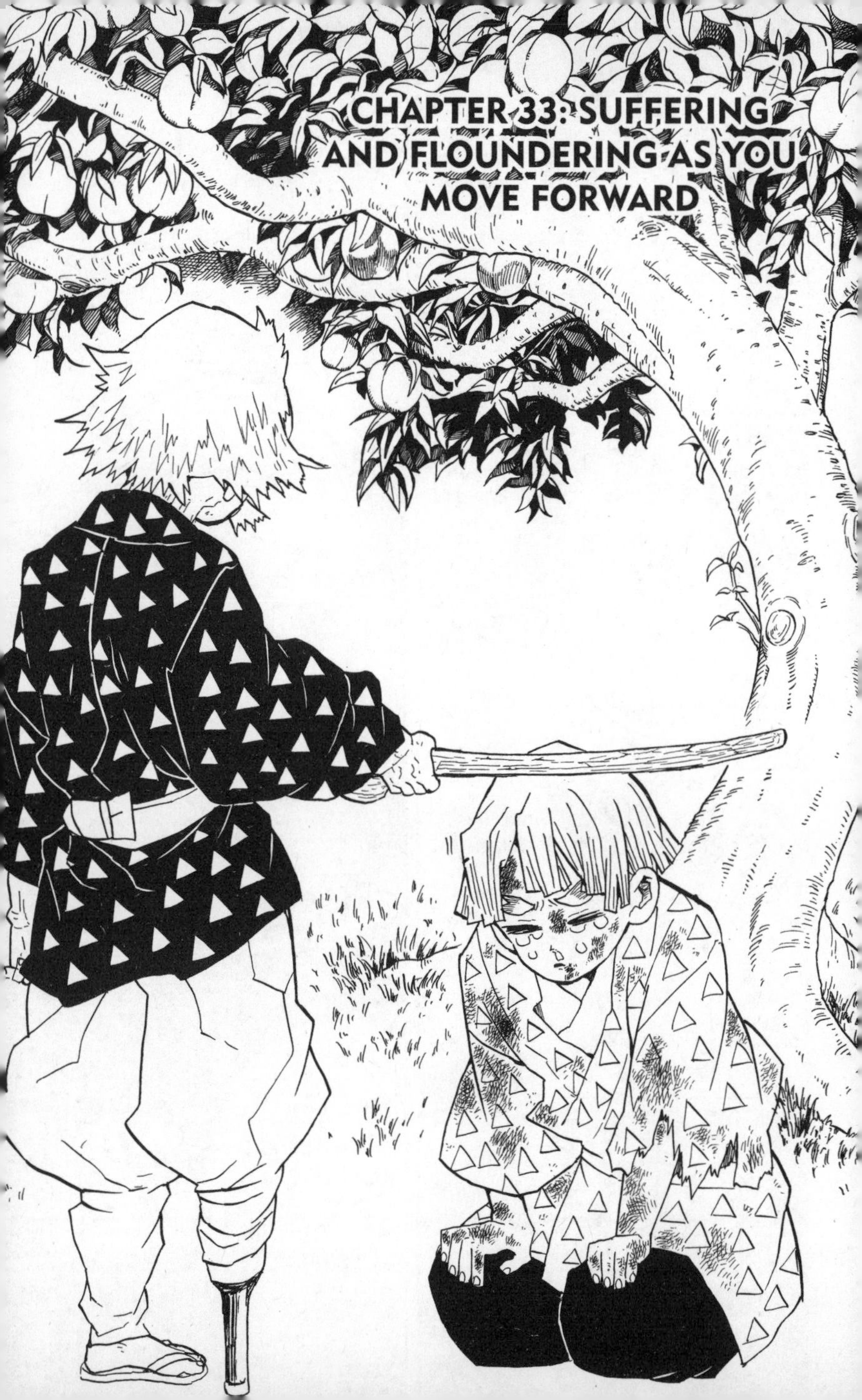
CHAPTER 33: SUFFERING AND FLOUNDERING AS YOU MOVE FORWARD

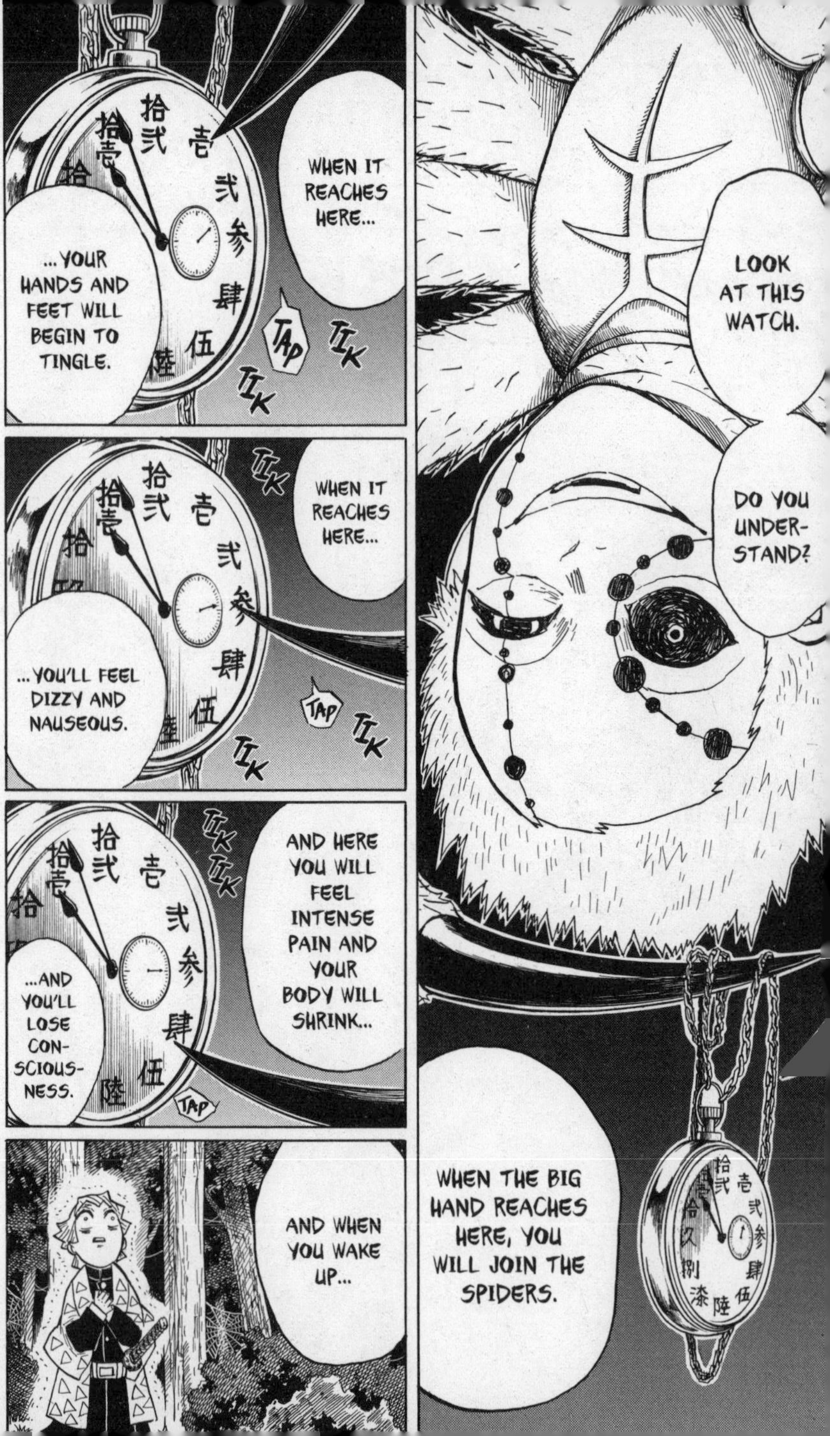
LOOK AT THIS WATCH.
DO YOU UNDERSTAND?
WHEN THE BIG HAND REACHES HERE, YOU WILL JOIN THE SPIDERS.
WHEN IT REACHES HERE...
TAP
TIK
TIK
...YOUR HANDS AND FEET WILL BEGIN TO TINGLE.
WHEN IT REACHES HERE...
TIK
TAP
TIK
TIK
...YOU'LL FEEL DIZZY AND NAUSEOUS.
AND HERE YOU WILL FEEL INTENSE PAIN AND YOUR BODY WILL SHRINK...
TIK
TIK
TAP
...AND YOU'LL LOSE CON-SCIOUS-NESS.
AND WHEN YOU WAKE UP...

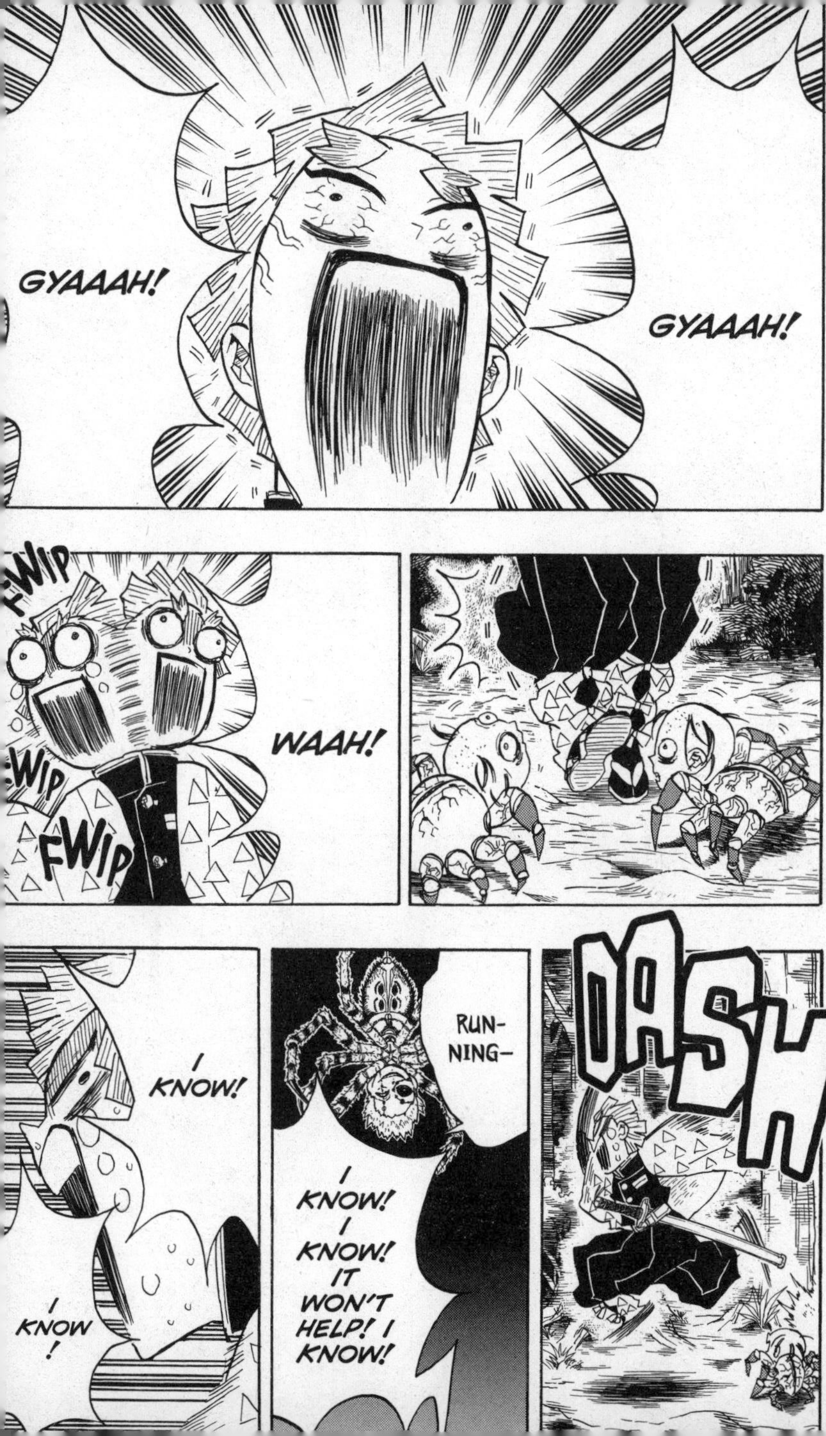
GYAAAH!
GYAAAH!
WAAH!
FWIP
FWIP
FWIP
DASH
RUN-NING—
I KNOW! I KNOW! IT WON'T HELP! I KNOW!
I KNOW!
I KNOW!

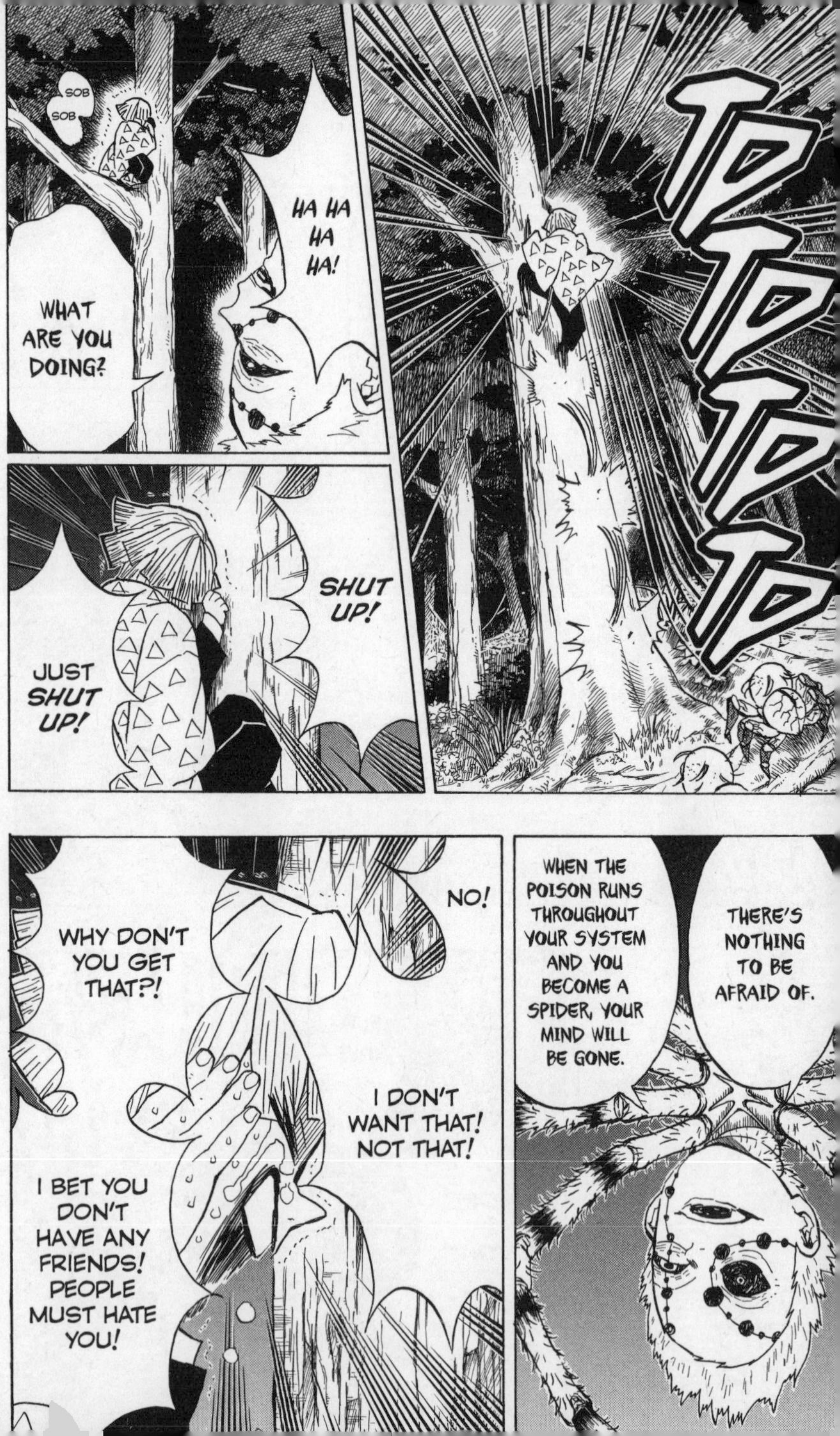
TP TP TP TP TP
HA HA HA HA!
SOB SOB
WHAT ARE YOU DOING?
SHUT UP!
JUST SHUT UP!
THERE'S NOTHING TO BE AFRAID OF.
WHEN THE POISON RUNS THROUGHOUT YOUR SYSTEM AND YOU BECOME A SPIDER, YOUR MIND WILL BE GONE.
NO!
WHY DON'T YOU GET THAT?!
I DON'T WANT THAT! NOT THAT!
I BET YOU DON'T HAVE ANY FRIENDS! PEOPLE MUST HATE YOU!

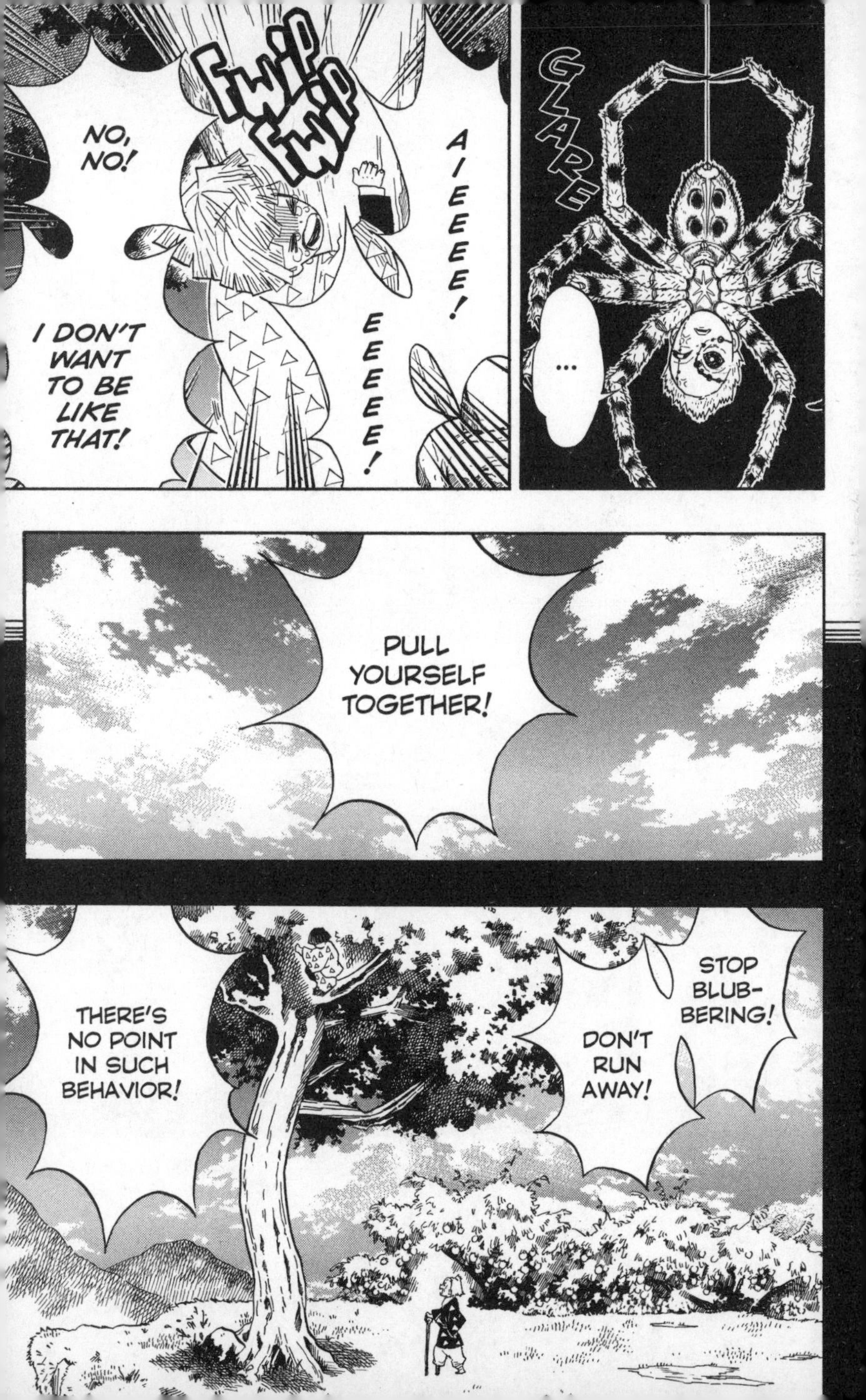
GLARE
...
FWIP FWIP
AIEEEE!
EEEEE!
NO, NO!
I DON'T WANT TO BE LIKE THAT!
PULL YOURSELF TOGETHER!
STOP BLUB-BERING!
DON'T RUN AWAY!
THERE'S NO POINT IN SUCH BEHAVIOR!

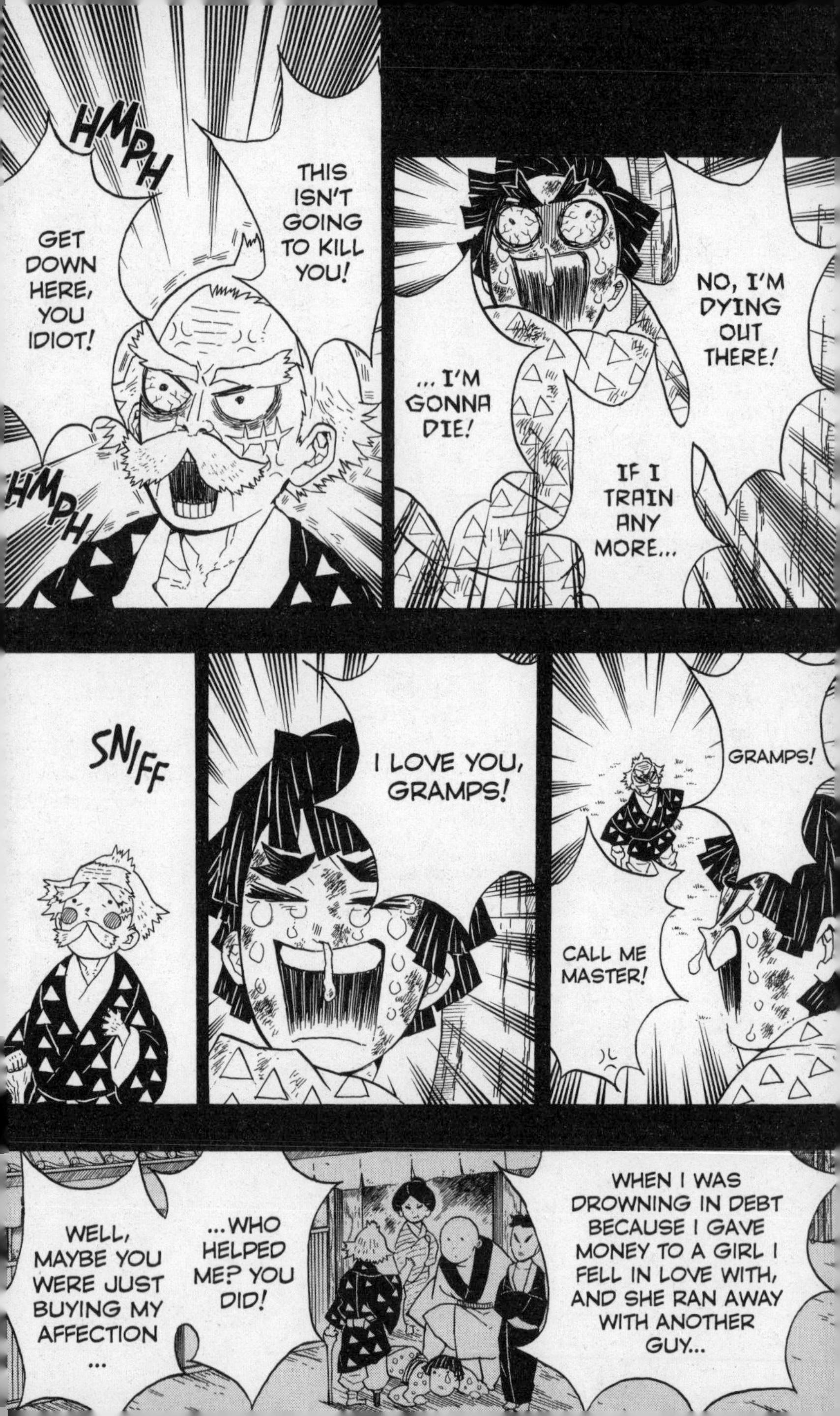
NO, I'M DYING OUT THERE!
IF I TRAIN ANY MORE...
... I'M GONNA DIE!
HMPH
THIS ISN'T GOING TO KILL YOU!
GET DOWN HERE, YOU IDIOT!
HMPH
GRAMPS!
CALL ME MASTER!
I LOVE YOU, GRAMPS!
SNIFF
WHEN I WAS DROWNING IN DEBT BECAUSE I GAVE MONEY TO A GIRL I FELL IN LOVE WITH, AND SHE RAN AWAY WITH ANOTHER GUY...
...WHO HELPED ME? YOU DID!
WELL, MAYBE YOU WERE JUST BUYING MY AFFECTION ...

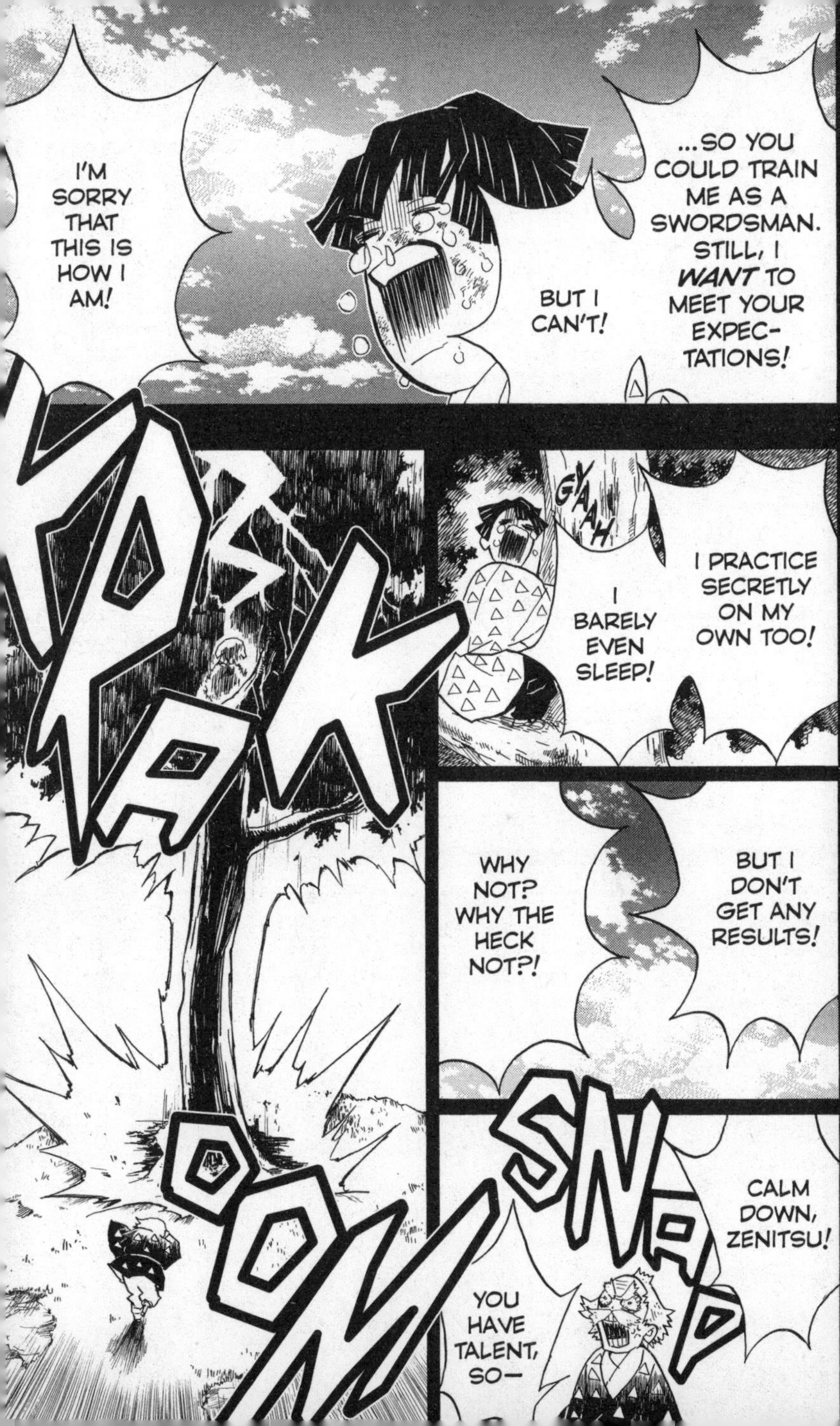
...SO YOU COULD TRAIN ME AS A SWORDSMAN. STILL, I *WANT* TO MEET YOUR EXPEC-TATIONS!
BUT I CAN'T!
I'M SORRY THAT THIS IS HOW I AM!
GYAAAH
I PRACTICE SECRETLY ON MY OWN TOO!
I BARELY EVEN SLEEP!
BUT I DON'T GET ANY RESULTS!
WHY NOT? WHY THE HECK NOT?!
SNAP
CALM DOWN, ZENITSU!
YOU HAVE TALENT, SO—

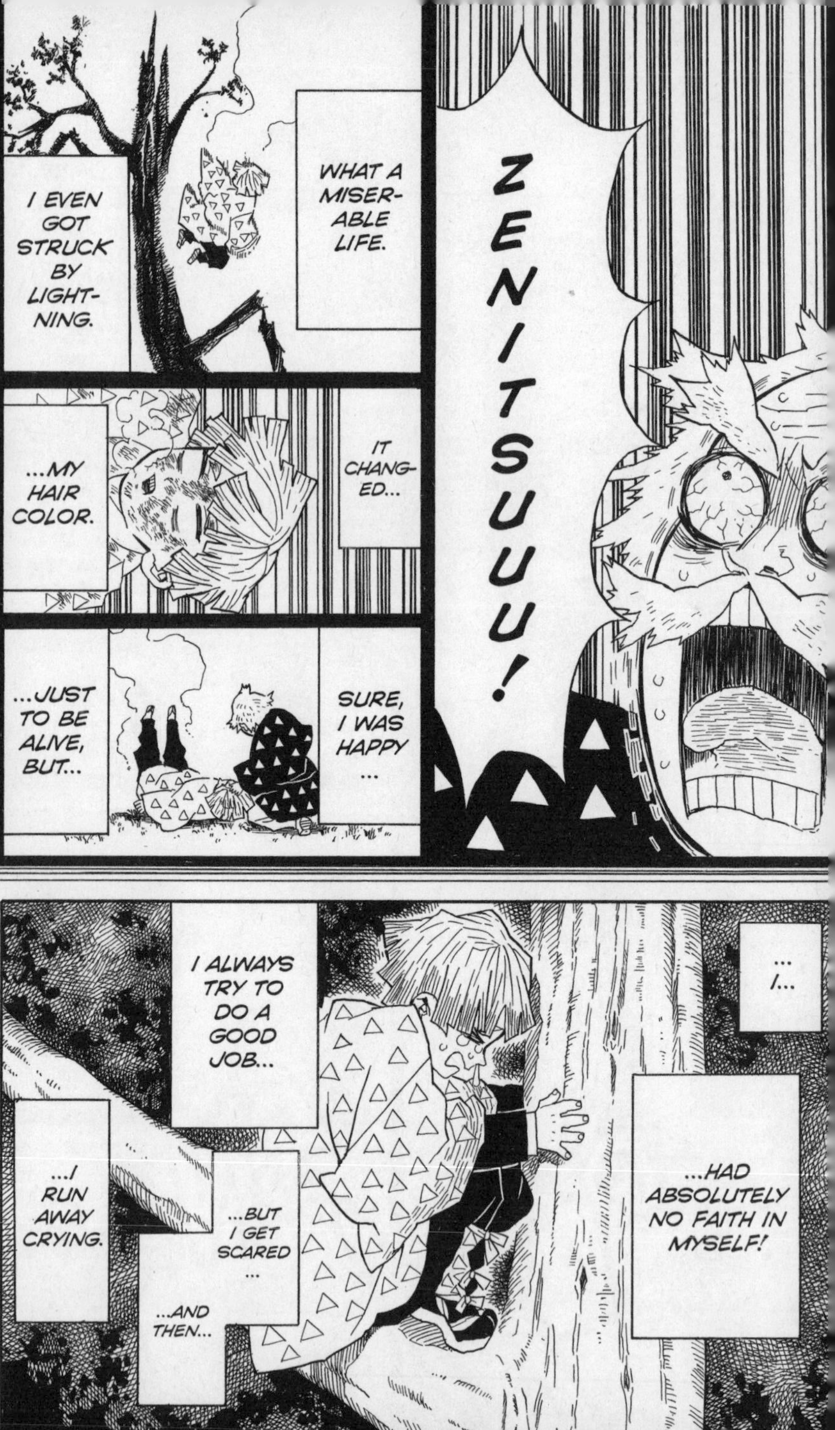
ZENITSUUU!
WHAT A MISERABLE LIFE.
I EVEN GOT STRUCK BY LIGHTNING.
IT CHANGED...
...MY HAIR COLOR.
SURE, I WAS HAPPY...
...JUST TO BE ALIVE, BUT...
... I...
...HAD ABSOLUTELY NO FAITH IN MYSELF!
I ALWAYS TRY TO DO A GOOD JOB...
...BUT I GET SCARED...
...AND THEN...
...I RUN AWAY CRYING.

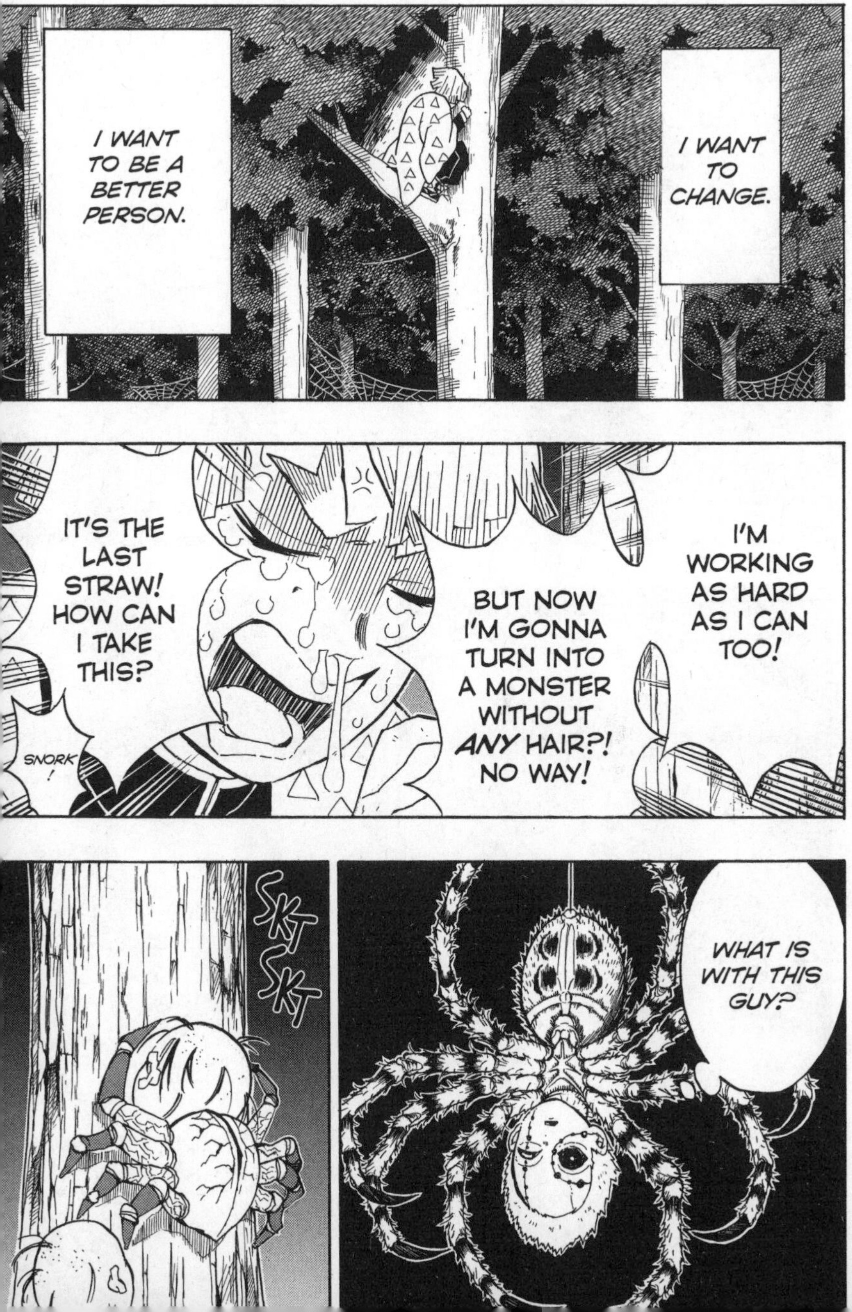
I WANT TO CHANGE.
I WANT TO BE A BETTER PERSON.
I'M WORKING AS HARD AS I CAN TOO!
BUT NOW I'M GONNA TURN INTO A MONSTER WITHOUT ANY HAIR?! NO WAY!
IT'S THE LAST STRAW! HOW CAN I TAKE THIS?
SNORK!
WHAT IS WITH THIS GUY?
SKT SKT

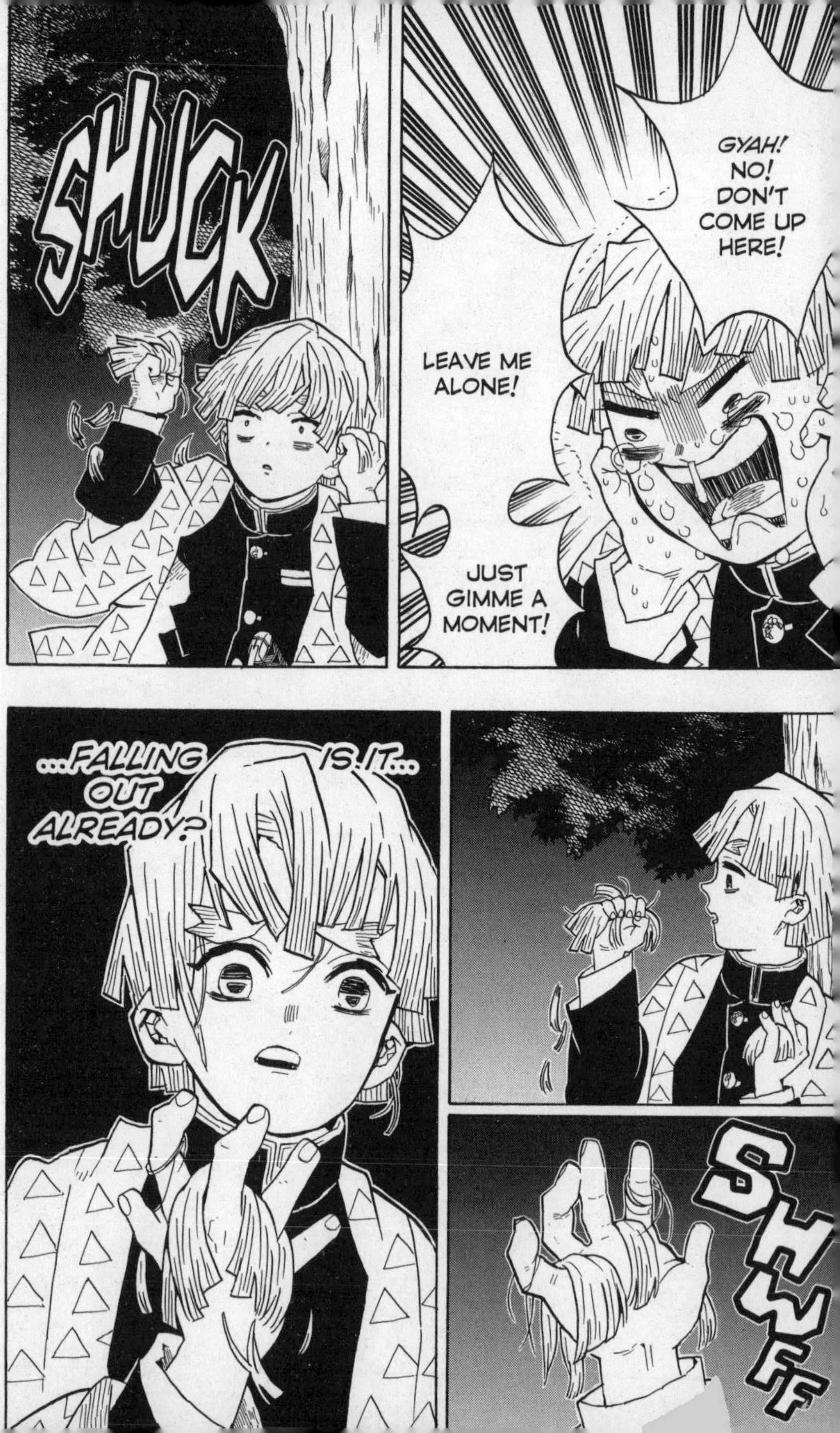
GYAH! NO! DON'T COME UP HERE!
LEAVE ME ALONE!
JUST GIMME A MOMENT!
SHUCK
SHWFF
IS IT...
...FALLING OUT ALREADY?

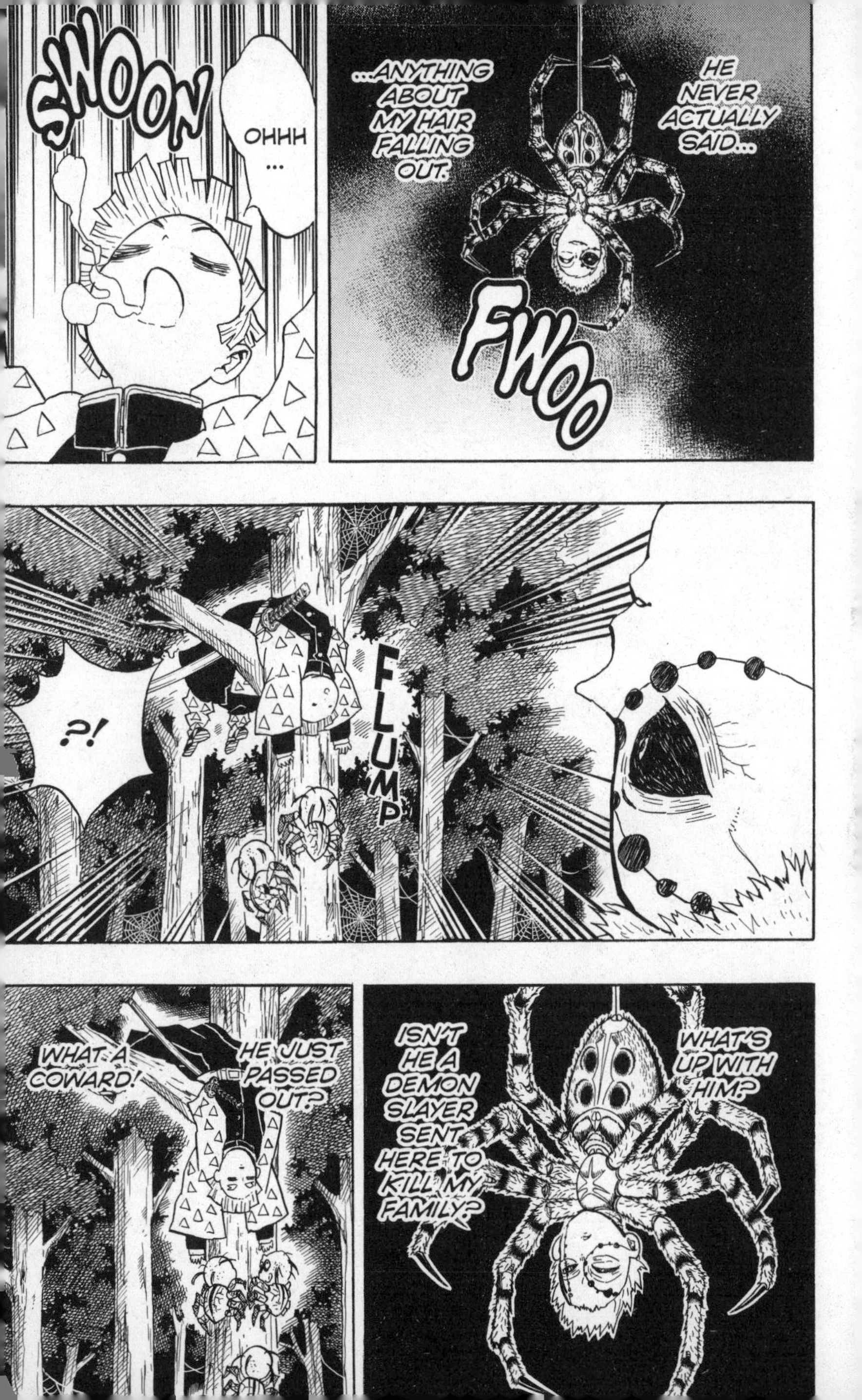
HE NEVER ACTUALLY SAID...
...ANYTHING ABOUT MY HAIR FALLING OUT.
FWOO
SWOON
OHHH ...
FLUMP
?!
WHAT'S UP WITH HIM?
ISN'T HE A DEMON SLAYER SENT HERE TO KILL MY FAMILY?
HE JUST PASSED OUT?
WHAT A COWARD!

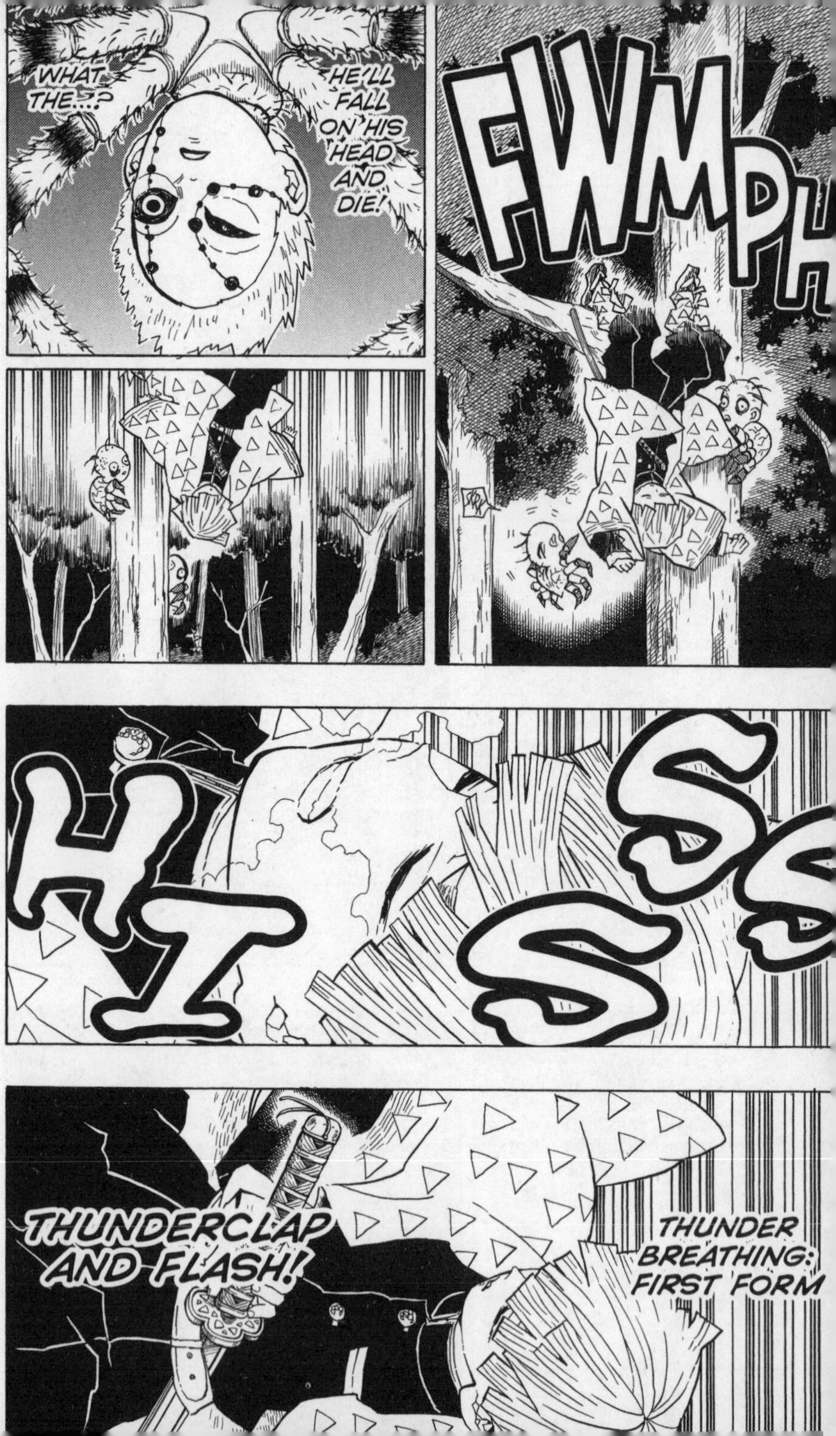
FWMPH
HE'LL FALL ON HIS HEAD AND DIE!
WHAT THE...?
HISSS
THUNDER BREATHING: FIRST FORM
THUNDERCLAP AND FLASH!

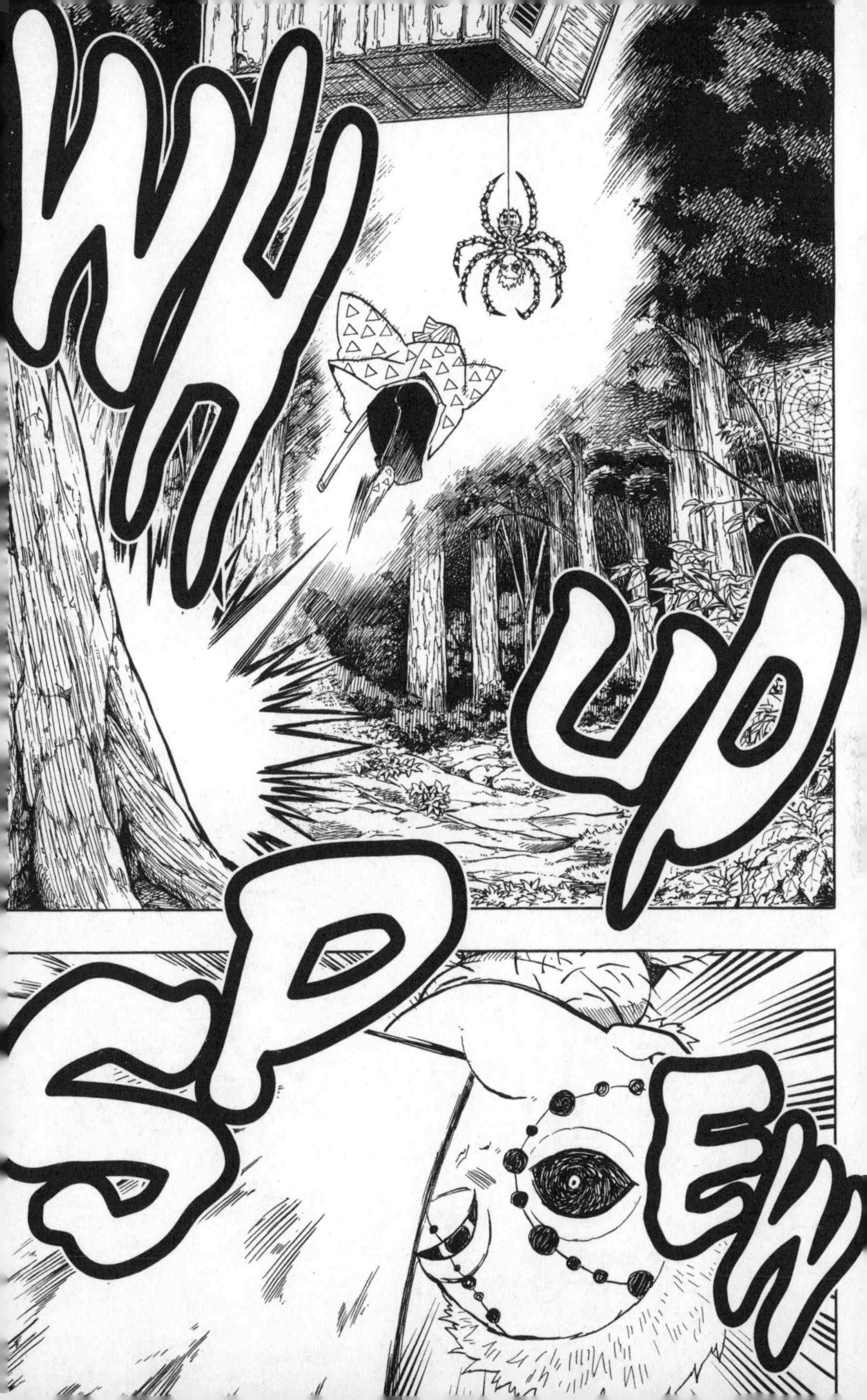
WHUP
SPEW

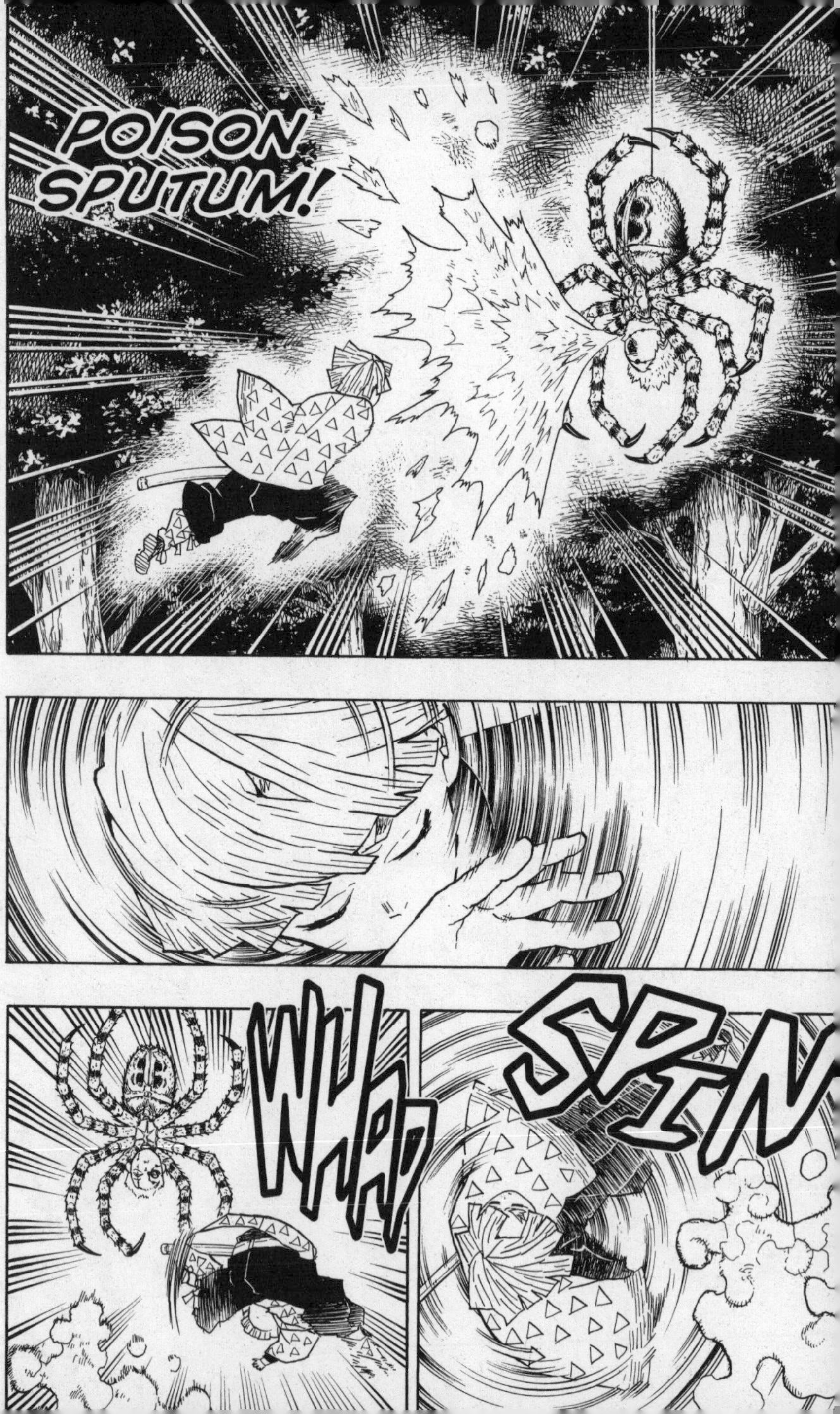
POISON SPUTUM!
SPIN
WHP

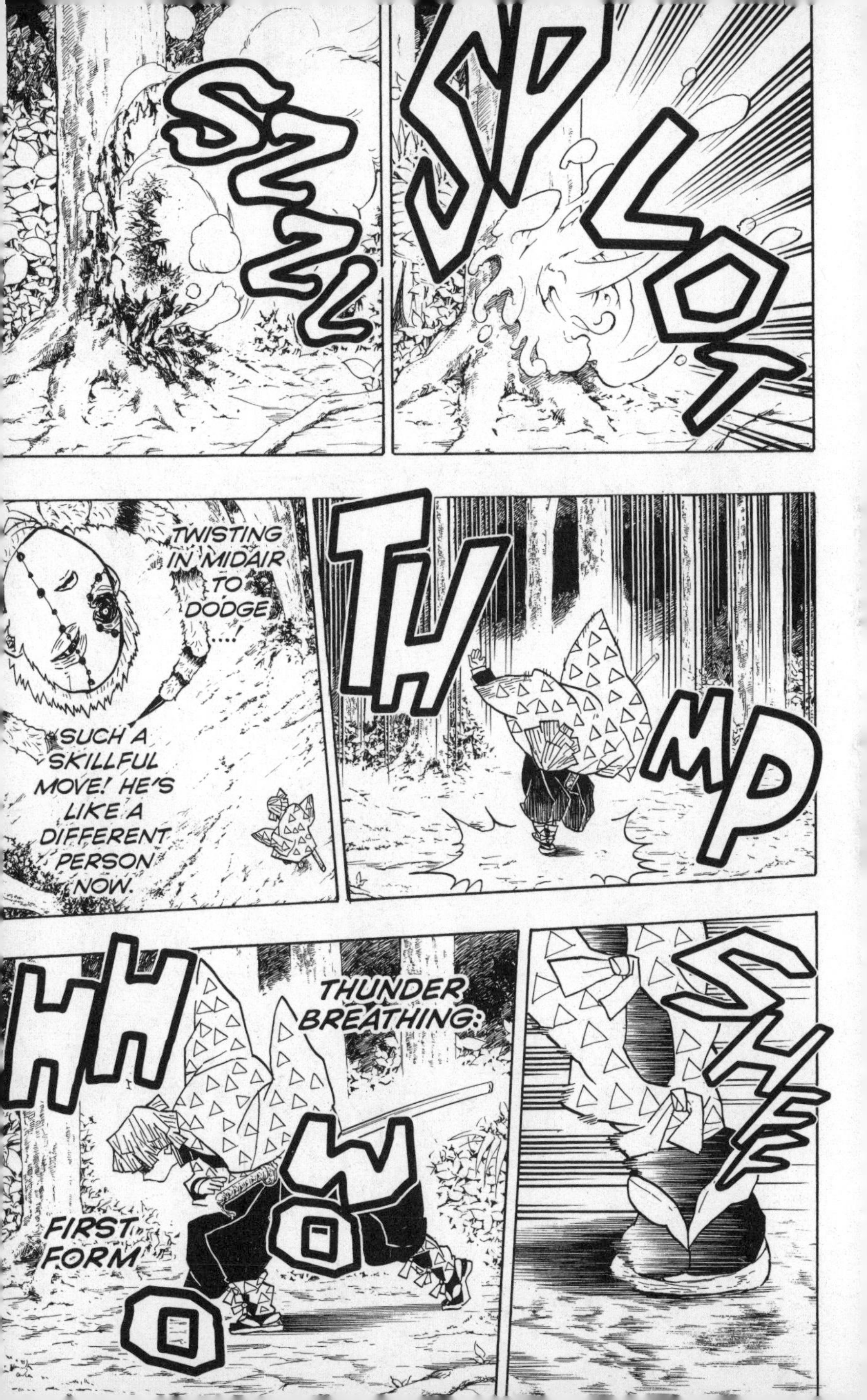
THUMP
TWISTING IN MIDAIR TO DODGE...!
SUCH A SKILLFUL MOVE! HE'S LIKE A DIFFERENT PERSON NOW.
THUNDER BREATHING:
FIRST FORM

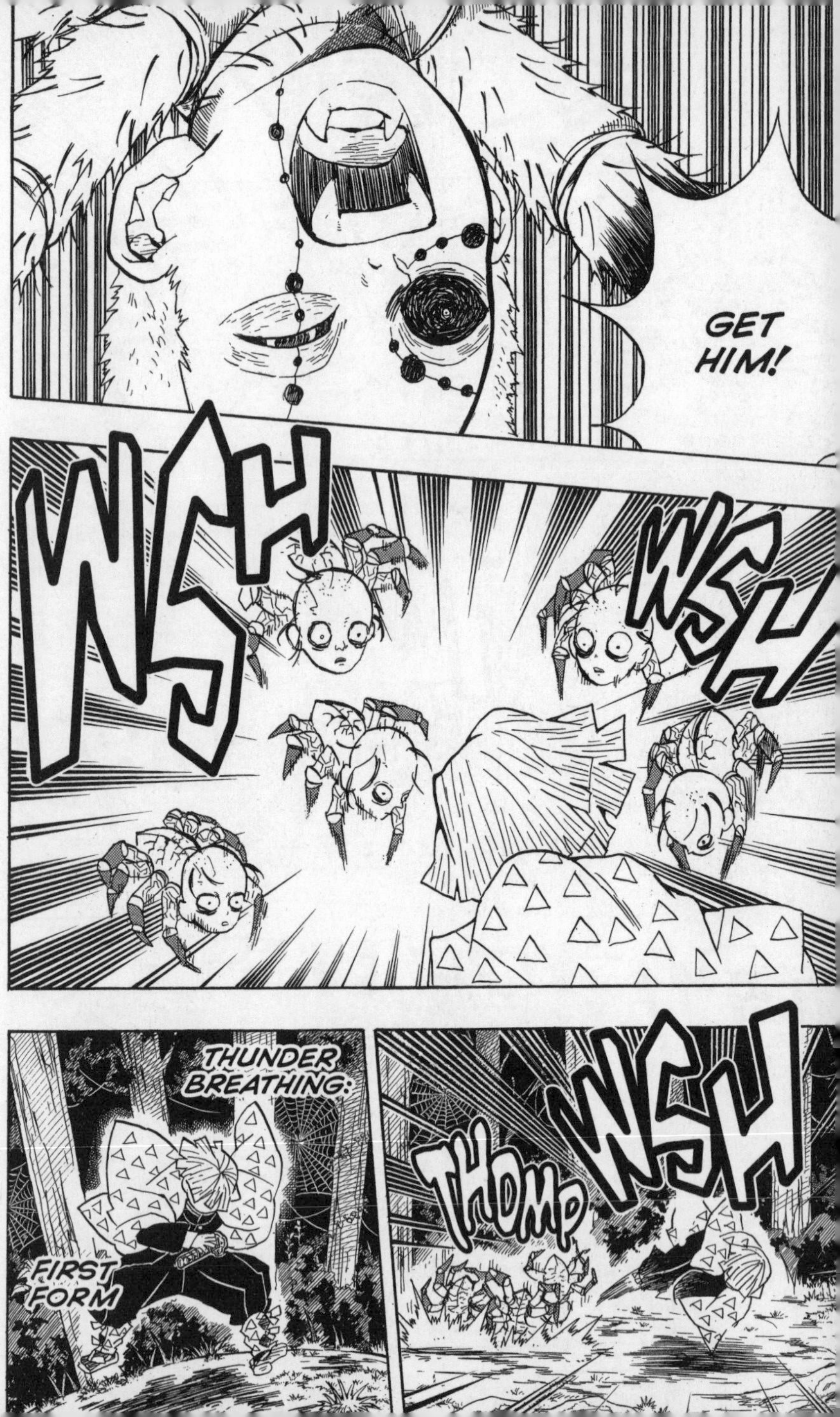
GET HIM!
WSH
WSH
WSH
THOMP
THUNDER BREATHING:
FIRST FORM

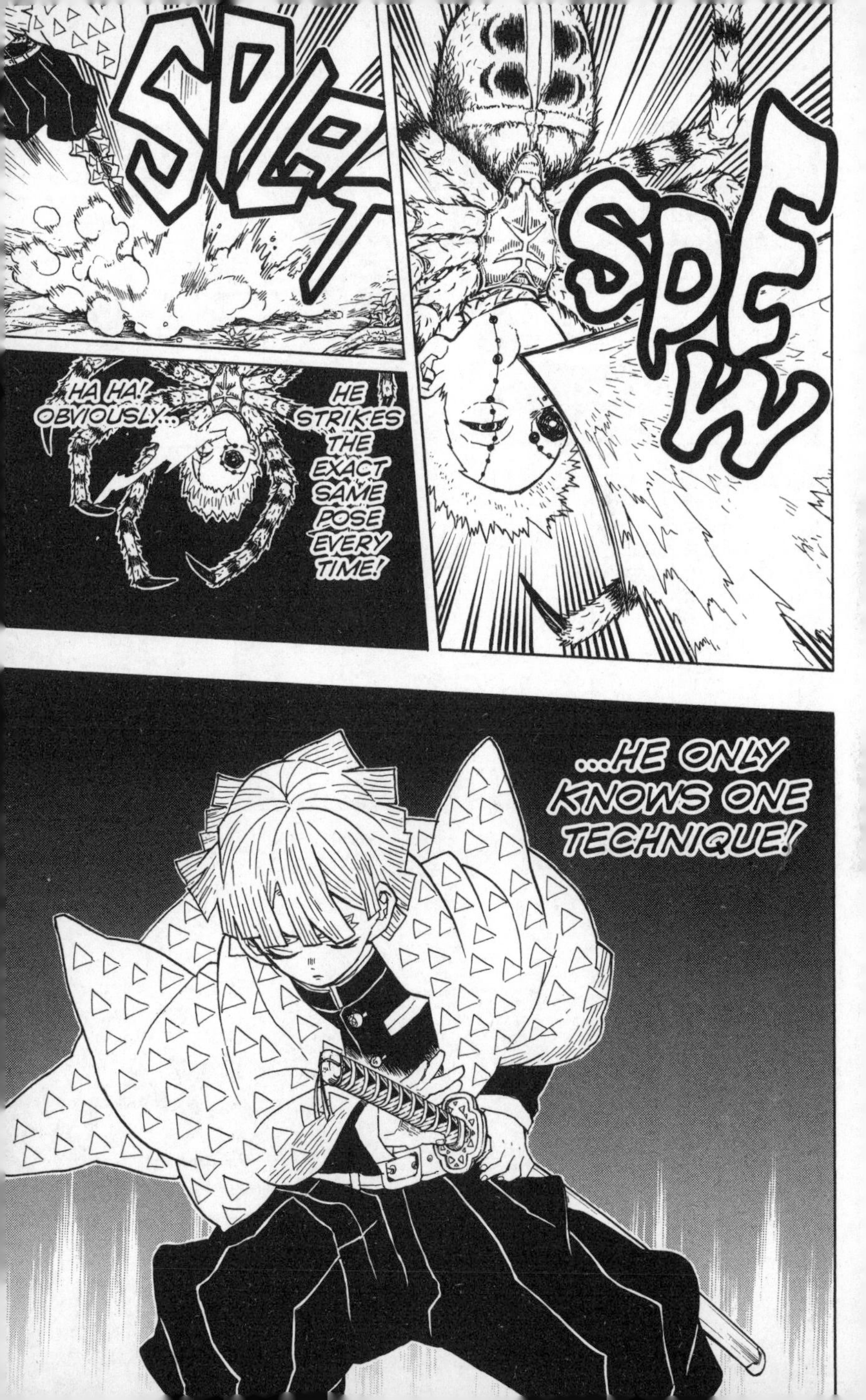
SPEW
SPLAT
HE STRIKES THE EXACT SAME POSE EVERY TIME!
HA HA! OBVIOUSLY...
...HE ONLY KNOWS ONE TECHNIQUE!

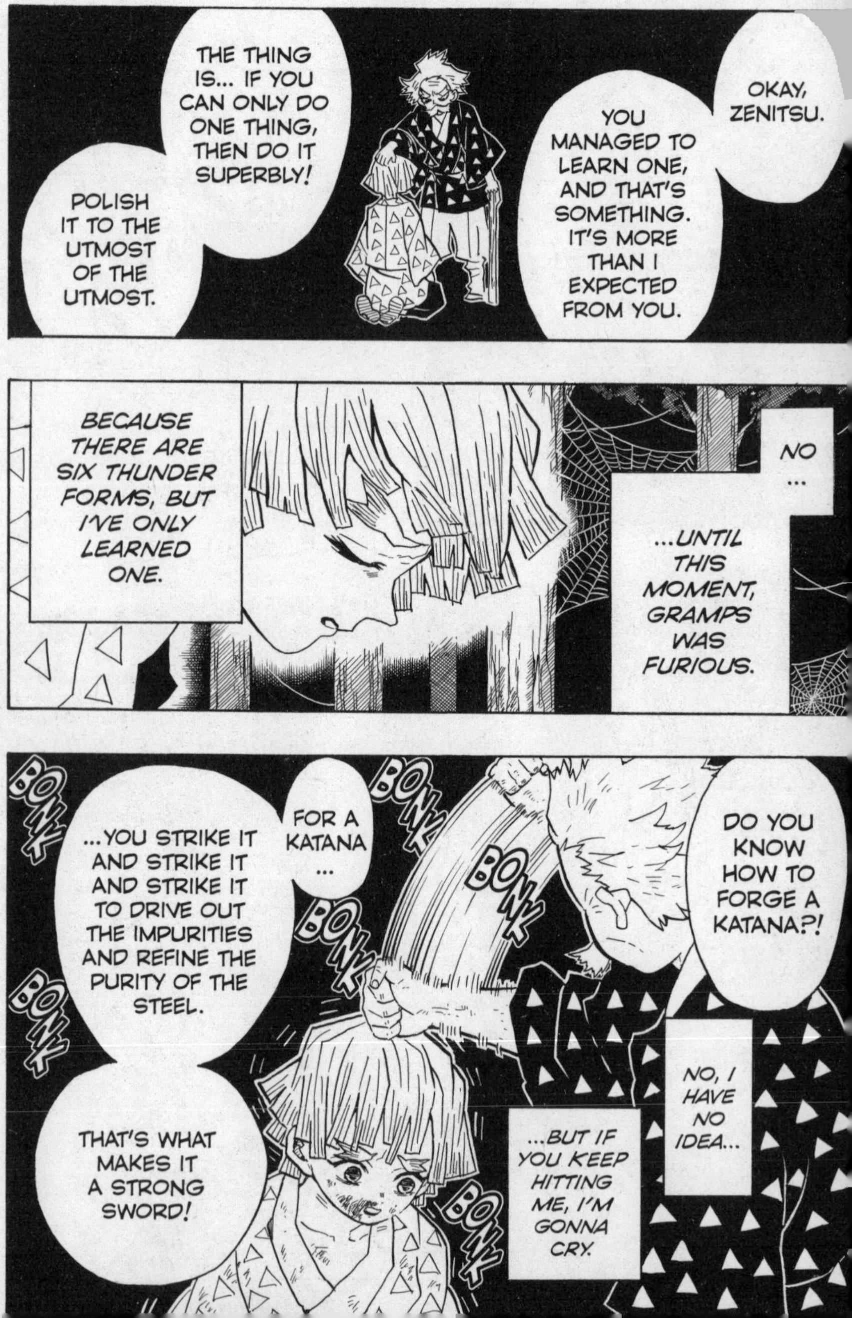
OKAY, ZENITSU.
YOU MANAGED TO LEARN ONE, AND THAT'S SOMETHING. IT'S MORE THAN I EXPECTED FROM YOU.
THE THING IS... IF YOU CAN ONLY DO ONE THING, THEN DO IT SUPERBLY!
POLISH IT TO THE UTMOST OF THE UTMOST.
NO ...
...UNTIL THIS MOMENT, GRAMPS WAS FURIOUS.
BECAUSE THERE ARE SIX THUNDER FORMS, BUT I'VE ONLY LEARNED ONE.
BONK
BONK
DO YOU KNOW HOW TO FORGE A KATANA?!
BONK
BONK
FOR A KATANA ...
...YOU STRIKE IT AND STRIKE IT AND STRIKE IT TO DRIVE OUT THE IMPURITIES AND REFINE THE PURITY OF THE STEEL.
BONK
BONK
NO, I HAVE NO IDEA...
...BUT IF YOU KEEP HITTING ME, I'M GONNA CRY.
BONK
THAT'S WHAT MAKES IT A STRONG SWORD!

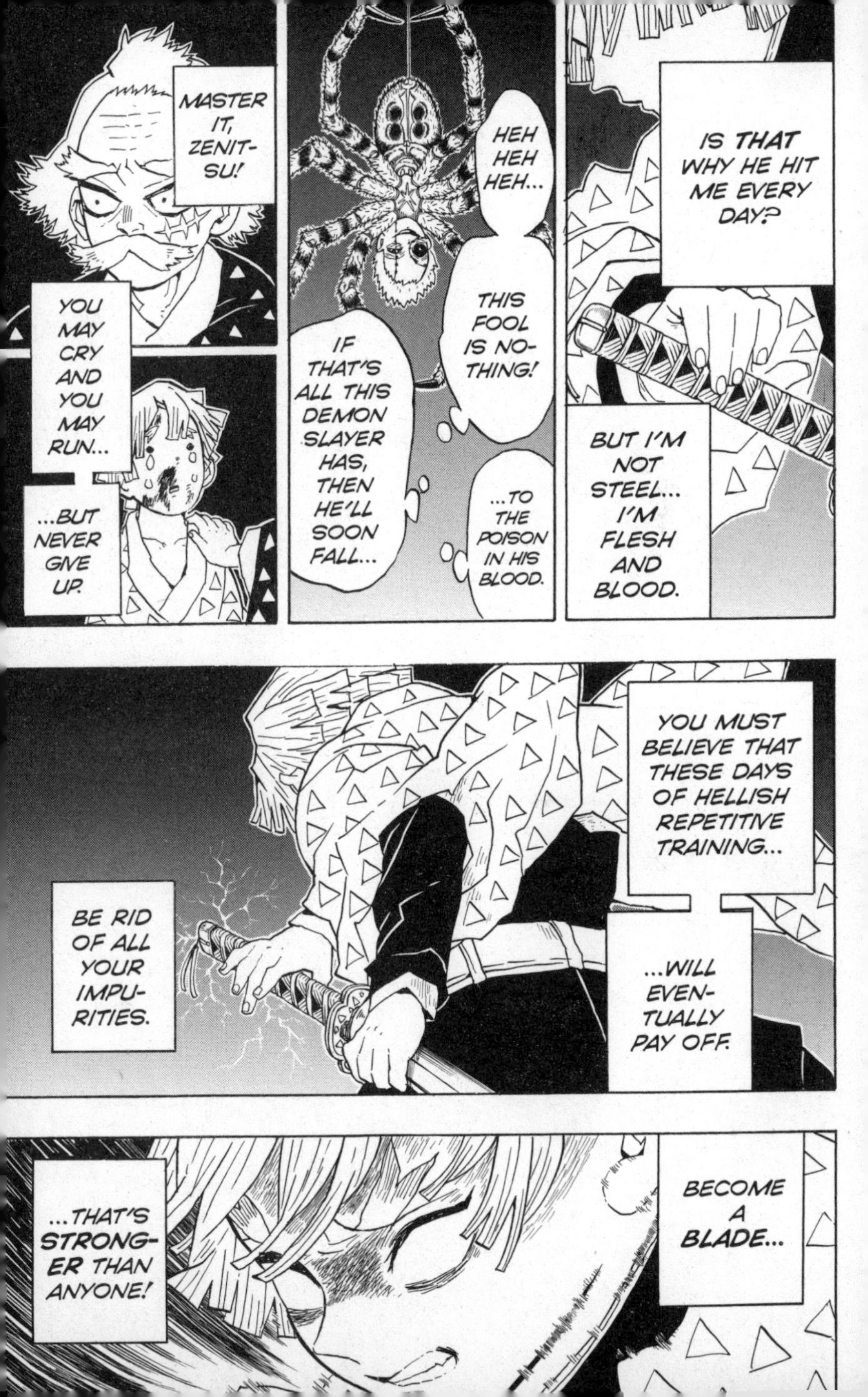
IS THAT WHY HE HIT ME EVERY DAY?
BUT I'M NOT STEEL... I'M FLESH AND BLOOD.
HEH HEH HEH...
THIS FOOL IS NOTHING!
IF THAT'S ALL THIS DEMON SLAYER HAS, THEN HE'LL SOON FALL...
...TO THE POISON IN HIS BLOOD.
MASTER IT, ZENITSU!
YOU MAY CRY AND YOU MAY RUN...
...BUT NEVER GIVE UP.
YOU MUST BELIEVE THAT THESE DAYS OF HELLISH REPETITIVE TRAINING...
...WILL EVENTUALLY PAY OFF.
BE RID OF ALL YOUR IMPURITIES.
BECOME A BLADE...
...THAT'S STRONGER THAN ANYONE!

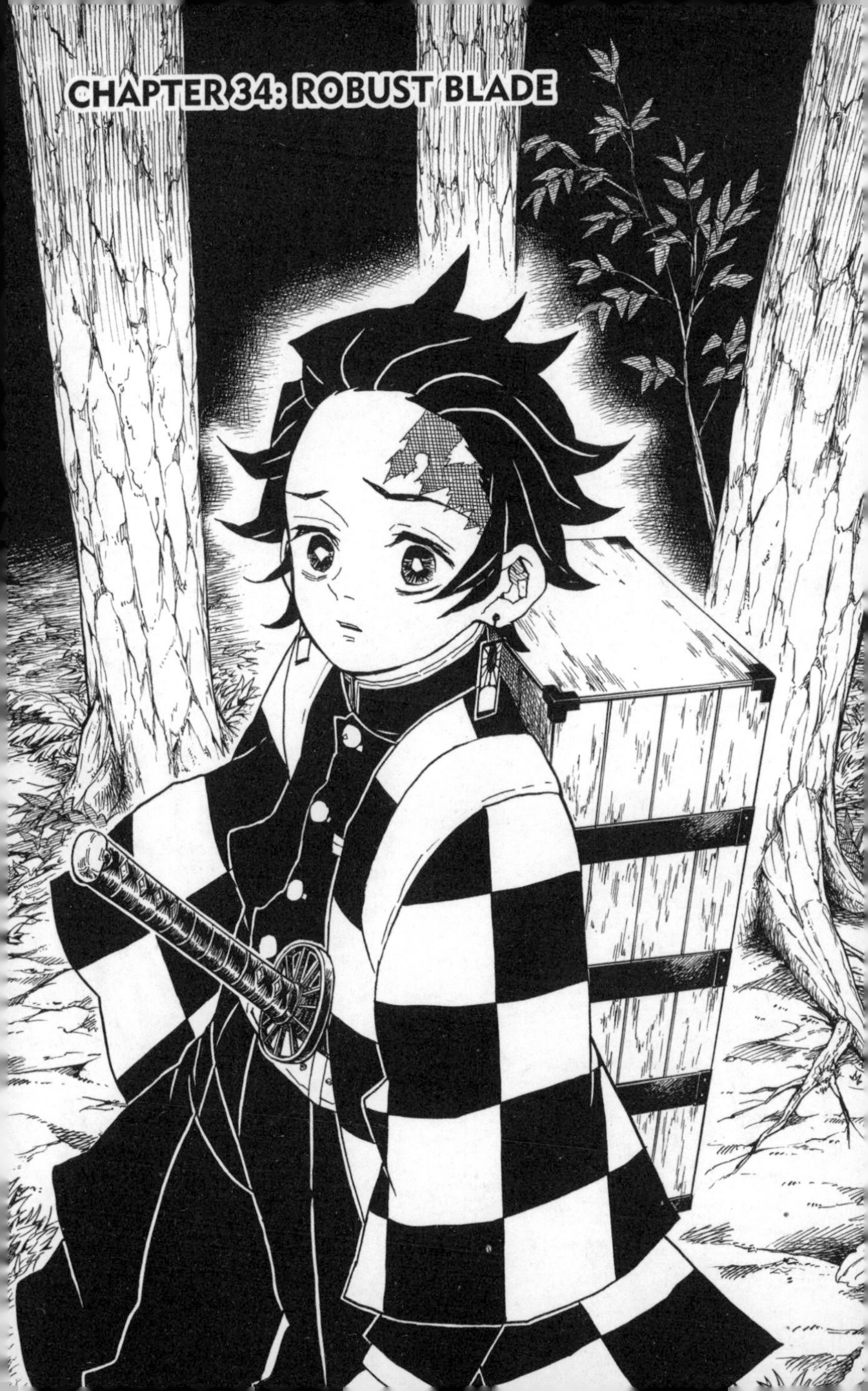
CHAPTER 34: ROBUST BLADE

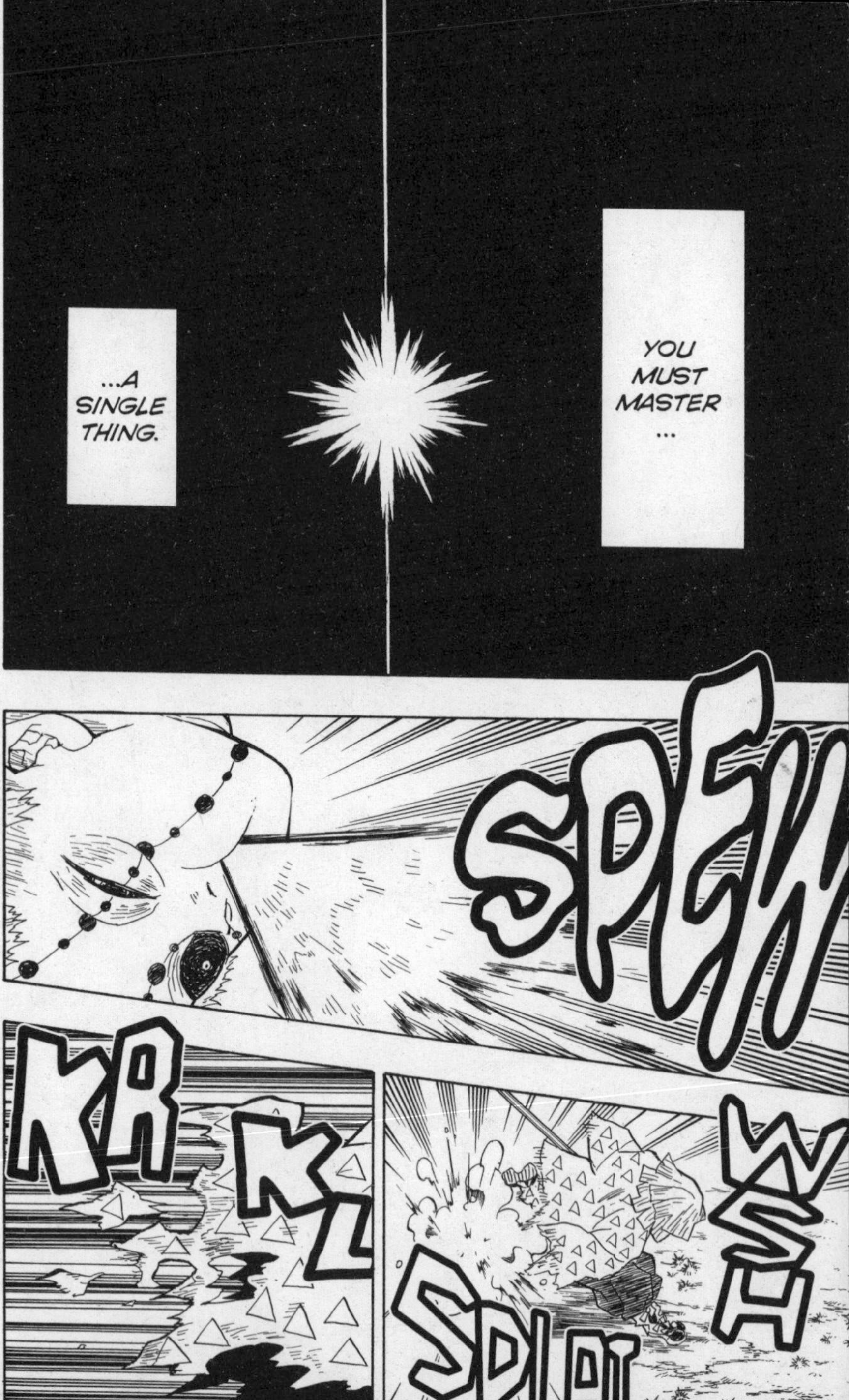
YOU MUST MASTER ...
...A SINGLE THING.
KRKL

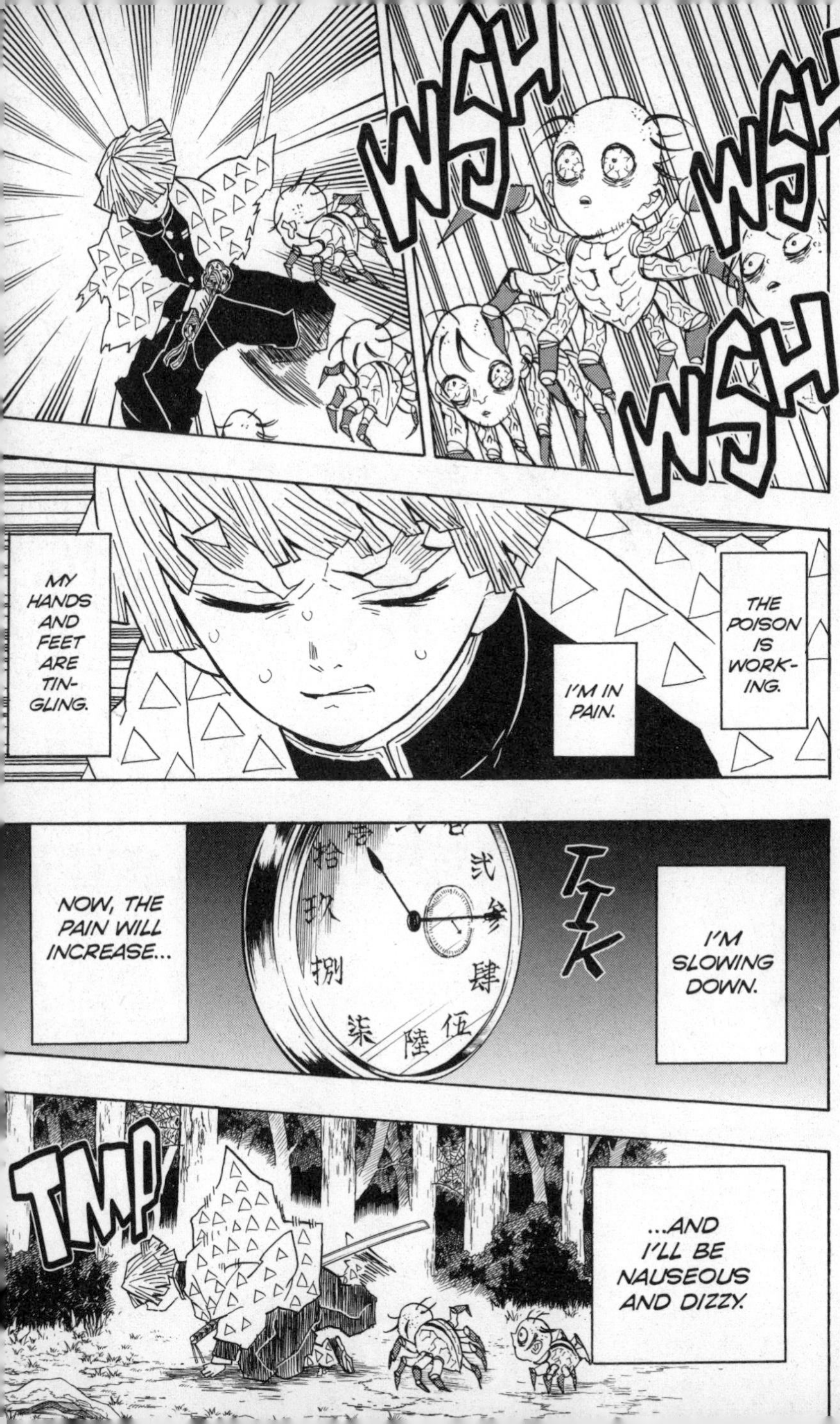
WSH WSH WSH
WSH
THE POISON IS WORKING.
I'M IN PAIN.
MY HANDS AND FEET ARE TINGLING.
I'M SLOWING DOWN.
TIK
NOW, THE PAIN WILL INCREASE...
...AND I'LL BE NAUSEOUS AND DIZZY.
TMP

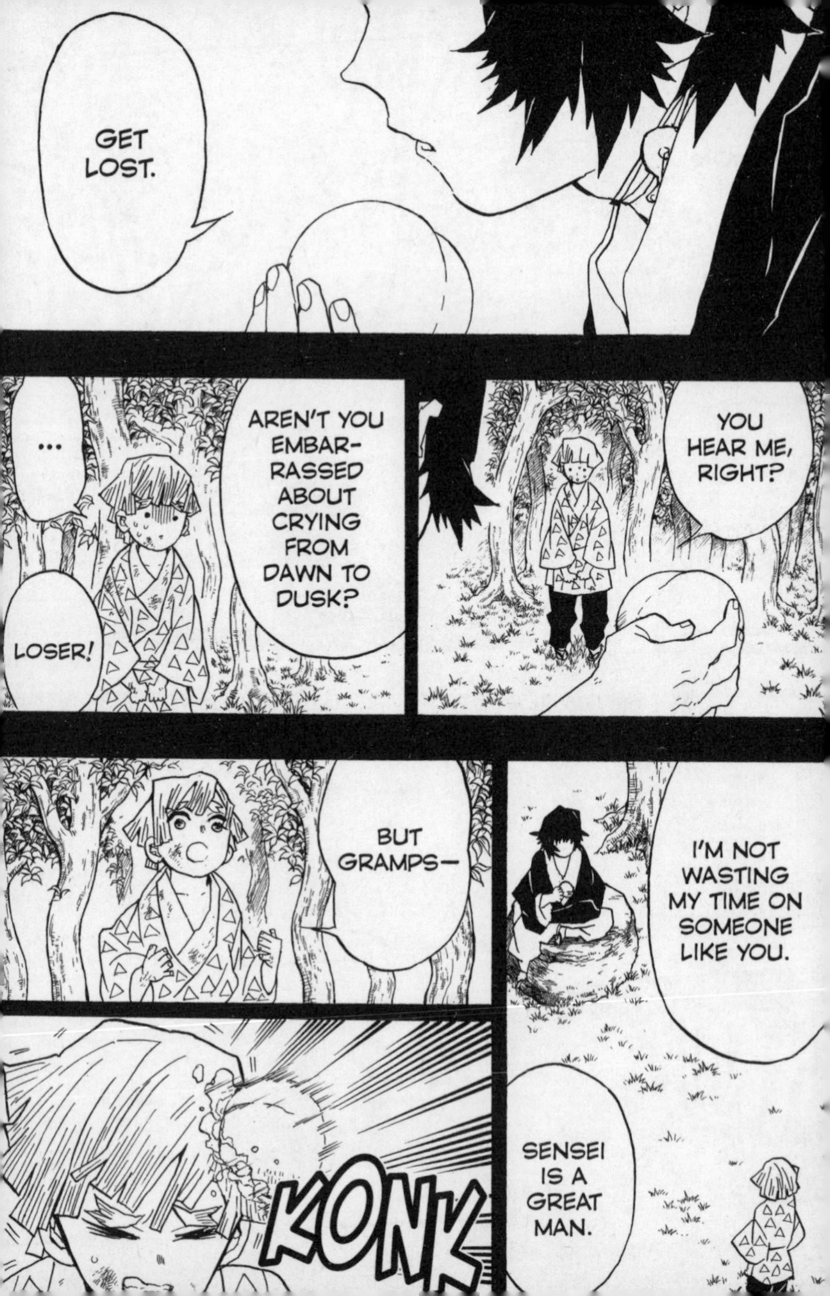
GET LOST.
YOU HEAR ME, RIGHT?
AREN'T YOU EMBAR-RASSED ABOUT CRYING FROM DAWN TO DUSK?
...
LOSER!
I'M NOT WASTING MY TIME ON SOMEONE LIKE YOU.
SENSEI IS A GREAT MAN.
BUT GRAMPS—
KONK

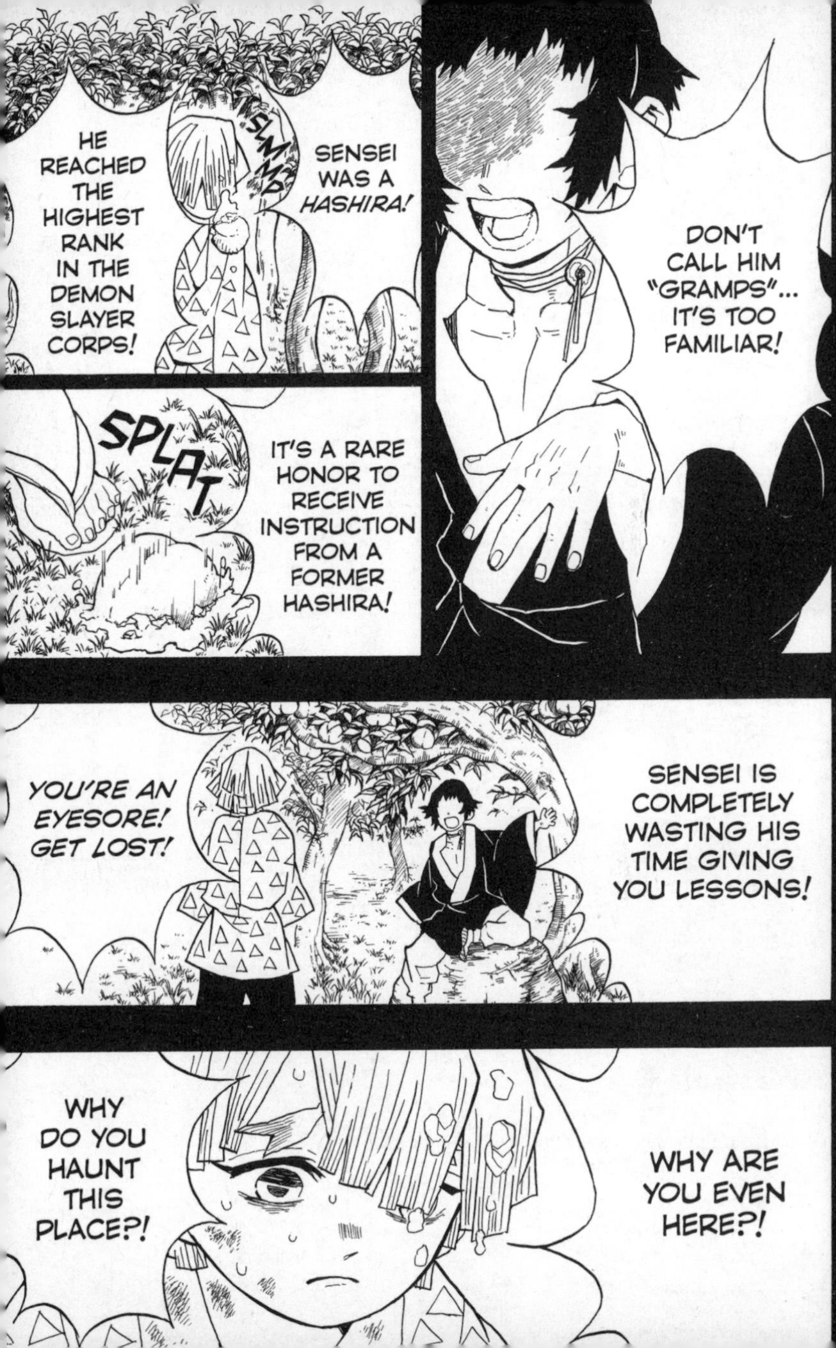
DON'T CALL HIM "GRAMPS"... IT'S TOO FAMILIAR!
SENSEI WAS A *HASHIRA!*
SLMMP
HE REACHED THE HIGHEST RANK IN THE DEMON SLAYER CORPS!
IT'S A RARE HONOR TO RECEIVE INSTRUCTION FROM A FORMER HASHIRA!
SPLAT
SENSEI IS COMPLETELY WASTING HIS TIME GIVING YOU LESSONS!
YOU'RE AN EYESORE! GET LOST!
WHY ARE YOU EVEN HERE?!
WHY DO YOU HAUNT THIS PLACE?!

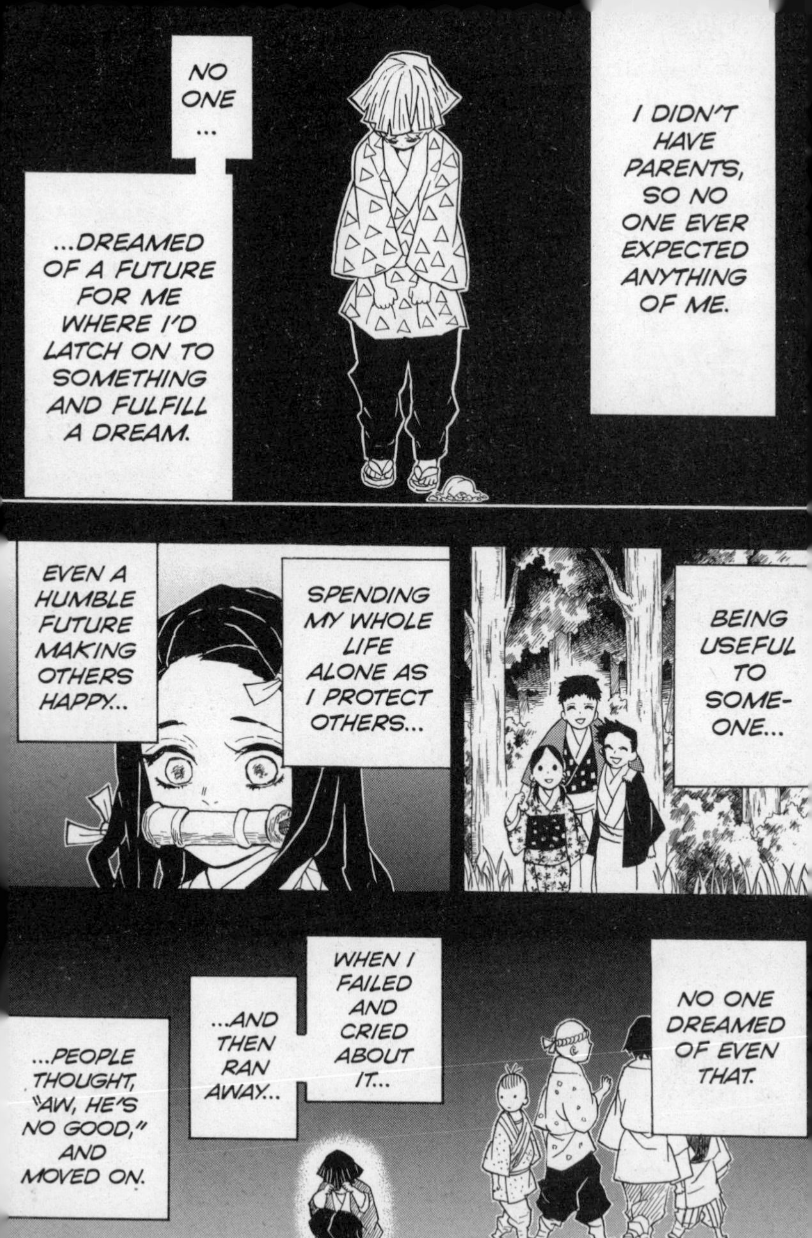
I DIDN'T HAVE PARENTS, SO NO ONE EVER EXPECTED ANYTHING OF ME.
NO ONE ...
...DREAMED OF A FUTURE FOR ME WHERE I'D LATCH ON TO SOMETHING AND FULFILL A DREAM.
BEING USEFUL TO SOME-ONE...
SPENDING MY WHOLE LIFE ALONE AS I PROTECT OTHERS...
EVEN A HUMBLE FUTURE MAKING OTHERS HAPPY...
NO ONE DREAMED OF EVEN THAT.
WHEN I FAILED AND CRIED ABOUT IT...
...AND THEN RAN AWAY...
...PEOPLE THOUGHT, "AW, HE'S NO GOOD," AND MOVED ON.

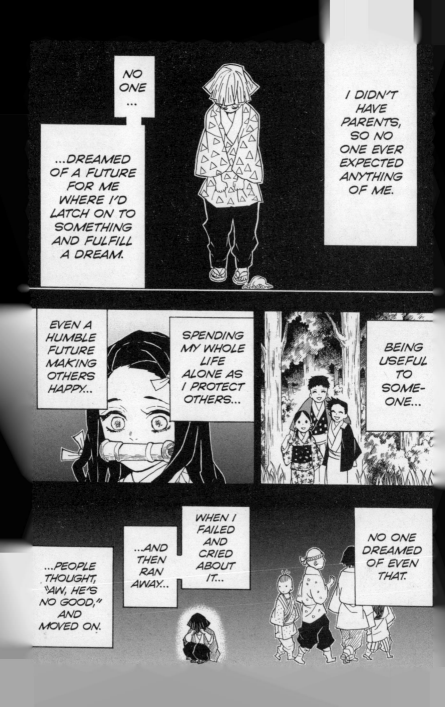

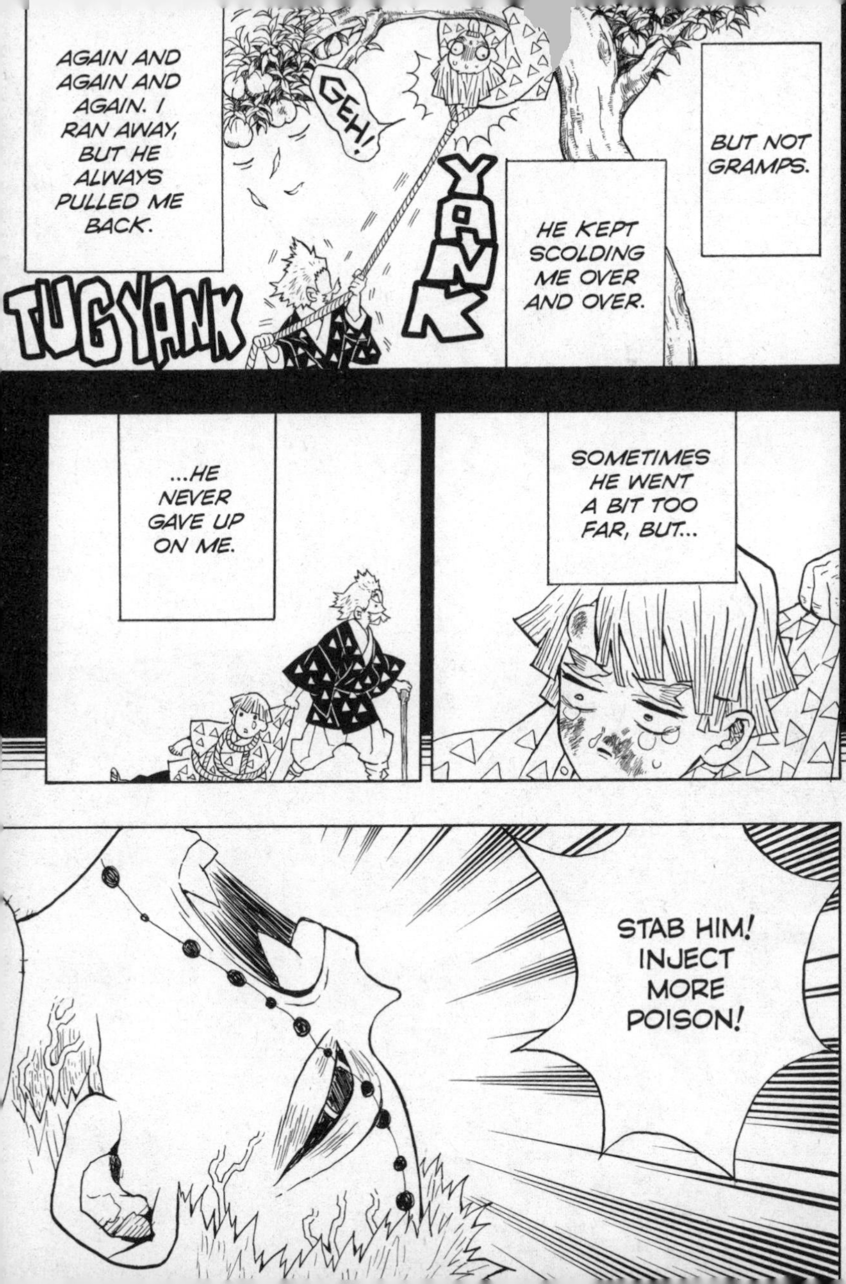
BUT NOT GRAMPS.
HE KEPT SCOLDING ME OVER AND OVER.
GEH!
YANK
AGAIN AND AGAIN AND AGAIN. I RAN AWAY, BUT HE ALWAYS PULLED ME BACK.
TUG YANK
SOMETIMES HE WENT A BIT TOO FAR, BUT...
...HE NEVER GAVE UP ON ME.
STAB HIM! INJECT MORE POISON!

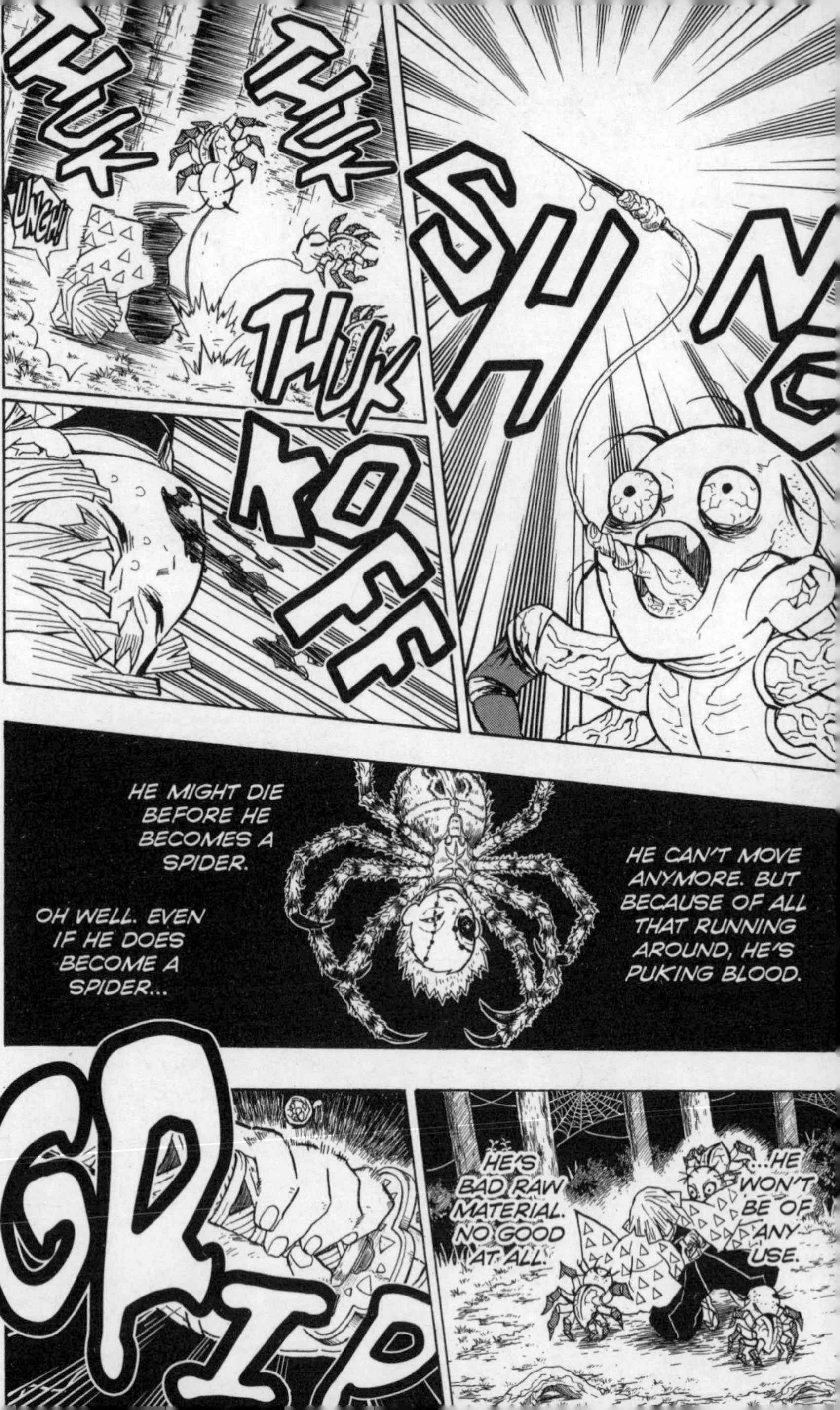
SHING
THUK
THUK
UNGH!
THUK
KOFF
HE CAN'T MOVE ANYMORE. BUT BECAUSE OF ALL THAT RUNNING AROUND, HE'S PUKING BLOOD.
HE MIGHT DIE BEFORE HE BECOMES A SPIDER.
OH WELL. EVEN IF HE DOES BECOME A SPIDER...
...HE WON'T BE OF ANY USE.
HE'S BAD RAW MATERIAL. NO GOOD AT ALL.
GRIP

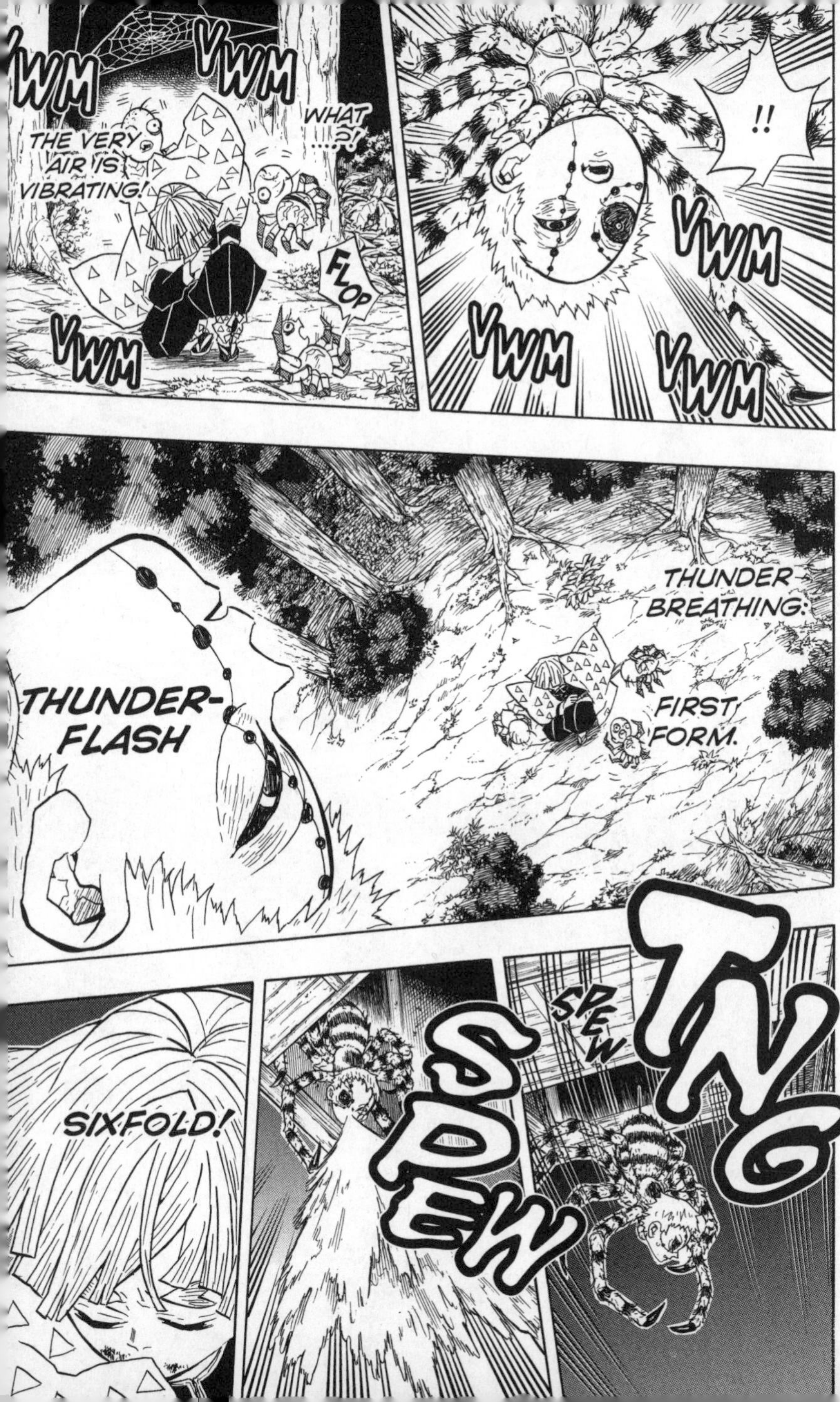
!!
VWM
VWM
VWM
VWM
VWM
THE VERY AIR IS VIBRATING!
WHAT ...?!
FLOP
VWM
THUNDER BREATHING:
FIRST FORM.
THUNDER-FLASH
TNG
SPEW
SPEW
SIXFOLD!

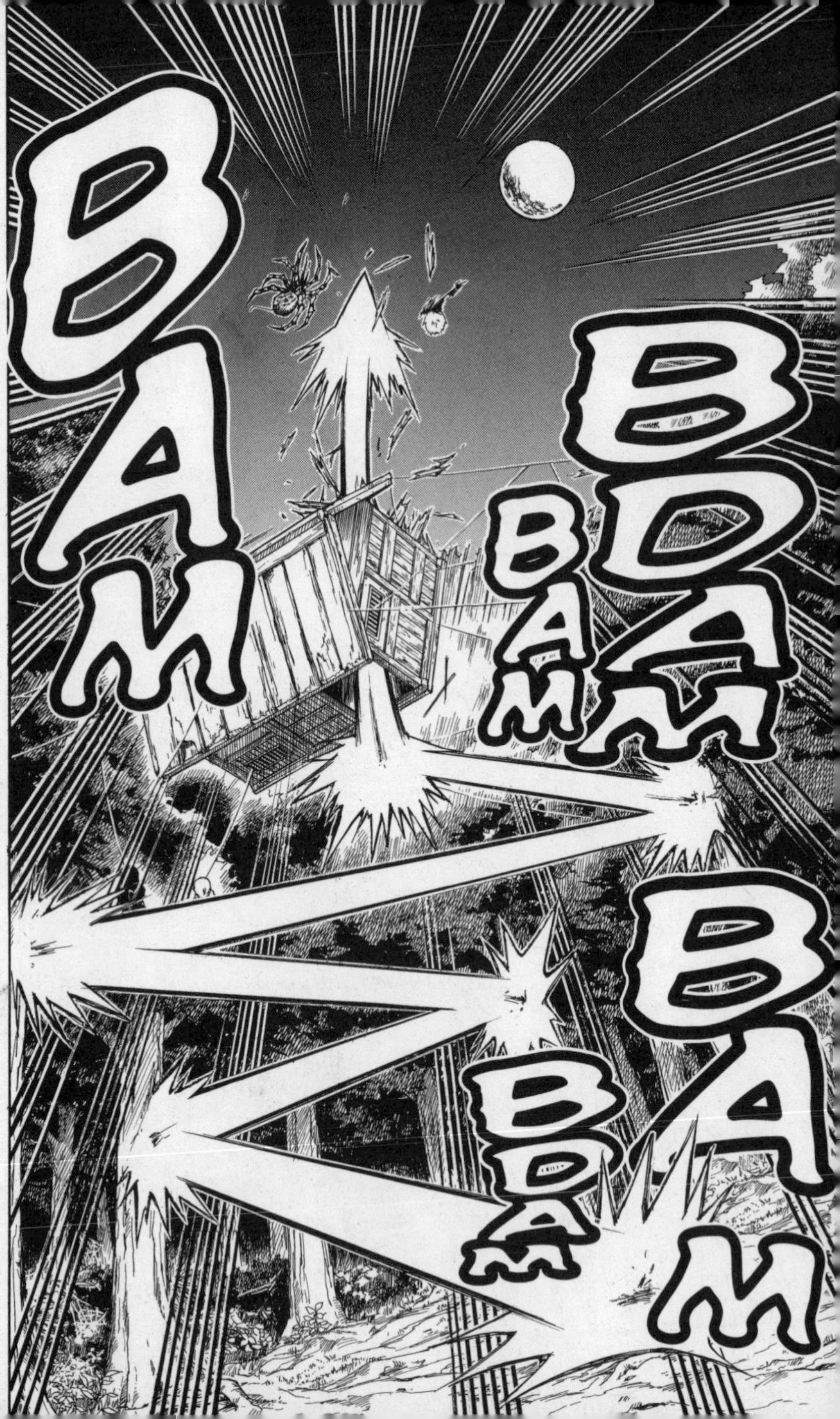
BDAM
BAM
BAM
BDAM
BAM

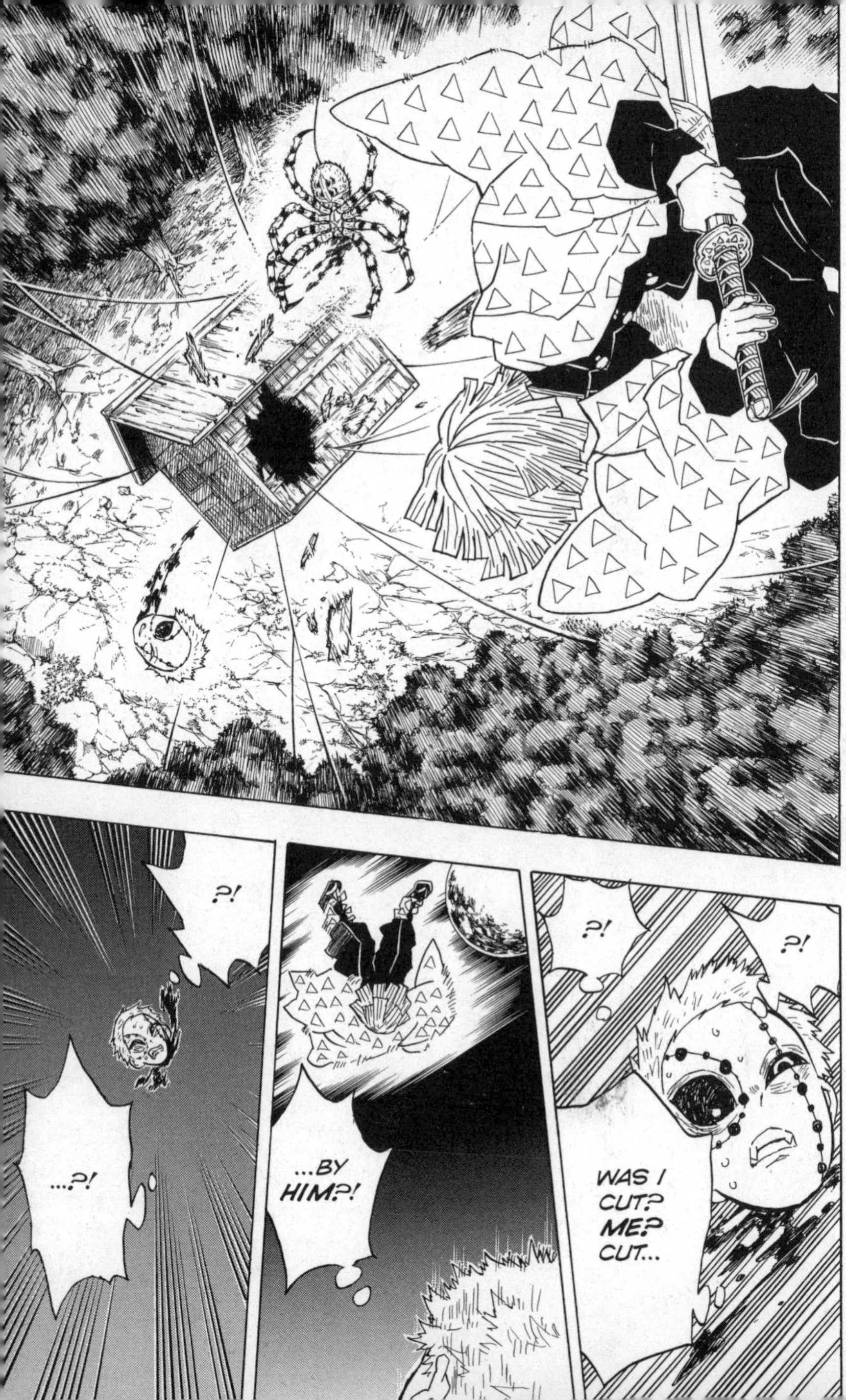
?!
?!
WAS I CUT? ME? CUT...
...BY HIM?!
?!
...?!

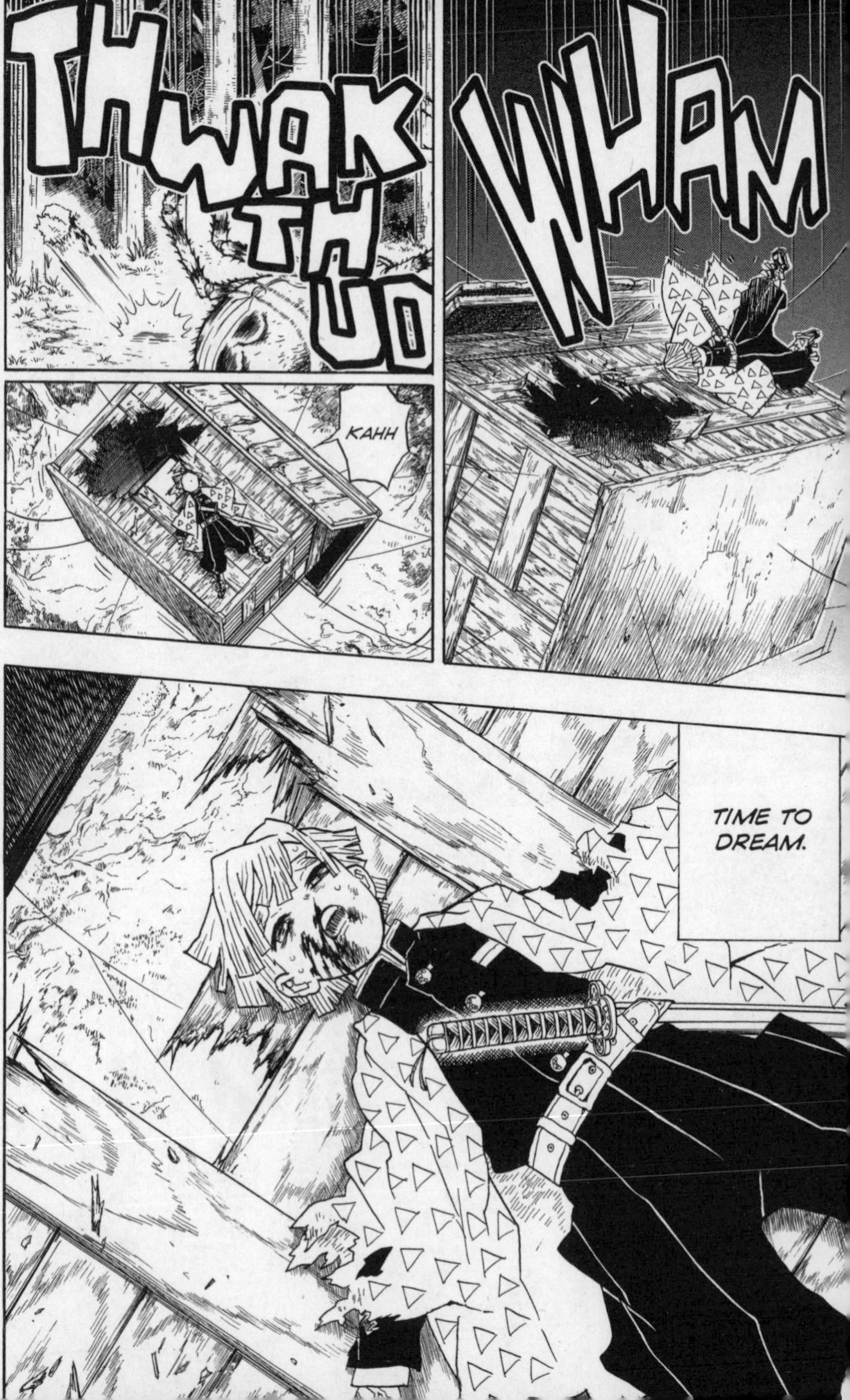
WHAM
THWAK
THUD
KAHH
TIME TO DREAM.

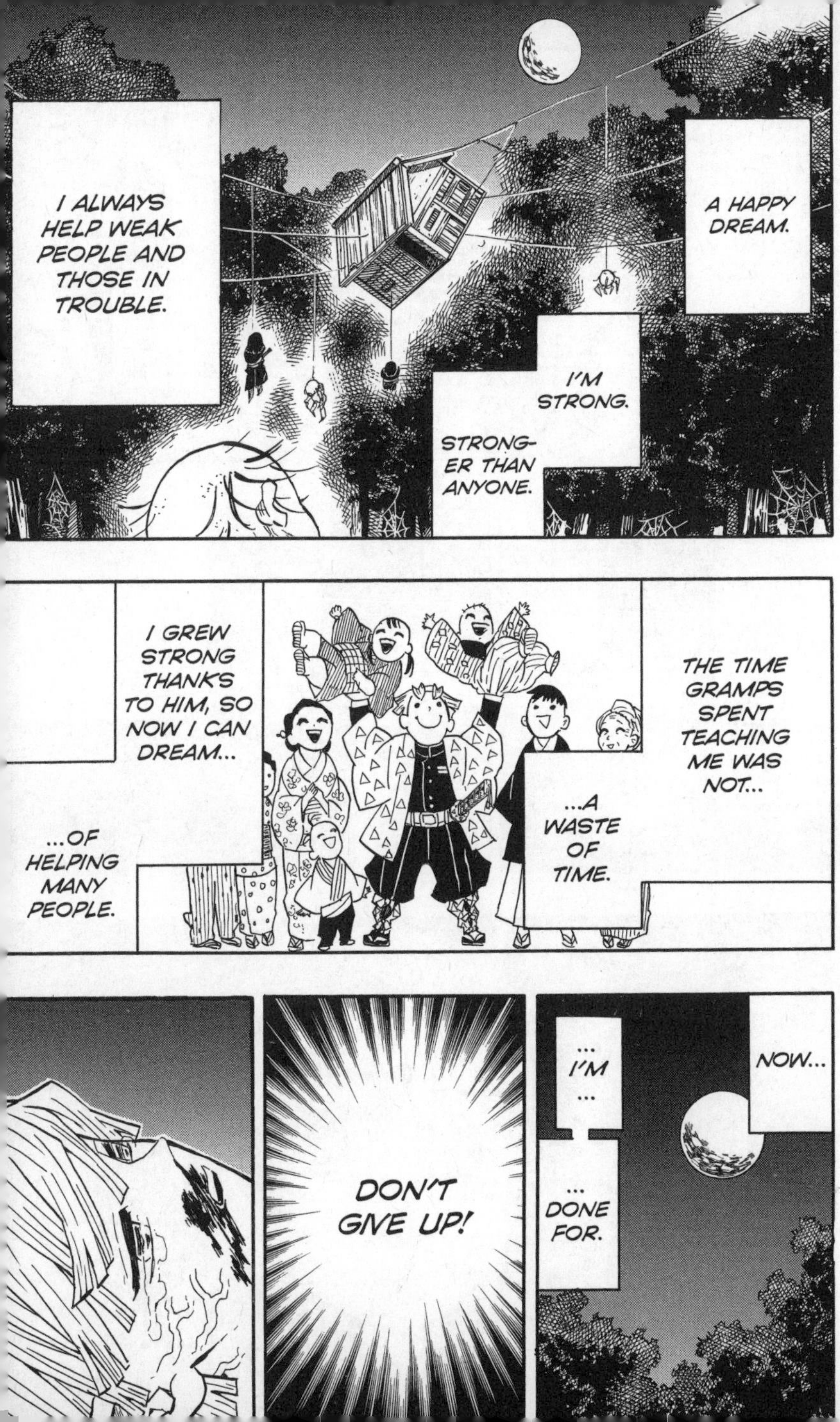
A HAPPY DREAM.
I'M STRONG.
STRONGER THAN ANYONE.
I ALWAYS HELP WEAK PEOPLE AND THOSE IN TROUBLE.
THE TIME GRAMPS SPENT TEACHING ME WAS NOT...
...A WASTE OF TIME.
I GREW STRONG THANKS TO HIM, SO NOW I CAN DREAM...
...OF HELPING MANY PEOPLE.
NOW...
...I'M...
...DONE FOR.
DON'T GIVE UP!

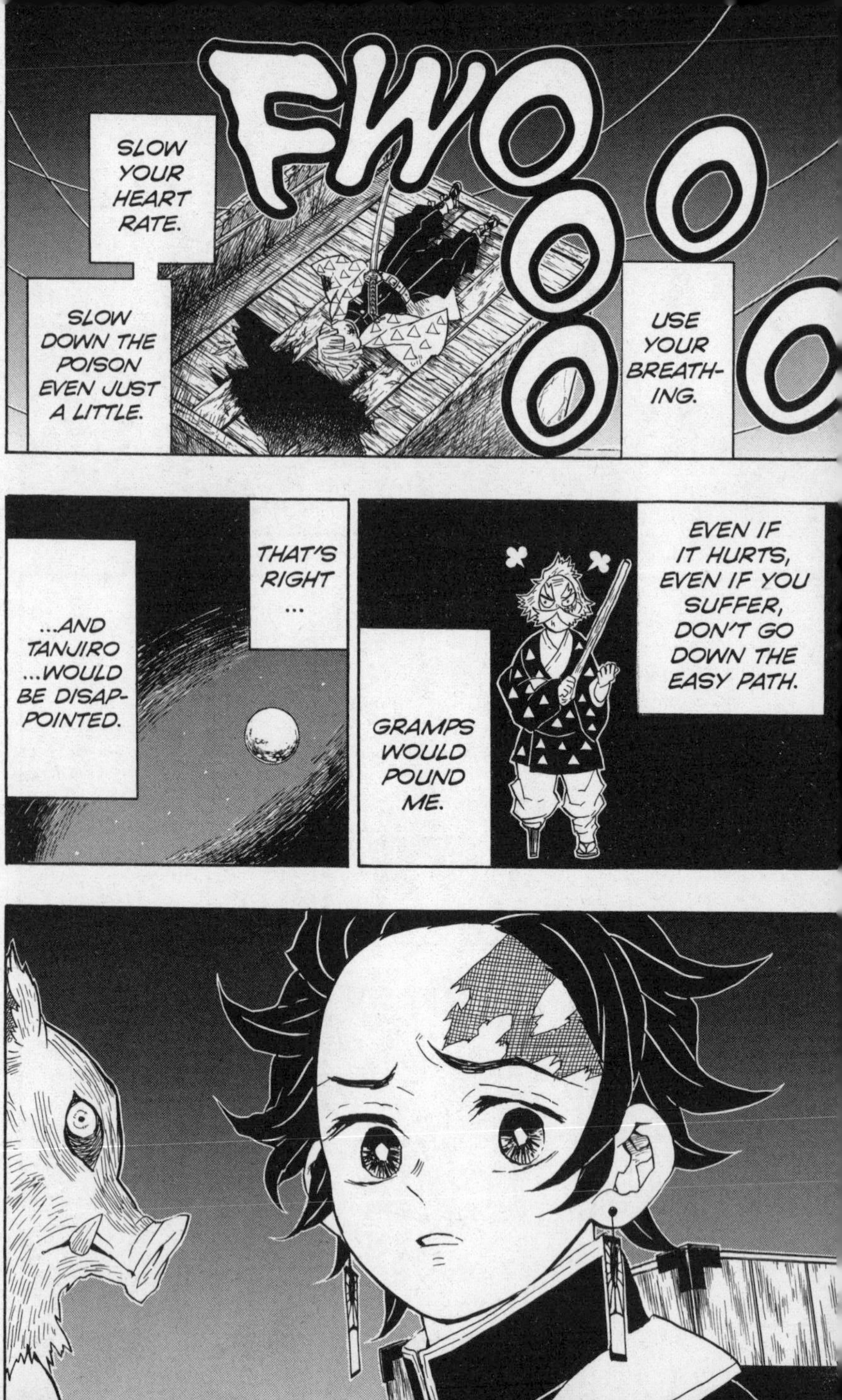
FWOOOOO
USE YOUR BREATHING.
SLOW YOUR HEART RATE.
SLOW DOWN THE POISON EVEN JUST A LITTLE.
EVEN IF IT HURTS, EVEN IF YOU SUFFER, DON'T GO DOWN THE EASY PATH.
GRAMPS WOULD POUND ME.
THAT'S RIGHT ...
...AND TANJIRO ...WOULD BE DISAPPOINTED.

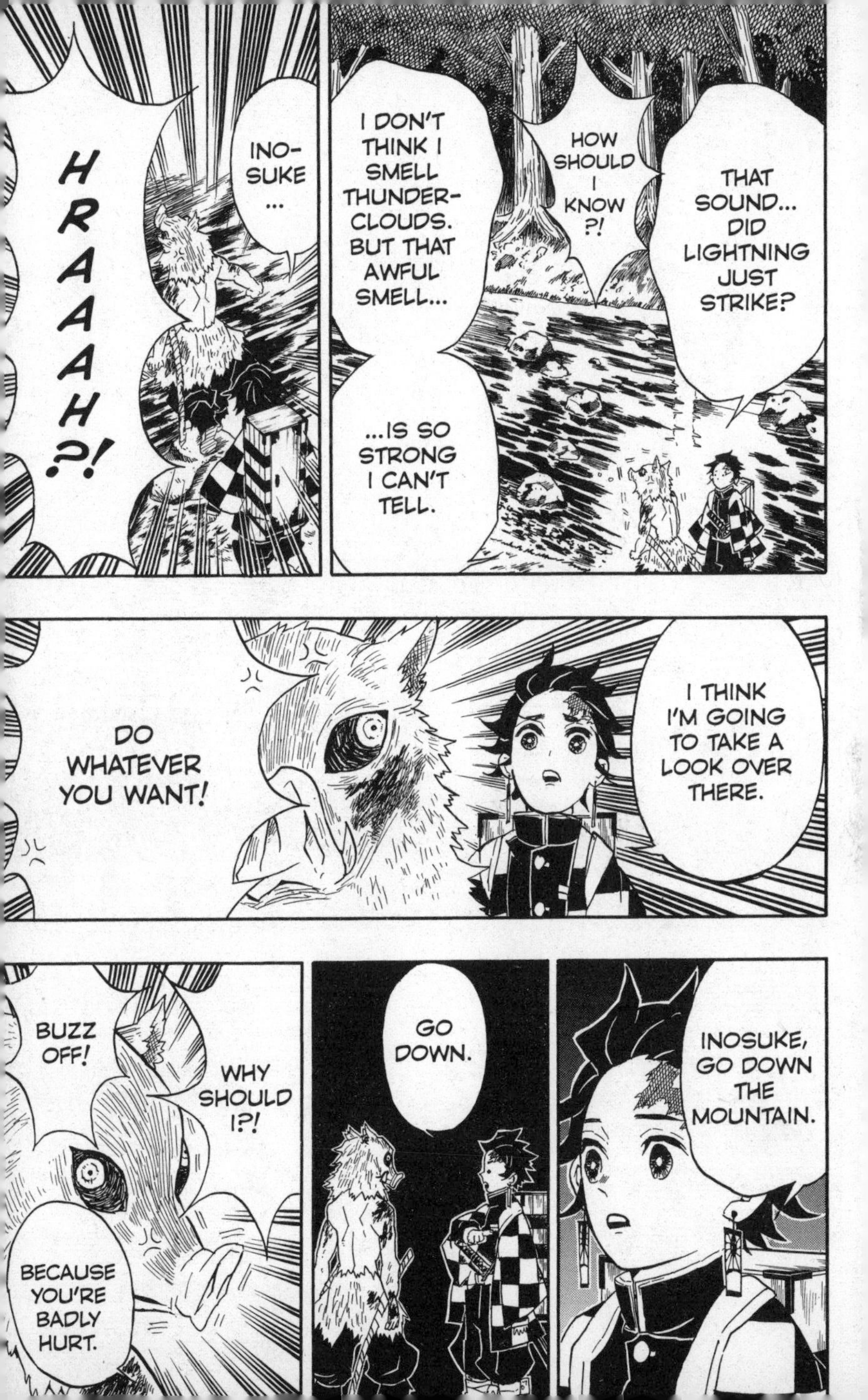
THAT SOUND... DID LIGHTNING JUST STRIKE?
HOW SHOULD I KNOW?!
I DON'T THINK I SMELL THUNDER-CLOUDS. BUT THAT AWFUL SMELL...
...IS SO STRONG I CAN'T TELL.
INO-SUKE ...
HRAAAAH?!
I THINK I'M GOING TO TAKE A LOOK OVER THERE.
DO WHATEVER YOU WANT!
INOSUKE, GO DOWN THE MOUNTAIN.
GO DOWN.
WHY SHOULD I?!
BUZZ OFF!
BECAUSE YOU'RE BADLY HURT.

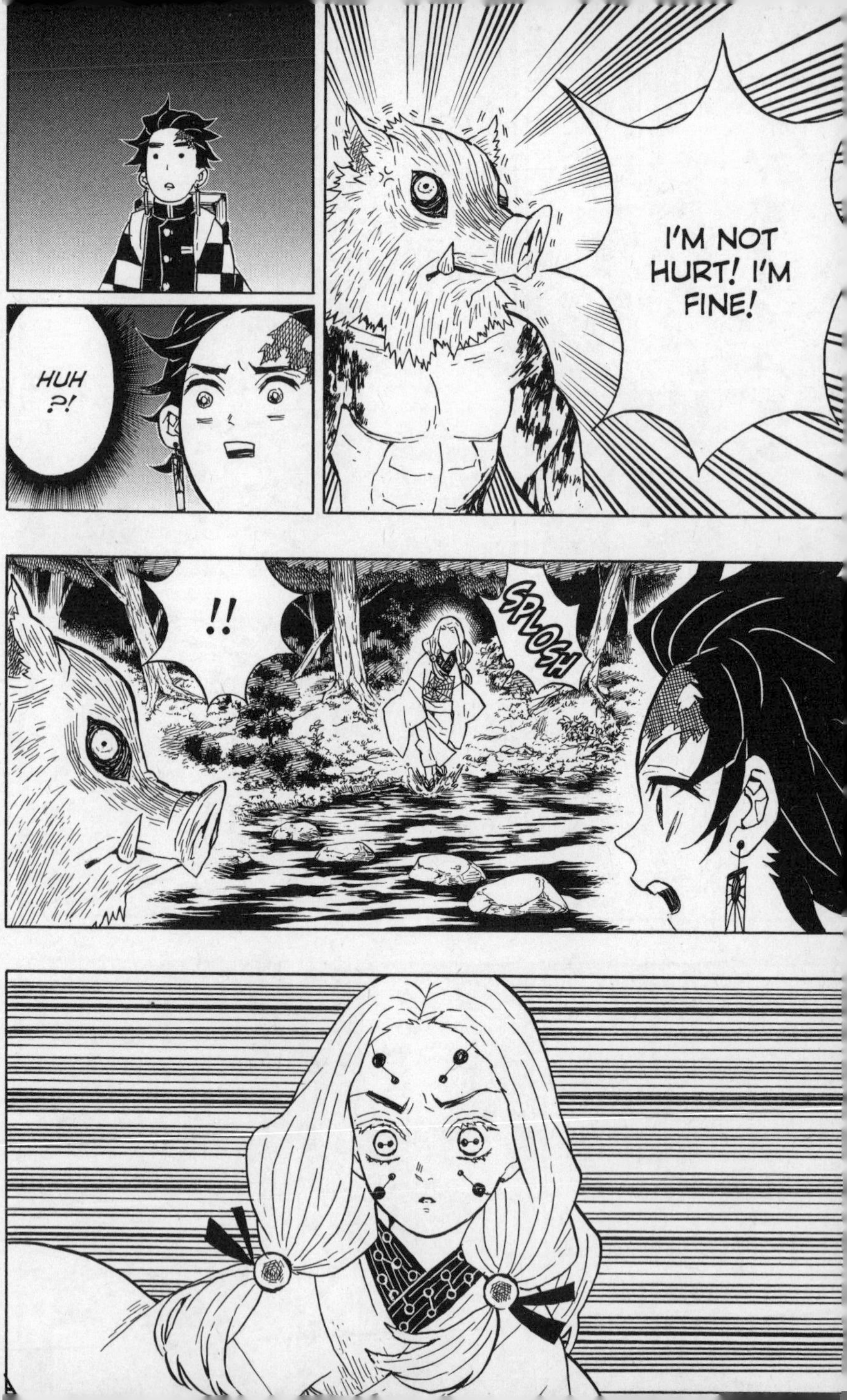
I'M NOT HURT! I'M FINE!
HUH ?!
SPLOSH
!!

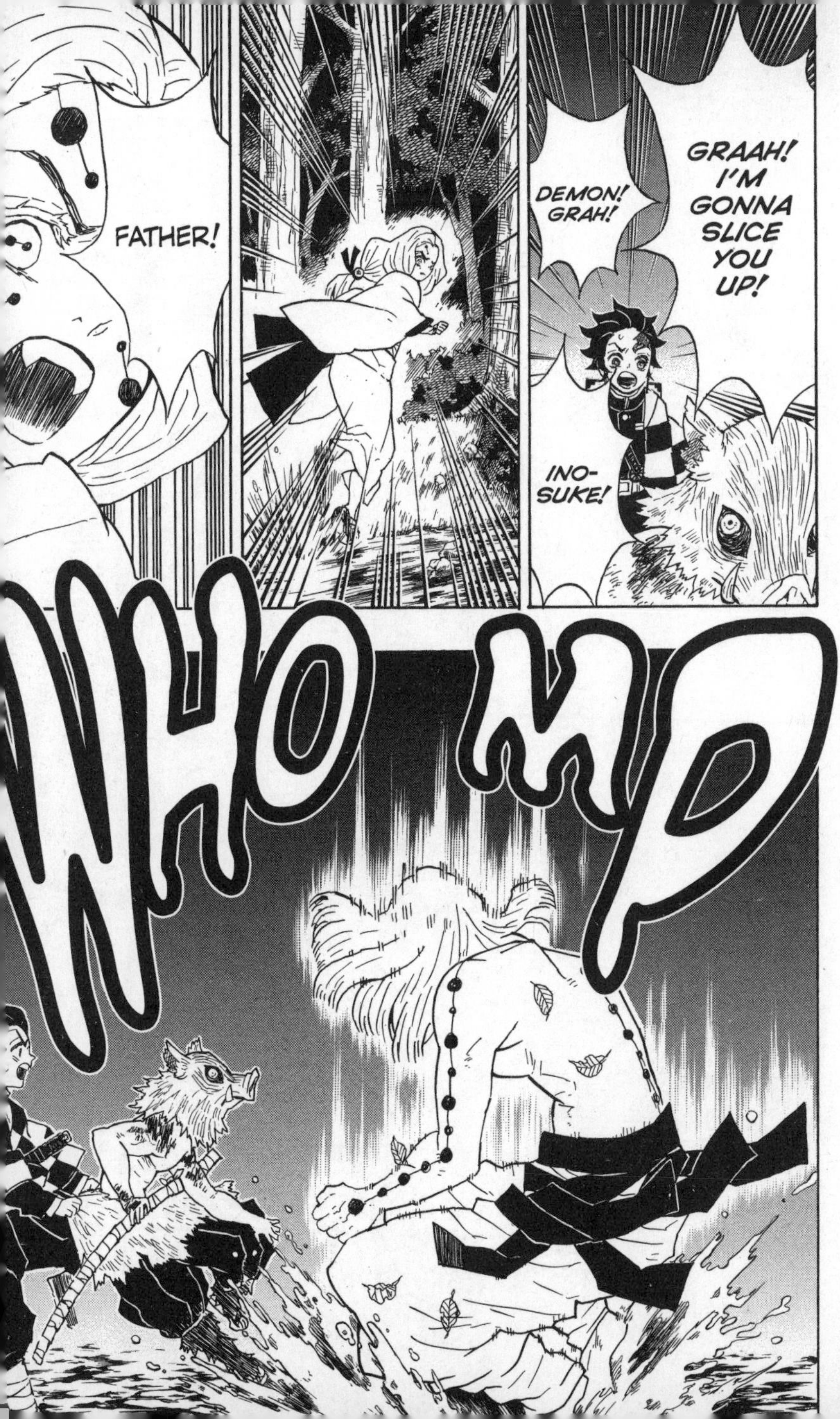
GRAAH! I'M GONNA SLICE YOU UP!
DEMON! GRAH!
INO-SUKE!
FATHER!
WHOMP

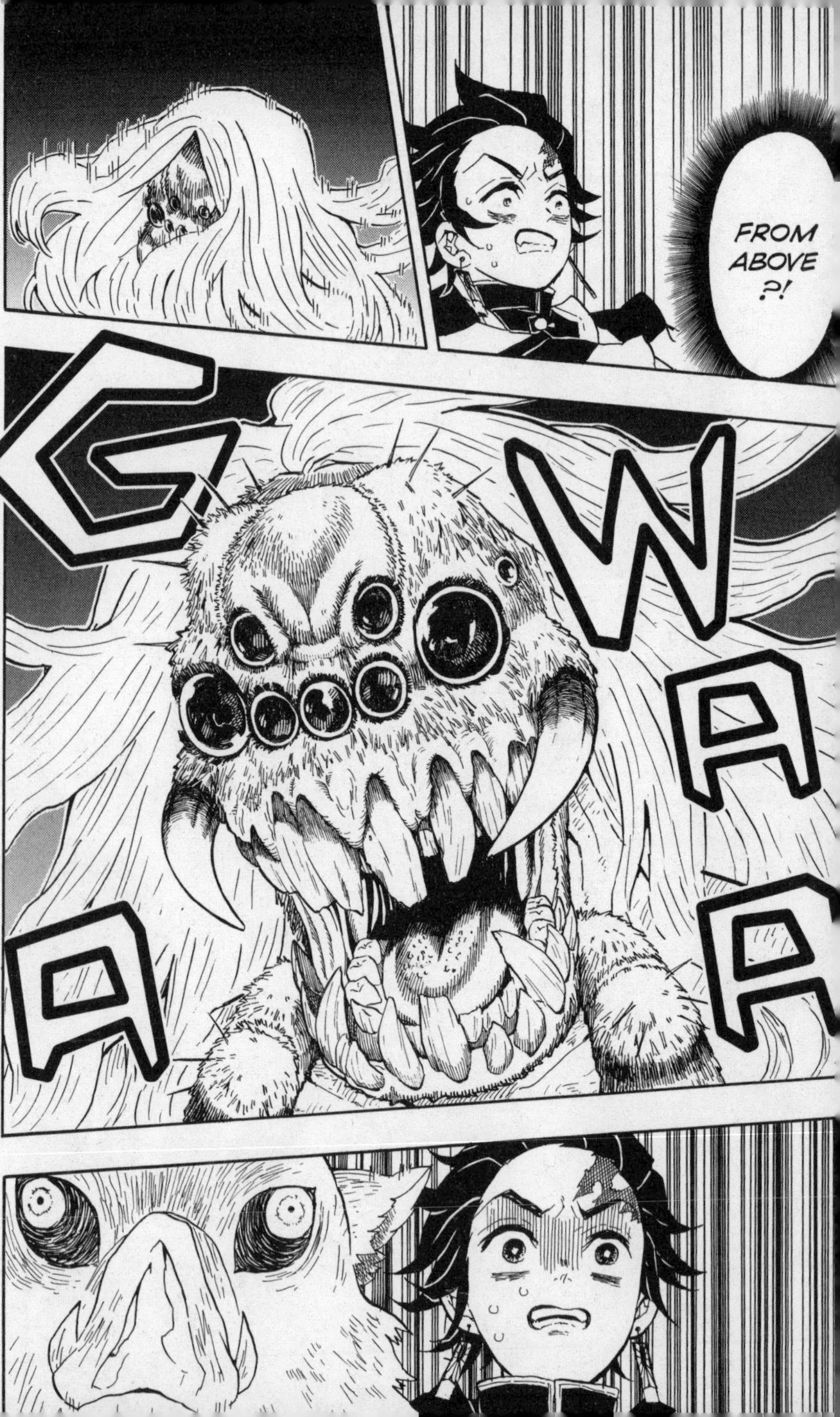
FROM ABOVE ?!
GWAAA

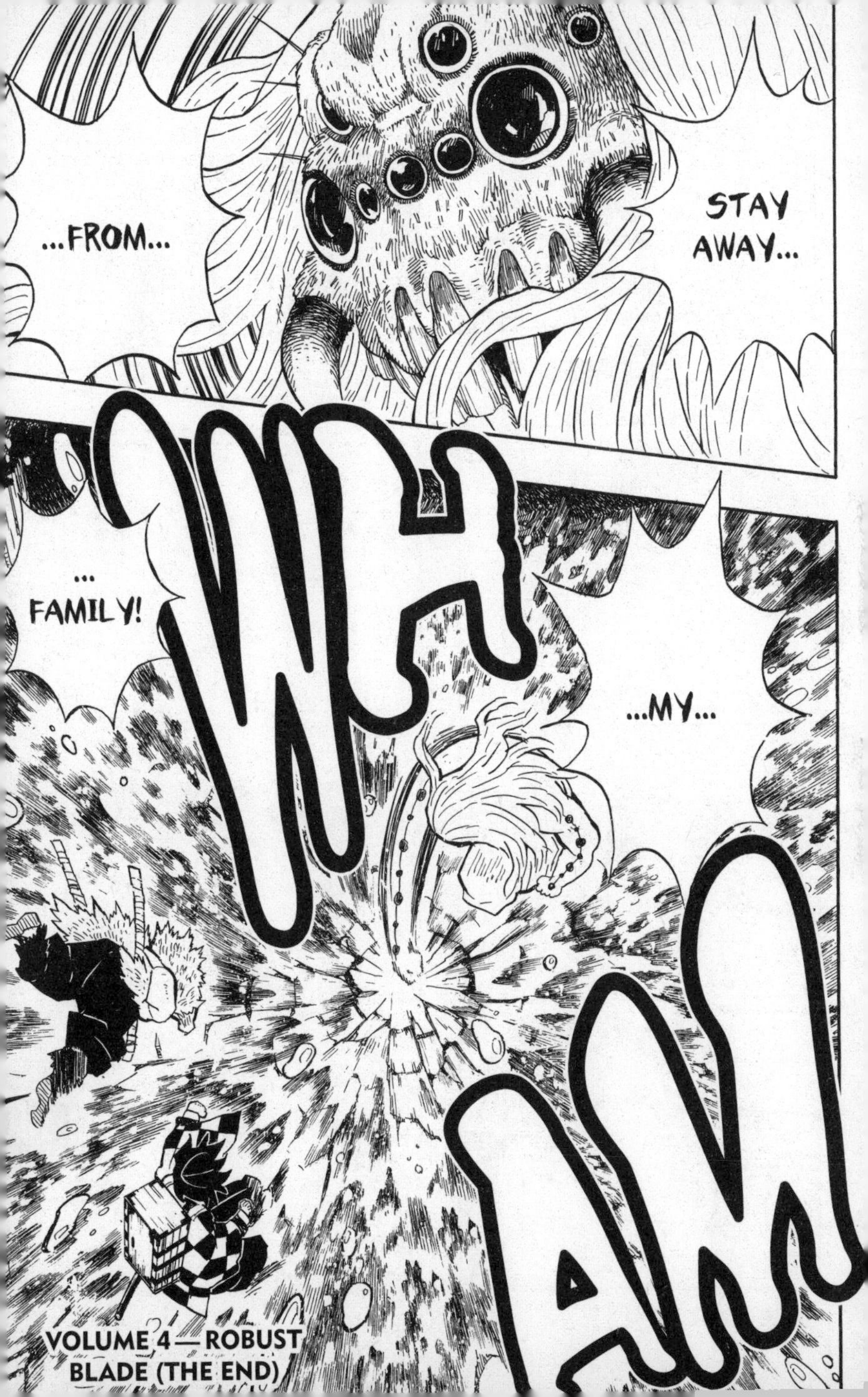
STAY AWAY...
...FROM...
...MY...
... FAMILY!
VOLUME 4—ROBUST BLADE (THE END)

STEEL HEAD

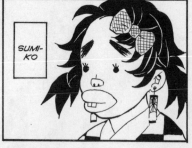

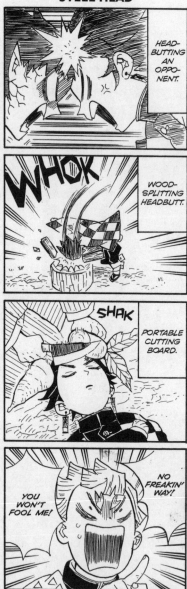

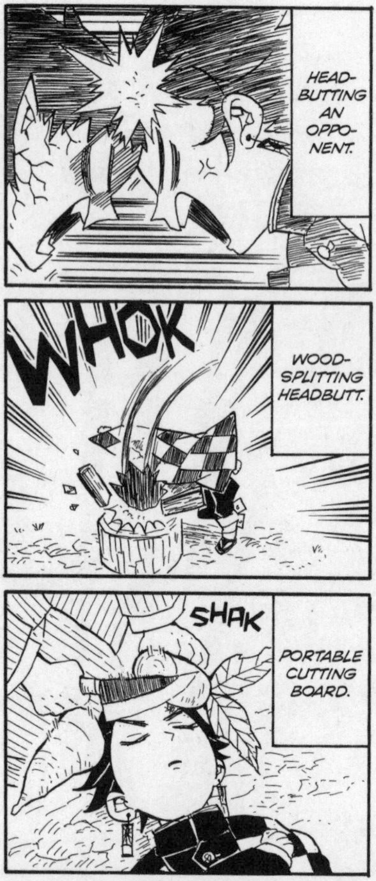
HEAD-BUTTING AN OPPONENT.
WHOK
WOOD-SPLITTING HEADBUTT.
SHAK
PORTABLE CUTTING BOARD.
NO FREAKIN' WAY!
YOU WON'T FOOL ME!

GENDER BENDING

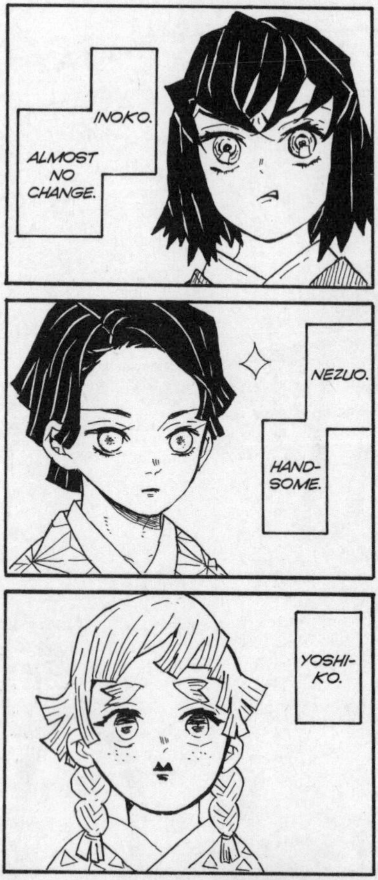
INOKO.
ALMOST NO CHANGE.
NEZUO.
HANDSOME.
YOSHIKO.
SUMIKO

THE END

Apology

Before Inosuke showed his true face in the regular storyline, I made a huge mistake by showing it in a comic strip in Jump GIGA, so I'd like to take this opportunity to apologize.

I've made many other mistakes, and all kinds of people are pointing them out. I intend to make as many corrections as possible, but I'm under strict time constraints and so I make mistakes (which I think bothers the readers).

I'll keep working as hard as I can, so I hope you'll stick with me!

We humbly beg your forgiveness.

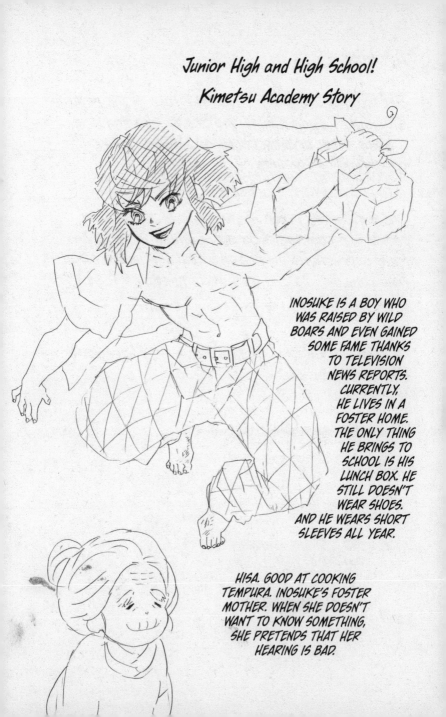

Junior High and High School!
Kimetsu Academy Story

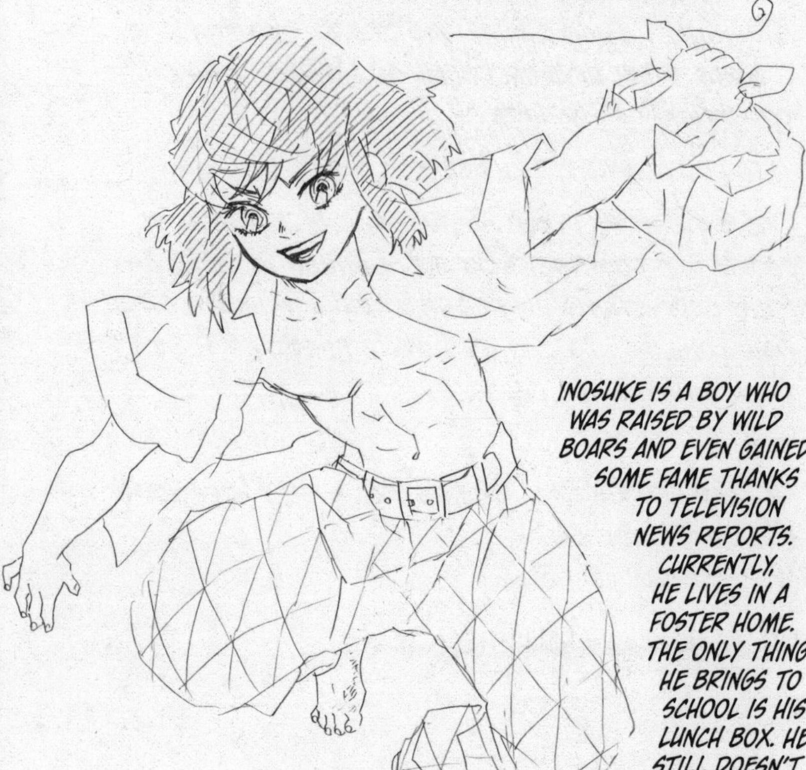

INOSUKE IS A BOY WHO WAS RAISED BY WILD BOARS AND EVEN GAINED SOME FAME THANKS TO TELEVISION NEWS REPORTS. CURRENTLY, HE LIVES IN A FOSTER HOME. THE ONLY THING HE BRINGS TO SCHOOL IS HIS LUNCH BOX. HE STILL DOESN'T WEAR SHOES. AND HE WEARS SHORT SLEEVES ALL YEAR.

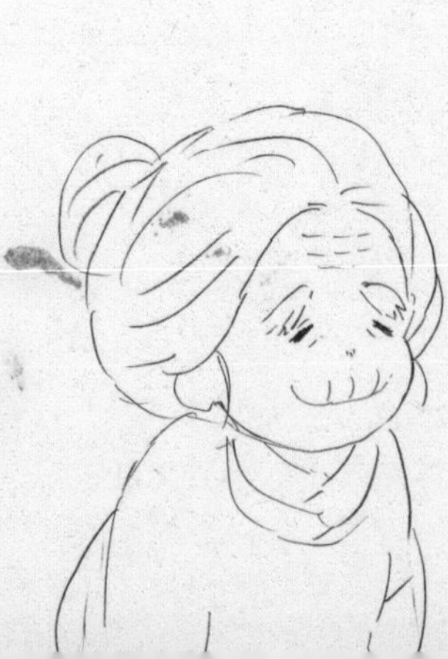

HISA. GOOD AT COOKING TEMPURA. INOSUKE'S FOSTER MOTHER. WHEN SHE DOESN'T WANT TO KNOW SOMETHING, SHE PRETENDS THAT HER HEARING IS BAD.

A WEIRDO WHO APPEARED IN THE TOWN OF KIMETSU. HE HOMES IN ON 16-YEAR-OLD GIRLS. THERE HAVE ONLY BEEN A FEW INCIDENTS, AND NO CORROBORATING WITNESSES, SO HE'S CONSIDERED AN URBAN LEGEND. TANJIRO SUSPECTS THERE ARE ACTUALLY TRIPLETS AND IS INVESTIGATING.

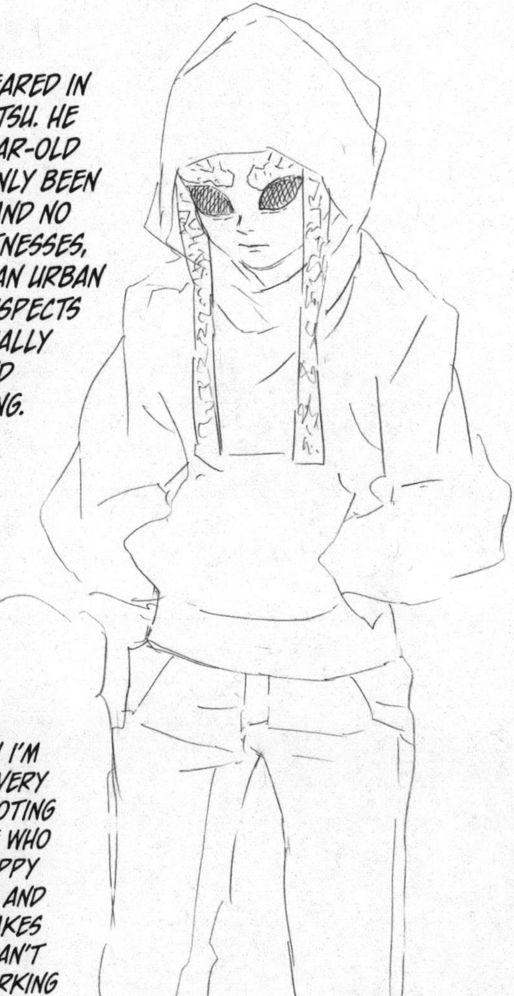

WORDS OF GRATITUDE

THANKS FOR READING! I'M GOTOUGE. THANK YOU VERY MUCH TO EVERYONE ROOTING FOR ME AND EVERYONE WHO HELPS OUT. I'M SO HAPPY ABOUT YOUR LETTERS AND PRESENTS THAT IT MAKES ME CRY. I'M SORRY I CAN'T RESPOND. I'LL KEEP WORKING AS HARD AS I CAN!

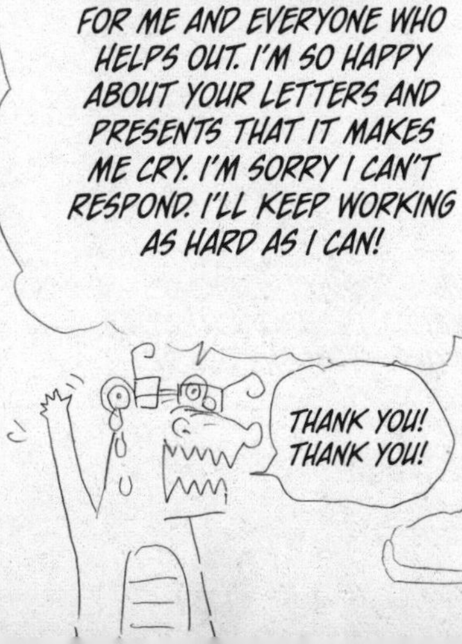
THANK YOU! THANK YOU!

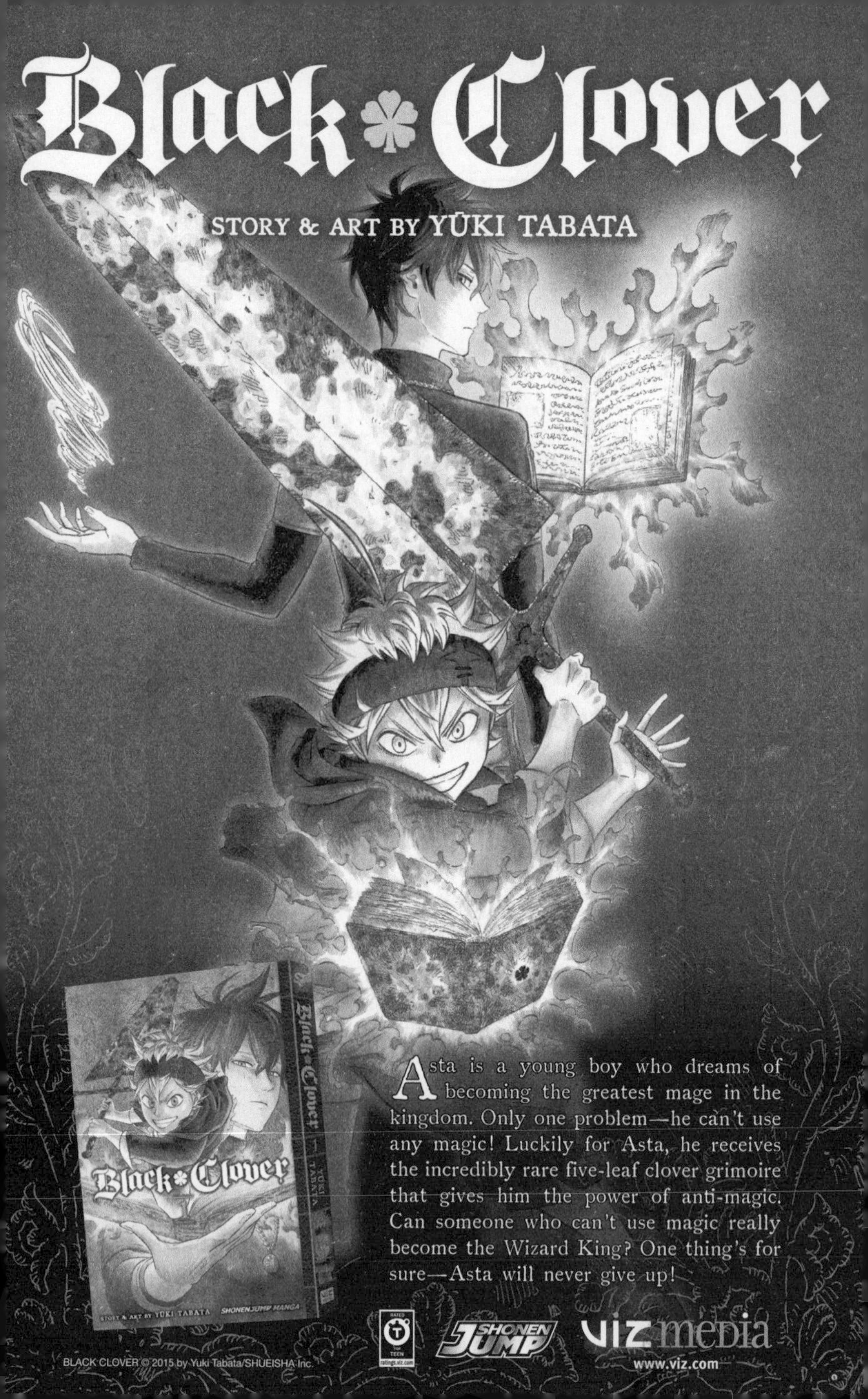
Black Clover
STORY & ART BY YŪKI TABATA
Black Clover
STORY & ART BY YŪKI TABATA
SHONEN JUMP MANGA
Asta is a young boy who dreams of becoming the greatest mage in the kingdom. Only one problem—he can't use any magic! Luckily for Asta, he receives the incredibly rare five-leaf clover grimoire that gives him the power of anti-magic. Can someone who can't use magic really become the Wizard King? One thing's for sure—Asta will never give up!
RATED T TEEN
ratings.viz.com
SHONEN JUMP
VIZ media
www.viz.com
BLACK CLOVER © 2015 by Yuki Tabata/SHUEISHA Inc.

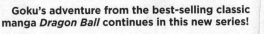

DRAGON BALL SUPER

STORY BY **Akira Toriyama**   ART BY **Toyotarou**

Goku's adventure from the best-selling classic manga *Dragon Ball* continues in this new series!

Ever since Goku became Earth's greatest hero and gathered the seven Dragon Balls to defeat the evil Boo, his life on Earth has grown a little dull. But new threats loom overhead, and Goku and his friends will have to defend the planet once again!

YOU'RE READING THE
WRONG WAY!

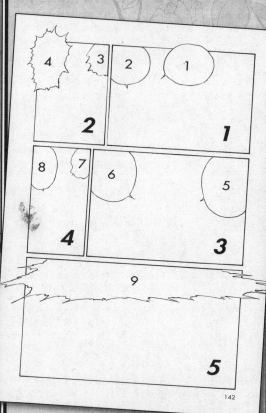

DEMON SLAYER: KIMETSU NO YAIBA
reads from right to left, starting in the
upper-right corner. Japanese is read from
right to left, meaning that action, sound
effects and word-balloon order are completely reversed from English order.